POCKET *A*DVENTURES
BELIZE

POCKET ADVENTURES
BELIZE

Vivien Lougheed

HUNTER

HUNTER PUBLISHING, INC,
130 Campus Drive, Edison, NJ 08818
732-225-1900; 800-255-0343; fax 732-417-1744
www.hunterpublishing.com

Ulysses Travel Publications
4176 Saint-Denis, Montréal, Québec
Canada H2W 2M5
514-843-9882, ext. 2232; fax 514-843-9448

Windsor Books
The Boundary, Wheatley Road, Garsington
Oxford, OX44 9EJ England
01865-361122; fax 01865-361133

Printed in the United States

ISBN 1-58843-508-3

© 2005 Hunter Publishing, Inc.

This and other Hunter travel guides are also available as e-books
in a variety of digital formats through our online partners,
including Netlibrary.com and Amazon.com.

This guide focuses on recreational activities. As all such activities contain
elements of risk, the publisher, author, affiliated individuals and companies
disclaim responsibility for any injury, harm, or illness that may occur to
anyone through, or by use of, the information in this book. Every effort was
made to insure the accuracy of information in this book, but the publisher and
author do not assume, and hereby disclaim, liability for any loss or damage
caused by errors, omissions, misleading information or potential travel
problems caused by this guide, even if such errors or omissions result from
negligence, accident or any other cause.

Cover photo: Diver with coral, compliments RFCP/Tony Rath
All interior images by Vivien Lougheed, unless noted.
Index by: Nancy Wolff

Maps by Kim André, © 2005 Hunter Publishing, Inc.

1 2 3 4

www.hunterpublishing.com

Hunter's full range of guides to all corners of the globe is featured on our exciting website. You'll find guidebooks to suit every type of traveler, no matter what their budget, lifestyle, or idea of fun.

Adventure Guides – There are now over 40 titles in this series, covering destinations from Costa Rica and the Yucatán to Tampa Bay & Florida's West Coast, Ecuador, Switzerland, Paris and the Alaska Highway. Complete with information on what to do, as well as where to stay and eat, *Adventure Guides* are made for the active traveler, with comprehensive coverage of the area's history, culture and wildlife, plus all the practical travel information you need. Details on the best places for hiking, biking, canoeing, horseback riding, trekking, skiing, watersports, and all other kinds of fun, are included.

Alive Guides – This ever-popular line of books takes a unique look at the best each destination offers: fine dining, jazz clubs, first-class hotels and resorts. In-margin icons direct the reader at a glance. Top-sellers include *St. Martin & St. Barts*, *The US Virgin Islands* and *Aruba, Bonaire & Curaçao*.

And Hunter has long been known for its **one-of-a-kind** travel books that focus on destinations and vacations rarely found in travel books. These include *The Best Dives of the Bahamas; Golf Resorts; Cruising Alaska; A Traveler's Guide to the Galapagos* and many more.

Full descriptions are given for each book at www.hunter-publishing.com, along with reviewers' comments and a cover image. You can also view pages and the table of contents. Books may be purchased on-line via our secure transaction facility.

Acknowledgments

My first appreciation goes to John Harris for sticking with me even when he is lost in some foreign landscape or in one of my manuscripts. His dedication to me makes all my writing possible (and readable).

My second appreciation goes to Kim André. I've never before worked so closely with an editor and had so much fun.

Paige Pedersen is a major inspiration for me in my incessant travels. Her enthusiasm helps me over the tough spots and her company makes the trips fun.

I cannot begin to thank all the people who have helped me with this book. The list includes those working in the tourist industry in Belize, whether they be guides, hotel managers, restaurant owners or artists. Their knowledge and willingness to help is a good indication of what visitors will receive when they arrive in the country. I also must thank those involved in the tourist industry who are not part of Belize's infrastructure, but contribute to it. These include tour operators, scientists, NGOs and professionals who have specialized interests. Last, I would like to thank all the travelers I met who gave me leads and information about places I had not yet found.

DEDICATION

I dedicate this book to Joyce Lancaster, who I hope one day will be able to visit this beautiful country.

Contents

THE NORTH

◆ Maps

Introduction

During winter, I often close my eyes and visualize Belize. I see sun, sand and sea. I see white beaches, blue skies and clear waters. My memory, like a television camera, continues to the largest coral reef in the Americas where there is a world seething with exotic life.

Most people who arrive from harsh climates head for the islands, where they snorkel, swim, dive, fish, sail and hang out in the sun. They play golf, eat spicy foods, read books and drink beer. Most of all, they relax.

However, there is more to Belize than a blissful rest in paradise. There are ancient Maya ruins to explore, animal preserves to visit, a jungle full of medicinal plants to study and an endless number of images to capture on film.

Belize also has a history involving pirates and buccaneers, wrecked ships, and the slave trade. Remnants of this history remain and someone is always willing to share a story. Belizeans are proud of the fact that their varied cultures live together peacefully, a big contrast to most of Central America.

The best time to come to Belize is between Nov. and May when a cloud is seldom seen and the winds are never more than a pleasant breeze. May to Nov. is when the waters can be a bit murky and the winds can increase to hurricane levels. But this is also a time when the jungle becomes lush and the flowers are abundant.

This pocket size travel guide is for the adventurer who has limited time but wants to see Belize's highlights. If you have longer to spare in this beautiful land and want more details on the country's fascinating culture and history, its people and wildlife, pick up a copy of my *Belize Adventure Guide*.

❖ AUTHOR'S CHOICE OF MUST DO'S

- ❖ Play Robinson Crusoe at Glover's Reef.
- ❖ Have dinner at Capricorn's on Ambergris Caye, then take the moonlight boat trip home.
- ❖ Try overnight caving at Caves Branch River.
- ❖ Explore unexcavated Maya ruins at Roaring River.
- ❖ Cycle to Rio Frio in Cayo District.

History

Anywhere I go, I want to know who was there before me. I want to know their stories. I've been traveling in Latin America for about 20 years now, so it is easy for me to get caught up in pre-Columbian history.

The history of Belize is part of the history of the greatest ancient American civilization. During the Classic Period of the Maya, Belize was the heart of the empire, with an estimated population of one million people.

But even before the Maya, who?

◆ Historical Timeline

The timeline below indicates the major triumphs and losses of various important groups, the development of cultures and ways of life, as well as other important dates in Belizean history.

20,000 BC	Paleo-Indians migrate down the continent along an ice-free corridor in search of large herbivores.
18,000 BC	First settlers arrive in Central America.
7000 BC	Nomadic tribes become farmers.
3000 BC	Pit houses become the common shelter.
2300 BC	Pottery replaces stone jars.
2000 BC	Arawak and Carib Indians occupy the Caribbean. The Garifuna are distant relatives of these tribes. Maya settle in Belize and start building stone structures.
AD 250-1000	Classic Period of Maya civilization when textiles and bricks were developed and ceramics were refined. There was a class structure in society. Pictorial symbols and numerology developed. Raised fields developed in the Pulltrouser Swamp. Religious ceremonial centers were built. Balche, fermented honey and bark, was made.
1527-1547	Francisco de Montego, father and son, carried out a 20-year conquest of the Maya but left Belize unconquered.
1630-1640	Baymen arrive in Belize to cut logwood and mahogany. The privateers (pirates) arrive and use the hidden coves from which to attack unsuspecting Spanish ships.
1798	Battle of St. George's Caye; 32 Spanish ships and 2,500 troops were defeated by 240 Baymen.
1802	Garafuna arrive on the shores of Belize.
1821	Spanish rule ended.
1823	First Garafuna arrive in Belize from Honduras.

1838	British abolished slavery. Slaves who were ill-treated in other countries started immigrating to Belize.
1848-1858	Caste War in Yucatán caused 5,000 Maya to take up farming in Belize.
1871	Legislative Council set up in Belize City.
1982	New constitution drawn up and Belize gains independence.

❖ A GAME TO DIE FOR

The captains of the losing teams in Maya ballgames were sacri-ficed to **Ek Chuah**, the Maya god of war and human sacrifice. The idea was to extract the victim's heart, while it was still pump-ing. This was usually done by plunging a dull knife into the chest of the captain. The blood from the heart was smeared on the stone image of Ek Chuah. If the sacrifice took place in a temple on top of a pyramid, the priests tossed the body to the pyramid's base, where it was skinned. The head priest then put on the skin and danced. Players, who earned less respect, were sometimes shot with bows and arrows rather than cut up with a knife.

Government

Belize is a constitutional monarchy. The monarch is the British King or Queen, but the constitution gives the monarch – or the monarch's repre-sentative, the Governor General – a ceremonial status only. The monarchy doesn't cost Belizeans a cent. However, they get the pleasure of participating in the royal family gossip as part of the family, rooting for favorites. Generally, the Queen is popular in Belize.

The **Constitution** of 1981 defines the structure of government, enforces universal suffrage (starting at age 18), defines certain rights and freedoms, and requires a general election every five years at least. Legislative power is in the 29-member **House of Representatives**, and executive power in the **Cabinet**, which is appointed by the Prime Minister, the leader of the party that got the most seats in the House. The Prime Minister chooses Cabinet members from both the House and the Senate. The Cabinet makes policy for the government. Its deliberations are secret; there is open debate in the Cab-inet, but Cabinet members must keep that debate confidential.

In effect, the Prime Minister has near-dictatorial powers for five years, as-suming that his majority in the House is solid. This is the major difference be-tween the British (Westminster) and the republican (i.e., US) systems.

There is no proportional representation; this also tends to make for a clear majority for one party. The country is divided into 29 constituencies; whoever wins in each one, goes into the House. Though a third of Belizeans live in Belize City, their representatives cannot dominate the Assembly.

There is a second house, the Senate. It has eight appointed members: five by the Prime Minister, two by the leader of the opposition, and one by a council that advises the Governor General. The Senate studies legislation and makes recommendations, but it cannot pass legislation.

> ❖ **CIVIL SERVICE**
>
> For the Civil Service, there are six administrative districts run by government functionaries: Belize, Cayo, Corozal, Orange Walk, Stann Creek and Toledo. Each district has a town board that runs the main city. However, Cayo has two boards; one for San Ignacio and the other for Benque Viejo. Belize is the only district that has a city council.

The slightly left-wing **People's United Party** (PUP) generally forms the government. This was the case before independence too. For years, **George Cadle Price** was its leader and the country's Prime Minister. The UDP is the slightly right-of-center party, usually but not always in opposition.

In its foreign policy, Belize tends to side with the US on international affairs and supports a moderate free enterprise line. Belize has closer ties to the Commonwealth Caribbean states than to the Central American ones. But those ties, formalized in CARICOM (created from the words, Caribbean Community), can bring only limited economic benefits.

The **Belizean Defense Forces** (BDF), which include an army of about 600 (including a few female platoons), a navy of some half-dozen patrol boats and 60 sailors, and an air force comprising a couple of transport planes and the people that fly them, gets aid and training from Britain, Canada and the US. The BDF's main base is near the international airport.

The **Belize Police Force** (BPF) is about the same size as the BDF and is the civilian police. There are also 32 members of the **Tourist Police Force**, 30 of them in Belize City and two on Caye Caulker. The Tourist Police fall under the jurisdiction of the Belize Tourist Board and are paid from the 7% hotel tax. San Pedro on Ambergris Caye pays 46% of this tax, but to date has no Tourist Police on the island.

Economy

Belize is mostly an agrarian society, so more than half of its export income is from the production of sugar cane, citrus, bananas and vegetables. Half of this production is exported to the United States.

Historically, Belize has been an exploited colony where the people worked for low wages, lived in poor housing, suffered malnutrition and had almost no health care. In 1950, the People's United Party was formed; their main aim was to gain political and economic independence for the people of Belize. Their leader was **George Price** and in 1981, when independence from Britain was finally gained, he became the first Prime Minister. Between those dates, the struggle for better working and living conditions continued. Finally, between 1971 and 1975, 525,000 acres of land was taken out of the hands of the few and redistributed.

◆ US Dollar & the IMF

Following land redistribution was the collapse of the Belize dollar. To keep the economy fairly stable, the government in 1976 pegged the currency to the American dollar at a fixed rate of two to one.

However, the plummeting value of sugar crops in the 1980s resulted in Belize taking out IMF loans that, in turn, put more stress on the economy. Because their export market is always below the import requirements (in 2004, it fell short by $149.7 million) Belize seems to be always in the red.

> **❖ ADD UP THE FIGURES**
>
> *Figures taken from the 2004 Index of Economic Freedom.*
> **EXPORT INCOME:** $434.3 million in 2002. 66% came from sugar, bananas, citrus & vegetables; 22% from textiles; 8% from seafood; 3% from lumber.
>   54% is traded with the US; 23% with Great Britain; 17% with the European Union; 6% with the Caribbean community; and 1% with Mexico.
> **BELIZE IMPORTS:** $584 million. 47% is from the US; 11% from Mexico; 5% from CARIBCOM; 3% from the UK.

◆ New Promise

Mining is beginning to show promise. The Toledo district has enough dolomite (used in fertilizer) to support a viable extraction and processing industry, but so far not enough has been processed to make a huge difference in attracting foreign dollars.

Tourism is a big factor. There is a belief that the travelers who patronize local businesses (this could be you), rather than the big resorts, benefit the people most. Some believe that the resorts take a lot of the profit out of the country. Bookings are arranged and paid for elsewhere and profits go to foreign banks. On the other hand, the larger resorts employ 25% of the working population, albeit at minimum wage and with no extra benefits like paid health care.

People & Culture

There are seven major languages used by the people who live in Belize.

- ❖ **BELIZE CREOLE ENGLISH:** 55,000 first-language speakers, plus about 103,000 second-language users, for a total of 158,000. Nearly everyone in Belize uses Creole. Belize Creole English is a heavily accented and bastardized form of English with loads of Misquiti, Spanish, Maya and African words thrown in for fun. An example: "Wat wi di du" means, What are we doing?

- ❖ **ENGLISH:** 60,000 speakers, although most use it as a second language. English is the national language, used in education, government and business.
- ❖ **SPANISH AND SPANISH CREOLE:** There are about 60,000 first- and second-language speakers, increasing as Maya and Mestizo refugees come into the country from Guatemala and El Salvador.
- ❖ **GARIFUNA OR CARIB:** 12,500 first-language speakers.
- ❖ **KEKCHI, MOPAN & YUCATECAN DIALECTS:** 16,000 first-language speakers.
- ❖ **MENNONITE GERMAN:** 5,800 first-language speakers.

◆ Cultural Groups

GARIFUNA: Garifuna number over 55,000, most of whom live in villages along the Caribbean coast from Belize to Nicaragua. Honduras has the largest Garifuna population.

Garifunas are a mixture of black African slaves and the Indians of the Lesser Antilles who migrated from Guyana and the Orinoco River area of Venezuela to St. Vincent Island. During a storm in 1635, two sailing ships capsized near St. Vincent, freeing the slaves. Some made it to shore.

> **FASCINATING FACT:** *In the Arawak language, Garifuna means "cassava-eating people."*

By 1700, the black-Indian mix had become the dominant group on St. Vincent, living in the mountains where they became good at guerrilla warfare. They actually controlled one end of the island, much to the disgruntlement of the British, who in turn treated the Garifuna harshly.

As conflicts continued, the Garifuna attempted to drive out the English, but were quickly defeated. In 1797, fearing more problems, the English decided to have the Garifuna shipped to Jamaica and then to Roatan Island in Honduras. The Garifuna were not satisfied with their new island and soon turned it over to the Spanish. They headed for the mainland of Central America and settled along the coast of Belize and Honduras.

The first to arrive in Belize came on Nov. 19th, 1823. Nine years later there were settlements at Stann Creek, Seine Bight, Punta Gorda and Barranca.

> **AUTHOR'S NOTE:** *Name calling, swearing and gossiping are considered aggressive acts and are highly frowned upon by the Garifuna.*

The Garifuna have their own unique language and maintain customs and traditions that reflect the mixing of the two cultures. The Garifuna are Catholic, but continue to tie many of the Afro-Indian rituals into church ceremonies.

Traditional Garifuna music is usually of the call-and-response nature, while drums beat in the background. The accompanying dances can be sexually segregated or sexually seductive, depending on the celebration. The songs often originate as working songs, the rhythm designed to make the chore easier.

MESTIZOS: Mestizos (a mix of Spanish and Indian) came as refugees escaping the Caste War in the Yucatán, and from Guatemala and El Salvador. They speak English with outsiders, but usually speak Spanish in the home.

Mestizo towns are traditionally Spanish in design, with a central town square bordered on one side by a Catholic church. Their food is also traditional Spanish-American, consisting of beans and rice or rice and beans (for variety). This is interspersed with handmade tortillas (a flat corn bread) or tamales, a corn paste with a piece of spiced meat in the center. The tamale is rolled into a banana leaf and cooked.

MENNONITES: The Mennonite church was founded in Zurich, Switzerland in 1525. These anti-Catholics were originally called Anabaptists because they insisted on the rebaptism of adults rather than infant baptism.

The church was named after Menno Simons, the Dutch leader who encouraged his followers to move into Holland.

Mennonites believe that they belong to the true Reformation of the Christian faith. They also believe that the state should be run separately from the church and they practice a loose form of communal living. This lifestyle has often been misunderstood and classified as communism.

Mennonites are a peaceful people who reject all violence and war. This pacifism caused some hard feelings during World War II when they became 40% of all conscientious objectors in the US and 80% of those in Canada.

As they searched for religious freedom, the acclaimed author, Emory King helped persuade the Mennonites to settle in Belize. They readily did this, working hard to make the land into productive farms.

Mennonites can be seen around the country in their distinct clothing; the women wear ankle-length dresses and head coverings in the form of a straw hat or a kerchief and the men have bibbed overalls, cleaned and ironed to perfection. Their farms are efficiently run and you'll often see Mennonites in towns selling their produce. They operate their own schools, banks and churches. Mennonites are an asset to the Belizean economy. Just purchase some vegetables or fruit from them some time and you will agree.

MAYA INDIANS: The Maya Indians of Belize include the **Kekchi**, the **Mopan** and **Yucatán** Maya. Each of these groups has its own language. Many Guatemalan Maya refuse to speak Spanish, the language of their oppressors.

Most of the Maya are farmers who grow corn, rice and wheat. They live in traditional villages with thatched-roof houses. Their religion is Catholic, with Maya rituals included in ceremonies and Maya gods personifying some saints. They use herbal medicines rather than Western chemical medicine.

EAST INDIANS: This group arrived after the emancipation of black slaves in 1838. They came as indentured servants. An indentured servant must work for his master for an agreed-upon number of years before he is free to work for himself. However, this indenture was often extended for long periods of time and the Indians found it difficult to start their own lives. The original East Indians kept up some of their cultural traditions.

Recently, a new wave of East Indians is migrating to Belize, but the people seem to be assimilating into the Mestizo society.

CHINESE: Chinese immigrated to many countries, including Belize, in the mid-1800s. They came as laborers and kept a close community of their own. When the Japanese invaded China just before World War II, another influx of Chinese immigrants came to Belize. The third and final group came in the 1970s from Hong Kong and Taiwan.

Presently, there is a solid community throughout Belize. They have integrated well with the other groups. Freedom of religion is tolerated in Belize, and some Chinese still practice Buddhism.

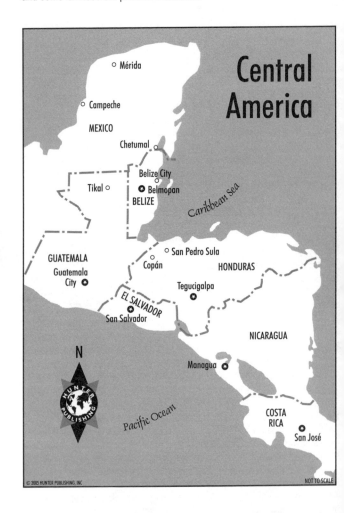

Geography

◆ How the Land was Formed

Belize and the Mexican states of Yucatán, Quintana Roo and Campeche, as well as parts of Tabasco and Chiapas, make up an 85,000 square-mile limestone platform that emerged from the ocean about 80 million years ago.

Because of tectonic movements and climatic changes, water covered and drained from the land many times. This affected the limestone. As the seeping water eroded the rock, caverns, caves and underground tunnels were formed. Probably the largest cave system in North and South America underlies the Maya Mountains near the Guatemala border in western Belize. It's known as the **Chiquibul** complex.

Due to the water and plate movements, ripples from the old seabed form valleys with low ridges. The valleys flow north to south and fill with water. These formations are clearly visible since the forests have been cleared, especially in Northern Belize.

 MYSTERIOUS MAYA: *The ancient Maya believed that the land on which they lived sat on the back of a turtle that floated in the sea.*

As the North American plate moved in a westerly direction, it collided with the Caribbean plate that was heading east. This activity caused the land to lift, forming the **Maya Mountains** of southern Belize, which are dated from between 65 and 34 million years ago and occupy almost half the land mass. They run northeast from the Guatemalan border for 70 miles. The mountains include limestone, dolomite and granite. **Mount Victoria**, standing at 3,680 feet (1,122 meters), has until recently been given credit as the highest mountain in Belize. In fact, Doyles Delight in the Cockscomb Range stands at 3,688 feet (1,124 meters) above sea level. The cave system lying under these mountains has caverns that run from three to nine miles in length.

◆ Environments

Moving from the Maya Mountains to the south and east towards the ocean, the land falls quickly; within 15 miles you're at sea level. The terrain along the edge of the sea is mostly **swamp** and **mangrove**, but the land between the higher peaks and the swamps is **rainforest**, with a dense cover of palms, ferns, lianas and tropical cedar. It rains most of the year in the south; annual precipitation can total 150 inches (380 cm) or more. The north gets less than 60 inches (150 cm) and is dry from Nov. to May.

The land falling to the west of the Maya Mountains is the "pine ridge," a **wet savanna** that has poor, sandy soil and grows little but pine trees. These lower hills, which are crossed by logging roads, cover hundreds of square miles.

The central and northern region is **savanna**. The river valleys that drain the mountains from the south have spread a thin layer of soil into the southern part of this savanna and in this soil grows some of the richest hardwoods in the world. **Hardwoods** cover about 70% of the entire savanna. Much to the credit of Belize, 44% of this hardwood forest is virgin.

The low-lying savanna in the north is spotted with swamps and large lagoons that drain into the Caribbean. Again, its depressions run north-south.

Along the Caribbean Sea, Belize's coastline is rimmed with **mangrove swamp**. Not good for human habitation, but rich ecologically, it houses hundreds of species of birds and a similar number of fish species.

◆ Offshore

Beyond the coast is a 150-mile **barrier reef**, the longest unbroken barrier reef in the Western Hemisphere, and second in size only to Australia's Great Barrier Reef.

The coral that is part of the barrier reef has been forming for millions of years. As the coral reef develops, the number and types of animals in and around the reef are constantly changing.

Coral is a small polyp that, for survival, requires saline water of a temperature between 70°F (21°C) and 86°F (30°C). Their life starts at about 125 feet (38 meters) below the surface, where they consume minute organisms and dissolved gasses. They form group colonies, attaching themselves to rocky coasts and other coral to build up skeletons. The cup-like cavities you may see in mature coral crustaceans were once occupied by the living polyps.

The skeletons that form the crustaceans are made of calcium carbonate and take three forms: fringing reefs, barrier reefs and atolls. Some of these formations descend to 5,000 feet (1,500 meters) below sea level.

- ❖ **Fringing reefs** extend outward from the shore of a mainland or island like a shelf. The outer edge occasionally rises like the edge of a saucer, forming a rim that is cut through by channels.
- ❖ **Barrier reefs** are characterized by a shallow channel or lagoon between reef and shore.
- ❖ **Atolls** are ring- or horseshoe-shaped reefs that surround lagoons. They can have breaks in them through which the tide rushes. A number of small atolls may form rings that surround larger lagoons. Some atolls originally surrounded volcanic islands that subsided below the surface, leaving the encircling coral reef. Coral islands are atolls with volcanic rock close to the surface. Wave action pushes up coral sand over the reef. This makes for poor soil, although palm trees and other salt-resistant plants can germinate in it.

As the most recent glaciers melted, the sea rose and the Caribbean Coral Reef ecological system became what it is today; a marine biological museum protected from the ravages of a raging sea by the coral walls. It has millions of fish.

DID YOU KNOW? *Black coral, now protected, grows one millimeter every hundred years.*

For today's traveler, Belize offers a diverse landscape of cool pine forests, sauna-like jungle, palm-dotted islands, parched brown savanna, majestic mountains both above and below sea level, and flat, muddy swamp.

INTRODUCTION

EARTH'S TIME

490-443 MILLION YEARS AGO. Oceans cover North America and then drain. Corals and clams evolve.

443-417 MILLION YEARS AGO. The earth floods and the seas recede leaving salt deposits. Sea life is dominated by corals and arthropods. Fish develop jaws!

417-354 MILLION YEARS AGO. Appalachian Mountains form in North America and South America takes on its present position. This is the age of fish, when armored fish, lung fish and sharks develop. Ozone layer forms around the earth.

354-290 MILLION YEARS AGO. The continents collide and the climate cools. Cockroaches emerge. The first reptiles emerge. Trees, club mosses and ferns evolve.

290-248 MILLION YEARS AGO. Glaciations occur and huge deserts abound; some corals become extinct. Herbivores and carnivores, terrestrial and aquatic divisions develop.

248-144 MILLION YEARS AGO. Continents separate and the climate warms; 75% of the earth's reptiles and amphibians die. Atlantic Ocean forms and the western mountains on the American continent form. Many dinosaurs disappear. First frogs, toads and salamanders appear. Small mammals like shrews develop.

144-65 MILLION YEARS AGO. Continents take their present shape. More mountains form and the climate warms; the remaining dinosaurs disappear.

65-34 MILLION YEARS AGO. Continental plates shift and the Maya Mountains in Belize form. Horse, rhino and camel can be found. Whales and dolphins develop.

34-5 MILLION YEARS AGO. Oceans become established. Early primates develop. Whales and walruses are now present, as are herons, ducks, eagles, hawks and crows.

5-1.8 MILLION YEARS AGO. Isthmus of Panama changes the ocean's circulation. Plates keep shifting. Primates evolve.

1.8 MILLION-10,000 YEARS AGO. Thirty percent of the earth is covered in ice. Moose, elephant, musk ox, saber-tooth cats and the sloth are now present.

10,000 YEARS TO PRESENT. Glaciers recede. Tourists evolve and roam the earth.

◆ Parks

There are eight protected areas in Belize that are managed by the **Belize Audubon Society**. Mandated by the government in 1984, the Audubon Society has worked hard toward the "sustainable use and preservation of natural resources." The society is a non-profit organization that is not affiliated with any political party.

To assist the society in protecting, administrating, researching and managing these areas, I encourage you to visit the parks, pay the foreigners' entrance fee and, if you can, leave the society an added donation.

AUDUBON SOCIETY-MANAGED AREAS

At present the following places are under the management of the Audubon Society:Guanacaste National Park, Blue Hole National Park, Community Baboon Sanctuary, Cockscomb Basin Wildlife Sanctuary, Crooked Tree Wildlife Sanctuary, Tapir Mountain Nature Reserve, Half Moon Caye Natural Monument, Blue Hole Natural Monument.

The Audubon Society on Fort Street in Belize City has a shop across from the Tourist Village (see page 60) selling souvenirs and t-shirts. The proceeds from these items go toward the society's operation. For more information, visit www.belizeaudubon.org.

The Cayes
1. Bacalar Chico Marine Park
2. Hol Chan Reserve
3. Caye Caulker Forest Reserve
4. Great Blue Hole
5. Half Moon Caye National Monument
6. Glovers Reef Reserve
7. South Water Caye/ Tobacco Caye Reserve; Laughingbird Caye National Park

The North
8. The Bermudian Landing Community Baboon Sanctuary
9. Crooked Tree Wildlife Sanctuary/Chau Hix ruins
10. Lamanai Archaeological Reserve
11. Altun Ha ruins
12. Cuello ruins
13. Nohmul ruins
14. Santa Rita ruins
15. Cerros ruins
16. Shipstern Wildlife Reserve
17. Rio Bravo Conservation Area/ La Milpa ruins

The West
18. Guanacaste Park
19. Belize Zoo
20. Monkey Bay Wildlife Sanctuary
21. Blue Hole/St. Herman's Cave
22. Five Blues Lake National Park
23. Mountain Pine Ridge Forest Reserve/ Slate Creek Preserve
24. Hidden Valley Falls
25. Caracol ruins/Chiquibul Forest Reserve
26. Xunantunich ruins
27. To Melchor, Tikal, Flores (Guatemala)

The South
28. Cockscomb Jaguar Reserve
29. Bladen Branch Nature Reserve
30. Nim Li Punit ruins
31. Lubaantun ruins
32. Uxbenka ruins
33. Monkey River Wildlife Sanctuary

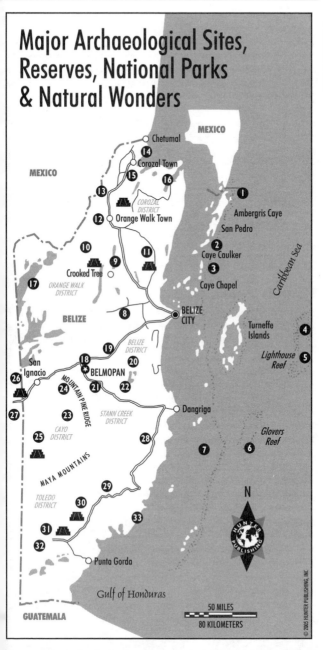

Major Archaeological Sites, Reserves, National Parks & Natural Wonders

MEXICO

MEXICO

MEXICO

Chetumal

Corozal Town

COROZAL DISTRICT

Orange Walk Town

Crooked Tree

ORANGE WALK DISTRICT

BELIZE

BELIZE CITY

BELIZE DISTRICT

San Ignacio

BELMOPAN

MOUNTAIN PINE RIDGE

STANN CREEK DISTRICT

CAYO DISTRICT

Dangriga

MAYA MOUNTAINS

TOLEDO DISTRICT

Punta Gorda

GUATEMALA

Gulf of Honduras

Ambergris Caye

San Pedro

Caye Caulker

Caye Chapel

Caribbean Sea

Turneffe Islands

Lighthouse Reef

Glovers Reef

N

50 MILES
80 KILOMETERS

© 2005 HUNTER PUBLISHING, INC.

Climate

Generally speaking, Belize has a sub-tropical climate tempered by trade winds. The dry season runs from Nov. to May. Temperatures range from 50°F (10°C) to 97°F (35.6°C), although the inland range is much greater.

Annual rainfall can be anywhere from five inches (12.5 cm) in the north to 300 inches (76 cm) in the south. But as you travel in Belize, you'll notice that few days go by without a little sunshine and, even during the height of rainy season, there are days without rain. It is the humidity of the country that makes the heat seem so oppressive. All year long, the humidity can run from 85% to 90% and occasionally it will go higher.

> ❖   **MAUGER WEEK**
>
> Mauger season in Aug. is when the trade winds stop and the mosquitoes start. Temperatures go up and rum supplies in stores throughout the country go down. The drinking is an attempt to nullify the discomfort. It lasts about a week.

◆ Forces of Nature

There are two climatic disturbances that can affect the general patterns in Belize. One is the northern wet air mass that is pushed south from Canada and the US between Nov. and Feb., bringing colder temperatures and widespread heavy rains. It causes choppy seas and forces small fishing vessels to run and hide in the mangrove swamps.

> **AUTHOR NOTE:** *Huracon is the Carib God of Evil. Once winds hit 156 miles an hour, the storm is categorized as class 5 and considered a hurricane.*

Hurricanes are the second type of disturbance that affects Belize. A hurricane is created when an area of low pressure forms in the upper atmosphere and the tropical waters of the Atlantic warm to over 80°F (26°C) to a depth of 200 feet (61 meters). The heat of the water causes circulation of the winds to accelerate. When the winds are less than 40 mph, it's called a tropical depression, but with winds above that speed, a storm is classified as a hurricane.

Hurricane season starts on June 1; most hurricanes hit Belize between mid-Aug. and mid-October. However, only 5% of the hurricanes that form in the western mid-Atlantic ever reach this little country.

> **HURRICANE FACT:** *The Hurricane of 1780 blew through the Caribbean and killed 22,000 people.*

Because the reefs protect waters closest to the mainland, usually the ocean tides and waves are not noticed. However, during a hurricane there can be waves as high as 16 feet (five meters). During hurricane conditions, the swing bridge in Belize City opens before its scheduled time so boats can go up the Belize River to relative safety.

There are times when hurricanes blowing 200 miles away from Belize still cause destructive wave action along the shores. On the bright side, a good emergency evacuation plan is in place and many of the resort owners on the cayes keep in contact with the hurricane center in Miami so that they can evacuate their patrons before the storm arrives.

❖ MAJOR HURRICANES OF BELIZE

- ❖ 1931 - An unnamed hurricane killed 1,000 people.
- ❖ 1955 - Janet destroyed the town of Corozal and left in its wake 681 dead.
- ❖ 1961 - Hattie had winds up to 186 mph and four-meter (13-foot) tides. The storm killed 275 people.
- ❖ 1974 - Fifi and Carmen. Fifi was a Class 1 storm (mildest on Saffer Simpson Scale), but it killed 8,000-10,000 people in Honduras and did a large amount of damage in Belize.
- ❖ 1978 - Greta left five dead and 6,000 lives affected.
- ❖ 2000 - Keith hit around Ambergris Caye causing over $500 million worth of damage.
- ❖ 2001 - Iris almost obliterated Placencia and killed 20 people when their boat tipped over.

Plant Life

With its diverse landscapes, Belize presents a whole world of trees, flowers, shrubs, grasses and bromeliads. Those are the natural plants. There are also a number of domesticated plants, like corn, sugar cane and beans. It is impossible to describe all 4,000 plants and 700 trees, but this general overview covers the most dominant plants and animals you will encounter.

FASCINATING FACT: *Of the 3,000 plants in the rainforest, about 2,000 are known and used by indigenous peoples. Modern science has tested about 1% of these plants for medicinal purposes.*

◆ The Rainforest

Rainforests are defined as areas that receive 160-400 inches (405-1,015 cm) of rain annually and have little temperature change throughout the year. This consistent environment supports an ecosystem of plants, animals and insects that struggle against each other for survival.

All rainforests are found between the Tropic of Cancer and the Tropic of Capricorn and they are on land that has never been glaciated.

Typically trees in the rainforest grow over 150 feet tall (45 meters) and their branches spread out, forming a lush canopy over the creatures living below. This canopy prevents most of the sunlight from reaching the forest floor, leaving the ground with few nutrients. Since the root systems of these trees must compete for the small amount of available nutrients, roots spread out sideways, rather than heading deep down into the ground. This type of growth leaves trees somewhat unstable. To counter this instability many trees, like the Ceiba, have developed buttresses at the base of their trunks that act like stabilizing arms.

Long woody vines called **lianas** often climb up trees in the rainforest and add to the dense canopy at the top. The many plants in the rainforest produce a tremendous amount of oxygen, which is soon consumed in the decomposition process occurring on the forest floor.

Orchids are parasitic and grow on a host plant. However, there are some that grow in the ground. Depending on which source you use, Belize has between 70 and 250 species of orchids natural to the country, 80% of which live on host plants. Orchids are members of the most highly evolved plant groups on the planet. There are about 25,000 species worldwide. Their evolution has resulted in thick leaves that hold moisture for the plant. Some of the flowers are highly perfumed, thus attracting more creatures for pollination.

> **FASCINATING FACT:** *The South and Central American Indians used vanilla, obtained from a highly perfumed orchid, as flavoring for drinks long before Columbus came to the continent.*

Similar in appearance to the orchids are the **bromeliads**, or air plants. Unique to the Americas, bromeliads grow at any elevation up to 8,000 feet (2,500 meters) and in any terrain from rainforest to desert. Some bromeliads can be as small as one inch across, while others grow to three feet (one meter). The pineapple is the most commonly known bromeliad. It originated in Brazil and Paraguay and was spread by the local Indians before Columbus arrived. He took the plant to Europe, where it was planted and taken on to other countries.

> **AUTHOR TIP:** *To determine if a pineapple is good to eat, snap your finger against it. If you hear a solid dull sound, then it is good to eat. If the sound is hollow, the fruit is of poor quality.*

> ❖ **PINEAPPLE HOSPITALITY**
>
> Over the years, the pineapple has become a symbol of hospitality. Legend says that it got its reputation from a sea captain who was living in the Caribbean. Whenever the captain returned from sea, he would stop at his friend's place and impale a fruit onto the fence. This would be taken as an invitation for the friend to visit. The symbol was later incorporated by innkeepers who had the pineapple added to their logos and even carved onto bedposts.

◆ Mangroves

Mangrove forests are found along the coast of Belize and on some of the cayes. Each species plays an important, slightly different, part in the ecological system.

Mangroves are often found parallel to coral reefs. It is believed that because the plants like brackish, nutrient-rich water, they clarify it for the coral that likes clear, nutrient-poor water.

Red mangroves, found closest to or in the water, trap silt and rotting leaves around their roots. As the debris turns into soil, the red mangrove dies (after sending seeds to other parts of the area) and the white mangrove moves in.

White mangroves are very salt-tolerant and have a unique root system that grows above high-water levels. Seed pods develop on the ends of these non-immersed roots and, after they ripen, fall into the ground and grow. The roots above the water also facilitate the exchange of gases.

Some mangroves are able to filter the salt water through their root system, while others release the salt through the pores of their leaves.

Besides being a protecting environment for hundreds of fish, mangroves are home to both birds and land animals. But mangroves help humans too. They keep soil erosion to a minimum and they absorb some of the harsh wave action caused by hurricanes and storms. The wood from the trees is used to make traps and nets and it can also be burned for fuel.

Since 1989, clearance of mangroves in Belize is illegal. Unfortunately, as pressure for more tourist facilities increases, the enforcement of this regulation decreases.

◆ Heliconias

Heliconias are a small group of plants found in the tropics that are characterized by their large leaves and striking flowers. Native to Central and South America, they grow in humid regions, usually at elevations below 1,500 feet (450 meters). Some of the more recognizable heliconias are the banana, the bird of paradise, ginger and the prayer plant.

◆ Trees

The **hardwood forests** of Belize were what drew many entrepreneurs to the country in the first place. It was **mahogany** and **ziricote** (or zericote) that put dollars into their pockets. But try as they might, they never stripped this little country completely of its forests. Today, about 44% of the original trees are still standing, an impressive statistic when compared to similar countries like El Salvador, which has less than 2% of virgin forest left.

The **bull horn acacia** has large spines on its body and will grow up to 12 feet high (3.5 meters). The shrub's spines are home to the Acacia ant; each tree can hold 10,000 to 100,000 ants. The tree and the ants have formed an interdependency that seems to work. The tree provides a home and food (the sweet nectar produced at the base of its leaves) and the ant in turn bites or stings anyone who comes near the tree. The shrub's violet-scented flowers are used in France's perfume industry.

Cacao, grown throughout the tropics, gives the world over one million tons of chocolate powder every year. This evergreen grows to 25 feet (7.5 meters). It likes a warm humid climate without much rain. The tree produces an oblong fruit, up to 12 inches (30 cm) long that, when ripe, can be yellow, red, purple or green. The fruit, which is usually harvested after the wet season, has between 20 and 60 seeds that grow in five even rows. The five-petaled cacao flower is pink and has five smaller yellow petals inside. It opens in the morning and lives for only one day. However, the plant produces flowers all year long.

The cacao tree likes shade and starts to produce fruit at three or four years of age. An adult grove, one acre in size, can produce between 300 and 1,000 pounds (136-450 kg) of cacao per year for up to 50 years.

Calabash trees can be identified by their white tubular flowers or gourd-shaped fruits that grow from their trunks. Up to 100 flowers or gourds can grow on a tree at any time. It takes seven months after pollination for the fruit to ripen and fall from the tree.

The **ceiba tree** is another deciduous giant of the forest and can be identified by its gray, fan-tailed trunk. The tree reaches 150 feet (50 meters) in height and is home not only to birds and animals, but also to many aerial plants. The tree sheds its leaves during dry season and seedpods can be seen dangling from branches.

 MYSTERIOUS MAYA: *The Maya believe that the ceiba tree connected the center of the earth to the heavens. The only time the tree is used by the Maya is when a dug-out canoe is needed.*

Fruit trees grow abundantly in the tropics of Belize. There are limes, oranges, grapefruit, apple, papaya, avocado and – my favorite – the **cashew**. Although I like the nut, it is the fruit with its tart pulp that makes my mouth water. Do taste it if you are there during its season, which is early May.

The **guanacaste tree** is a fast-growing tree that reaches a height of 130 feet (40 meters), a significant portion of which is trunk. Gunacaste trunks often have a diameter of over six feet (1.8 meters). The seed pods are broad and flat, about three or four inches across, and curled into a tight circle so they resemble a human ear.

The **gumbo limbo tree** is also called the tourist tree because it has a red bark that peels, much like the pale skin of tourists. It grows well in shade and is often found in the jungle or on an island that has not been cleared. The Maya used its bark to treat rashes caused by the poisonwood tree.

The **palm tree** is everywhere in Belize and comes in a number of varieties such as the cahune, banana, palmetto, silver thatch, queen and royal palms. Since lethal yellow (a palm tree bacteria) has invaded and killed many of the trees, some land owners are replanting with the dwarf palm, a species that is supposed to be resistant to bacteria.

Palms like to live near the coast, although they can be seen at elevations of up to 2,000 feet (600 meters). They grow to 100 feet (30 meters) and have feather-like fronds that reach out 35 feet (10 meters). Their seeds are the coconuts that, once opened, produce a sweet drinkable nectar and a pulpy fruit that lines the shell.

INTRODUCTION

The **mahogany tree** is the national tree of Belize, a magnificent deciduous
giant. A mature tree stands well over 75 feet tall (25 meters) and the foliage
offers a great amount of shade. The trunk has a red, scaly bark and there are
four to eight leathery leaves on each branch. Tiny white flowers appear in
clusters and bear a pear-shaped fruit that has noticeable grooves along its
length. The fruit produces wing-shaped seeds.

The **pine tree** grows most abundantly in the Mountain Pine Ridge area.
Unlike its northern relative, this softwood evergreen has long flowing needles. The bark of one species is thick and rough and more fire-resistant than
the bark of a second type that grows on the ridge. Some pine trees in Belize
have been invaded by the pine beetle. This little beetle, barely 1/8th of an
inch long, is the most aggressive of the five known species. A mating pair will
produce up to 160 kids. While in the larvae stage, these kids feed off the inner bark. Then, as they mature, they devour the outer bark.

The **poisonwood tree** is a species you should be able to identify and
avoid. The alkaloid sap from this tree causes a skin irritation. The
poisonwood is related to poison ivy, only a poisonwood infection is more severe. The tree grows to about 25 feet (seven meters) and has a short trunk,
stout limbs and drooping branches. The bark is reddish-brown and covered
with thin oily patches of sap. The leaves cluster in groups of five, all about six
to 10 inches long (15 to 25 cm). They are smooth and glossy on top, but dull
and pale underneath.

The leaves of the poisonwood are broad at the base and thin to rounded at
the ends. The leaves may be blotched with irregular black spots. The fruit
looks like a yellowish berry and grows on the stem. There is almost always a
gumbo limbo tree growing near a poisonwood. This is convenient as the
gumbo limbo tree's sap is the antidote to the poisonwood's infection.

The **sapodilla** or **chicozapote tree** is the source of our chewing gum. It
produces a cream-colored latex and grows in northern Belize to heights of
150 feet (45 meters). The latex makes the wood of the tree rot-resistant.

The **strangler fig** is actually a parasite that chokes other living trees. Its
seed is usually deposited on the host tree by a bird or insect, and a tiny root
starts to twist its way down the trunk of the host while tiny branches and
leaves begin to sprout. As the root moves down, it develops leaves and
branches and more roots, that eventually wind around the host. The fig lives
off the host plant until its nutritional value has been devoured.

The **tamarind tree**, with feathered foliage and tiny red and yellow flowers,
is seen everywhere in Belize. It produces a brown fuzzy pea pod from which
a drink called tamarindo is produced.

The **ziricote tree** is also known as ironwood because it is so dense that it sinks in water. Ziricote grow up to 100 feet (30 meters) in height. They are found in the drier areas of the tropics. Their bright orange flowers, shaped like a forget-me-not, make them easily recognizable.

Animal Life

Belize has become conscious of preserving its wildlife and the habitat in which it lives. Although this may be stimulated by tourism, the results are good. There are almost as many sanctuaries, parks and reserves offering protection to everything – from animals to butterflies to snakes to orchids – as there are missionaries trying to preserve the souls of the people.

> **AUTHOR TIP:** *Rainforests are host to a huge number of birds and animals, many of which are active at night, when it is cooler. Be aware of this when taking a tour. If someone promises to show you a tapir (a night-time hunter), for example, be sure to take an early-morning or evening tour, as the animals are never seen at midday.*

◆ Rodents

Belize has the usual array of rodents, including squirrels, gophers, rats, moles, rabbits and porcupines. Distinct for their gnawing abilities, these animals have teeth that never stop growing and must be worn down in order for the animal to survive. Rodents are generally small and eat mostly vegetation, although their diets are often supplemented with eggs, birds and insects. This highly reproductive group sometime has numerous litters every year.

◆ Amphibians

Amphibians include frogs, toads, newts, salamanders, sirenians (sea cows) and caecilians (creatures that look like earthworms). Although amphibians have lungs, they also do some air exchange through their skin. They are found world wide, except on the poles and in extreme deserts.

Amphibians are hatched from eggs and usually go through a tadpole or larvae stage where breathing is done through gills. They metamorphose and in their new form they breath with lungs. Their skins are moist, glandular and pigmented, although if living away from light, pigmentation is minimal. Some, like the salamander, are able to rejuvenate lost body parts (for some reason, the back end of the creature is quicker to respond to re-growth than are the front limbs). The most endearing feature of the amphibian is its ability to consume large amounts of insects, especially mosquitoes.

◆ Reptiles

Reptiles are prominent in Belize, and it would be a rare visit if you didn't see at least one iguana, snake, turtle, gecko or toad while there. Reptiles control their temperature by moving in their environment. If it is too hot in the sun, they move to the shade. They all have a tough dry skin that is used primarily to preserve body moisture. Reptiles are the first creatures along the evolutionary ladder to have developed lungs.

Reptiles have evolved a number of protective devices. Some have hard shells or scales, while others inflict a poisonous venom. Yet others just change color so they blend into their environments and can't be seen. Reptiles always live in vegetated areas and prefer warm climates. More reptiles live on land than in fresh water and more in fresh water than in salt water.

TURTLES: The **hawksbill** is endangered due to the commercial value of its shell, meat and eggs. In recent years, this turtle's presence has drastically declined in the Caribbean Sea and Atlantic Ocean. The hawksbill is different than other turtles in that it has a beak-like mouth and two claws on each flipper. It generally grows to around 34 inches (87 cm) and weighs 175 pounds (80 kg). However, the biggest ever found weighed in at 280 pounds (127 kg).

> **FASCINATING FACT:** *The turtle's shell makes the animal's ribs immoveable. In order to breath, turtles either swallow air or they kick their legs and pump the air into their lungs.*

The hawksbill can nest over a span of six months, between July and October. During this period the female nests four or five times, allowing a 14-day interval between each nesting. She lays around 140 eggs each time and the eggs hatch about 60 days after being laid. At birth, each hatchling weighs 12-20 grams (less than an ounce).

Generally, hawksbills eat sponge from around a reef and they use the ledges of the reef for resting spots.

> **❖ BEKKO**
>
> Bekko is a Japanese word meaning shell. For centuries, bekko has been used for making jewelry and decorating things like cabinets, door posts and mirrors. The hawksbill's shell is considered the most beautiful, colored orange, gold and dark brown.

The **loggerhead turtle** can grow up to three feet (one meter) and weigh up to 250 pounds (115 kg). Loggerheads are named for their large heads and short necks. They can be found in the coastal bays and estuaries of the Atlantic, Pacific and Indian Oceans. In the Western hemisphere, they can be found from the east and west coasts of Canada down to the tip of Argentina. They are carnivores and like shellfish; the turtle's powerful jaws can easily crush the shells of clams and shrimp.

Female loggerheads nest every two or three years. Every season they may nest four or five times and lay 100-125 eggs at each nesting. The eggs incubate for about 60 days. This period, along with the sex of the turtle, is dependent on the temperature.

The **green turtle** is so named because of the color of its fat. This slow grower does not reach sexual maturity until at least 20 years of age and some are believed to wait for 50 years. The green turtle will grow to about 39 inches (one meter) and weigh about 330 pounds (150 kg). However, in the recent past these creatures would grow to twice that size. Today, we harvest them so rapidly that they no longer have time to grow to their maximum size.

The green turtle is vegetarian and likes to graze on meadows of sea grass that grow in warm ocean waters. However, immature green turtles are known to eat a bit of meat. The females nest once every two to four years. Each nesting season results in two or three breeding sessions, about 14 days apart. The female lays around 100 eggs each time and the youngsters hatch about 60 days later.

◆ Cats

Jaguars are the largest and most powerful cats in the Americas. Often referred to as *el tigre*, the jaguar stands around 20-30 inches (51-76 cm) at the shoulder and has an overall length of six to eight feet (two to three meters). The jaguar's slender but strong body can weigh 250 pounds (115 kg).

The jaguar is built to hunt, with strong shoulders, sharp teeth, good eyesight and hearing, and claws that can rip the hamstring of a deer with one powerful swipe. The jaguar's short fur is usually yellow with black spots, or black circles with a yellow dot in the center. Some jaguars, however, are black in color, which makes their dots almost invisible.

There is no specific breeding season for the jaguar. The kittens are cared for by both parents for about one year, then everyone splits and fends for themselves. With good luck and lots of food, a jaguar lives about 20 years.

The red tiger or **puma** is also called the mountain lion, cougar or panther. Just a bit smaller than the jaguar, this animal can be found throughout North and South America wherever deer, its main source of food, is found. The puma is comparable in strength to the jaguar, and has been known to haul an animal five times its size for a considerable distance. The puma's life expectancy is only 15 years.

The **coati** is a tree-climbing mammal related to the raccoon. It has a long snout (tipped white) and an even longer tail that is usually the same length as its body. It keeps its striped tail high and, as it walks, the tail swings from side to side. Coatis are sociable animals and the females often travel with their young in groups of up to 20. When a group of these animals attacks a fruit tree, it can devour the entire crop in a few minutes. A full grown male stands about 10 inches (25 cm) at the shoulder and will grow to about two feet (half a meter) in length. This omnivore hunts both in the day and at night and eats just about anything, so your chances of seeing one moving along in tall grass or along rocky hillsides are good.

Margay and **ocelots** are both cats. An ocelot can weigh in at 35 pounds (16 kg), while the margay is not much bigger than a domestic cat. Both have black spots or rings and broken stripes on their fur.

> ❖   **ANIMAL RESCUE**
>
> If you come in contact with an injured, orphaned or troublesome animal in Belize, please call the wildlife hotline at ☎ 614-3043, a service funded by the Woodland Park Zoological Gardens.

◆ Other Mammals

Skunks are related to weasels, and their reputation for defense (spraying a horrid perfume up to 12 feet/3.5 meters), is well known. The skunk aims for the eyes of its enemy, and the liquid it emits produces temporary blindness.

Another night hunter, the skunk comes out of its den when the temperatures cool. It forages for insects, larvae, mice and fallen fruit. Skunks mate in spring and have litters of up to six young that are ready to look after themselves after about two months. The life span of a skunk is around 10 years.

The **tapir** or mountain cow is related to the horse and rhinoceros, but it is unique in the fact that it is the last surviving ungulate with an odd number of toes and it bears its weight on the middle toe. The animal's name was derived from the Brazilian Indian word meaning thick, which refers to its hide. This short-haired cow stands about four feet (1.2 meters) at the shoulder and weighs in at around 600 pounds (275 kg) when fully grown. It has a trunk-like snout that grabs leaves from aquatic plants or forest foliage for food.

The tapir is an excellent swimmer and can stay underwater for long periods, especially when hiding from its worst enemies, the jaguar and puma.

The **red deer** is the most common of all deer. It stands four feet (1.2 meters) at the shoulder and can weigh up to 300 pounds (135 kg). This deer always has a white rump patch around its short tail. A five-year-old stag is full-grown and has antlers with six points on each side. The stag usually grows one point every year until he reaches this six-point stage and then point growth is arbitrary. Once a year, female red deer give birth to one fawn that can stand within an hour of life.

The **peccary** is a small pig-like creature that has been around for 40 million years (according to fossil finds). It weighs about 65 pounds (23 kg) and travels in herds of a few individuals to as many as 300.

The peccary has two distinct features. One is the smell it exudes from a musk gland on its back when irritated. The second is its amazing nose, the tip of which is flat and reinforced with a cartilaginous disk that can lift logs and dig underground for roots and insects. A true omnivore, the peccary will eat anything from poisonous snakes to cactus.

The ant bear or **great anteater** is known for its lack of teeth. It has an elongated head has a small hole about the size of a pen from which a tongue, that can extend up to 19 inches (48 cm), whips out and snatches up termites and other insects. Its front toes and claws curl under, so it seems to be walking on its knuckles. It stands about two feet (60 cm) at the shoulder and is (including tail) about 6.5 feet (two meters) long.

The **armadillo**, also known as the dilly, is an insect-eating mammal that has a bony-plated shell encasing its back. This shell is the animal's protection. Although of the same family as the anteater, the armadillo has teeth that are simple rootless pegs in the back of its mouth. Because of these teeth, the armadillo is able to eat snakes, chickens, fruit and eggs. It also likes to munch on the odd scorpion.

 MYSTERIOUS MAYA: *The Maya believe that the black-headed vulture, rather than dying, becomes an armadillo when it gets old.*

◆ Monkeys

The **spider monkey** is not as common as the howler, nor is it as noisy. Spider monkeys have grasping hands that have no functional thumbs and a grasping tail that is hairless at the end. These five "hands" make the spider monkey very maneuverable. They travel in bands of 20 to 30 and will attack threatening invaders. They use fruits and branches as weapons, and some are known to urinate on enemies walking below.

The baboon or **black howler monkey** makes a horrid howling, growling sound that, if heard when you are walking alone through the jungle, will spook the hell out of you. And that is what it is meant to do. This leaf-eating primate has little facial hair, except on its chin. Like the spider, the howler has a long grasping tail. Its skin is black and its jawbone protrudes to accommodate the bladder-like resonating chamber found in the throat. It is this chamber that allows the monkey to make the frightening racket it does.

Howlers live in troops of up to 10 and have one dominant male leader. Once a troop is formed, they eat, sleep and travel together. Howlers weigh up to 25 pounds (11 kg) and mothers nurse their young for about 18 months.

◆ Spiders & More

Insects and arachnids are everywhere and play an important part in the cycle of tropical life. You are sure to encounter some critters from this group. Included are mosquitoes and cockroaches, botflies and butterflies, houseflies and fireflies, fire ants and leaf cutter ants, termites and scorpions. Some bite and others don't. Some are good to eat (chocolate-covered ants) and some (such as fireflies) are not even wanted by birds, toads or frogs.

Scorpions should be avoided as they do bite; when in the jungle, shake out shoes and clothes before putting them on. Apparently, the smaller the scorpion, the more lethal the bite. These anthropods are characterized by a long body and a segmented tail. Death from a sting results in heart or respiratory failure some hours after the bite.

For the most part, **ants** work in the service industry, cleaning up garbage left around the jungle floors (and your room if you are careless). Their highly organized colonies can be many feet across and equally as high. A colony of **leaf cutter ants** (also called wee wee ants) can strip a full-grown jungle tree within a day. The ants chew and swallow the leaves, which they regurgitate.

From that vomit, a fungus grows. They eat the fungus. The excretion from these ants helps fertilize the jungle floors.

Other insects are everywhere. Those huge blobs of gunk that cling to trees are the homes of **termites**. If you sleep under a thatch roof, be aware of **chagus**, the insect that sucks your blood and replaces it with its own excretion. Lethal cysts can develop if the infected area is not treated immediately. Everyone should avoid **mosquitoes** (use something with DEET) and if you ever step on a **fire ant's** mound, you'll be really sorry.

◆ Birds

Birds are plentiful and varied. Some are common while others are rare. Along with the indigenous birds of the country, Belize lies in a migratory path and thus has many visiting birds during spring and fall. It also has varied environments (islands in the Caribbean, rainforests, drier savannas and grasslands, swamps and lagoons), so it attracts birds needing those habitats.

> The most comprehensive tome available is the *Field Guide to the Birds of Mexico and North Central America* by Steve Howell and Sophie Wedd, published by Oxford Illustrated Press. It has both color plates and black and white drawings that cover 750 species. The book is 1,010 pages and heavy to carry.

> The second guide to look for is the *Field Guide to Birds of Mexico and Adjacent Areas: Belize, Guatemala and El Salvador* by E.P. Edwards and E.M. Butler, published by University of Texas Press. This book is a mere 209 pages and much better for carrying.

> A more practical and general guide to the wildlife in Belize is *Belize and Northern Guatemala: Ecotraveller's Wildlife Guide* by Les D. Beletsky. It's published by Harcourt Brace and endorsed by the Wildlife Conservation Society. It has 80 pages on birds alone, but covers everything from environmental concerns to animals.

The endangered **jabiru stork** is the largest bird in the western hemisphere, with a wing span of nine-12 feet (three-four meters). The stork has a large bill that is good for scooping up fish and frogs. The jabiru is found in Belize only from Nov. to June. Its most popular place to stay during while nesting is the Crooked Tree Wildlife Sanctuary, where a total of 24 have been seen together at one time.

The **frigate bird** or iwa can soar for hours over the sea, although it seldom goes more than 50 miles away from its home island. Because it does not lift off from water very well, the frigate steals from other birds or swoops down and catches fish swimming near the surface. It is big, black and beautiful. You will see many.

Underwater Life

After you've been in Belize for a short time, some form of underwater life will have crossed your path. There is coral or sponge that has broken off from the reef and washed up onto the shore. The sand itself is ground coral and sea shells. Walking along the beach, you may come upon tiny fish trapped in a tide pool. Most restaurants have shrimp, lobster or conch listed on their menus and there are few hotels that don't have a bowl of shells decorating the hall or stairway. Souvenir shops are inundated with shell crafts and most of the tourist industry revolves around snorkeling, fishing and deep-sea diving.

❖ CURIOUSLY CORAL

Coral reefs, formed millions of years ago, lie a few miles off the mainland. Composed of organic skeletal deposits from both plants and animals, this land of calcium carbonate (limestone) is fascinating to explore.

- ❖ **Stony corals**, such as brain and star corals, the main builders of reefs and atolls, are found exclusively in warm waters no deeper than 80 feet (25 meters). Stony corals are arranged in multiples of six polyps to each tentacle.

- ❖ **Horny corals**, with eight polyps to each tentacle, include organisms like sea fans and elkhorn corals. These corals have a supporting spine and can have over a million polyps. There are thousands of types of horny corals in the waters around Belize, and just being able to identify the stony from the horny is a good start.

- ❖ **Soft corals** do not deposit or contribute to the construction of a barrier reef as they totally disintegrate after death.

- ❖ There are also **false corals**, such as the prized black coral used for making ebony-colored jewelry.

Within the coral reef are underwater plants and grasses, some that flower and all with roots. Living in this environment are barnacles and conch, crabs and lobster, and fish of every color, size and shape.

The **manatee**, or sea cow, is a favorite attraction for tourists. This gentle aquatic animal weights about 400 pounds (180 kg) and is around seven feet (2.1 meters) long, although some large males have been known to grow up to 1,500 pounds (680 kg) and reach 15 feet (4.5 meters). The manatee has a torpedo-like body with a long flat tail that is used for propulsion. Its two forepaws are like paddles with tiny claws on the ends. Its upper lip is cleft and dotted with a few whiskers.

FASCINATING FACT: *The 11 teeth growing on the manatee's bottom jaw rotate. As the front two wear out, they drop off and the entire row moves forward. In the space where the very back molars were located, a new set develops.*

Dolphins are plentiful in the waters of Belize. Playful and intelligent, dolphins mature between five and 12 years and a female gives birth to one calf every second or third year. The life span of a dolphin is up to 48 years.

Dolphins travel in pods and it is suspected that each member of a pod is related. They like to stay near their home waters for their entire lives. They hunt for fish using an echo-location method similar to bats. A dolphin will eat up to 150 pounds (68 kg) of fish a day.

Whale sharks can be seen during the snapper moon, the full moons of Mar., Apr. and May. At that time, snapper and grouper are spawning and whale sharks like the taste of those newly fertilized eggs.

A whale shark is the largest fish known. It can grow to 50 feet (15 meters) and weigh 20 tons. That is a lot of animal.

National Emblems

Belize has an entire plethora of official national emblems and a story that intertwines each emblem with the history of the people.

National Anthem
Land of the Free
O Land of the free, by the Carib Sea,
Our manhood we pledge to thy liberty,
No tyrants here linger, despots must flee,
This tranquil haven of democracy.
The blood of our sires which hallows the sod,
Brought freedom from slavery oppression's rod,
By the might of truth and the grace of God,
No longer shall we be hewers of wood.
Arise! Ye sons of the Baymen's clan,
Put on your armours, clear the land.
Drive back the tyrants, let despots flee,
Land of the free, by the Carib Sea.
Nature has blessed thee with wealth untold,
O'er mountains and valleys where prairies roll,
Our fathers, the Baymen, valiant and bold,
Drove back the invader; this heritage bold,
From proud Rio Hondo to old Sarstoon,
Through coral isle, over blue lagoon,
Keep watch with the angels, the stars and moon,
For freedom comes tomorrow's noon.

◆ Coat of Arms

The Belizean Coat of Arms, first designed in 1907, is a circle representing a shield. It is featured on the national flag, shown on the following page.

◆ National Flag

The national flag is royal blue with a horizontal red stripe at the top and bottom. The Coat of Arms sits in a white circle in the center. The flag was first adopted in 1950 when Belize, then called British Honduras, first decided to move toward independence from Britain.

◆ National Motto

Sub Umbra Florero is Latin and means "under the shade I flourish." The shade is assumed to be that of the giant mahogany tree, but it is also metaphorical for "quiet or cool" political times.

◆ National Flower

The **black orchid** grows in damp areas and flowers all year. It has greenish yellow petals, except for the one prominent petal at the top, which is shaped like a clam shell and is such a deep purple that it appears to be black. A short flower, it grows in clusters not much higher than six inches.

◆ National Tree

The **mahogany** is one of the most magnificent deciduous trees. In spring, red buds appear, causing the hills to glow as if on fire. They soon turn into clusters of white flowers that in turn produce a pear-shaped fruit. When the fall rains end, leathery leaves appear, usually six or eight to a cluster.

◆ National Bird

The sociable **keel-billed toucan** has a canoe-shaped bill and bright yellow cheeks and it loudly croaks its presence from large trees in the lowland rain forests. The bird's serrated beak looks heavy but in fact is remarkably light. Toucans use the serrated edges of their beaks to cut fruit, their main diet. They also eat insects, lizards, snakes and the eggs of smaller birds.

◆ National Animal

The **tapir** or mountain cow has a fat body, short legs, a long snout and white-tipped ears. Despite its name, the tapir is more closely related to the horse and rhinoceros than the cow. This poor-sighted herbivore has excellent hearing and smell. The tapir is shy, hunts at night, and is rarely seen in groups larger than three or four. It breeds all year long. Full maturity is reached at one year and the life span of this animal is about 30 years.

Travel Information

Facts at Your Fingertips

CAPITAL: Belmopan.

HEAD OF STATE: Queen Elizabeth II of England, since Feb. 6, 1952.

GOVERNOR GENERAL: Sir Colville Young is the Queen's representative. He has been in office since Nov. 17, 1993.

PRIME MINISTER: Said Musa, leader of the PUP since 1997, is the nation's third Prime Minister.

DEPUTY PRIME MINISTER: John Briceño. He is appointed by the Prime Minister and is a member of the cabinet and the ruling party.

POPULATION: 262,299 people. Forty-two percent of the population is under 14. Ethnic groups are 29-40% Creole, 33-43.7% Mestizo, 10% Mayan, 8% Garifuna, 8% white and 1% other.

AREA: 8,868 square miles. Of that, 62 square miles is water.

BORDERS: Guatemala 165 miles, Mexico 155 miles.

COAST: 240 miles.

CURRENCY: Belizean dollar; US $1 = BZ $2 (2002). This is a fixed rate.

HOSPITALS: There are eight government-run hospitals, one in Belize City, one in Belmopan and one in each of the six districts.

RELIGION: 92% Christian, with 62% of that being Catholic.

EDUCATION: Compulsory for everyone between six and 14 years of age. The literacy rate is 70.3% and is equal for men and women.

LIFE EXPECTANCY: 69 for men and 73.5 for women. On average, four children are born to each woman.

NATURAL PRODUCTS: Bananas, cocoa, citrus, sugarcane, lumber, fish and cultured shrimp. Industrial production includes garment factories, food processing, tourism and construction. Belize produces its own electricity by using either fossil fuels (43%) or water (57%).

GDP: $276 per year, but the adult unemployment rate is 11.8%.

When to Go

◆ Seasonal Considerations

Belize is pleasant at any time of year. The off-season, mid-May to mid-Sept., brings the best prices for hotels and tours, as well as fewer tourists. Mid-May is the start of rainy season. However, it does not rain all day every day during that time. Usually, there are a few torrential downpours during the night or for an hour during midday. This is the most hot and humid time of year. Sept. and Oct. are the worst months for hurricanes. **Temperatures** peak at 90°F (32°C) and can go as low as 19°C. If a north wind blows, even the cayes can be 70°F (21°C). **Humidity** is always high, averaging between 87% and 90%, and **rainfall** is anywhere from 1.5 inches (38 mm) to 12 inches (305 mm) per month. **Christmas** and **Easter** are when Belizeans like to vacation so hotel rooms are scarce. This is high season.

◆ National Holidays

National holidays are a big thing. Shops are closed, restaurants are full and everyone is out enjoying the festivities. Special foods are sold on the streets. People are friendlier than usual. Baron Bliss Day is especially good as the entire nation participates in events like bike, horse or sailboat racing.

For more information about particular events during national holidays, contact the **tourist office** in Belize City, New Central Bank Building, Gabourel Lane, ☎ 223-1913. For information in Corozal, ☎ 422-3176; New River Orange Walk, ☎ 322-0381; Punta Gorda, ☎ 722-2531; and San Ignacio, ☎ 824-4236. Or you can e-mail them at info@travelbelize.org.

FEBRUARY: One week before Lent the **Fiesta del Carnival** is held. It has evolved into a costume party where people use paint and face makeup to hide their identity. There is usually lots of noise attached to this event.

MARCH: Mar. 9 is **Baron Bliss Day**. Henry Edward Ernest Victor Bliss IV was a wealthy Englishman who received his title from the Portuguese. In 1926, when Bliss learned of his impending death due to food poisoning, he willed all his money, rumored to be about one million pounds sterling, to Belize. The country received it after Bliss's wife died. Each year a ceremony is held at his tomb below the lighthouse in Belize Harbor, Belize City. This is followed by sailing regattas.

MARCH/APRIL: There is a four-day holiday for **Easter** sometime during Mar. and Apr.; the exact date depends upon when Easter falls. The vacation includes Friday, Saturday, Sunday and Monday.

MAY: May 1st is **Labor Day**, celebrated (after a speech from the Minister of Labor) with kite-flying contests, a sailing regatta, horse races and a bicycle race. May 24th is **Commonwealth Day**. A general celebration of Belize's place in the British Commonwealth, its most popular events are horse races in Belize City and Orange Walk.

JUNE: June in San Pedro offers a three-day festival in honor of St. Peter, the town's patron saint. All the people who fish for a living are blessed at a special mass, followed by music, dancing and food.

AUGUST: San Antonio in the Toledo District celebrates the **Maya Deer-Dance Festival**. The celebration, which lasts for one week, offers historical plays, music and dancing. The **Costa Maya Festival** (formerly the International Sea & Air Festival) is held in San Pedro in mid-Aug. to celebrate the friendship of all neighboring countries. There is music, dance and food.

SEPTEMBER: Sept. 10th is **St. George's Caye Day**. This national holiday commemorates the battle of St. George in 1798. There are carnivals, sporting events, parades and music concerts. This is a very big celebration. Sept. 21st is **Independence Day**. Independence from Britain was granted on that day in 1981; it is when the Constitution of Belize came into effect.

OCTOBER: Oct. 12th, **Columbus Day**, brings a two-day, international cross-country hike and bike race to bring attention to the national rainforests.

NOVEMBER: Nov. 19th is **Garifuna Settlement Day**. It was on this day in 1823 that Garifuna first arrived in Dangriga. To commemorate this event, they paddle in canoes laden with traditional foods, drums and household utensils. Once at the village they dance, sing and eat until late into the night.

DECEMBER: December 25th and 26th has the festival of **Christmas** followed by the English holiday called **Boxing Day**. Originally an English tradition, Boxing Day or St. Stephen's Day was when those of lower classes received boxed gifts of goods or money from their bosses/lords/employers.

What to Take

◆ Required Documents

You must have a valid **passport** that will be good for six months after your entry into the country. No visas are required for citizens from Canada, the United States, England, Belgium, Denmark, Finland, Greece, Iceland, Italy, Liechtenstein, Luxembourg, Mexico, Spain, Switzerland, Tunisia, Turkey and Uruguay for stays of up to 30 days. If your visit exceeds one month, a permit must be obtained from Immigration at the airport.

Everyone entering Belize must have a travel permit, given free at the border or port of entry. You will be returned a portion of the form to carry with you. This tiny piece of paper must be submitted to the border guard on your departure. Loss of the paper could cost you in time and headaches. Technically, you must also have an onward ticket when entering Belize, although this is seldom checked.

Your pet must have all shots and vaccinations required for international travel. Rabies shots must be no older than six months.

An AIDS test is required for those staying more than three months in Belize; a US test is accepted if it was done within three months of your planned visit.

For further information about regulations, call one of the **Immigration and Nationality Departments**: ☎ 822-2423 in Belmopan; ☎ 222-4620 in Belize City. Or see the websites www.travel.state.gov or www.ambergriscaye.com/economics/entryreq. This second site also has a list of Belize Foreign Offices around the world.

◆ Packing List

Binoculars are a must, even if you are not a bird watcher.

Everyone in Belize wears shorts, so pack **shorts** and **t-shirts**. Revealing outfits are not acceptable; shorts should fall to mid-thigh. Keep your clothing loose and comfortable.

Sandals are good at the beach and on the cayes, but **running shoes** or light **hiking boots** are needed for jungle walks.

On public beaches you will need a **bathing suit**. Most beach-goers bring a beach towel or grass matt to lie on.

Cameras are a great way to record a memory. Humidity is high in Belize, so keeping the camera dry is a concern. Because of the intense sunlight, a slow-speed film is recommended.

> **AUTHOR TIP:** *A flash should be used when photographing people during the day so that the harsh shadows are eliminated.*

The underwater photography is splendid. However, I suggest you take an introductory course before leaving home.

A **money belt** should always be made of a natural-fiber so that it's comfortable worn under your clothes.

❖ KEEP IT SAFE

Keep important documents in plastic bags inside the money belt, protected from sweat. Always place some money and/or travelers' checks in different places, so if you are robbed you will have some money to live on. There are belts that have zippered pockets on the underside. These comfortable and inconspicuous belts are worn as ordinary belts would be. Money must be folded lengthwise to fit. Tiny pockets can also be sewn into clothing, in the hem of a skirt or the cuff of a shirt.

Daypacks are convenient and hard to pickpocket or snatch. In cities, on buses or crowded places like markets, wear your daypack at the front, with the waist strap done up. Keep only the amount of money you need for the day in your daypack and the bulk of your money elsewhere. Keep your camera in the pack (not hanging around your neck) so that it is easily accessible and easy to hide.

It seems to me that a map is really hard to follow if you don't have a **compass**. Purchase a simple one.

If you find yourself stuck in a noisy hotel room, **earplugs** are essential.

Dive gear can be brought from home or rented from the dive shops at around US $25 for a complete diving outfit ($8 for a wet suit). You will need your **PADI diving certification** ticket.

An **umbrella** keeps off both sun and rain. It is also a nice little defense tool.

A **walking stick** is useful if you plan to visit caves, or go hiking or walking along rivers, where rocks are usually slippery.

Your **first aid kit** should include prescription medications.

Make **photocopies** of your passport and other documents and store them somewhere other than with your passport. In our technological age you can also scan your passport and e-mail the scan to a traveling e-mail address (i.e., Yahoo or Hotmail).

Reading material is available in English at magazine stands and book stores and many hotels have book-trading services. But for the most part, Belize is in need of books. Take some and leave them there.

A **sleeping sheet** is advisable if staying in the cheaper places or camping; a sleeping bag is not necessary.

Sunglasses and **sun hat** should be worn all the time you are in the sun.

Sunscreen and **insect repellent** are necessities.

Health Concerns

Belize does not have the same quality of medical services as North America, so purchase **medical insurance**. The cost is anywhere from US $1 to $5 per day, and many policies include ticket cancellation insurance and coverage against theft.

Before purchasing travel insurance, read the fine print. Some insurance companies give discount coupons for museums/parks. Some will cover you for adventure sports like climbing, but only if ropes are NOT used. A good place to look at insurance options is www.internationalplan.com.

◆ Common Ailments

General health and nutrition should be kept at an optimum level when traveling. Make certain you have rest, lots of clean water and a well-balanced diet that is supplemented with vitamins. This is not difficult to do in Belize. The tap water is safe; it is collected rain water. If you feel squeamish about drinking tap water, bottled mineral water is available everywhere.

Salt intake is important as it helps prevent **dehydration**.

Should you get a mild case of **diarrhea**, take a day of rest, drink plenty of water and do not consume alcohol. This common condition, often caused by the change in diet, usually clears up quickly. The mineral water can be supplemented with yogurt tablets. Imodium AD should be used with caution.

Eat at places where others are eating. If the sanitation looks dubious, don't eat the salad; have some hot boiled soup instead.

Fevers & Worse

Malaria, according to the World Health Organization, is a possibility in Belize any time of the year and anywhere at elevations below 400 feet (120 meters). The danger of infection increases during rainy season. In the event that you develop a fever for no explicable reason, like a cold or flu, especially if you are in mosquito country or have been bitten by a mosquito, you should treat the condition as if it is malaria. Some forms of malaria are lethal, so immediate attention is imperative.

Keep exposed skin covered early in the morning or at dusk when the mosquitoes are most active. Using repellents laced with DEET is also recommended. Although traces of DEET have been found in the livers of users, it is still better than the instant death of malaria. Using a sleeping net in infected areas is highly recommended.

Other protections against malaria-bearing mosquitos are to spray or soak your clothes and sleeping gear (including net or tent) with permethrin. Protection lasts for up to three washings. Permethrin can be purchased in any garden shop that sells pesticides.

Dengue fever and **dengue hemorrhagic fever** is caused by four related but distinctly different viruses that are spread by daytime-biting mosquitoes. Infection from one of the viruses does not produce immunity toward the other three. Dengue cannot be transmitted from person to person. Symptoms of dengue are high fever, headache, backache, joint pain, nausea, vomiting, eye pain and rash. There is no treatment except to take painkillers with acetaminophen rather than those with aspirin (acetylsalicylic acid decreases your blood's clotting abilities thus increasing the possibility of hemorrhage). Drink plenty of fluids and rest. If dengue hemorrhagic fever is contracted fluid replacement therapy may be necessary. The illness lasts about 10 days and total recovery takes two to four weeks.

Yellow fever is present in all the jungles of Central America. Though inoculation is not required for entrance to Belize, it may be required for re-entry to your own country (check with your immigration office). Inoculation, good for 10 years, is recommended if you want to avoid a lengthy stay in quarantine. Children must also have a certificate of inoculation, but it is not recommended to inoculate those who are less than one year of age.

Routine inoculations common in your home country should be up to date. Besides these, immune globulin is recommended against **viral hepatitis**, the shots are good for about six months. If you have had viral hepatitis, you are already immune. Inoculation against **typhoid fever** is highly recommended. This inoculation is good for 10 years.

Bugs

Worms and **parasites** can be a problem in the tropics. Keep your feet free of cuts or open sores so that worm larva or parasites cannot enter. Use sandals in the showers, especially if cleanliness is in question. Wear closed shoes (running shoes or hiking boots) when outdoors, especially in the jungle.

If staying in lower-end hotels, where **bed bugs** or **fleas** can be a problem, keep your sleeping gear in mothballs during the day.

The **tumbu fly** transports its eggs into its host by way of the mosquito. Once in its host, the egg hatches and the fly lives under the skin. However, it must have air. If you have a red swelling that is larger than something from a mosquito bite, look closely. If you see a small hole in the swollen area cover it with petroleum jelly to prevent the fly from breathing. Without air, it dies.

Chagas, also known as the kissing bug, exists in Central America and infection can become either chronic or acute. The parasite enters the bloodstream when the infected oval-shaped insect inserts its proboscis into your skin. Once the parasite is in your bloodstream, the larva migrates to the heart, brain, liver and spleen, where it nests and forms cysts. If you wake up with a purplish lump somewhere on exposed skin, you may have been bitten. Symptoms include fever, shortness of breath, and vomiting or convulsions. See a doctor immediately.

◆ Treatment Options

If you become sick, contact your own consulate for the names of doctors or medical clinics. The consulates can usually recommend doctors who have been trained in your place of origin. For minor ailments that need attending, you may want to try one of the local clinics or hospitals in Belize. See *Emergency Contacts*, page 305, for a complete list of embassies and consulates.

To reach these hospitals by phone, you need dial only the number given here if you are in Belize. There are no area codes to incorporate.

Karl Heusner Memorial Hospital, Belize City, ☎ 223-1548
Cleopatra White Outpatient Clinic, Belize City, ☎ 224-4012
Matron Roberts Health Center, Belize City, ☎ 227-7170
Port Loyola Health Center, Belize City, ☎ 227-5354
Rockview Hospital, Rockville, ☎ 220-6074
Orange Walk Hospital, Orange Walk, ☎ 322-2072
Corozal Hospital, Corozal, ☎ 422-2076
Dangriga Hospital, Dangriga, ☎ 522-2078
Dr. Price Memorial Clinic, Independence, ☎ 523-2167
Punta Gorda Memorial Hospital, Punta Gorda, ☎ 722-2026
Belmopan Hospital, Belmopan, ☎ 822-2264
Caye Caulker Health Center, Caye Caulker, ☎ 226-2166
San Pedro Health Center, San Pedro, ☎ 226-3668
San Ignacio Hospital, San Ignacio, ☎ 824-2066

TRAVEL INFORMATION

You can also contact the **IAMAT** (International Association for Medical Assistance to Travelers) clinic at 99 Freetown Road in Belize City, ☎ 224 5261. IAMAT's mission is to provide competent medical care to travelers anywhere in the world by doctors who have been trained in Europe or North America.

Herbal medicines are popular among the Maya and Garifuna. If you are away from the kind of medical care you are accustomed to, you may want to try a local "curandero," or healer. Ask a local where one can be found.

> **HERBAL LAXATIVE:** *Tamarind fruit (in a long brown pod) is often seen in the market. From this fruit a tart drink is made. If the fruit is soaked in water for a while, the water can be used as a laxative.*

For official government updates on outbreaks, advisories and more, visit the Centers for Disease Control & Prevention run by the US Health Department at http://www.cdc.gov.

◆ Water

Tap water is safe to drink; it is usually rain water collected from the roofs and stored in wooden or cement vats. If you feel uncomfortable with this, purified water is available throughout Belize. The cost is about BZ $1 per liter.

> **STAYING HEALTHY:** *Signs decorate many buildings in Belize warning people to pay attention to thirst, and not to dehydrate themselves.*

If traveling where creek/lake water must be used, add a chemical such as iodine for purification. There is also a tablet available with a more palatable silver (as opposed to an iodine) base. Mechanical filters take a long time to process the water and they do not filter out all organisms that could cause problems.

Money Matters

Belize is not a cheap place to visit. It is the most expensive Central American country. Budget travelers will have a hard time living in Belize for less than US $25 a day, which puts it almost on par with Canada. The (almost) all-inclusive resorts are expensive, ranging from about US $100 to $200 per day. Plus, the non-inclusive part of these packages are drinks, tours and diving.

Be aware of which currency is being quoted. Occasionally, a taxi driver will tell you that your fare is $5, and he silently hopes you pay in US dollars even though he meant the fare to be in Belize dollars. On the other hand, as soon as a hotel owner sees that you are a foreigner, he will almost always quote you a price in US dollars. Since Belize has an informal policy of double-pricing for tourists, deliberately confusing US and Belize dollars is common.

◆ Price Scales

In the hotel/restaurant/tours sections of this book, I give a price range. The price for a single and double room is the same, unless otherwise stated, and all prices are in US dollars. Use these rates as a guideline only; always call and verify current prices.

❖ HOTELS		❖ RESTAURANTS	
$	$10 to $20	$	under $5
$$	$21 to $50	$$	$5-$10
$$$	$51 to $75	$$$	$11-$25
$$$$	$76 to $100	$$$$	$26-$50
$$$$$	over $100	$$$$$	over $50

TRAVEL INFORMATION

For each restaurant/hotel, I give my personal impression, followed by a brief review. My impressions may have been influenced by who I saw and how they treated me. Once you have used the book for a while, you will have an idea as to what events and experiences interest me and what level of service impresses me.

◆ Banking/Exchange

One domestic (**Belize Bank**) and three foreign-owned banks (**Barclays**, **Nova Scotia** and **Atlantic**) operate in Belize. Banking hours are Mon. to Thur., 8 am to 2:30 pm, and Fri. from 8 am to 4:30 pm. You can exchange currency in either cash or traveler's checks and draw money from your Visa/MasterCard account.

If you're used to relying on **ATMs** for cash withdrawals, you'll have to plan differently in Belize. The ATMs are not hooked up to the international system, so they work only for Belizean bank accounts.

The Belize dollar is tied to the American dollar and is half the value: BZ $2 = US $1. Both currencies are readily accepted anywhere in the country. You can change foreign currency at the airport, at your hotel or at any bank in the country. However, it is best to carry US dollars. Belize dollars can be exchanged back into US dollars at the airport in Belize City or with money changers at all land borders (although anything less than BZ $5 will not be accepted at the airport). Belize dollars can also be exchanged at some US airport money exchange offices for a charge.

Traveler's checks in American currency can be cashed almost anywhere. If you are charged a fee for cashing American Express travelers' checks, insist on obtaining a receipt. Send the receipt into American Express, Salt Lake City, UT 84184-0401 and they will refund these charges.

If you are charged an extra fee (sometimes up to 8%) for using Visa/MasterCard, report this to the Visa/MasterCard office in your home city or call the international office at ☎ 800-336-3386. This extra charge violates the contract agreement between the credit card companies and the merchant.

Should you need money sent to you, contact **American Express Travel Service**, 41 Albert Street, Belize City, ☎ 227-7363, or **Western Union**, 63 Regent Street, Belize City, ☎ 227-0014. There are Western Union substations throughout the country and they offer the quickest service.

◆ Taxes & Tipping

Sales tax is 15% on all goods and services (called the VAT, or value added tax), except food (no tax) and accommodations (8%). Some hotels charge a 10% service charge over the quoted price and tax of the room; be sure to ask before checking in.

Once you have paid the foreigner's fee, the tax and the service charge, tipping is not necessary. Taxi drivers do not expect a tip. However, if you receive good service in a local restaurant, a tip is a nice gesture of appreciation. Ten-15% of your bill is a reasonable amount.

> ❖ **DUAL PRICING**
>
> Dual pricing is in effect and, in fact, is encouraged by the government. This means that Belize citizens are charged a much lower price for some hotels and all park entrance fees. For example, the entry fee to Cockscomb Basin Wildlife Reserve is BZ $4 for nationals and US $8 for foreigners. And when hotels fill out their application forms for licensing, one of the questions asked is what will the proprietor charge locals and what will he charge foreigners for the same room.

The official justification for dual pricing is that Belizeans would not be able to afford to visit attractions if prices were not lower. Ironically, what is happening is that Belizeans are buying the tickets at their lower price and selling them to tourists for a significant mark-up, though still lower than the suggested tourist price.

◆ Planning your Expenses

If you make all your own arrangements, your cheapest day could run about US $25. This would include a basic room with a slow-moving fan, two good meals in a traditional restaurant and a visit to one tourist attraction that you reach on foot. Should you want to do some of the fun things like snorkeling or diving, you will have to budget US $50 to $75 a day. To go first class in Belize – enjoy a rum punch at sunset and spend a few hours scuba diving with rented gear – budget US $200-$400+ per day.

Measurements

Officially, Belize recognizes the metric system. However, car odometers show miles, and everyone talks in miles, so we use miles as forms of measurement in this book. Other measurements are not so cut and dry, so we give both. If ever you are in doubt, use this chart to convert the figure into a measurement you can work with.

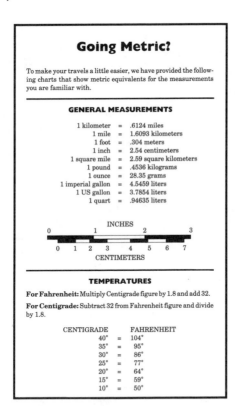

Going Metric?

To make your travels a little easier, we have provided the following charts that show metric equivalents for the measurements you are familiar with.

GENERAL MEASUREMENTS

1 kilometer	=	.6124 miles
1 mile	=	1.6093 kilometers
1 foot	=	.304 meters
1 inch	=	2.54 centimeters
1 square mile	=	2.59 square kilometers
1 pound	=	.4536 kilograms
1 ounce	=	28.35 grams
1 imperial gallon	=	4.5459 liters
1 US gallon	=	3.7854 liters
1 quart	=	.94635 liters

INCHES

0   1   2   3

0   1   2   3   4   5   6   7

CENTIMETERS

TEMPERATURES

For Fahrenheit: Multiply Centigrade figure by 1.8 and add 32.

For Centigrade: Subtract 32 from Fahrenheit figure and divide by 1.8.

CENTIGRADE		FAHRENHEIT
40°	=	104°
35°	=	95°
30°	=	86°
25°	=	77°
20°	=	64°
15°	=	59°
10°	=	50°

Dangers & Annoyances

If you hang out in the very poor sections of a city where you are unknown, if you are staggering drunk in a back alley, if you trust a stranger to hold your cash while you run to the washroom, you are going to have a sad tale to tell.

◆ Common-Sense Precautions

When out, **be aware** of what is around you. If you are being followed, go into a store or knock on someone's door. Predators look for single travelers.

Make certain that expensive items like your camera are **out of sight**. Carry only a bit of cash in your pocket and the rest in your money belt.

Be inside at night and take a **taxi** back to your room if you have been out late. **Don't be drunk** in public. A drunk is a great target. Don't get mixed up in the **dope** trade.

Women should walk with confidence. If you appear frightened or lost, you are a target. Don't walk alone in non-populated places like the jungle or along a secluded beach. In the event that you are grabbed or accosted in any way, create a scene. Holler, scream, kick and fight with all your might. However, if you are approached by someone with a weapon, let them have it all.

◆ In the City

Belize City has the reputation of being dangerous. With an unemployment rate of almost 13% and the average employed person earning US $3,200 a year, money is in short supply. I have never had a problem anywhere in Belize. However, caution is advised. Be alert, confident and careful.

◆ Emergency Assistance

In the event of a **robbery**, call the local police. Phone numbers are given at the beginning of every telephone book. The police, for the most part, are not corrupt. Once you have reported the incident, call your embassy or consulate. See the *Appendix*, page 305, for a list of embassies and consulates in Belize.

Communications

◆ Telephone

To call anywhere in Belize, you dial only the seven-digit number. If calling from out of the country, dial your country's international access code (in the US, this is 011), Belize's country code, **501**, and then the seven-digit number.

Using the telephone is not difficult. Purchase a **telephone card**, available in BZ $5, BZ $10 and BZ $20 denominations. Go to a telephone that is programmed to accept cards, pick up the receiver and wait for the operator to tell you to punch in the PIN shown on the back of the card (you must scratch off the silver in order to see the PIN). Assuming the number is accepted (often it is not, so you have to punch it in again), you will be instructed to enter the number you are calling. To make more than one call, hit the pound sign and punch in the next number. If you run out of funds during a call, the operator will come on the line, tell you that you are out of money, and then cut you off. There is very little time to punch in another PIN; you will need to redial.

◆ Internet

It is cheaper to use Internet service at a Belize Telephone Limited (called BTL) office than it is in an Internet café. The only BTL office I found without Internet service was in Orange Walk. Rates at BTL offices are US $3 an hour. The machines are generally fast, but the downside is that you can use them only during business hours, Monday through Friday, 8 am to 5 pm. The cost of service at commercial Internet cafés range from US $6 for five minutes (on Ambergris Caye) to US $3 per hour (San Ignacio).

◆ Postal Service

The postal service is good. It takes about a week for a letter to reach North America and costs about 30¢ for a card or one-page letter. Parcels do not have to be inspected before being mailed and insurance is available. You can have mail sent to General Delivery at any post office in Belize and it will be held for you.

Culture Shock

◆ Public Affection

Belize is a conservative country, so physical affection in public is not encouraged. Remember, this is a country with a strong religious tradition and a place where even abortion is not yet legal.

◆ Gay & Lesbian Travel

It is still illegal to be gay in Belize. My feeling is that until we stop making distinctions, there will still be discrimination. However, I understand the need for information, so I mention whether a hotel is liberal in my review.

◆ Human Rights

Although women are not considered equal to men in any setting, for the most part human rights are respected. The government never stops international groups from checking on the rights of Belizeans and women's groups are free to educate and promote equality.

There have been few reports of **police brutality**. Arbitrary arrest, limited to 72 hours, is seldom abused. All accused are innocent until proven guilty and family court issues are usually settled behind closed doors. There have been no political assassinations nor are there any political prisoners in Belize.

Food

Traditional foods in Belize are often good and some are exceptional. Chicken, beef, pork and seafood can be purchased almost anywhere, and it's the way they are prepared that makes for a culinary adventure. Always go to an eatery that is patronized by locals.

If you are on the islands, seafood will be your main staple and Creole food may be more common than anything else. Chinese restaurants are abundant and there are even some ethnic places, including a Lebanese restaurant on Ambergris Caye and an Indian restaurant in Belize City.

◆ Traditional Dishes

I wouldn't hesitate to eat food cooked over a fire by street vendors, nor would I ever go hungry if a market stall serving food was nearby. Belizeans are clean and their food is no exception.

Cassava (or yucca) is a root that is boiled and then strained for the pulp. It is dried and pounded into a white flour which, in turn, is made into a bread. Cassava is a traditional food of the Garifuna.

Fry jacks are a cornmeal bread substitute that's fried to a crisp. They are half moon-shaped and hollow inside. For breakfast, fry jacks are often served in restaurants instead of toast.

Rice and **refried beans** are the national staple. Since they have no taste they need no explaining.

Tamales are made from a gob of corn paste with a spicy piece of meat in the center rolled into a banana leaf and boiled. These are very good.

Escabeche is an onion soup flavored with copious amounts of spices. It is not only spicy hot, but the flavor is such a complicated mix of spices, it is difficult to put a finger on any particular one.

Relleno soup is made with stuffed chicken, ground pork and eggs. This is one of my favorites.

Gacho is a flour tortilla stuffed with vegetables, cheeses or meats and baked in the oven.

Sere is a soup made with fish and coconut milk.

Conch and **lobster** are offered almost everywhere. **Stewed chicken**, like rice and beans, is on every menu.

Ice cream is often homemade. But even the commercially made ice cream is good in Belize.

Booking a Room

Many people book their accommodations over the Internet. This is okay, but photos probably show only the best side of an establishment, and lighting plays a big part in making something look far more attractive than it is. You may not see the cockroaches in the corners or the bus terminal next door. Be sure to ask some questions.

- ❖ Is there air conditioning or a fan?
- ❖ Is there hot water? How is it heated?
- ❖ Where is the water obtained and is there a cost for it? Water stored in a vat is different from water in a well. Water on an island may be filtered by the sand and discolored by the roots of the palm trees.
- ❖ Is there electricity, or will you listen to a generator all night? Some islands do not have any electricity, while others use solar paneling to generate it.
- ❖ What exactly does "meals included" mean?
- ❖ How far is this establishment from other life?
- ❖ Do the prices include taxes and service charges?
- ❖ Does the hotel accept credit cards and do they add a fee for this?
- ❖ What kind of fun activities are nearby? Can you ride a horse, windsurf or fish? Are guides licensed? Note that it is illegal for a person to act as a guide without being licensed.

If you do book ahead, print out all correspondence and keep the documentation with you. Some proprietors have been known to offer one rate, but charge another after the customer has arrived.

Getting Here

There are many options. You can have a tour agent book your flight and hotels so all you need to do is pack, grab your cash and credit card, and get yourself to the airport. Or you may be on a long trip and arrive in Belize overland. You may want to do nothing but drive or cycle from one archeological site to the next before heading to Guatemala or Mexico. If you have specialized activities you'd like to pursue, like kayaking around Glover's Reef or diving the Blue Hole, consider using a tour group, such as Slickrock Adventures or Island Expeditions. They do all the work while you have all the fun.

◆ Outfitters Who Do All the Work

Some tour companies will be mentioned more than once in this book because they specialize in many types of tours. All offer photography, wildlife viewing and natural history information.

Slickrock Adventures, PO Box 1400, Moab, UT 84532, ☎ 800-390-5715, www.slick-rock.com, US $200+ per day. Slickrock has been around for over 25 years. For 17 of those years, it has been offering tours into Belize. They offer professional instruction in sea kayaking and windsurfing and are safety conscious. Highly respected in Belize and highly recommended.

Eco Summer Expeditions, PO Box 1765, Clearwater, BC, V0E 1N0, Canada, ☎ 800-465-8884, www.ecosummer.com, US $100-200 per day. This company offers a number of expeditions. Trips can be either a combination land/sea experience or a kayak/dive/snorkel/sail trip. Their reputation for safety in Canada is excellent. Their meals are popular too.

Island Expeditions Co., 1574 Gulf Road, #156 Point Roberts, WA 98281, ☎ 800-667-1630, www.islandexpeditions.com, US $100-200 per day. Island Expeditions has been running specialized kayak tours into Belize for 16 years. Trips range from seven to 12 days, and can include hiking, sea kayaking, river rafting or exploring Maya sites. Trips are all-inclusive (except for airfare, departure taxes and diving costs) and accommodations are in either tents or lodges.

Sunny Skies Adventures, TMM Bareboat Vacations, Coconut Drive, Ambergris Caye, Belize, ☎ 226-3026, www.sunnyskyadventures.com, US $100-200 per day. This company offers a bareboat (that means no crew and you do everything) catamaran that holds eight people comfortably.

GAP Adventures, 19 Duncan Street, Toronto, ON M5H 3H1, Canada, ☎ 800-465-5600, www.gap.ca, US $75-100 per day. If you are looking for a more relaxed adventure, GAP kayaks around the southern cayes. Sleeping accommodations are in a tent or hammock.

◆ Arriving by Air

Aircraft arriving from outside the country land at the **Philip Goldson International Airport** in Ladyville, nine miles from Belize City. Those transferring directly to a domestic flight within Belize must pay a US $7.50 security charge. When leaving Belize by air, the departure tax is US $20.

Many major centers in North America and most capital cities in Central America have direct flights to Belize. **American** (☎ 800-433-7300, www.aa. com), **Continental** (☎ 800-525-0280, www.continental.com) and **TACA Airlines** (☎ 800-535-8780, www.grupotaca.com) all fly out of at least one major North American city. **Mexicana** (☎ 800-531-7921, www.mexicana.com) and **Aeromexico** (☎ 800-237-6639) also have flights from many of the major North American cities, although they don't offer direct flights to Belize (they stop in Mexico). As of 2002, **Cayman Airways** (☎ 800-422-9626, www. caymanairways.com) started flying a charter plane to Belize. Starting Nov. 2002, **Air Jamaica** flies into Belize four times a week. They make connections from many major American cities and their prices are good. www. airjamaica.com, ☎ 800-523-5585.

Instead of flying directly into Belize, a more economical option is to take a flight to Cancún, Mexico, and bus/drive/cycle/hitch down to Belize. Since Cancún receives two million vacationers a year, hundreds of planes go in and out of there daily from places around the world; deals are easy to find.

There are air-conditioned, first-class buses leaving for Chetumal from the main terminal in Cancún five times a day.

There are no flights arriving or departing Belize City after dark. This is why it's so difficult to get a flight into the country without spending a night en route.

Of course, if you live in a major US city (Houston, Dallas, Miami), direct flights are available.

Internet Search Sites

The cost of flights changes all the time. Although this can be frustrating, it can also work to your advantage, especially if you're willing to book on-line. Use the travel-oriented sites listed below or go to each individual airline (see websites listed above). Alternately, go to a general search engine, such as www.google.com, type in "discounted airline tickets" and let your search engine start the process.

www.cheapflights.com sells to those in Canada and the US.

At **www.priceline.com**, you place a bid on an airline ticket. The bid, if accepted, is a binding contract.

www.latintickets.com sells to those in the United States only.

www.vacationweb.com, which sells to those in the US or Canada, offers the best prices of all.

◆ Overland

You can reach Belize by bus from either Mexico or Guatemala. Mexican lines go as far as Chetumal, and Guatemalan buses go as far as Melchor de Mencos on the Guatemala/Belize border. However, in Mexico you can catch a Novelo bus that will take you all the way to Belize City. At the Guatemalan border, you must walk across and catch a bus in Benque Viejo.

If driving your own car, you must fill out a form at immigration indicating the type and condition of your vehicle. You must post a bond on your credit card as insurance that you have the same vehicle when you leave the country. You must also purchase Belizean car insurance. The Insurance Corporation of Belize has agents at the border just waiting to take your cash.

◆ Arriving by Sea

You can cross by ferry from Puerto Barrios, Guatemala to the Belizean ports of Punta Gorda or Placencia.

Getting Around

◆ Air Travel

There is just one international airport in the country, in Ladyville, nine miles out of Belize City. Municipal airports vary in their regulations. Only local flights can use the municipal airport in Belize City.

AUTHOR NOTE: *If transferring directly from an overseas flight to a domestic one at the International Airport, there is a US $7.50 fee.*

From the Ladyville airport, you can fly to many destinations within Belize with local airlines. **Tropic Air** (☎ 800-422-3435, 226-2012 in Belize, www.tropicair.com) has numerous flights every day from either the international or municipal airports. They also offer air tours that fly over the cayes. **Maya Air** (☎ 422-2333, www.mayaair.com) offers many flights to various points in Belize. Because the prices become repetitious, I have omitted them from all but the Belize City flights.

When leaving Belize by air, the departure tax is US $20, which includes a US $3.75 Protected Areas Conservation Trust fee that is good for one month and must be paid only once even if you leave the country many times.

Getting From the Airport to Your Hotel

Taxis run from the airport to the city for a set rate of US $17.50. You can share a taxi with up to three other people, but make arrangements before leaving the terminal building; the taxi drivers become quite hostile if they catch you trying to get a group together once outside.

A **shuttle van** goes from the airport to San Ignacio and costs US $5. The vans meet all TACA, American Airlines and Continental Airlines flights. You can get from Ladyville (where the airport is located) by **public bus**, but you must walk out to the main road and wait for a local bus. **Water taxis** are available at the Marine Building in Belize City if you want to go to the cayes. The last one leaves at 5 pm. **Caye Caulker Water Taxi**, ☎ 203-1969 or 209-4992, www.gocayecaulker.com, offers a good schedule. **Thunderbolt Water Taxi** (Captain Cesario Rivero) is based on Ambergris Caye, ☎ 226-2217.

◆ By Bus

Three major bus companies travel to different parts of the country. **Venus Bus**, ☎ 207-3354, travels north to Corozal and the Mexican border; **Novelos**, ☎ 207-2025/3929, travels west to the Guatemala border; and **James**, ☎ 702-2049, travels south to Punta Gorda. Smaller companies can take you to outlying villages three or four times per week; ask the locals.

◆ Car Rentals

Four big American franchises offer service in Belize – **Budget** (☎ 800-404-8033, www.budget.com), **Hertz** (☎ 800-654-3131, www.hertz.com), **Thrifty** (☎ 800-847-4389, www.thrifty.com) and **Avis** (☎ 800-230-4898, www.avis.com). Or you can rent from one of the smaller companies in Belize City. Prices are always quoted in US dollars and you must have a major credit card. Some companies allow you to take your rental vehicle off the major highways and onto secondary roads. Some don't.

Insurance is mandatory, with a deductible of US $750 is payable by both parties involved at the time of an accident. A refund is forthcoming if you are proven the innocent party. The only other document you will need is a legal **driver's license** from your own country or an International Driving Permit.

Gasoline is expensive, about BZ $7.25 per gallon, US 81¢ per liter. Car rental rates range from US $88-95 per day, usually with unlimited mileage.

Crystal Auto Rental, International Airport, ☎ 223-1600 or 800-777-7777, www.crystal-belize.com, offers a 10% discount for rentals of over three days and a 5% discount for cash. This includes insurance and unlimited mileage.

JMA Motors Ltd., 771 Bella Vista, Belize City, ☎ 223-0226, jmagroup@ btl.net. If reserving a vehicle through this company, you can work through Budget (see above). The staff was helpful and supplied a car within an hour.

TRAVEL INFORMATION

> ❖ **WATCH YOUR CAR, MISTER?**
>
> If asked by a local if your vehicle needs to be watched (for a fee) I would suggest paying and, after you leave with your vehicle intact, report the incident and give a description of the "protector" to the police. If you elect not to pay the protection fee, you may find your tires poked full of holes from an ice pick.

Driving

In Belize City the traffic is heavy during rush hours. Most streets are narrow and all are one-way. Roads often have potholes and everyone travels slowly. Off the highway, the roads are deplorable – all gravel with huge potholes.

Driving is on the **right** and road signs are international. If turning left, first pull onto the right shoulder. Check both ways and wait until there is no traffic, then pull across both lanes and onto the road you want. **Seat belts** are mandatory in the front seat and failing to use them can result in a US $12.50 fine.

◆ Hitchhiking

Because of the heat, people are quick to pick up hitchers, and drivers always offer anyone walking on a secondary road a ride. Those waiting at bus stops are also often offered a ride. Hitching is probably safe if you are a group of two or three people. I would avoid hitching when alone.

Directory

GENERAL DIRECTORY

■ OUTFITTERS & TOUR OPERATORS

Eco Summer Expeditions	☎ 800-465-8884	www.ecosummer.com
Gap Adventures	☎ 800-465-5600	www.gap.ca
Island Expeditions	☎ 800-667-1630	www.islandexpeditions.com
Slickrock Adventures	☎ 800-390-5715	www.slickrock.com
Sunny Skies Adventures	☎ 226-3026	www.sunnyskyadventures.com

■ WATER TAXI SERVICE

Caye Caulker	☎ 203-1969, 209-4992	www.gocayecaulker.com
Thunderbolt	☎ 226-2217	

■ CAR RENTAL COMPANIES

Avis	☎ 800-230-4898	www.avis.com
Budget	☎ 800-404-8033	www.drivebudget.com
Crystal Auto Rental	☎ 223-1600, 800-777-7777	www.crystal-belize.com
Hertz	☎ 800-654-3131	www.hertz.com
JMA Motors	☎ 223-0226	jmagroup@btl.net
Thrifty Car Rental	☎ 207-1271, 800-847-4389	www.thrifty.com

■ AIRLINES

Air Jamaica	☎ 800-523-5585	www.airjamaica.com
Aeromexico	☎ 800-237-6639	www.aeromexico.com
American Airlines	☎ 800-433-7300	www.aa.com
Cayman Airways	☎ 800-422-9626	www.caymanairways.com
Continental	☎ 800-525-0280	www.continental.com
Maya Air	☎ 422-2333	www.mayaair.com
Mexicana	☎ 800-531-7921	www.mexicana.com
TACA Airlines	☎ 800-535-8780	www.grupotaca.com
Tropic Air	☎ 800-422-3435, 226-2012	www.tropicair.com

■ BUS COMPANIES

James Bus	☎ 702-2049
Novelo Bus	☎ 207-2025
Venus Bus	☎ 207-3354

■ EMBASSIES

Belize Embassy	☎ 202-332-9636	www.embassyworld.com/

For foreign embassies within Belize, see *Emergency Contacts*, page 305, in the *Appendix*.

GENERAL DIRECTORY

■ EMERGENCIES

American Express	☎ 227-7363	www.americanexpress.com
US Center for Disease Control & Prevention		www.cdc.gov
Visa/Mastercard	☎ 800-336-3386	www.visa.com www.mastercard.com
Western Union	☎ 227-0014	www.westernunion.com

■ USEFUL WEBSITES

Belize Discover	www.belizediscover.com
Belize Now	www.belizenow.com
Belize Online Tourism & Investment Guide	www.belize.com
General Travel Information	www.belizereport.com
Travel Belize	www.travel-belize.com

TRAVEL INFORMATION

Belize

To Francsico Escárcegaa

MEXICO

Chetumal
Santa Rita
Corozal Town
Cerros
Sarteneja

COROZAL DISTRICT

Orange Walk Town

MEXICO

Blue Creek
San Felipe
Lamanai
La Milpa

Crooked Tree

ORANGE WALK DISTRICT

Chan Chich

NORTHERN HWY

Altun Ha

Ambergris Caye

San Pedro
Caye Caulker

Caye Chapel

Blue Hole

BELIZE

Burrell Boom
Bermudian Landing
Ladyville
BELIZE CITY
Hattieville

WESTERN HWY

BELIZE DISTRICT

Northern Lagoon

BELMOPAN

Caves Branch
HUMMINGBIRD HWY

San Ignacio
Xunantunich

Georgeville
Benque Viejo
Melchor de Mentos
Augustine
CAYO DISTRICT

To Flores & Tikal

MOUNTAIN PINE RIDGE

Caracol

MAYA MOUNTAINS

COCKSCOMB RANGE

Victoria Peak (3,680 feet)

STANN CREEK DISTRICT

Gales Point
Southern Lagoon

COASTAL RD

Dangriga

Hopkins
Sittee River

SOUTHERN HWY

Independence
Seine Bight Village
Placencia

GUATEMALA

TOLEDO DISTRICT

Nim Li Punit
Lubaantun
San Pedro
Jalade
San Antonio
Pusilhá

Monkey River

Punta Gorda

Barranco

Gulf of Honduras

GUATEMALA

Caribbean Sea

Turneffe Islands

Lighthouse Reef

Glovers Reef

N

HUNTER PUBLISHING

50 MILES
80 KILOMETERS

© 2005 HUNTER PUBLISHING, INC.

Belize City

Introduction

Although not the capital of the country, Belize City is the largest city in the nation. It is also the center of commerce, culture and transportation. The 2003 census showed a population of 64,100, although unofficial estimates go as high as 80,000 residents, a third of the country's total population.

BC, as the city is commonly called, is a collection of majestic colonial houses interspersed with clapboard shacks rigged

with huge wooden vats that collect rain water from the tin roofs. Decorating the vats and roofs of these buildings are palm trees and flowering bougainvillea. Mosquitoes breed in the open sewers border the black-topped streets and in the swamps beyond the sea walls.

The city's populace is as colorful as its buildings. It is a mixture of black and white, brown and yellow. For a developing nation, Belize has citizens that look healthy and dress well. All have smiles (even if they rob you) and the time to talk.

◆ City Life

In the past, Belize City was considered a dangerous and crime-riddled place. Built on a history of rum running and buccaneering pirates, at one time it may have been more intimidating. Today, there are fewer pan-handlers in the crowded and busy streets than there are in Seattle or Vancouver. On my most recent visit, I was not bothered even once by hustlers trying to sell me something.

Like any major center in the world, Belize City does have robberies and murders. There are organized gangs and drug runners, thugs and petty criminals. As an obvious foreigner, you should be as cautious in Belize City as you would be in Los Angeles, London or Nairobi.

Because tourism is an important part of the economy, Belize established a **Tourist Police Force** in 1995. These officers can be seen walking or riding bicycles on the streets in the core of the city, alert to the presence of trouble. Since their formation, petty crime against foreigners has decreased. They will come and speak with you or shadow you if they feel you are in a danger-ous situation.

But don't let potential crime deter you. I hope you take the time to enjoy the city by exploring historical spots, eating in great restaurants, and talking with those who call BC home. It is an interesting and friendly place to be.

◆ Orientation

The heart of Belize City is split by **Haulover Creek**, at the mouth of the Belize River. The most common landmark and reference point is the **Swing Bridge** that goes over the river as it flows into the Caribbean Sea. The only one of its kind in the Americas, the bridge separates the residential north part of the city from the commercial south. Once a day, at around 5:30 pm, this hand-op-erated bridge swings open to allow ships up or down the river.

In contrast to the rest of the country, which is laid back and easy going, the southeastern side of the Swing Bridge, in the commercial area of Regent and Albert Streets, is a cauldron of human activity. It's an interesting part of town during the day, but a place that foreigners should avoid at night as this is where a lot of the crimes occur. Taxis are plentiful and cost US $2.50/BZ $5 to anywhere in the city. Use them as an inexpensive safety precaution.

Another area that seems busy and intimidating is where the out-of-town buses arrive and depart near the Belchina bridge, also in the southeastern part of town. Again, take a taxi to and from this area, especially if you have baggage that makes you look like a tourist.

AVERAGE TEMPERATURES & RAINFALL			
	Daily temp.	**Humidity**	**Monthly rainfall**
JAN	74.6°F/23.7°C	74%	54.9 inches/139.6 cm
FEB	77.2°F/25.1°C	69%	26.6 inches/67.8 cm
MAR	61.8°F/16.5°C	68%	21.8 inches/55.4 cm
APR	82.1°F/27.8°C	71%	24.1 inches/61.5 cm
MAY	84.0°F/28.9°C	69%	42.7 inches/108.6 cm
JUN	83.4°F/28.5°C	75%	25.5 inches/64 cm
JULY	83.7°F/28.7°C	73%	92.4 inches/235.2 cm
AUG	83.8°F/28.8°C	74%	72.5 inches/184.4 cm
SEPT	83.3°F/28.5°C	76%	72.5 inches/184.4 cm
OCT	81.5°F/27.5°C	74%	98.3 inches/250.1 cm
NOV	79.2°F/26.2°C	77%	77.9 inches/198.3 cm
DEC	77.2°F/25.1°C	76%	69.1 inches/175.8 cm

Information provided by Historical and current records at the National Meteorological Service at Philip SW Goodson International Airport in Ladyville.

History

Some locals claim that Belize City is one of the swampiest, hottest and most humid places in the country, but is in no danger of sinking into the bog because it is built on a solid foundation of mahogany chips, sand ballast and empty rum bottles.

◆ Historical Timeline

1600	Logging is established in Belize.
1690	Slaves are brought from Africa to help with logging.
1786	Belize City is established.
1787	Hurricane destroys all of Belize City except for one building.
1790	Yarborough Cemetery is established. Residence of city number 2656.
1800	Fort George Island is inhabited by British. St. John's Church is built in Belize City.
1806	Fire destroys much of the city.
1819	Court House is built.
1856	Fire destroys west side of the city.
1857	Prison is built.
1859	The city has 6,000 residents.
1862	Belize City becomes the capital of British Honduras.
1863	Arsonist begins fire that destroys south side of city.
1918	Angry over racism, rioters destroy many public buildings.
1931	There are 16,687 residents in BC. In Sept., a hurricane destroys many parts of the city.
1961	Hurricane Hattie destroys much of the city and Belmopan is made the country's new capital.
1981	Independence from Great Britain is earned.

BELIZE CITY

❖ EMORY KING

Emory King, a colorful local character, was shipwrecked on the cayes of Belize in 1953. This compelled him to make Belize his home and, as it turned out, the country became his passion. He has authored many history and travel books about Belize, is a newspaper columnist, a broadcaster and realtor. King is quoted by Fodor as saying, "In the north we raise sugar cane. In the south we raise citrus and bananas and rice. In the west we raise cattle and pigs and corn. In Belize City we raise hell."

Getting Around

Walking is the best way to get around in the center of the city. Most places of interest are within a short distance of each other.

> **AUTHOR NOTE:** *Cycling in the city is not advisable because the streets are narrow and the traffic heavy. Also, motorists are not accustomed to cyclists, so courtesy toward them is not common.*

Public **buses** go anywhere in the city for BZ $1. You may have to take more than one bus to get where you want to go, but those living in the city can give you directions on which bus to take and where to catch it. As a general rule, once out of the heavy traffic common in the core of the city, the bus will stop to pick you up almost anywhere; just put your arm out to indicate that you want the bus to stop. Otherwise, you must go to a marked bus stop – there will be a sign on a post indicating the spot.

Taxis have green license plates (as opposed to white ones on private vehicles) and will go anywhere in the city for BZ $5. Because the price of gas is high (BZ $7/gallon), taxis often take more than one passenger along a route. If you are coming from the bus station, a popular point of origin, you can be almost certain there will be more than one person riding with you. Each person will pay BZ $5. Taxis from the airport to anywhere in town cost BZ $35 and the drivers get very angry if you try to share a taxi with someone not in your party. I suggest teaming up with others *before* you leave the terminal building. These drivers have a monopoly on the trade and are protective of their fares.

Driving your own vehicle in the core of Belize City requires a lot of nerve. The streets are all one way, narrow and busy and there are also a few traffic circles to tackle. However, once in the suburbs and not during rush hours, driving is no problem.

Adventures & Sightseeing

◆ Adventures on Foot

WALKING TOUR ~ DAY 1

Start at the swing bridge and walk on the northwestern side of the city. This will introduce you to the sometimes intimidating pace and activities of the city.

The first **wooden bridge** over Haulover Creek was built in 1818 so that those transporting cattle would no longer have to drag them across the water with ropes. Because of the humidity and constant use, the first bridge soon rotted and a second wooden structure was built in 1859. When this had to be replaced, residents built a swing bridge to accommodate boats that traveled up and down the Belize River. Finally, a metal bridge, made in Liverpool, England, was brought over and put across the water.

On the corner of North Front Street beside the swing bridge is the **Marine Terminal**, where the water taxis depart for the offshore cayes. The terminal has always been a bustling and colorful place. Logs were floated down the river and sold to waiting merchants here who, in turn, shipped the logs around the world. The terminal is also where slaves were displayed before they were sold to landowners. Fishermen have always congregated at this junction of fresh and salt water, offloading and selling their daily catch. Built in 1923, the building was originally the city's fire station.

The terminal also houses the **Maritime Museum** and the **Coastal Zone Museum**. Both are open daily from 8 am to 4:30 pm; tickets are sold just outside the door, at the same booth where water taxi tickets are sold, and are good for both museums. The cost is BZ $4 per person, but US $4 for foreigners. The museum's main floor has model boats and documents on display. Upstairs is a collection of shells and corals. The entire museum is in dire need of repair and care. ☎ 223-1969. *very cool place*

Continuing along North Front Street to the northeast is the Sea Sports Belize office (an easy-to-spot landmark) and just beyond, at 91 North Front Street, is the **Image Factory**, ☎ 223-4151. Since its inception in 1995 it has had over 30 exhibitions, some from as far away as New York, England and Australia. Numerous Belizean artists – such as Richard Holder, a street-life photographer, Hugh Broaster, a sculptor, Betty Cooper, a painter from Dangriga, and Pamela Brown, a natural life painter – display their work here.

Continue along until North Front Street hits Handyside. Cross over and follow Fort Street past the Wet Lizard (where you might like to stop for lunch), and you will come to the entrance of the new **Tourism Village**, www.belizetouristvillage.com, built in part by the rich Belizean entrepreneur Barry Bowen as a duty-free shopping center. His plan was to attract the cruise ship tourist business. The mall is open until 6 pm daily.

She Sells Sea Shells, ☎ 223-7426, open same times as the Tourist Village, is in booth 21A. It's an exquisite shop that sells and trades in rare shells. It is the most interesting shop in the mall. Continuing along Fort Street you will come to the **Audubon Society**, ☎ 223-4987.

The next landmark is the **Bliss Lighthouse** and **Tomb of Baron Bliss**, Belize's greatest benefactor. Each year on Mar. 9th a ceremony is held at his tomb below the lighthouse in Belize Harbor. This is followed by sailing regattas. You cannot enter the lighthouse. Read the full story of Bliss on page 30.

Across from the lighthouse is the **Radisson Fort George** as well as numerous colonial mansions. Next, continue up Cork Street to **Memorial Park**, where World War I heroes are commemorated.

The **National Handicrafts Center**, 2 South Park Street, ☎ 223-3636, bcci@btl.net, was established in 1992 to help local artists. It is a cooperative that has a wide range of goods such as zericote and mahogany carvings, slate sculptures, oil paintings and jippi jappa baskets.

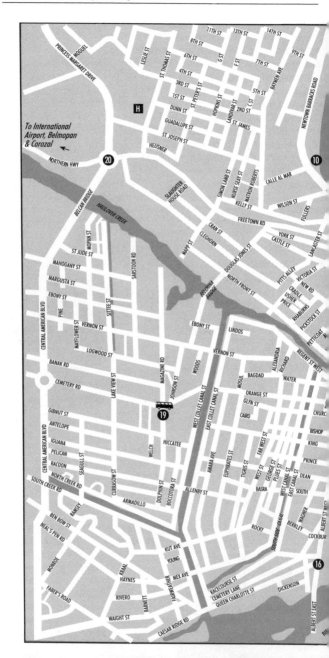

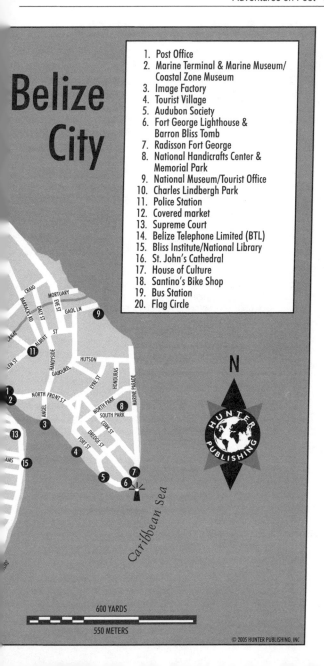

Belize City

1. Post Office
2. Marine Terminal & Marine Museum/ Coastal Zone Museum
3. Image Factory
4. Tourist Village
5. Audubon Society
6. Fort George Lighthouse & Barron Bliss Tomb
7. Radisson Fort George
8. National Handicrafts Center & Memorial Park
9. National Museum/Tourist Office
10. Charles Lindbergh Park
11. Police Station
12. Covered market
13. Supreme Court
14. Belize Telephone Limited (BTL)
15. Bliss Institute/National Library
16. St. John's Cathedral
17. House of Culture
18. Santino's Bike Shop
19. Bus Station
20. Flag Circle

BELIZE CITY

Caribbean Sea

600 YARDS
550 METERS

© 2005 HUNTER PUBLISHING, INC

The **Chamber of Commerce** is in the same shop/building/office and shares the same staff. Both places are open from Monday to Friday, 8 am to 5 pm and Saturday from 8 am to 1 pm.

Walk south past the American Consulate on Gabourel Street until you see the Central Bank building, where the **tourist board** (☎ 223-1913 or 223-1910, www.travelbelize.org) is located. This office, open from 8 am to 5 pm, Monday to Friday, has information about upcoming cultural events in town, but few advertising pamphlets. The Central Bank building in front of it is the old prison that has been converted into the new **Museum of Belize**, ☎ 223-4524, www.museumofbelize.org. It opened in Feb. of 2002 and is Belize's first national museum. The building was constructed in 1857 from ballast bricks and was used as a prison until 1993. $10 BZ worth it

To provide us with a glimpse of what the building once was, one cell has been restored. A cell was originally built to hold one man; at the time of the prison's closing each cell held six to eight men. Among other things, the museum's exhibition shows how, in the 1870s, hard prison labor included chopping mangroves at Prisoners' Creek. The second floor of the museum is dedicated to Maya culture and holds such treasures as the buenavista vase found in Cayo.

 If Maya history intrigues you, pick up a copy of the excellent full-color book *Maya Masterpieces*, for sale at the museum. It describes some of the treasures found in the Maya display.

The entrance fee to the museum is US $5 (for foreigners) and it is open Tuesday to Friday, 10 am until 6 pm, and Saturdays, 10 am until 4 pm. All the staff, from the curator to the janitor, is fully trained to answer any questions you may have about the museum or its contents.

Going north from the museum to the sea wall and beyond, you will come to the **Charles Lindbergh Park**. The park was dedicated to Lindbergh because he landed his famous plane, *Spirit of St. Louis*, in Belize in 1927.

This completes the first day of your walking tour. Meet again at the swing bridge in the morning and we'll head over to the other side of the city.

WALKING TOUR ~ DAY 2

Cross the swing bridge and walk along Albert Street, going first past the **covered market**, built in 1993 to replace the original one that was established in 1820. There is mostly produce for sale here, but just outside the door and beside the swing bridge local artisans sell handmade jewelry, hats, carvings and beaded works. Next to the market is the banking district, set in the pie-shaped corner where Albert and Regent Streets meet. This was the location of the original courthouse, but the fire in 1918 destroyed the building.

Cutting across to Regent Street, you will come to a white colonial building with ornate iron works along the stairs and balcony. This is the **Supreme Court Building**, featuring a four-sided clock as its crown. The original building was constructed in 1818, but the court was not used until 1820. In 1918 the building was destroyed by fire. The building is across from Central Park, now called **Battlefield Park**, where a bust of labor leader **Antonio Soberanis** sits.

Just beyond the Supreme Court and down along the ocean on Southern Foreshore Street is the **Bliss Institute**, named after the famous benefactor Barron Bliss. Today, it is the cultural center of Belize City and it hosts plays, concerts, and exhibitions. There is a permanent exhibition of Maya artifacts from Caracol. The display is open Monday to Thursday from 8 am to 5 pm and Friday until 1 pm. ☎ 227-2458. The Institute also houses the Belize Arts Council (same phone number).

Leave the ocean and go inland on any appealing street to Albert Street, where you will find **St. John's Cathedral**, the oldest Anglican church in Central America. It had its foundation stone laid in 1812.

West of the cathedral is **Yarborough Cemetery**, which has gravestones dating back to 1781. Unlike other cemeteries, where bodies have been buried on top of one another when space got tight, Yarborough was declared full in 1870 and a new cemetery, located on Cemetery Road by the bus stations, was established.

Turn back toward the water to Regent Street and Government House, now renamed the **House of Culture**, ☎ 227-3050. Built in 1814, it is one of the oldest buildings in the city and was the seat of government for over 150 years. Now a historical museum, it is open Monday to Friday, 8:30 am to 4:30 pm. The gardens are open to birdwatchers for a mere US $2.50.

At the very end of land is a causeway joining Bird's Isle with the mainland. The island is a favorite spot for impromptu outdoor concerts.

As you stroll back along Albert Street toward the swing bridge, take note of the colonial houses that have what appear to be brick basements. In fact, it was here that slaves were chained at the end of their working days.

◆ Adventures on Wheels

Cycling

Although I don't recommend cycling in the city itself, I do encourage cyclists to connect with Belizean cycling groups so they can get to places out of town. If you must cycle in Belize, you should bring your own bicycle.

Santino's Bike Shop, 18 New Road, ☎ 223-2500, santinos@btl.net, is a great repair shop. Stop here to catch up on the latest cycle news or to make a connection so you can enter one of their monthly races.

Mr. Perry Gibson of the **Belize Cycle Association**, 7202 Caesar Ridge Road (no telephone listed), wallen@btl.net, can be contacted for information about upcoming races or practice runs.

Organized cycling events have a huge number of contestants and some of the races offer large prizes. Other races have prizes that you couldn't take home with you, such as goats and chickens; however, the fun of participation is worth forfeiting your winnings. A list of scheduled races throughout the year is available at Santino's.

Shopping

Most tourists buy sculptures made from mahogany or zericote hardwood. There are men throughout the country who can sculpt your profile onto something like the handle of a cane or into a bust.

Another common art is **slate carving**, drawn from the Maya tradition. The reproductions are all copies of those found at one of the ruins in Belize.

Calabash painting is another popular gift. Calabash is a piece of dried gourd that Belizean artists use as a medium. These can be purchased at souvenir shops throughout Belize.

The **National Handicraft Center**, 2 South Park Street, ☎ 223-3636, has many unique designs on display and they vary from finely crafted toy sailboats to smooth wooden tapirs. *very cool place*

In Belize City you can buy **handmade jewelry** and a few crafts from the artists located outside the Market beside the swing bridge. For these items you must barter.

I was amazed at the variety and quality of products at the **Wet Lizard Gift Shop**, 1 Fort Street, ☎ 223-5973. Many of the pieces cannot be found anywhere else in Belize.

The Tourism Village next door to the Wet Lizard has craft shops that carry things like clothes made from local cotton, painted gourds (calabash), seashell chimes, black coral jewelry and paintings by local artists. The top painters in Belize are Jason Bennett, Carole Bowman, Carolyn Carr, Edwardo Alamilla, Marcos Larios and Walter Castillo. Some of these paintings can be found at **Fine Arts**, ☎ 227-5620.

My favorite shop is **She Sells Sea Shells**, ☎ 223-7426, described in the walking tour of Belize City, page 55.

Gallon Jug Agro-industry Ltd., #1 King Street, ☎ 227-7031, has items for sale that are grown and produced on the Chan Chich estate. The most are their Mango Tango Gourmet Coffee and Lissette's Sweet Mango Jam and Secret Sauce of Spicy Mango.

Places to Stay & Eat

◆ Accommodations

Accommodations are scattered throughout the city and run from basic to luxurious. Price ranges are per room, per night. Usually the price for a single and a double is the same.

Barrack Guest House, 8 Barrack Road, ☎ 223-6671, $, has five rooms, three with

❖ HOTEL PRICING	
$	$10 to $20
$$	$21 to $50
$$$	$51 to $75
$$$$	$76 to $100
$$$$$	over $100

baths. All have fans, and all are basic and clean. Complimentary morning coffee and fruit is offered at this family-run operation.

Seaside Guest House, 3 Prince Street, ☎ 227-8339, seasidebelize@btl.net, $$, is decorated in bold colors and is safe, even though it is not in the best area of town. There are six basic rooms and cheaper dorm beds. You can order breakfast or purchase refreshments.

Freddie's Guest House, 86 Eve Street, ☎ 223-3851, $$, has three rooms, two that share a bath and a third with private bath. This clean and spacious house is only one block

AT A GLANCE ACCOMMODATIONS	
ACCOMMODATION	PHONE
Bakadeer Inn ($$$)	☎ 223-0659
Barrack Guest House ($)	☎ 223-6671
Belize Biltmore Plaza ($$$$)	☎ 223-2302
Bellevue Hotel ($$$)	☎ 227-7051
Chateau Caribbean ($$$$)	☎ 223-0800
Colton House ($$$)	☎ 203-4666
Coningsby Inn ($$$)	☎ 207-2710
Freddie's Guest House ($$)	☎ 223-3851
Grant Residence B & B ($$$)	☎ 223-0926
Great House ($$$$$)	☎ 223-3400
Mopan Hotel ($$)	☎ 227-7351
North Front St Guest House ($)	☎ 227-7595
Princess Hotel & Casino ($$$$$)	☎ 223-2670
Radisson Fort George ($$$$$)	☎ 223-3333
Seaside Guest House ($$)	☎ 227-8339
Three Sisters Guest House ($$)	☎ 223-6729
Villa Boscardi ($$$)	☎ 223-1691

BELIZE CITY

from the sea, and even offers its guests a garden in which to sit. Call ahead to book.

Three Sisters Guest House, 55 Eve Street, ☎ 223-5729, $$, is set in a large wooden house across the street from Freddie's. Its guest rooms are set around a main common area, where cable TV is available. The four rooms are large and two have private baths. Each room has a good fan.

Mopan Hotel, 55 Regent Street, ☎ 227-7351, hotelmopan@btl.net, $$, is across the street from the Coningsby. This 200-year old colonial house is newly painted in bold colors. There is a bar and restaurant on site.

Colton House, 9 Cork Street, ☎ 203-4666, coltonhse@btl.net, $$$, is a colonial home built in 1928 with local woods. The rooms are all exquisitely decorated and have private baths. Each of the four rooms on the main floor opens onto the wrap-around porch. Children over the age of nine are welcome. There is an information library and videos available in the common room. Complimentary coffee is offered in the mornings, but no food is served.

Bellevue Hotel, 5 Southern Foreshore, ☎ 227-7051, bellevue@btl.net, $$$, is on the south side of town on the water. The hotel offers clean rooms with private bathrooms. There is a pool, bar, restaurant and Internet café.

Coningsby Inn, 76 Regent Street, ☎ 207-2710, coningsby_inn2001@yahoo.com, $$$, is a well-kept colonial home with comfortable rooms, air

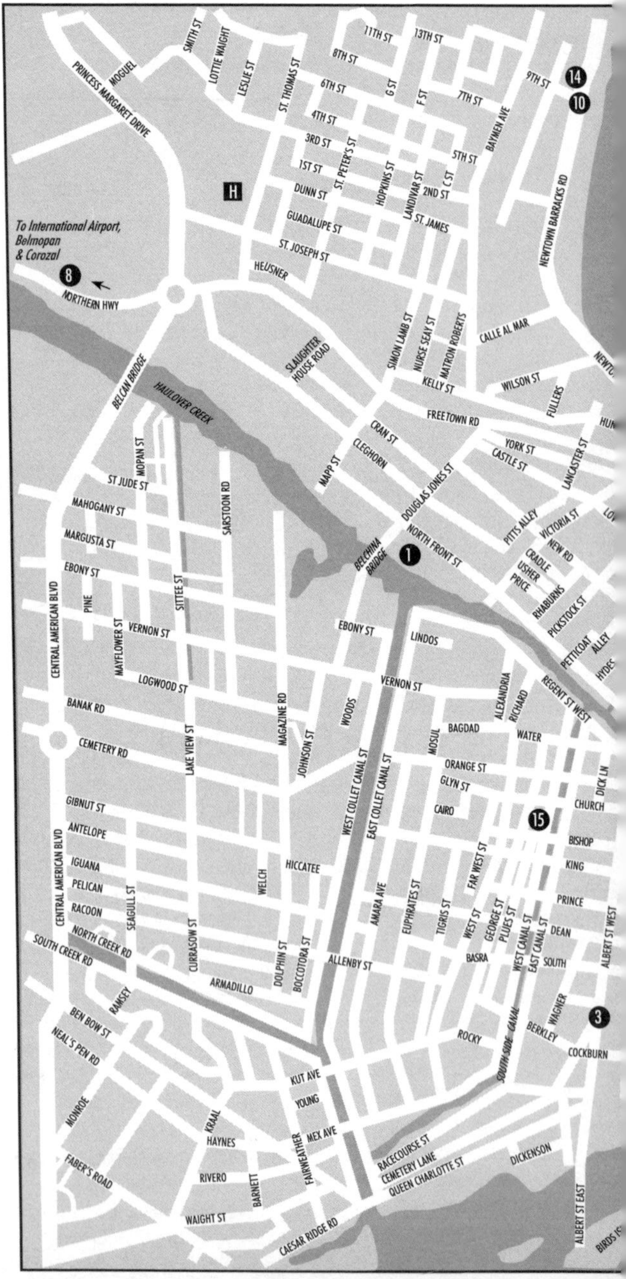
To International Airport, Belmopan & Corozal
NORTHERN HWY
BELCAN BRIDGE
HAULOVER CREEK
PRINCESS MARGARET DRIVE
MOGUEL
SMITH ST
LOTTIE WAIGHT
LESLIE ST
ST. THOMAS ST
11TH ST
13TH ST
8TH ST
6TH ST
4TH ST
3RD ST
1ST ST
DUNN ST
GUADALUPE ST
ST. JOSEPH ST
HEUSNER
ST. PETER'S ST
G ST
F ST
7TH ST
9TH ST
BAYMEN AVE
5TH ST
HOPKINS ST
LANDIVAR ST
C ST
2ND ST
ST. JAMES
NEWTOWN BARRACKS RD
CALLE AL MAR
SLAUGHTER HOUSE ROAD
SIMON LAMB ST
NURSE SEAY ST
MATRON ROBERTS
KELLY ST
WILSON ST
FULLERS
FREETOWN RD
CRAN ST
CLEGHORN
MAPP ST
YORK ST
CASTLE ST
LANCASTER ST
DOUGLAS JONES ST
NORTH FRONT ST
PITTS ALLEY
VICTORIA ST
NEW RD
CRADLE
USHER
PRICE
RHABURNS
PICKSTOCK ST
PETTICOAT
ALLEY
REGENT ST WEST
BELCHINA BRIDGE
MOPAN ST
ST JUDE ST
MAHOGANY ST
MARGUSTA ST
EBONY ST
PINE
SARSTOON RD
SITTEE ST
MAYFLOWER ST
VERNON ST
LOGWOOD ST
BANAK RD
CEMETERY RD
CENTRAL AMERICAN BLVD
LAKE VIEW ST
MAGAZINE RD
JOHNSON ST
WOODS
EBONY ST
LINDOS
VERNON ST
ALEXANDRIA
RICHARD
BAGDAD
WATER
MOSUL
ORANGE ST
GLYN ST
CAIRO
DICK LN
CHURCH
BISHOP
KING
PRINCE
DEAN
SOUTH
ALBERT ST WEST
WEST COLLET CANAL ST
EAST COLLET CANAL ST
FAR WEST ST
GIBNUT ST
ANTELOPE
IGUANA
PELICAN
RACOON
SEAGULL ST
NORTH CREEK RD
SOUTH CREEK RD
HICCATEE
WELCH
CURRASOW ST
AMARA AVE
EUPHRATES ST
TIGRIS ST
WEST ST
GEORGE ST
PLUES ST
WEST CANAL ST
EAST CANAL ST
BASRA
ALLENBY ST
DOLPHIN ST
BOCCOTORA ST
ARMADILLO
RAMSEY
BEN BOW ST
NEAL'S PEN RD
ROCKY
SOUTH SIDE CANAL
WAGNER
BERKLEY
COCKBURN
KUT AVE
YOUNG
MEX AVE
KRAAL
HAYNES
FAIRWEATHER
MONROE
FABER'S ROAD
RIVERO
BARNETT
RACECOURSE ST
CEMETERY LANE
QUEEN CHARLOTTE ST
DICKENSON
WAIGHT ST
CAESAR RIDGE RD
ALBERT ST EAST
H
1
3
8
10
14
15

Belize City
Accommodations
& Restaurants

1. North Front St Guest House
2. Freddie's & Three Sister's Guest House
3. Mopan Hotel
4. Colton house
5. Bellevue Hotel
6. Coningsby Guest House
7. Chateau Caribbean
8. Belize Biltmore Hotel & Restaurant
9. Radisson Fort George Hotel & Restaurant
10. Princess Hotel, Casino & Restaurant
11. Neries Hotel
12. Big Daddy's
13. Wet Wizard
14. Sumati Indian Restaurant
15. Macy's Restaurant

CRAIG
DRAKES RD
DALY ST
EVE ST
MORTUARY
GAOL LN
ALBERT
HANDYSIDE
GABOUREL
HUTSON
EYRE ST
HONDURAS
MARINE PARADE
NORTH FRONT ST
ANGEL
NORTH PARK
SOUTH PARK
COOK ST
DREDGE ST
FORT ST

11
7
13
4
9

Caribbean Sea

N

HUNTER PUBLISHING

600 YARDS
550 METERS

© 2005 HUNTER PUBLISHING, INC

conditioning, private baths and a view that overlooks a littered backyard. The restaurant is famed for its good food. The hotel was named by the owner's father (it was his middle name).

North Front Street Guest House, 124 North Front Street, ☎ 227-7595, thoth@btl.net, $, is a rambling old building run by Miss Matilde Speer who has lived here all her life. The eight rooms have shared bath and large porch. Stand here at night and watch the street action in safety.

> ❖ **BURIED TREASURE**
>
> Henry Robateau was a pirate who ran rum between Jamaica and Belize in the fastest schooner on the high seas. During his last visit to Jamaica he got into too much rum and wild women, which resulted in his losing every penny he had. He decided that to get his money back he would have to put up a wager and race his boat against anyone willing. The challenge was met, the wager set and the men took off. Robateau won the race and with his winnings bought the house on 124 North Front Street. He buried the keel of his boat under the house and never left home to carouse again. As far as we know, the keel is still under the house.

Chateau Caribbean, 6 Marine Parade (next to Memorial Park), ☎ 223-0800, chateaucar@btl.net, $$$$, is an old colonial house that was once a hospital. The house, which overlooks the ocean, has recently been renovated. Each room has air conditioning, a tiled bathroom, cable TV and a good view. The wrap-around porch dotted with wicker furniture is a real draw. The hotel's restaurant has a notably good reputation. I did not find the staff particularly friendly.

Belize Biltmore Plaza (Best Western), Mile 3, Northern Highway, ☎ 223-2302, Biltmore@btl.net, $$$$, is elegant. It has 80 spacious, air-conditioned rooms with cable TV and private baths. There is a safe deposit box, parking lot, business center, pool and gardens, gift shop, bar and restaurant. The staff is friendly and helpful and the tour office can arrange all trips from horseback riding to jungle river expeditions and fishing.

Radisson Fort George Hotel & Marina, 2 Marine Parade, ☎ 223-3333, 800-333-3333 (US), rdfgh@btl.net, $$$$$, has 102 rooms in two buildings. Each room has air conditioning, private bath, coffee maker, hair dryer, mini bar, radio, data port, direct-dial telephone and cable TV. The rooms overlook either the Caribbean Sea or a well-tended garden. There is a restaurant, tavern, pool, dive shop, tour agency and gift shop. Even if you don't stay here, you should visit for a cocktail one evening.

Princess Hotel & Casino, Newtown Barracks in Kings Park area, ☎ 223-2670, resprincess@btl.net, $$$$$, has a total of 181 first-rate rooms with all the amenities of a first-rate hotel. It also has a plethora of entertainment facilities. There is the usual dining room and bar, along with a conference room and business center (for Internet and e-mail), swimming pool and air conditioning throughout. It also has a casino with dance hall girls, two of the largest movie theaters in Belize, a fitness center with massage parlor, a bowling alley and an arcade room. The staff can be quite aloof.

The Great House, 13 Cork Street, ☎ 223-3400, www.greathousebelize. com, $$$$$, is a colonial masterpiece that was built in 1927 as a family home. It still holds its original charm. There are 12 rooms with glistening hardwood floors, balconies, private baths, air conditioning, cable TV, minibars and fridges, coffee makers and hair dryers. The colonial-style décor is pleasing. Shops on the main floor offer souvenirs and newspapers, and you can also book a tour here. The hotel's Smoky Mermaid restaurant is a popular place to hang out (see below).

Bakadeer Inn, 74 Cleghorn Street, ☎ 223-0659, $$$, has 12 rooms, all with private bath, air conditioning, king-size beds and cable TV. There is secure parking and a common room and garden for guests to enjoy. This tutor-style house sits alongside the river and its name is tied into the lumber business. Bakadeer is Creole for "landing area." The McFields are an active family in Belize. Kent has an art/frame shop across the street from the hotel where local artwork can be purchased. Ian is involved in the real estate business. If you want to be in Belize on a more permanent basis, he will help you out. Melony is a marine biologist who has been the director of the Shipstern Reserve in Corozal District.

Grant Residence Bed & Breakfast, 126 Newtown Barrack Road, ☎ 223-0926, www.grantbedandbreakfast.com, $$$, is a family run establishment that makes personalized service their greatest feature. This spacious colonial home, luxuriously decorated, offers an open living/dining room for guests to use. Each bedroom faces the sea, has private bath, ceiling fan and cable TV. There is private parking and Internet service, and the house is just one block from the casino at the Princess.

Breakfast is a culinary adventure at this B&B. The owners, Ward and PJ, offer exciting dishes like a papaya boat – half a papaya topped with banana slices and drizzled with lime and coconut yogurt. Fry jack fans will be pleased to hear that their favorite Belizean breakfast item is also available here. In the evenings, Ward and PJ offer guests a complimentary drink. This gesture seems to reinforce the hosts' desire to make everyone feel welcome. Longer stay guests get every eighth day free.

Villa Boscardi, 6043 Manatee Drive, Buttonwood Bay, ☎ 223-1691, www.villaboscardi.com, $$$, has five rooms. Soon, it hopes to have 10. The spacious rooms, decorated in the finest European style (with cleanliness to match) all have private bath, cable TV, hardwood floors and air conditioning. There is also Internet service. Complimentary transportation to and from the airport is available every day except Sunday and on holidays, and a shuttle service runs into the center of the city. A unique feature is that guests can rent a 4X4 vehicle for US $78 a day, including insurance.

BELIZE CITY

*✗ Bellove Hotel- Southside of swing bridge
clean, no curfew, but kind of pricey
not safe @ night*

[handwritten top margin] Moon Clusters cafe - cholis funky place are yumm

[handwritten left margin, vertical] Riverside tavern - classy place, nice atmosphere

◆ Restaurants ✳ *[handwritten]* Pandoras cafe - So cool!

While there is good food in Belize, no one comes here to eat. Rice and beans often alternates with beans and rice. This, of course, can be spiced up with hot sauce. The plus is that there is real coffee, as opposed to instant Nescafé, country-wide. This is a real attraction for me. But unless

you dine at resorts, you will have to work hard to find culinary excitement. If you are unsure of where to go and nothing in this book appeals to you, follow the locals. Their restaurants often look shabby, but the rice and beans at least will be good.

Another option is to purchase your food in the market and prepare it at your hotel. Cooking can be a problem, but I found that salads were seldom on café menus and, since I craved them, I had to purchase veggies in the market and eat them at home.

[handwritten] cashew wine has a gross aftertas'

❖ WHAT'S THE SEASON?

Lobster is unavailable from Valentine's Day on the 14th of Feb. to the middle of June. However, if **cashew** is your culinary dream, this pepper-shaped fruit with a large seed hanging from the bottom is ripe in May. The Guatemalans claim that they gave the English the seed and kept the succulent fruit for themselves.

Most eateries do not require reservations. However, I do suggest you avoid the main rush hours as the more popular places fill up quickly for lunch and dinner. Places like Capricorn on Ambergris Caye need as much as two day's notice before you can get a table. During high season, all up-scale restaurants require reservations except those with a buffet.

Neries 2 Restaurant on the corner of Queen and Daly Streets, ☎ 223-4028, $, is by far the most popular and famous place in BC. Offering traditional foods, it opens at 7:30 am. They make fry jacks for breakfast and cow foot soup for lunch. Sere, made with fish and coconut milk, is a favorite soup. According to the menu, relleno soup, made with stuffed chicken, ground pork and eggs, is available only on government paydays. There is a second Neries at 124 Freetown Road near the Cinderella Plaza.

Big Daddy's Diner, ☎ 227-0932, $, is on the second floor of the Commercial Center. Take the stairs at the back of the Albert Street market on the south side of the swing bridge. If going for lunch, arrive by 11:30 am because workers from the downtown area flock to this popular place and it holds only 66 people. Big Daddy's is famous for its fresh salads.

The Wet Lizard, #1 Fort Street, ☎ 223-5973, $, is next door to the Tourist Village. The restaurant overlooks the Village and the water. This is a good place to stop for lunch and a rest on your walking tour of the city.

Macy's Café, 18 Bishop Street, ☎ 207-3419, $$, specializes in wild game such as venison. Iguana (banana chicken) and seafood are also on the

[handwritten] bamboo

menu. Once you are seated, look for the photo of Harrison Ford taken while he was starring in the film *Mosquito Coast*. His table was the one by the door. This is a busy restaurant during lunch hour, when it gets packed with locals.

Sumathi Indian Restaurant, 190 Newtown Barracks, ☎ 223-1172, sumathi@btl.net, $$, has moved here from its old location in the center of town. It also changed

AT A GLANCE RESTAURANTS	
EATERY	PHONE
Big Daddy's Diner ($)	☎ 227-0932
Biltmore Plaza Hotel ($$$)	☎ 223-2302
Bob's Bar & Grill ($)	☎ 223-6908
Macy's Café ($$)	☎ 207-3419
Neries 2 Restaurant ($)	☎ 223-4028
Planet Hollywood ($$)	☎ 223-2429
Princess Hotel Restaurant ($$$)	☎ 223-2670
Radisson St. George's ($$$)	☎ 223-3333
Sumathi Indian Restaurant ($$)	☎ 223-1172
Smoky Mermaid ($$$$)	☎ 223-4759
Wet Lizard ($)	☎ 223-5973

BELIZE CITY

its name; it was previously called Memories of India. The restaurant opens from 10:30 am to 11 pm and features north Indian foods, even though the owners are Tamil, from southern India. Sumathi means "bright light" in Tamil. The prices are reasonable and, much more important, the meals are a welcome change from beans and rice. → *pretty pricey*

Radisson's St. George's Dining Room, 2 Marine Parade, ☎ 223-3333 ext 654, $$$. The Sunday brunch here, open from 11:30 am to 2 pm every week, always has a huge variety of foods. The restaurant also has theme nights like the Seafood Dinner Buffet, the Mexican Dinner Buffet or the Oriental Lunch Buffet. You can call for information or stop in the lobby and ask for a calendar that shows the features for the month.

Princess Hotel Restaurant, Newtown Barracks in Kings Park, ☎ 223-2670 or 800-451-3734, resprincess@btl.net, $$$, has an all-you-can-eat buffet for less than US $10. In competition with the Radisson, the Princess also tries to do theme nights. However, the Radisson has a better reputation. For the most part, the food here is North American in style and content – chicken, steak and roast beef.

Biltmore Plaza Hotel, Mile 3, Northern Highway, ☎ 223-2302, $$$, has both good food and good service in an elegant setting. It opens at 6 in the morning and serves a bottomless cup of coffee. The North American-style food is well prepared and tasty.

The Smoky Mermaid, 13 Cork Street, ☎ 233-4759, $$$$, is open from 6 am to 10 pm every day and offers special dishes like coconut shrimp, Jamaican chicken and ribs, and Smoky's banana chimichanga, their specialty. I am not going to tell you what this is. You must go and give it a try.

Bob's Bar & Grill, 164 Newtown Barracks Road, ☎ 223-6908, $, has a verandah where you can sit and watch the action on the street. This is a comfortable and popular place to hang out. Reservations are recommended.

[handwritten: the burrito stand on the Northside of swing bridge- so good! garnache's too!]

Nightlife

The nightlife in Belize City is fun and a lot of it revolves around the strip of **Newtown Barracks Road**. If you plan to bar-hop or be out late, take a cab.

◆ Performing Arts

[handwritten: MJ's on PR has really bad karaoke!]

If you are a concert/symphony/theater fan, call the **House of Culture**, ☎ 227-3050, or the **Belize Arts Council**, ☎ 227-2458, for information on what's happening in the city.

[handwritten: Putt Putt Bar+grill! Friendly and safe but kind of boring]

◆ Lady Luck

Princess Hotel Casino on the strip (Newtown Barracks in Kings Park), ☎ 223-2670, is open daily from noon to 4 am. Near the door are almost 500 slot machines and video poker games. The serious gamblers are farther back. You can play blackjack, roulette or get into a game of poker. All players get free drinks and snacks. Twice a night Russian dance hall girls do a Los Vegas-style performance. Conservative dress code; no sandals. *[handwritten: not if yo]*

◆ Flicks

[handwritten: Club Next - $15 BZ in PR. ALWAYS AN ADVENTURE! go for the free drinks!]

You'll find **movie theaters** at the Princess Hotel, Newtown Barracks in Kings Park, ☎ 223-2670. The two theaters show movies that change every week.

◆ Sports

[handwritten: ✗ Sneak into Radisson or Princess swimming pool]

Soccer (called football, and pronounced fooot-BAL) is popular. To see a game, go to the MCC grounds on Newtown Barracks Road (past the Princess). Call ahead to see who is playing and when, ☎ 223-4415.

Bowling is offered at the Princess Hotel, Newtown Barracks in Kings Park, ☎ 223-2670. There are two lanes with all the latest equipment.

◆ Music, Bars & Clubs

The Tourist Office, Central Bank Building, Gabourel Lane, ☎ 223-1913 or 223-1910, www.travelbelize.org, keeps track of **local bands**. Contact them to find out where the best Belizean pop music bands are playing. The office is open from 8 am to 5 pm, Monday to Friday.

Bars are everywhere in Belize and they range from sleazy, smoky dumps to sophisticated verandah lounges. There is live music poolside at the Radisson and Biltmore every weekend.

Belize Biltmore Plaza offers the prize-winning Blue Hole Drink, which consists of dark rum, blue cacao, grapefruit juice, lime concentrate and coconut cream. The drink won the Belize Signature Drink Award.

Planet Hollywood, 35 Queen and Handyside Streets, ☎ 223-2429, and the **Ambassador Lounge**, 69 Hydes Lane, ☎ 223-1723, are places to try for a drink if you want familiar surroundings.

[handwritten note: go to Angelus Press for internet - AC + $3.03 BZ for 1 hr!]

Day Trips

Except for visiting the cayes, these trips can be done using public transportation, your own bicycle, a car or with a tour.

> ### ❖   SUGGESTED DAY TRIPS
>
> ❖   Hike to and around the education center at the **Belize Zoo**; see page 120.
>
> ❖   Go horseback riding at **Banana Bank Lodge**; see page 122.
>
> ❖   Cycle or drive to **Altun Ha ruins**; see *The North* chapter, page 80.
>
> ❖   Hike through the sanctuary and canoe the river at the **Baboon Sanctuary/Bermudian Landing**; see *The North*, page 77.
>
> ❖   Take an historical exploration of **St. George's Caye**; see page 281 in *The Cayes* chapter.
>
> ❖   Play golf at **Chapel Caye**; see page 280.
>
> ❖   Bird watch in a protected area of **Swallow Caye**; see page 282.

BELIZE CITY

◆ Tour Operators

❖   If you want **ruins**, the best are Actun Tunichil Muknal, Xunantunich, Caracol, Lamanai and Altun Ha.

❖   For **wildlife** go to the Belize Zoo, Crooked Tree, Baboon Sanctuary, Manatee Lodge or Lamanai Outpost.

❖   For **jungle hiking** go to Chaa Creek, Jaguar Preserve and Chan Chich.

❖   And I must add that for the best **diving/snorkeling**, go to Glover's Reef.

Mayan Travel & Tours Ltd., 10 North Park Street, ☎ 223-3289, nigelm@btl. net. Besides the most popular tours (the Lamanai ruins or manatee watching), this company also offers city tours in a comfortable air-conditioned van if walking is too much.

   Sea Sports Belize, 83 North Front Street, ☎ 223-5505, www.seasports-belize.com, are experts in water sports. The company was nominated for Best Tour Operator in 2000.

   Slickrock Adventures are highly experienced in Belize.

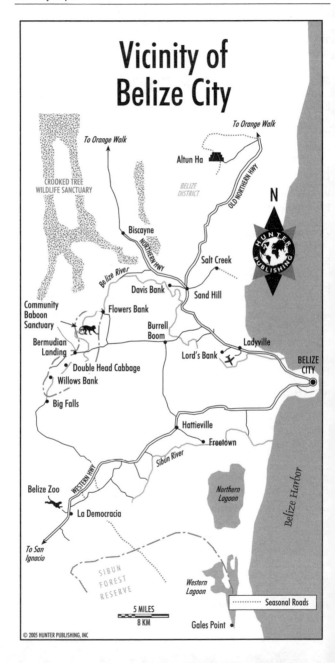

Vicinity of Belize City

Maya Travel Services, 42 Cleghorn Street, Caribbean Tobacco Building, ☎ 223-1623, 223-1241 or 223-2886, www.mayatravelservices.com, have "hiked, paddled, galloped, driven and flown across Belize." They seem to like river travel; if you want to visit one of the ruins and to get there by river (a must while in Belize), then give Maya Travel a call.

Belize Close Encounters, Box 1320, Detroit Lakes, MN 56502, ☎ 888-875-1822 or 218-847-4441, www.belizecloseencounters.com, has been operating in Belize for over 13 years. Their best skill is creating custom trips, whether it be caving or diving, museums or horseback riding. The San Ignacio area is their specialty.

Birding Tour Agencies

Wildside Birding Tours, 14 Marchwood Road, Exton, PA 19341, ☎ 888-875-9431, www.wildsidebirding.com.

Bird Treks, 115 Peach Bottom Village, Peach Bottom, PA 17563-9716, ☎ 717-548-3303, www.birdtreks.com, is run by avid birders.

Borderland Tours, 2550 West Calle Podilla, Tucson, AZ 85745, ☎ 800-525-7753, offers one specialized birding tour to Belize annually.

Caligo Tours, ☎ 800-426-7781 or 914-273-6333, www.caligo.com, takes birders to Chan Chich lodge in the Rio Bravo area.

BELIZE CITY

❖ BIRDING GUIDES IN BELIZE CITY

If you want a private tour, hire one of the bird specialists living in Belize City. The cost of a birder is usually US $50-$100 a day.

- ❖ Edward Allen, 6413 Fer Lane, ☎ 223-4660
- ❖ Ed Herrera, 98 George Street, ☎ 227-7413
- ❖ Peter Faria, 11 Belama Site, ☎ 223-1745
- ❖ Nathan Forbes, 7061 Racoon Street, ☎ 227-0049

Directory

GENERAL DIRECTORY		
■ INFORMATION SOURCES, WEBSITES		
Audubon Society	☎ 223-4987	www.belizeaudubon.org
Belize Arts Council	☎ 227-2458	
Chat About Belize		www.chatboutbelize.com
Nationality Dept	☎ 822-2423	www.travel.state.gov
Tourist Office	☎ 223-1913	www.travelbelize.org
■ TOUR OPERATORS & OUTFITTERS		
Belize Cycle Association		wallen@btl.net
Bird Treks	☎ 717-548-3303	www.birdtreks.com
Borderland Tours	☎ 800-525-7753	
Caligo Tours	☎ 800-426-7781 or 914-273-6333	www.caligo.com
Close Encounters	☎ 888-875-1822	www.belizecloseencounters.com
Maya Travel Services	☎ 223-1623, 223-1241	www.mayatravelservices.com
Mayan Travel & Tours	☎ 223-3289	nigelm@btl.net
Sea Sports Belize	☎ 223-5505	www.seasportsbelize.com
Slickrock Adventures	☎ 800-390-5715	www.slickrock.com
Wildside Birding Tours	☎ 888-875-9431	www.wildsidebirding.com
■ SHOPS & ART GALLERIES		
Belizean Style	☎ 223-4660	www.gographicsbz.com
Gallon Jug Agro-industry Ltd.	☎ 227-7031	
Image Factory Art Gallery	☎ 223-4161	
National Handicrafts Ctr	☎ 223-3636	bcci@btl.net
She Sells Sea Shells	☎ 223-7426	
■ NIGHTLIFE		
Ambassador Lounge	☎ 223-1723	
Princess Casino	☎ 223-2670	resprincess@btl.net
■ ATTRACTIONS		
House of Culture	☎ 227-3050	
Marine/Coastal Museum	☎ 223-1961	
MCC Soccer Grounds	☎ 223-4415	
National Museum	☎ 422-4524	www.museumofbelize.org

The North

The Northern Highway and its side roads take you from Belize City to the northern region of Belize. Whether you go by bicycle, bus, canoe or car, the lands surrounding the Northern Highway will give you a different view of Belize than you get from the Cayes or Mountain Pine Ridge areas.

In the north, there are **Maya ruins**, some of which are not yet excavated. It is a popular sport to cycle to Altun Ha and rent at Pueblo Escondito. Opportunities to spot rare wetland birds are found at places like **Crooked Tree**. Virgin jungle foliage can still be found around places like **Gallon Jug**. **Cycling** is safe and a pleasant method of travel, and **canoeing** at least once on a jungle river in Belize is a must. In the north, the New River runs to Lamanai and the Belize River goes from Bermudian Landing to the sea. Both are gentle runs.

Although there are some upscale accommodations available in unique settings, they are the exception in this area. Often, food is local rather than international.

Along the Highway

Below, I describe the road going north from Belize City. As we come to secondary roads leading to other places of interest, we detour to visit them before returning to the New Northern Highway.

MILEAGE FROM BELIZE CITY TO MEXICAN BORDER	
Mile 10	**Airport/Ladyville**
Mile 15.5	Turn west onto a secondary road for **Burrel Boom/ Bermudian Landing/Baboon Sanctuary**
Mile 19	Turn east onto the Old Northern Highway/**Altun Ha**
Mile 30	Turn west onto a secondary road for **Crooked Tree**
Mile 49	Old Northern Highway joins New Northern Highway

MILEAGE FROM BELIZE CITY TO MEXICAN BORDER	
Mile 52	Turn west onto a secondary road for **Guinea Grass/Lamanai** and **Blue Creek**
Mile 57	**Orange Walk Town**. Turn east (over the New River) onto a secondary road for **Copper Bank/Progresso/Sarteneja**
Mile 83	**Corozal Town**
Mile 92	**Mexican border**

Although there are few mileage signs on the Northern Highways, people refer to locations by the number of miles along the road. To make things easy, I give all directions this way. If you lose track, ask a local resident.

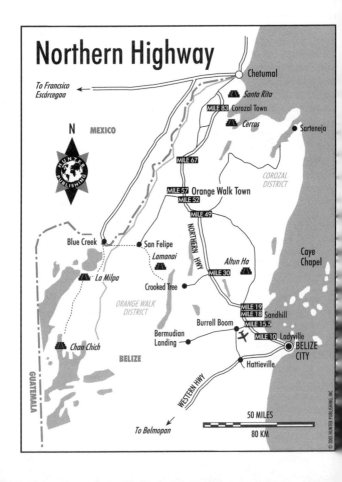

Leaving Belize City

◆ How to Travel

If traveling by **bus**, take a taxi to the **Venus bus station** at the main terminal and buy a ticket for the town you wish to visit. Corozal, the farthest town north of Belize City along the highway, is only three hours by express bus. All buses will stop anywhere along the road, except for express buses, which stop only in the major centers.

    Driving, **cycling** or **hitching** requires a bit more work. From the Swing Bridge in Belize City, follow Queen and then Albert Street to Eve Street. Turn north and continue along the road that skirts the water. Eve Street becomes Barracks Road and, after it curves, turns into Princess Margaret Drive. When you arrive at a large traffic circle that has many flags in its center, take the first road to the right off the circle. This is the New Northern Highway.

Belize City to Bermudian Landing

◆ Attractions

Travellers Liquors, Ltd., 2.5 miles along the New Northern Highway, ☎ 223-2855, www.travellersliquors.bz, was first established in 1953 as a store that sold liquor mainly to travelers going to and from Belize City.

    Ladyville, 10 miles from Belize City along the New Northern Highway, is a small suburb with about 1,500 residents. Because Belize is growing fairly rapidly, Ladyville is now almost a suburb of Belize City. The most notable landmark in Ladyville is the **Philip S.W. Goldson Airport**.

    A trip to the **Belikin Brewery and Coca-Cola plant** (in the same building) just a mile or so past the airport on the old airport road (turn left off the New Northern Highway) may also be of interest. ☎ 225-3195. Call in advance for tour times.

◆ Places to Stay

There are a few places to stay as you head out of town. **Belize River Lodge**, Mile 8.5 Belize River Road, ☎ 225-2002, bzelodge@btl.net, $$$$, is a first-class fly-fishing lodge that has been operating since 1960. Situated on the Belize River, the lodge is just four miles from the Caribbean. Besides a **restaurant** and bar, the hotel offers tours to other must-see spots in the country. All-inclusive prices are available.

    Embassy Hotel, Airport Ring Road, ☎ 225-3333, www.embassyhotel-belize.com, $$, is the only hotel close to the airport. Since there is no flying after dark in Belize, there is no possibility of the planes keeping you awake.

Each of the 40 rooms has air conditioning, fan, TV and bath with hot water. Private parking is offered and there's a restaurant that opens early for breakfast, a roof-top courtyard and hammocks around the verandah. The hotel is clean and the hosts are hospitable. For the economy-minded you can have a car, room and breakfast for US $99 a day.

▶▶ *To reach **Burrel Boom** and **Bermudian Landing**, turn west off the New Northern Highway at Mile 15.5 onto the secondary road. The communities along this stretch of road each have a population of between 500 and 1,500 residents.*

Bermudian Landing Area

◆ Getting Here

BY CAR OR BICYCLE: From the New Northern Highway, turn west at Mile 13 onto an unnamed secondary road. Drive for three miles and cross the Belize River. Less than two miles farther, you will pass a road going south (it leads past a Methodist school and the El Chiclero Hotel). Continue straight ahead on the secondary road and you will arrive at Bermudian Landing and the farming villages beyond.

> **AUTHOR NOTE:** *A "sleeping policeman" is the local name for those speed bumps found at the entrance and exit of every town.*

BY BUS: Two bus companies travel to this area; **Pooks** leaves from the main bus station area in Belize City and **Russells** leaves from Cairo Street two blocks east of the main station and one block north. Pooks buses leave at 5:10 pm, Monday to Friday, and at 2 pm on Saturday. Russells buses leave at 12:15 and 4:30 pm, Monday to Friday, and 12:15 and 1 pm on Saturday.

TAXI OR TOUR: Almost every tour agency or taxi driver will take you to the Baboon Sanctuary. A half-day tour would include only the sanctuary. A taxi would charge about the same as a tour. Hitching is possible, but there is little traffic to the villages.

◆ Introduction

The greatest draw to this area is the **Community Baboon Sanctuary**. The sound of these animals howling through the jungle is a thrill that should not be missed. If you happen to be alone when they start their lament, it will raise the hair on your neck.

Having your own transportation makes it easier for you to visit villages in the area. Tenting is permitted near the sanctuary.

There are also two **canoe** routes that can be enjoyed along this stretch of the **Belize River**. One is the 60-mile run from Bermudian Landing to the Haulover Bridge in Belize City and the other is the 60-mile run from Guanacaste Park to Bermudian Landing. If you are really ambitious, have the time, and enjoy jungle rivers, do both of these trips.

◆ History

This area was a logging center from the 1700s until the end of Belize's mass-logging period. Now the area is farmland. Burrel Boom got its name from a time when logs that were floating loose down the river were "boomed." Booming is the process of grouping a large amount of logs together and holding them together by a chain or rope. The "boom" is then floated downriver in a controlled fashion. Loose timbers were stopped from floating past Burrel Boom by a huge chain strung across the river. Parts of the chain and chain anchors can still be seen along the river near the village.

◆ Things to Do

Community Baboon Sanctuary

A **Natural Wildlife Museum and Visitor Center** at the far end of Bermudian Landing (there's only one street) is the official headquarters for the sanctuary. Their mailing address is PO Box 1428, Belize City, ☎ 220-2181 or 220-2158, www.howlermonkey.bz. The center is open daily from 8 am to 5 pm. The entry fee is US $5 and the ticket is good all day. You can leave and return to the sanctuary at no extra charge.

I highly recommended hiring a local guide, available at the center, to take you through the jungle. The best time to see the monkeys is in the early morning or at dusk. The shorter trails take as little as 10 minutes, while longer ones can take two to three hours.

The modest natural wildlife museum, opened in 1989, takes only a few minutes to visit, but the information will fill in details not always available elsewhere. The museum is open during the same hours as the park.

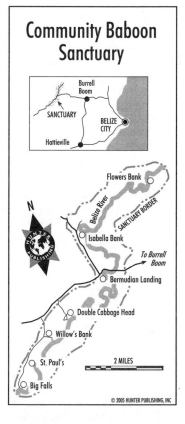

THE NORTH

Community Baboon Sanctuary

© 2005 HUNTER PUBLISHING, INC

> ### ❖ MONKEY BUSINESS
>
> The sanctuary offers a Sponsor a Monkey program. The annual cost is $20 for adults, $10 for children. Supporters are supposed to receive quarterly updates and photographs of their adopted monkeys. I found that this does not happen.

 The center sells the book, ***Belizean Rain Forests; Community Baboon Sanctuary, 3rd edition***, by Robert Horwich and Johnathon Lyon. Previously used copies are available at www.amazon.com.

The Community Baboon Sanctuary is operated by the citizens of the surrounding communities who have cooperated with each other to create an environmental haven for the black howler monkey. The management of the sanctuary is completely voluntary, as is the agreement to practice farming techniques that will not harm the natural habitat of the monkeys. Before the formation of the sanctuary, these creatures were endangered due to loss of habitat.

The sanctuary has also been generously supported by the United Nations Development Program. The UN's latest project is to set up an education center at the museum so that both locals and visitors can learn more about the area in general and the monkeys in particular.

The sanctuary is bordered by the banks of the Belize River, with its riparian and broad-leafed forests that are abundant in vines so popular with baboons. Inland from the river are marsh, pasture and farmland. The eastern end of the sanctuary has cohune palm, while the west is bordered by pine trees and savanna.

The monkey species found in the sanctuary is one of six similar types living in Central and South America. This particular species dwells only in southern Mexico, northern Guatemala and Belize. After the sanctuary had been in operation for three years, the monkey population had grown to about 1,000. But there were still many unnecessary deaths. Monkeys were caught in barbed wire fences or run over by cars at night. Bridges, ropes and wooden ladders were placed in strategic places so the animals could travel over and around these hazards safely. This has contributed to the increase of the population that is now believed to be over 3,000. One such bridge can be seen strung high above the road as you enter Bermudian Landing.

Besides the howler monkey, the sanctuary has Baird's tapirs, Morelet's crocodiles, iguanas and Central American river turtles. There are over 250 birds hanging around the 100 or so species of trees that border many of the Maya house mounds still unexcavated in the sanctuary.

Adventures

Crocodile hunting is a two-hour, after-dark activity. You can rent a canoe and guide for this either at the Howler Monkey Lodge or at the Nature Resort for US $40 per person. Hunts offer views of more than crocs. Bats come out to feed during these early evening hours, as do some birds. Insects seem to sing more at dusk and blooming flowers are most pungent at this time of day.

Horseback riding through the sanctuary is available, but should be booked ahead of arrival. Call the sanctuary, ☎ 220-2181 or 220-2158, for information. Rates are US $10 per hour.

Canoeing from Big Falls to the sanctuary takes one day and is highly recommended. Canoe rentals and shuttles can be arranged from either lodge in Bermudian Landing or from the sanctuary. The cost is dependent upon the length of your trip.

The canoe ride from Bermudian Landing to Belize City is in deep water that is slow and flat. There is lush jungle on both banks. After Flowers Bank the river really gets boring (there isn't even a riffle) as you push your way through mangrove swamp. If you are a birder, this section will be anything but boring. The greatest draw during dry season is the possibility of seeing sharks that come up the main channel from the coast.

I highly recommend at least one river trip while in Belize and if your skills and confidence are low, this may be a good one. The worst that could happen is that you could tip, get wet and then be attacked by a shark.

◆ Places to Stay

The Nature Resort, next to the sanctuary's visitor center, ☎ 604-9286, naturer@btl.net, $$, has spacious and clean cabins beside the river. Each thatched-roof building has a fan, writing desk and fridge. The shared bath is about 20 feet from the front door.

Howler Monkey Lodge, ☎ 220-2158, h_monkey@btl.net, $$, is just before the visitor center and a short distance off the main road. Each little cabin, nestled in the jungle on the banks of the river, has two double beds, a fan and a private bath with hot water. The lodge has a reference library and a one-for-one book exchange. **Tenting**, $, along the river at the Howler Monkey Lodge is permitted. Camping in the sanctuary is not permitted.

El Chiclero, Burrell Boom, ☎ 225-9005, soffit@io.com, $$, is a stucco building, clean and neat, with air conditioning. Each room has two double beds, private bathrooms with tile floors and hot water. There is a swimming pool on the grounds and the sundeck overlooks the town. Special weekly or monthly rates are available.

◆ Places to Eat

The **Baboon Sanctuary Restaurant**, $$, beside the visitor center, is open from 8 am to 5 pm seven days a week. The food is cooked and served by local women, who use their own secret recipes.

Howler Monkey Lodge, $$, run by the Womens' Conservation Group, offers Creole and international cuisine, all home-cooked. Vegetarian and special dietary requirements can be met as long as the cook knows in advance. The meals are family style; you get what everyone else gets.

There's a **supermarket** just half a mile past the visitor center on the road going to Double Head Cabbage. It's not a long walk and is a good spot to buy groceries and snacks for your cabin.

El Chiclero, Burrell Boom, ☎ 225-9005, $$. The owners take pride in serving some of the best meals available in the north. Although El Chiclero has a two-star price, it has five-star hospitality and quality.

▶▶ *Return to the New Northern Highway at Mile 15.5 and continue north. Turn east off the New Northern Highway at Mile 19, just past Sandhill.*

Old Northern Highway

The Old Northern Highway is single lane and paved for most of the way, but also dotted with numerous potholes. Occasional extensions in the width of the road allow vehicles to pass each other. There is one bridge with no side guards. This style of roadway encourages careful driving. However, the road is excellent for cycling.

A bus goes from Belize City, past the turn for Altun Ha, to the village of **Maskall** three times a day; at 1, 3:30 and 5:30 pm. The **Maskall Bus Company** vehicles leave from Mosuel Street, just off Princess Margaret Drive (near the Flag circle) in the city and **Russell's** buses leave from Cairo Street, just two blocks from the main bus terminal. The bus drivers will let you off at the road to Altun Ha and you can walk the rest of the way.

▶▶ *If driving or cycling , turn off the Old Northern Highway at Mile 10.5 to reach Altun Ha.*

hard to get to w/out a tour guide. hitchiking not recommended but people will STOP

◆ Altun Ha

Altun Ha Maya ruins are three miles along an unnamed secondary road. The ruins are open daily from 8 am to 4 pm and the entrance fee is US $5 per day for foreigners. Trained tour guides are available and they can give you tons of information about the area. There is also a confectionary, a gift shop and toilet facilities at the entrance to the ruins.

HISTORICAL TIMELINE

200 BC	Earliest settlements are at Altun Ha.
100 AD	Most of the larger structures are built during this century.
550 AD	Temple of the Green Tomb was built.
600 AD	Tomb with jade head carving of Kinich Akau constructed.
1963	Archeologist AH Anderson finds jade pennant in BC that led to money being awarded for more exploration at the ruins.
1968	Seven tombs found, one that had cable markings where the body was lowered into the tomb. Other tombs had been vandalized.

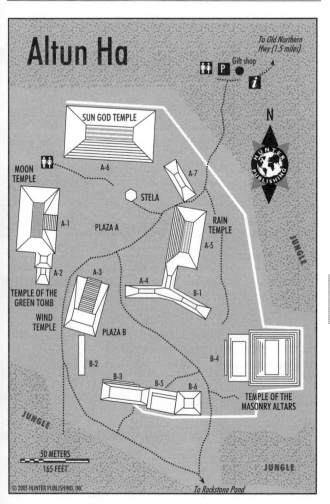

Exploring the Ruins

Although the earliest settlements are thought to have been around 200 BC, most of the large structures were built about AD 100. At its peak Altun Ha had over 3,000 people living in the center and an additional 5-7,000 people living in the vicinity.

The ruins consist of two main **plazas** surrounded by 13 **temples**. The ceremonial center sits inside a 1.5-square-mile area and is surrounded by about 500 **residential mounds**.

❖ **"ALTUN HA"**

Altun Ha means "stone water" and was named after the rockstone pond beside which a small reservoir was built. However, the main 71,000-square-foot reservoir is southwest of the ceremonial complex along a trail leading from Plaza B. It has a stone and clay dam at its south end. Beside it was where the first temple was built. Because of the plentiful water supply, the housing density near the reservoir is higher than elsewhere in the site.

Altun Ha's temples are unique in structure. Most were built in four phases and each phase had an altar on top. At the altar, carved jade objects were thrown into a fire and burned, along with incense. The next phase was then built over the altar and sacrificial objects. In Plaza B at the **Temple of Masonry Altars**, there were eight phases of construction.

 MYSTERIOUS MAYA: *Kinich Akau was the patron God of Uxmal and father of Itzamna, lord of night and day. It is believed that Kinich Akau descended into the city of Uxmal every day at noon in the form of a macaw and ate the offerings left on the altar. Kinich Akau often appears with filed teeth similar to those of a jaguar and wearing Kin, the symbol of the Maya day.*

In Plaza A, at the **Temple of the Green Tomb**, which was built around AD 550, over 300 items were found. Some items were of carved jade, others were pieces of stone jewelry. Numerous stingray spikes were also found. These were used by the Maya for bloodletting.

It is believed that Altun Ha fell due to peasant revolts in the Late Classic Period. Following that, the trade center for the region moved to Lamanai.

Today, under the leadership of German archeologist Andrea Ruf, many of the temples and masks are being restored.

◆ Belize Jungle Gardens & Aquarium

The Jungle Gardens, Rockstone Pond, ☎ 609-5523, are open Sunday to Friday, 9 am to 5 pm, and are located a half-mile from the ruins on the way back toward the Old Northern Highway. This tastefully designed garden has a river-to-reef aquarium, and cages that contain reptiles and amphibians. Another building displays insects and plants, and a saltwater touch tank is filled with touchable marine animals and plants. There's also a butterfly garden, nature trails, reptile cage, gift shop and a healing herb garden.

Belize Jungle Gardens offers educational workshops and river snorkeling tours or survivor-island (as in the TV program on Discovery Channel) camping. Ask at the desk or phone for details.

◆ Places to Stay & Eat

El Pescador Restaurant, ☎ 609-5523, $$, on the Belize Jungle Garden's grounds, can seat 70 people in its covered gardens. It serves gourmet food and specializes in seafood.

❖ HOTELS		✱ RESTAURANTS	
$	$10 to $20	$	under $5
$$	$21 to $50	$$	$5-$10
$$$	$51 to $75	$$$	$11-$25
$$$$	$76 to $100	$$$$	$26-$50
$$$$$	over $100	$$$$$	over $50

Maya Wells Restaurant, ☎ 209-2039, $$, opens Tuesday to Saturday from 9 am to 5 pm. They are reputed to serve good local cuisine. The restaurant is in a covered garden similar to El Pescador.

▶▶ *Return to the Old Northern Highway and continue north. The road is riddled with potholes.*

Along the Old Northern Highway at Mile 30 is the popular cycling destination of **Pueblo Escondido**, ☎ 614-1458, www.pueblo-escondido.net, $, a "farm and observation garden," where **tenting** is permitted. Some sites are under covered huts for protection against rain. There are hiking trails, fishing ponds and wetland birding sites on the property. There is also a good cycling road at the back of the property that leads to the Altun Ha ruins.

THE NORTH

On the Old Northern Highway at Mile 39 is the **Pretty See Jungle Ranch**, ☎ 209-2005, $$$$, which was once a macadamia nut plantation. It is located on 1,300 acres of pasture land and jungle. The opportunity for seeing wildlife along its many trails is good. The hardwood, octagonal-shaped cabins sleep four. There is a bar and restaurant on the premises.

> ❖ **COOL ABODE**
>
> It is believed that houses built in an octagonal shape are easier to keep cool. Thatch huts should never have air conditioning as the cold air goes up through the roof. It is much better to have a fan.

Maruba Jungle Resort and Spa, Mile 40.5 on the Old Northern Highway, ☎ 322-2199, www.maruba-spa.com, $$$$$, is *the* luxury accommodation on this stretch of road. There are standard rooms, suites and villa suites ($450/day) tucked into the jungle on the property. For entertainment, you can go to a Maya psychic reader, rent a car with a chauffeur, ride horses or soak in the Japanese hot tub. There is a mineral bath and a viewing tower. For those who want to relax by the pool but have gone through all their reading material, there is a one-for-one book exchange. Other amenities include a restaurant and bar, laundry service and airport pick-up service. The resort offers honeymoon and wedding packages, as well as "mood mud therapy." Best of all, a waiter can deliver tropical drinks made from local fruit to anywhere on the property. The owners speak Spanish, English and German, and any tour you may want can be arranged from the reception desk.

The Old Northern Highway joins the New Northern Highway at **Carmelita**. This little village, with its great community spirit, uses some of the profits from its sand pits to fund the primary school.

▶▶   *You'll return to the New Northern Highway at Mile 19 and continue to Mile 31. Turn west onto a secondary road that leads to Crooked Tree Village and Sanctuary. The secondary road goes for three miles until it reaches a causeway that takes you across the Northern Lagoon to the village. Prior to the building of the causeway in 1984, the village was accessible only by boat.*

Crooked Tree Village & Sanctuary

Crooked Tree Village and Wildlife Sanctuary is located on an island that covers about 20 square miles and has a population of about 900.

◆ Introduction

Serious **birders** can't afford to miss this spot, considered the top birding site in Belize. The wetland bird population is second to none, plus there are two families of the rare Jabiru storks that make the sanctuary their yearly nesting place.

A second important draw to this little island is the **Cashew Festival** that takes place over the first weekend in May every year. Attending will give you a pleasant memory of Creole culture (see below).

Crooked Tree is set up for outdoor exploration. Tenting, canoeing and hiking are popular pursuits.

◆ History

The village of Crooked Tree has been around for over 300 years and is thought to be the oldest settlement in Belize. There are three popular stories about the naming of the community.

- ❖   The first is that three **buccaneers** came to the area and called themselves the "crooked three." It is reported that the three hid a bucket of gold in the swamps north of the village.

- ❖   The second story is that it was the **logging** industry that first settled in the area and named the place after the crooked branches of the logwood trees.

- ❖   The third story concerns the **cashew tree**, which grows abundantly in the area. During storms, it has been known to topple over but continue to grow, crookedly.

❖ **LUCRATIVE LOADS**

During the 1500s logwood sold in England for £100 per ton. One ship could carry about 50 tons of logwood, which could be sold for a total of £5,000, more than a year's profit from any other merchandise shipped during that time. In the mid-1700s a total of 13,000 tons of logwood left Belize in one year. That comes to a total £65 million paid for the one export product. It was only after the aniline dyes made from coal tar were discovered that the use of logwood decreased.

◆ Getting Here

BY BUS: There are four direct **Jex Busses** going from Belize City to Crooked Tree. They leave daily at 10:30 am, 4:30 and 5:30 pm from Pound Yard Bridge in Belize City. The fourth bus departs at 4 pm from the Novelo Bus station (main terminal).

If these times are not convenient, take any non-express bus going north and ask to be let off at the junction going to the sanctuary. The walk to the village takes about an hour, and you stand an excellent chance of seeing a lot of birds along the way. Returning buses leave Crooked Tree at 6 am, 6:30 and 7 am daily.

◆ Crooked Tree Wildlife Sanctuary

Crooked Tree Wildlife Sanctuary is under the care of the Belize Audubon Society, 12 Fort Street, Belize City, ☎ 223-5004 or 223-4987, www.belize-audubon.org. The visitor center, located beside the causeway at the entrance to the village, is open daily from 8 am to 4:30 pm. The cost to enter the sanctuary is US $5 per day for foreigners.

> **AUTHOR NOTE:** *In 1998 the sanctuary became the 108th member of the Ramsar Convention, at which time it was declared the first wetland of international importance.*

There are three ways to visit the sanctuary: on foot, by boat or on horseback. Boats and horses are available in the village and at the resort within the sanctuary.

The 16,400 acres of waterways and swamps make up two groups of lagoons that, in turn, make up the sanctuary. The largest group includes the Calabash Pond, Southern Lagoon, Western Crooked Tree, Revenge and Spanish Creek. They are linked to the Belize River by Black Creek. The second group, located south and west of the first group, includes Jones and Mexico Lagoons. They run into the Belize River via Mexico Creek. Until 1984 when the causeway was built, these linking waterways were the only highways into the area.

The lagoons are as much as one mile wide and 20 miles long (1.6 km by 32 km). During high water, Northern Crooked Tree Lagoon reaches a depth of eight feet (2.4 meters), while in May, the peak of dry season, it can be dry.

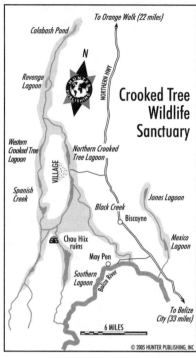

The lagoons and creeks are inundated with logwood thickets, marsh and broadleaf forests and pine/oak savannas. This makes them a haven for both migratory and indigenous birds. The lagoons also house manatee, crocodiles, iguanas and every species of freshwater turtle found in Belize.

Interpretive trails lead through the sanctuary. Ask for directions at the visitor center or follow any of the sandy trails from the village – they go for miles. The sanctuary has the longest elevated boardwalk in Belize and it stretches .6 miles across a section of the wetlands. This walk has signs along the way.

Although waterfowl are the most prominent birds found at the sanctuary, the greatest draw for birders is the possibility of spotting a jabiru stork with its three- to four-meter (10- to 12-foot) wingspan. Belize has the largest nesting population of jabirus in all of Central America and the sanctuary has two pairs that nest there every year. They arrive in Nov. and build stick nesting platforms in the lowland pine savannas. The birds remain until Apr. or May, when they join other jabirus and head out, leaving just as the rains arrive.

Apr. and May is also when migratory birds are passing through. The bird population at this time is immense; to date, a total of 276 species have been seen.

◆ Adventures

Canoe rentals and **horseback riding** can be arranged either at **Sam Tillett's Hotel**, ☎ 220-7026, or at the **Bird's Eye View Lodge**, ☎ 225-7027. The cost of a canoe is US $15 per day. Taking a motorboat tour with four people will cost the same (per person) and you have the advantage of a guide. However, the canoe is far more ecologically sensitive to the lagoons and less intrusive to the birds. Horses can be rented from both places and cost US $10 an hour from Bird's Eye without a guide and US $15 from Tillett's with a guide.

Cashew Festival, on the first weekend of May, is actually a three-in-one event. There is the harvest of the cashews, an agricultural show and a display of Creole village life at its best. During the festival, cashew wine (which is sweet) flows into the mouths of all except the very young or very weak and counters the spices of the Creole foods that are served. The wine, in turn, makes the Punta Rock music (see Dangriga, page 196) less abrasive and the greased pole climb more appealing. There is also a story-telling event, a beauty pageant and Creole games of every kind.

> **❖ IN THE EYE OF THE BEHOLDER**
>
> During the beauty contest, "E too maaga," meaning "she's too thin" in Creole, can be heard often as the beauties line up for the pageant. "Manfi" is the desired requirement. Manfi means shapely bust and hips. Besides not being too thin, the beauty pageant contest winner must also be a local girl with good moral conduct, top grades at high school and a polite manner.

Overnight hiking can be arranged at **Sam Tillett's**, above. He will take you into the jungle where you can spot many inland birds and possibly see some animals. Prices can be negotiated and depend upon where you go, services required and the number of people in your group. Having your own equipment will save on rental fees.

> **AUTHOR TIP:** *Gasoline can be purchased from a private house, even though there is no service station in the village. Ask locals for directions. The lady purchases the gasoline by the barrel in the duty-free zone and sells it to locals for less than the cost at service stations. However, she will sell only the amount needed to get you to a service station.*

Birding Pals, www.birdingpal.org, is a networking group who try to put birders from different countries in contact with each other. The purpose of the group is to have people share the special interest in birds and learn about one another's cultures. The list of participants is growing daily, so check the website just before heading to Belize if you would like to develop such a friendship.

The group also lists professional guides available for hire. These listings give the qualifications of each guide so you can satisfy your own special needs. This list is also growing rapidly, so log on to their website just before you leave and see who's available.

Birding Pals was started in Apr., 2000 by Knud Rasmussen of Toronto, Canada. Since the group's inception, the list of members has become substantial. There are over 1,500 pals in 166 countries. Mr Rasmussen gets no funding for this, nor does he charge for the immense amount of work he does. His motivation is his love of birds and he believes that birders are very special people.

THE NORTH

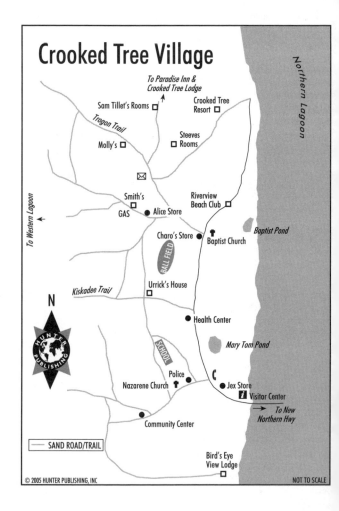

◆ Places to Stay

Bird's Eye View Lodge, at the south end of village along the lagoon, ☎ 225-7027 or 570-588-1184, www.belizenet.com/birds-eye, daacker@ptd.net, $-$$$. This is a bustling place where excited birders gather in the guest lounge to talk about the day's sightings. There is a mixed selection

❖ HOTEL PRICING	
$	$10 to $20
$$	$21 to $50
$$$	$51 to $75
$$$$	$76 to $100
$$$$$	over $100

of accommodations, from inexpensive dormitory beds or tenting space to rooms that offer private baths.

Sam Tillett's Hotel is in the center of the village, set back from the lagoon. ☎ 220-7026, samhotel@btl.net, $-$$$. Tillet's is another busy spot. It offers comfortable suites and single rooms with fans and private bathrooms. There is also tenting in the yard with access to a shower. If Sam is full and you have no place to stay, he may even rent you a hammock on the porch. There is a restaurant at the hotel. Sam is known as the best bird guide in the village and his zest for life is infectious.

Paradise Inn is right on the lagoon at the north end of the village. ☎ 220-7044, www.adventurecamera.com/paradise, $$$$. There are a group of palmetto palm and thatch cabins with private baths and balconies overlooking the lagoon. The food served in the dining room is excellent. The hotel has been recommended by many travelers.

Tenting is available at Tillett's and at Bird's Eye View Lodge. A home stay can be arranged at the visitor center if you would like to be with a family. The center closes at 4:30 pm, so plan to be there at least an hour before closing to give the worker time to arrange a place for you.

◆ Places to Eat

The hotels listed above all offer meals that can be ordered and/or included with your room package.

Tree's & Vee's, $, in town, serves traditional Creole food with fresh seasonal wines (cashew and berry).

❖ RESTAURANT PRICING	
$	under $5
$$	$5 to $10
$$$	$11 to $25
$$$$	$26 to $50
$$$$$	over $50

Ms. Suzette's, $, offers the best fried chicken and fries, or fresh fish and fries, in the village. Both dishes come with a coleslaw that has a unique dressing and an admirable reputation.

Ms. Judith's, $, offers the traditional beef, pork or chicken with rice and beans. Although the choice of dishes is limited, the quality of food is high.

If you're looking for something to do after dinner, head to the disco near the lagoon on the north side of the island.

▶▶ *Return to the New Northern Highway at Mile 31, the Crooked Tree Village turnoff, and head north. The next 24 miles go through farmland.*

Crooked Tree Village to Orange Walk

The toll booth at **Tower Hill Bridge**, Mile 51, will cost about US 50¢ if you are driving. Tower Hill is the only toll bridge in the country.

The sugar cane area around Orange Walk is also known as **Little Columbia** because of the ganja and coca that is illegally grown and shipped from here. The side roads in this area should not be traveled at night either by foot, bike or car. Drug enforcement officers are often in the area, but they my not be around when you need protection.

▶▶ *Just after the toll booth on the New Northern Highway is the secondary road going west to **Guinea Grass** and the Mennonite community of **Shipyard**. It's nine miles to Guinea Grass and 18 miles to Shipyard. From the booth on the New Northern Highway at Mile 51, it is four miles to Orange Walk Town.*

Orange Walk Town

Orange Walk town has a population of about 12,300 people and is locally called **Sugar City**.

AVERAGE TEMPERATURES & RAINFALL		
	Daily temp.	**Monthly rainfall**
JAN	74.6°F/23.7°C	30.2 inches/76.8 cm
FEB	77.0°F/25.0°C	13.3 inches/33.7 cm
MAR	78.8°F/26.0°C	11.3 inches/28.8 cm
APR	82.6°F/28.1°C	18.1 inches/45.9 cm
MAY	84.2°F/29.0°C	39.0 inches/99.1 cm
JUN	84.9°F/29.4°C	79.7 inches/202.5 cm
JULY	84.0°F/28.9°C	75.5 inches/191.7 cm
AUG	84.2°F/29.0°C	80.9 inches/205.6 cm
SEPT	84.2°F/29.0°C	67.3 inches/171.0 cm
OCT	82.2°F/27.9°C	74.3 inches/188.7 cm
NOV	79.5°F/26.4°C	40.0 inches/101.6 cm
DEC	76.8°F/24.9°C	30.5 inches/77.4 cm

Source: Belize Sugar Industries located at Towerhill, two miles from Orange Walk Town.

◆ Getting Here

BY CAR OR BICYCLE: If driving or cycling, stay on the New Northern Highway. The road is good and decorated on each side by sugar cane fields.

> **TAKE NOTE:** *Do not drive at night, especially on the secondary roads. This is a drug-running area and night travel is not for visitors.*

BY BUS: Buses going north and south pass along the New Northern Highway through Orange Walk every half-hour. Take a bus from the main terminal in Belize City. An express bus will take half as long as a regular bus, but it isn't nearly as interesting. Regular buses can be caught anywhere along the highway. Flag one down and the driver will stop.

◆ Introduction

The town, sitting on the banks of the New River, is a bustling hodge-podge of animals, cars, buses, sugar cane trucks, garden goods and friendly people. It's also the transfer place if you want to reach some of the fishing villages on the Caribbean coast.

Orange Walk is believed to have gotten its name from the orange trees that at one time decorated the banks of the New River. If this is true, the town council should plant more because the quiet walk near the river is a delightful contrast to the bustle of the center and orange trees would add to the beauty.

There are two important Maya sites near Orange Walk. **Lamanai** is best reached by boat up the New River and **Cuello** is close enough to town that it can be reached by bicycle. Other attractions are the **Rio Bravo Conservation Area** and **Chan Chich Lodge**. Both are exquisite for wildlife viewing.

Orange Walk itself has decent hotels, good restaurants, Internet cafés and sleazy bars. The surrounding area is dedicated mostly to sugar cane farming or Mennonite settlements. The drug running mentioned earlier seems to be just an extension of the rum running that was done during the 1800s.

◆ History

Prior to Europeans arriving in Belize, this area was densely populated with **Maya**. For some unknown reason they abandoned most of the area before Columbus arrived. The latest theory is that severe drought caused starvation.

The re-entry of the Maya occurred in 1849 when they were fleeing from the wars in Mexico caused by the Spanish elite enforcing servitude and confiscating land. These acts of oppression left the Maya in poverty.

The **British** welcomed the Maya, hoping that they would set up farms and grow much needed produce for the loggers who were denuding the land at that time. As the wood disappeared and the prices for logs dropped, the landowners rented their land to the Maya. But not all was amiable and peaceful. Fort Cairn and Fort Mundy were built to protect the settlers from the warring Mexicans, who felt that a lot of Belize belonged to them. The final battle occurred in 1872 and a sort of peaceful co-existence began until 1892 when an actual treaty was signed between the British and the Mexicans.

As logging disappeared, the **chicle** business flourished. It was later replaced with **maize**. In the early 1900s an old sugar mill was imported from Leeds Foundary in New Orleans and installed north of town. The **sugar** business was started and is still the main source of income today.

Orange Walk and Corozal Districts were one large district until 1955, when Orange Walk split from Corozal and became a separate district with its own government. This seems to have been good for the area. In the last 50 years, Orange Walk District has quadrupled its population to about 40,000 people, one quarter of the population of Belize.

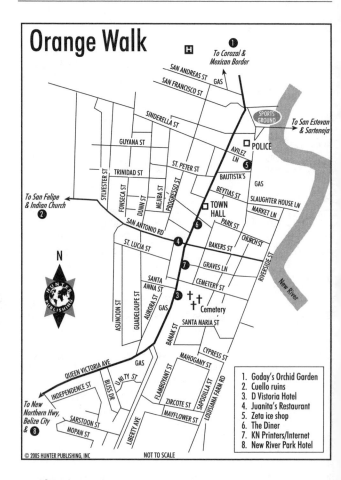

Orange Walk

To Corozal & Mexican Border ❶

To San Estevan & Sarteneja

To San Felipe & Indian Church ❷

To New Northern Hwy, Belize City & ❽

NOT TO SCALE

© 2005 HUNTER PUBLISHING, INC

1. Goday's Orchid Garden
2. Cuello ruins
3. D Vistoria Hotel
4. Juanita's Restaurant
5. Zeta ice shop
6. The Diner
7. KN Printers/Internet
8. New River Park Hotel

◆ Things to Do

Godoy's Orchid Garden, 4 Trial Farm, ☎ 322-2969, has a huge display of orchids and bromeliads. There is no charge to visit and Godoy's is open during regular business hours. In its fall blooming season, the national flower, the black orchid, can be viewed.

> **AUTHOR NOTE:** *Belize has nine major religious groups practicing in the country. Churches are exempt from paying property taxes and this may be one reason there are so many.*

Cuello Ruins

Cuello ruins, ☎ 322-2141, are just 1.8 miles along Yo Creek Road, west of Orange Walk Town and easily walked to in less than an hour. Cycling would take even less time. The ruins are on the Cuello family land, where rum is made at the distillery. You must ask permission to enter the ruins. Call ahead. To visit the ruins, go west on Baker Street, cross the highway and continue along San Antonio Road (Yo Creek Road) until you arrive at the Cuello Farm, about two miles along the road. If you haven't phoned ahead, stop at the first building you pass on the property.

The oldest pyramid on the site, built in nine layers, is believed to have been constructed about 2600 BC. This date is controversial; other experts think the pyramid was built about 1000 BC. Regardless, the ruins are an early example of how the Maya plastered over their structural stones to give the pyramid a smooth finish. This style of finishing is similar to the Cahal Pech ruins in San Ignacio, Cayo District and to the Zaculeu ruins, located just out of Huehuetenango in Guatemala. The Zaculeu ruins are believed to date from the Mam Dynasty, built during the late post classic period (AD 1400).

The most interesting discovery was the bodies with ceramic head coverings found at some of the 180 graves unearthed. There were also bodies found in a mass grave showing evidence of torture.

Damage to Cuello happened due to road construction in recent times. Building stones were removed for this work and graves were looted. The remaining objects found here are now part of the national exhibition.

 MYSTERIOUS MAYA: *The Maya are believed to have domesticated several breeds of dogs, one of them barkless (too bad they aren't still around). The Maya used to fatten dogs and sacrifice them. I'd love to sacrifice some of the barking dogs found in Belize City, especially around 3 am.*

Nohmul Ruins

The Nohmul ruins are just north of Orange Walk Town. To get there, take any vehicle heading north and get off at San José. It is just seven miles from town along the New Northern Highway. At the crossroads, walk west for one mile. This stroll will take less than 20 minutes each way.

Nohmul, meaning Great Mound, was at one time a major ceremonial center. However, its greatest fame comes from the ability of the Maya living there to conquer the Pulltrouser Swamp area and transform the land into productive farms.

Occupied from about 350 BC to AD 250 and then again from about AD 600 to 900, the town was the government seat for the settlements around San Estevan and San Luis.

The two ceremonial sites contain 10 plazas connected by a raised causeway. In total there are about 81 buildings in the city. The site covers 12 square miles and overlooks the Hondo River. Some of the architecture found at Nohmul is similar to that of the Yucatán in Mexico. This supports the idea that the Maya did migrate to the area from the north.

❖ **LESSONS**

Before Nohmul was established, trading was already popular between those living in Mexico and those near Corozal. Mik Chan (850 BC) was one such Maya trader, but during a drunken spree someone went off with all his goods, leaving him with nothing. Times have not changed. Get drunk in public and you could lose all your money.

◆ Places to Stay

D' Victoria Hotel, 40 Belize/Corozal Road, ☎ 322-2518, www.d-victoriahotel.com, $$, is at the south end of town. There is air conditioning, cable TV, parking, private bath with hot water and a swimming pool in the courtyard. Although a bit run down, the hotel is not noisy and it has pleasant staff. There is a bar and restaurant.

❖ HOTEL PRICING	
$	$10 to $20
$$	$21 to $50
$$$	$51 to $75
$$$$	$76 to $100
$$$$$	over $100

St. Christopher's, 10 Main Street, ☎ 302-1064, $$$, is across from the Zeta Ice Factory and faces the New River. It is, by far, the best place in town to stay, offering clean rooms and private baths with hot water. There is a restaurant and bar on the premises.

The New River Park Hotel, by the Tower Hill toll bridge, ☎ 322-3987, $$$, is a new place on the river. It offers private baths, hot water and air conditioning. The hotel is close to the dock, making it a convenient spot if you wish to catch the boat for Lamanai in the morning.

◆ Places to Eat

Juanita's Restaurant, 42 Staines Alley, ☎ 322-2677, $, is across from the Shell gas station just off the main road. It opens early in the morning for breakfast and serves large portions of excellent food at reasonable prices. Only the coffee needs to be improved.

❖ RESTAURANT PRICING	
$	under $5
$$	$5 to $10
$$$	$11 to $25
$$$$	$26 to $50
$$$$$	over $50

The Diner, 44 Queen Victoria Avenue, ☎ 302-3753, $$, is by far the best place to eat in Orange Walk. Presented buffet-style, the food is better and the variety larger than the usual fare found in other restaurants. Dishes such as pepper steak and fish in a rich white sauce, are on the menu too.

Excellent ice cream is available at the **Zeta Ice Shop**, 31 Main Street.

◆ Nightlife

Both the **D' Victoria** and **Mi Amor Hotel** have discos, where Punta Rock isn't quite so popular as Latin music. If you don't like marimba, maybe do the nightlife in some other town.

◆ Services

K & N Printers on Belize Road, ☎ 322-2473, south of the telephone company, has eight computers and they work well. K & N charges the same price as the telephone company in other towns, but it doesn't open its doors until 9:30 am at the earliest.

Orange Walk to Indian Church

▶▶ *Go west on Baker Street in Orange Walk Town, cross the New Northern Highway and continue along the secondary road called San Antonio Road or Yo Creek Rd for eight miles to Yo Creek. At Yo Creek, turn south and continue for 18 miles to San Filipe. Along the way you will pass San Lazaro, Trinidad and August Pine Ridge. At San Filipe, continue straight (the road veers to the southeast) along the dirt road for another 12 miles. You will then reach Indian Church, location of the Lamanai ruins. This is an all-season road, paved in some spots, red clay in others and potholed all along.*

◆ Getting Here

BY BUS: A bus goes to Lamanai three times a week, on Monday, Wednesday and Friday. It leaves Orange Walk Town around 4 pm from the fire station. Traveling by bus usually means that you will have to stay at the lodge near Lamanai for two nights (one when you arrive and the next day while you tour the ruins), then catch the 6 am bus back on the morning of your return.

BY BOAT: Jungle River Tours, 20 Lovers Lane (southeast corner of the park in Orange Walk), ☎ 302-2293, runs a boat service for the 26-mile run upriver. The cost is US $50 per person, with a minimum of four persons sharing the boat. The trip takes about 1.5 hours and includes lunch and pop.

Lamanai Lady Boat will pick up passengers at the Tower Hill toll bridge where it crosses the New River along the highway. Catch a bus going south (not an express) and get off at the bridge. The boat leaves at 9 am and a round-trip costs US $80. Again, the trip upriver takes 1.5 hours. I have heard reports that if there are not enough passengers, the boat will not go.

◆ Indian Church

Indian Church is the village where Lamanai ruins are located. Of the few buildings in town, some contain attractions. You might like to stop at the **Xochil Ku Butterfly Farm** (no phone). Built especially to promote ecological ideas among the local children, the farm is open during daylight hours at no cost to locals. You, on the other hand, are asked for a small donation.

Another in-town attraction is the **Chujue Xux Honey Project** (no phone). Here, African bees make honey, which is available for sale and makes a great gift. African bees are used because of their high quantity of production.

> ❖ **DOING GOOD**
>
> The **Tropical Rainforest Coalition**, 21730 Stevens Creek Boulevard, Cupertino, CA 95014, www.rainforest.org, has been very active and successful in this area. For US $50 you can preserve an acre of rainforest. The donation is tax deductible. Should you donate more than US $200, your name goes on their website.

Las Orquidias is the watering hole in Indian Church. If you have finished chugging around the ruins and need a beer, it is cold at this little tienda.

◆ Lamanai Ruins

Lamanai ruins are open daily from 8 am to 5 pm and the entry fee is US $5. The ruins are impressive, especially if arriving by boat. Long before you reach the dock you will see one of the temples (N10-43) peaking through the jungle roof. I recommend doing at least one river trip while in Belize and if Lamanai is a desired destination then I urge you to consider taking a boat.

At the ruins is a **cultural museum**. Maya Indians elders have donated objects that they are no longer using but consider to hold historical value. Inside, the well-exhibited display has numerous figurines depicting crocodiles.

This is not only one of the oldest Maya sites in Belize, it is the one that had the longest continual occupation. This occupational span started about 1500 BC and continued until the 1800s.

Lamanai was the original Maya name for this city and it means "submerged crocodile." The name was recorded in church records when two priests visited the city and then described their findings.

> **MYSTERIOUS MAYA:** *The Maya used the concept of "zero" one thousand years before Western civilization started using it.*

Lamanai sits on the New River Lagoon and some ceremonial sites are close to the water. This is unusual; Maya usually have the ceremonial temples and plazas in the center of town with the residences circling beyond. However, at Lamani, the houses splay out from the water to the south, north and west.

The most dominant structure and the one most thoroughly excavated is called N9-56 or the **Mask Temple**. It is so named because of the large mask on one corner of the building. A second mask that has no face (only the back panel remains) is on the upper side. These masks were cut from blocks of limestone, rather than the more common method of sculpting from a stone covered in plaster. The mask here is believed to depict someone from the Olmec society in Mexico. It is also believed by some to depict Kinich Ahau, the Mexican Sun God. The mask is adorned with a crocodile crown or head-dress. This building, from the early classic period, stands at 56 feet (17 meters). A tomb uncovered in this building had jade earrings and wooden figurines inside. One necklace found at the site has 90 jade beads, some carved, and is occasionally on display at the National Museum. The coffin, in which one body was found, was covered in chert chips, possibly from Colha ruins near Altun Ha.

 MYSTERIOUS MAYA: *No crocodile remains have been found in Maya tombs, and t is believed that the creatures were protected.*

P 9-2 is a structure that sits next to the Mask Temple. P 9-2 had no temple chambers on its top, but it did have an extension that overlooked the harbor. Today, it is nothing more than a depression in the earth. However, ceramic pieces have been found near the harbor.

P 9-25 is the largest set of buildings. They sit around a plaza that is over 300 feet long (100 meters). This group of buildings is just north of P 9-2. The tallest building around this plaza is 30 feet high (10 meters).

N 10-43 is the tallest building and the one seen from the river when Lamanai first comes into view. Standing a majestic 108 feet (33 meters), it is understandably often called "the castle." Built around the 2nd century BC, it was the Empire State building of the Maya. This pre-classic building was as tall then as it is now. In other words, no layers have been added. The transition from the lower buildings like those around the P 9-25 group to the huge one here suggests an economic upswing.

Just below N10-43 is a small **ball court**. Under the court's marker disc was a vessel sitting on a container of mercury, a substance believed to be known only to the highland Maya. The vessel had smaller vessels inside, along with shells and jade.

❖ POK A TOK

The ball game, called Pok A Tok in the Maya language, was played by young warriors who wanted their blood sacrificed to the Sun God. It was believed that the sacrificed blood could re-new the god's life. The winners/losers(I've never been sure which is which) were the ones who died on the high altar.

Farther south of the ball court are about 50 burial sites believed to be from the post classic period. The identifying trait for these tombs was the breaking of a clay vessel over the burying container before final covering.

The southern group of ruins also had a stelae with **Lord Smoking Shell** carved on it and incorporates a date, "tun 7 ahau 3 pop," which translates into a festivity that ended on Mar. 7th AD 625. It is an elaborate carving, with the lord dressed in rich adornments and holding a shell.

THE NORTH

◆ Places to Stay & Eat

Speak to **Nazario Ku** at the cultural museum about a place to stay. You can **tent** or rent a hammock from him, or he can arrange a **home stay** with one of the villagers. In the second case, meals will be available. If staying with Nazario, you should have some food with you.

Lamanai Outpost Lodge, ☎ 223-3578 or 888-733-7864, www.lamanai. com, $$$. The lodge, just 15 minutes from the ruins, is an upscale luxury place sitting on a knoll above the lagoon. The screened mahogany huts have thatched roofs and come with good ceiling fans, 24-hour electricity, laundry service and private baths with hot water. E-mail access is offered. There is a gift shop, swimming dock, bar and **dining room** ($$$) called **Bushey's Palace** that serves excellent food. The owners, Mark and Monique Howells, rescued two orphaned black howler monkeys and, with the help of those at the Lamanai Research Field Station, got them ready for reintegration into the jungle. The lodge won the 1999-2000 Hotel of the Year award. Their Spotlight River Tour may allow the guest to see a bulldog bat, the world's largest fishing bat, a flowering cactus whose flower opens only at night, or the Morelet's crocodile. It is believed that the world's largest population of Morelet's crocs lives around Lamanai.

 MYSTERIOUS MAYA: *According to Maya legend, the Creation Tree (bearer of all life) came from the head of a crocodile.*

◆ Rio Bravo Management Area

Programme for Belize, 1 Eyre Street, Belize City, ☎ 227-5616 or 227-1248, www.pfbelize.org, was established in 1988 to protect the forest that is now the Rio Bravo Management Area. The forest was under threat of being cleared by an international company. Environmentalists stepped in and convinced the company to use other land for their purposes.

To date there are 260,000 acres holding two research stations. Hill Bank is at the far end of the New River Lagoon and La Milpa Field Station is on the road to Gallon Jug. According to reports procured by these stations, this land holds around 400 species of birds, 200 varieties of trees and about 70 different kinds of animals. That makes it quite a natural zoo.

Hill Bank Field Station, ☎ 221-2060, at the south end of New River Lagoon, is best reached by boat. Boats head to Lamanai from Orange Walk Town or you can call the station to see if you can hook up with someone else who is going. Profits from overnight guests go to the preservation of the rainforest. The purpose of the station is to give the visitor an introduction to and education about the delicate balance of the rain forest and to promote environmental awareness.

At the station there are dorms that sleep 30 people. The dorms cost US $80 per person, and the fee includes three meals. There are compost toilets and showers heated by solar panels.

San Filipe to Blue Creek

▶▶ *If you wish to drive or cycle to the Mennonite settlement of Blue Creek and then continue on to Gallon Jug, you must backtrack from Indian Church 12 miles to San Filipe. At San Filipe, turn left (west) onto the main road. Continue along the road (rather than going back to Orange Walk) for about five miles and cross the Rio Bravo River Bridge. After 2.5 miles, turn left and you will be in the center of Blue Creek, by the Linda Vista Shopping Center.*

◆ Blue Creek

Blue Creek has gasoline available. The town is on the Rio Bravo Escarpment and on the confluence of the three waterways – the Rio Bravo, the Rio Hondo and Blue Creek.

◆ Places to Stay & Eat

Hillside Bed and Breakfast, ☎ 323-0155, $$, is the first Mennonite B & B established in Belize. Ask in town for directions to the house. If you are interested in the Mennonite way of life, you can get first hand experience by partaking in the ranching life of the Klassens. The food at Hillside is exceptional and the hospitality is the same.

La Rosita Store, about two miles west of Linda Vista Shopping Center, ☎ 323-0445, $$, has rooms for rent above the store. The rooms are basic and very clean. They are run by Jacob Neufeld and his wife, who will make you feel welcome.

Cornerstone Café, ☎ 323-0905, $, near the Linda Vista Shopping Center, has meals and refreshments. Prices are low and portions big.

Blue Creek to Gallon Jug

▶▶ *The all-weather road continues west out of Blue Creek through small settlements to Newstadt. A three-season road heads south. The one going to Gallon Jug and Chan Chich starts just before the village of Tres Leguas. This is a well-maintained road. To go to La Milpa, phone ahead to find out about the road conditions out that way.*

◆ La Milpa Research Station & Ruins

La Milpa Research Station, ☎ 323-0011, www.pfbelize.org, is one of two stations in the Rio Bravo Management Area. La Milpa charges US $20 for foreigners to visit (it's free for nationals). This is where I think the "scalp the tourist" game has gone too far. However, the money goes for a good cause and Programme for Belize needs the local support. If you want to visit, let them know in advance. The entry fee includes a guided walk along one of

THE NORTH

their trails, plus a guide at the ruins. Lunch will cost another US $8. There are thatch hut cabanas for overnight stays (US $100 per person) or dorm beds (US $80); prices include three meals.

This field station has some sponsorship from National Geographic Society and from Boston University and works in cooperation with Programme for Belize (see above) and all the profits from tourists' visits are going into more conservation for Belize. This site is deemed so important that when Princess Anne of England visited in 2001, she was given a tour. I wonder if she had to pay the twenty bucks.

From the visitor center at the station it is a one-hour walk through the jungle to the ruins. The ruins are called La Milpa, which means corn field in Maya. The land that holds the ruins was destined to be made into a corn field by local farmers before the area was saved by the Programme for Belize.

Under the leadership of Drs. Norman Hammond, Francisco Estrada-Belli and Gair Tourtellot, excavations at the site uncovered the **Great Plaza**, believed to be the largest Maya plaza ever discovered in Belize. It covers six square miles. The plaza is surrounded by four temples, three of which stand about 80 feet (24 meters) high. The plaza also contains two ball courts. During its peak, it is believed that 46,000 people lived in the 20,000 houses surrounding the center. There was also terracing done in the nearby fields.

So far, 19 stelae and 20 courtyards have been found. One building that was never completed had a stone throne in it. But the most important find was a **royal tomb** with a man inside. Archaeologists think his name was **Bird Jaguar**. Across his chest was a huge jade necklace. They think he lived around AD 450, just before La Milpa started its first decline. There was a revival in about AD 600 and then habitation continued until 1600. La Milpa peaked around AD 900.

▶▶ *To reach Gallon Jug, continue along the well-graded gravel road above the Rio Bravo for 35 miles to Barry Bowen's exquisite resort, Chan Chich.*

Gallon Jug/Chan Chich

Chan Chich, ☎ 800-328-8368, www.chanchich.com, $$$$$, is reputed to be one of the world's best lodges. Owned by Barry Bowen, the richest man in Belize and owner of Belikin Beer, the 250,000 acres of land backs onto the Rio Bravo Management Area. Because the lodge is ecologically sympathetic, it makes the two parcels of land one huge environmental reserve. Ten thousand acres of Bowen's land is being managed by the Programme for Belize.

The history of Bowen's 250,000 acres is interesting. Up until the 1960s Belize Estates, an international logging company, owned about one-fifth of the land in Belize, some of it around Gallon Jug. The main headquarters for the area was at Hill Bank on the New River Lagoon, not far from Lamanai. Logs were cut and hauled to the lagoon and then shipped downriver to the ocean.

However, in 1943 it was decided to move the headquarters from New River Lagoon to the Gallon Jug area. The foreman from New River Lagoon, Austin Felix, wanted to move to the new location. He chose a spot in the high bush near the present site of Gallon Jug. After the logging crews moved into the area, they called their home town many names, but nothing fit. Then Felix found three old jugs beside his house. It is believed the jugs were left many years before when the area was a Spanish camp. Felix named the area **Campamente Galon de Jarro**, but that name was too long. Gallon Jug was the name that stuck.

In 1988, Bowen completed the lodge facilities on one of the plazas in the Chan Chich Maya ruins. The thatched-roof cabins are surrounded by jungle and grass-covered temples. Made of local hardwoods, each cabin has two beds, screened windows, a ceiling fan and a large bathroom with hot water.

The jungle outside the cabins is home to about 350 species of birds and 150 different types of butterflies. A large number of cats also live here. If you want to walk in the jungle, guides are available all day long.

This resort offers numerous packages, all of which include birding. Some packages also have diving, some have ruins tours, some focus more on animal sightings. There are horses available for riding and the coffee served at the lodge is grown on the property. You can also rent a cabin without any other services.

> **AUTHOR NOTE:** Humans use only 7,000 of the 75,000 known edible plants found in the rainforests around the world.

There are nine miles of trails through Bowen's jungle that can be hiked or ridden. There are canoes for use at the spring-fed Laguna Verde and the larger Laguna Seca. There are unexcavated ruins to explore and birds to spot. Don't forget to look for jaguars and the fer-de-lance snake.

Sarteneja

▶▶ *Return to Orange Walk at Mile 56 on the New Northern Highway. To get to Sarteneja, follow Main Street north through Orange Walk and over the New River Bridge. This secondary road leading to Sarteneja starts to get bad at the bridge and gets progressively worse all the way to the village. Once across the bridge, take the left fork after one mile. Drive 5.5 miles to the town of San Estevan. Stay on the pavement. Six miles past San Estevan, take the road to the right. The road straight ahead goes to Progresso and Copper Bank (directions to these villages are below). Going to Sarteneja, take the left-hand turn at the next crossroad and drive past the Progresso Lagoon, Chunox Village and finally the Shipstern Reserve. Sarteneja is next.*

◆ Getting Here

BY BUS: Buses for Sarteneja leave the Zeta Ice Factory in Orange Walk Town, 31 Main Street, at 2 pm, 3 pm and 3:30 pm. It takes almost two hours to reach Sarteneja. This road is the worst in Belize.

Returning to Orange Walk Town, the buses leave Sarteneja at 4:30, 5:30 and 6:30 am. They drive around town quite a few times, making sure no one has been missed before they start down the highway.

BY BOAT: Boats can be hired at Ambergris Caye, Caye Caulker and Corozal Town for the short trip to Sarteneja. It takes about 30 minutes from Corozal and about an hour from Ambergris. The boat should be arranged with a tour agency of your choice or with a local fisherman who has his own boat. The cost by boat from Corozal to Ambergris Caye is US $20, so expect to pay around that price from the cayes to Sartenejo and less from Corozal.

◆ Introduction

A sleepy fishing village with about 700 residents on Corozal Bay, Sarteneja is just waiting for the tourists to start flocking in and, when they do, the village will loose a lot of its charm. However, I can't be selfish. My job is to tell you about such places. There are three hotels and one restaurant in town. Fishermen sit on the sandy beach mending nets and boats bob in the bay, waiting to be photographed. A constant breeze comes in off the bay and the dogs don't bark all night. The people are friendly and helpful. If you need to chill out, come here. Spanish is spoken more than English.

◆ History

"Tzateb-ey-ha" means water between the rocks or pool in the Maya language. Two Mayans, Mr. and Mrs. Aragon, came to Sarteneja from Valladolid to escape the hardships in Mexico. As they walked through the jungle, they came upon a spring that had formed a pool of fresh water. The Aragons decided to settle near the pool. They were joined by others from Tulum, who were also escaping harsh treatment from the Mexicans.

As time passed, they switched from farming to the more lucrative fishing industry. This proved to be a good move. Soon others came and the village grew to its present size.

◆ Things to Do

The two **graves** of the Aragons can be visited. The white plaster graves sit above ground near the ocean, within view of Krisami's Hotel. The fresh water **well** is still being used, although it is now encircled with cement. It is on Cola Aragon's property at 114 Conlos Street. Ask for directions. Drinking the water from the well will ensure that you return to Sarteneja before you die.

At Camdalie's Sunset Cabanas, there is a mural depicting the history of the town.

Bicycles can be rented from Krisami's Rooms. These bikes are available for guests first so you may have to wait. Cycling to Shipstern Nature Reserve is highly recommended. You see so much more along the way when on a bike or walking.

◆ Shipstern Nature Reserve

Shipstern Nature Reserve is three miles from Sarteneja. The bus will let you off at the reserve if you want to stop on your way to the village. Entrance fees are US $5 per person, payable at the park. The visitor center is open 24 hours a day.

The reserve covers 22,000 acres. It has north-wood forests, salt-water lagoons and mangrove shorelines. The forests are interspersed with limestone hillocks. First purchased in 1989, the reserve was managed solely by the International Tropical Conservation Foundation, Box 31, Ch 2074 Marin, Neuchatel, Switzerland. In 1996, the Belize Audubon Society joined in management of the reserve.

The **butterfly breeding center**, next to the visitor center, was started by two English people who eventually sold the entire reserve to the ITCF. It was established to help local people with sustainable development. By breeding the butterflies and selling the pupae to European butterfly houses, the locals attempted to make a little money. However, it was not cost-efficient and the export of the pupae was stopped.

About 200 species of butterflies are found on the reserve and, because they are enclosed at the station, the different stages of development can easily be seen and photographed. The best time to visit is on a sunny day. Rain and clouds cause the butterflies to hide in foliage.

There is also a short trail called the **Chiclero Botanical Trail** that leads from the parking lot into the forest. Because of the hurricane in 1955, much of the area's forest was destroyed and reforestation practices can now be observed. Along the trail you will encounter three different types of hardwood forests with about 100 varieties of trees. Many are labeled with their Latin names, their family names and their local names. A booklet available at the visitor center has a detailed description of the trail.

Just past the forested area is a wide savanna with mudflats and hillocks of limestone, vegetated with palms and hardwoods. The savanna is visited by white-tail deer and brocket deer. Tapirs, ocelots and jaguars are also reported to cross this area, although tracks are seen more often than the animals themselves.

Beyond the savanna is **Shipstern Lagoon**, where large numbers of North American birds take refuge before continuing their migration either north or south, depending on the time of year. One of the most fascinating birds that can be seen here is the black catbird, so named for its mew that often fools people into thinking that a cat, rather than a bird, is in the vicinity.

There are also about 60 species of reptiles and amphibians lurking about the lagoon. The Morelet's crocodile, an endangered species, has been spotted on the reserve.

At the very south end of the park is an abandoned village called Shipstern, from which the park derived its name.

THE NORTH

◆ Tour Operator

Wildtrack, ☎ 423-0232, at the Environment Center in Sarteneja, is run by Paul and Zoe Walker. It's associated with Raleigh International, 27 Parsons Green Lane, London SW6 4HZ, www.raleighinter-national.org. The Walkers will take you on an overnight trip to Fireburn Village, where the mostly unexcavated Shipstern Maya ruins are located. In this area, Raleigh is known for its work on the ruins, measuring and recording elementary details before intense excavations can take place. For US $50 per trip, the Walkers can also take you to Xo-Pol Pond for wildlife viewing. Overnight excursions are more.

Fernando/Verde Tours, Sarteneja, ☎ 423-2085 or 423-2283, will take you on a snorkeling trip to the reef or out fishing. The cost for fishing is US $150 a day, while a snorkeling trip with other people cost US $40 for each person for half a day.

◆ Places to Stay

Fernandos Rooms, on the main street facing the water, ☎ 423-2085, $$, has four rooms, all with double beds, private bath, hot water and fans. The establishment is very clean and the owners are friendly. There is a common room and a balcony on

❖ HOTEL PRICING	
$	$10 to $20
$$	$21 to $50
$$$	$51 to $75
$$$$	$76 to $100
$$$$$	over $100

the second floor where you can sit. Guests can order meals from Ciela, Fernando's wife, for reasonable prices. A large portion of fresh fish with vegetables and rice is about US $7.

Krisami's Motel, on the main street beside the water, ☎ 423-2283, krisamis@msn.com, $$, has only two rooms available. Each is clean and exquisitely decorated, with private bath, hot water and cable TV. This is a family-run establishment and Maria Verde, the owner, goes out of her way to make guests welcome. She also has family-style meals (often fresh fish) available for her guests. In fact, if you spend a day fishing and catch something good, Maria will cook it up for you. Her costs are reasonable.

Camdalie's Sunset Cabanas are next to Kisami's, no telephone, $$. There are two thatched-roof cabins with two double beds, a private bath and hot water in each. One has air conditioning, while the other has a fan. The main room next to the cabins contains the mural mentioned above.

Shipstern Nature Reserve has dormitory beds for US $10 per person and all profits go into the maintenance of the reserve. The beds are rented on a first-come, first-gets basis. Contact the Audubon Society for availability.

◆ Places to Eat

Lily's Restaurant is just off the beach. Follow the water to the east until you see a blue building with one or two tables outside. There is a sun porch and inside there are two booths. Lily's is a tiny establishment. Order your meals ahead of time and give her about two hours to prepare. She makes traditional rice and beans, eggs and tortillas, but she also offers a fish dish cooked in foil with vegetables and rice or French fries. Her meals are not scanty and her costs (US $3.50) are not high.

◆ Nightlife

Nightlife in Sarteneja consists of a book which you brought yourself, a hammock swinging in the ocean breeze and a rum punch that you made yourself.

Progresso & Copper Bank

▶▶ *Return to Orange Walk at Mile 56 on the New Northern Highway. To reach Progresso and Copper Bank, follow Main Street north through Orange Walk and over the New River Bridge. After crossing the bridge there is a fork within the first mile. At this fork go to the left and then drive 5.5 miles to the town of San Estevan. Stay on the pavement. Six miles past San Estevan there is a road to the right. Do not take this one. Take the road straight ahead. Belize First magazine rates this stretch of road as the third most beautiful in the country.*

Progresso and Copper Bank are two tiny villages situated on Progresso Lagoon, one of the prettiest stretches of water in the country. The villages can be reached from either Orange Walk Town or the shorter route from Corozal.

◆ Getting Here

BY FERRY: From Corozal, the trip is eight miles and includes a ride on the largest ferry in Belize. Leave Corozal going south and turn left at the sign indicating "Tony's." Turn right at the end of the road. After driving/cycling about 4.5 miles, make a left. Follow this road along the river for three miles.

The ferry is an old sugar barge donated to Belize from the Belize Sugar Industry. The government supplied workers for the restoration of the barge. This ferry has cut the distance to Copper Bank from 42 miles to eight miles.

BY BUS: A bus leaves daily from Zeta Ice Factory in Orange Walk Town at 11:30 am and 5:30 pm or from the bus terminal in Corozal at 11 am and 4:30 pm.

◆ History

The lagoon has been occupied by **Maya** for centuries. The small islands of Caye Coco, Caye Muerto and Caye On in the lagoon have Maya **ruins**. The ancient Maya city of **Chanlacom** is believed to be on the western shore of the lagoon. The Maya lived in small settlements around this lagoon and worked as farmers who traded with fishers along the Caribbean. These settlements were occupied until the 1600s.

THE NORTH

◆ Adventures

Rent a canoe from **Last Resort** in Copper Bank (see below) and visit one of the cayes. The ruins are still being excavated and burial sites have been found containing ceramics and spindle beads, bowls and, of course, skeletons of early people who lived here. The wildlife on this lagoon is exceptional and the area is not densely populated with locals or foreigners.

Canoeing from Copper Bank to Progresso during orchid season is one of the best trips in Belize. The plants hang from the banks and trees over the river, making them visible right from the canoe. Manatees and crocodiles are also living along this stretch of water. Because the lagoon hasn't yet been developed and inundated with visitors, the area is quiet. Rent a canoe at the Last Resort in Copper Bank, ☎ 606-1585. The cost is US $50 a day.

If you are not an experienced canoeist, join a guided tour organized by Last Resort. The guides will point out things that you would probably otherwise miss.

Hikers may want to undertake the three-mile trail from Copper Bank to Cerros ruins. The trail meanders through the jungle. Donna, at the Last Resort, will give you directions to the trailhead. Take a bird book to help you identify some of the birds.

Although there is not a tremendous amount to see, the area is a good place for a restful Caribbean experience.

◆ Places to Stay & Eat

Last Resort, PO Box 260, Copper Bank, Corozal, ☎ 606-1585, www.belizenorth. com/last_resort.htm, $. The people who run the resort, located just past the village, describe their establishment as offering "primitive luxury." It has 10 thatched-roofed cabins that have fans or air conditioning, shared baths and hot water. **Tenting** is also available for US $7.50 per person. The place is clean and homey and was recommended by some foreigners working in Belize. There's a reference library and a **restaurant** that serves a great variety of dishes, from lasagna to beef to lobster and homemade ice cream.

Regular live entertainment is available by the almost-famous Paradise Wranglers. This fun group started their musical career at Last Resort and have now been invited to play at other resorts in Belize. The hospitality here is exceptional.

Primitive Lodge, ☎ 337-662-6401, www.ambergriscaye.com/progresso, is located on five acres of heavily vegetated property that skirts the edge of the lagoon. The five thatched-roof huts are spacious and have private baths with hot water. There is a bird-viewing station tucked into the fruit trees and rock garden.

Corozal

▶▶   *Return to Orange Walk at Mile 56 on the New Northern Highway. Continue
north to Corozal, Consejo and the Mexican Border. About 20 miles on the
New Northern Highway takes you from Orange Walk Town to Corozal
Town. You'll see sugar cane fields that support the Libertad Sugar Refinery
just beyond San Pablo. The area is dotted with houses on stilts that seem
well cared for. The roads are often cycled by both locals and foreigners.
Once past Concepcion, just east of Louisville, the New Northern Highway
ends at Mile 79. Turn left for Corozal.*

◆ Getting Here

Driving/cycling is described here from south to north. If you are fresh from
Mexico, you will find driving/cycling in Belize to be a cake walk.

BY AIR: Both **Maya Air** (☎ 422-2333) and **Tropic Air** (☎ 800-422-3435,
226-2012) fly between Corozal and Belize City, Ambergris Caye and Caye
Chalker. See *Getting Around*, page 45, for flight schedules.

BY BUS: Buses from Chetumal go to Corozal daily. **Venus Bus**, 7th Avenue,
☎ 402-2132, and **Novelo's Bus**, 13-14th Avenue, ☎ 402-3034, have buses
going to the border, 20 minutes away, at least once every hour. Buses also go
to Belize City, three hours away, every hour, beginning at 5:30 am and quit-
ting at 9 pm.

BY WATER TAXI: A water taxi/boat from Ambergris Caye and Caye Caulker
arrives at the town wharf just beside the museum. It leaves daily at 3 pm and
costs US $20 per person. It takes 1.5 hours to reach San Pedro. Returning,
the taxi leaves San Pedro at 7 am.

◆ Introduction

Corozal is a colonial town that sits on the shores of the Caribbean Sea in
Chetumal Bay. The town has the lowest crime rate in all of the country and
residents are rightly proud of this fact.

This clean little city has been ignored by the tourist for far too long. Although there isn't enough to keep one busy for weeks, it is a place for those
who want a break after or before the hassles of Mexico.

Corozal has a population of around 10,000 people; most are fishers, farmers or sugar production workers.

◆ History

Corozal was the Maya city of **Santa Rita**. The old city was sporadically occupied and deserted for about 2,000 years. Then, in the mid-1800s when the
Caste Wars of Mexico were at their height, about 10,000 refugees crossed
the Rio Hondo into Belize and made their home at the present site of
Corozal. Some of these refugees were helped by gun runner James Blake.

Mexico wanted the territory that was now in the hands of the British, so skirmishes occurred often, forcing locals living near Corozal to build **Fort Barlee** for protection. That was 1870 and part of the fort still sits where the present day central park is located. The bricks used for construction of the fort and its adjoining buildings were originally used as ballast for ships that were coming from Europe to pick up wood.

As the village increased in size, residences were built over old Maya houses. Stones from Maya buildings were used as road fill. Today, the Maya city has but one pyramid left sitting about a mile northwest of town.

❖ **"COROZAL"**

Corozal derives its name from the Maya word for the Cohune Palm, once abundant in the area. The Maya considered the palm a sign of fertility.

After Hurricane Janet destroyed most of the town in 1955, it was rebuilt using professional planners. The rebuilding cost US $3.5 million and Corozal was the first town in Belize to have electricity, water and sewer throughout. It also has a logical grid street pattern.

> **AUTHOR NOTE:** *Corozal District was the first area in Belize to have a sugar cane industry and it is still the largest area for production of sugar.*

◆ Things to Do

Santa Rita Ruins

Walk to Santa Rita ruins just north of town (about one mile). The ruins are open from 8 am to 5 pm and entry fee is US $5. From the central park on 1st Street, walk north past the Venus Bus Station, veering half a block east at the station. Continue northwest along the Santa Rita road. You'll pass the hospital and town reservoir before you reach the ruins and, just beyond them, is the New Northern Highway.

At the beginning of the 20th century, Thomas Gann, an archeology buff, drew pictures of the frescoes he found at Santa Rita. The paintings showed figures roped together at the wrist. They were decked in tassels, garlands and jewelry – a distinctive characteristic of the Santa Rita frescoes. The paintings here resemble the paintings found on copper disks at Chichen Itza. Before the value of the paintings, frescoes and carvings was really appreciated, they were destroyed; mostly they were used as road fill. This is why Gann's pictures are so important. Later (1979-85), Dr. Chase from the University of Southern Florida excavated the remaining post classic buildings.

Early-style pottery found in graves indicates that the site has been occupied since about 2000 BC. As time passed, trade replaced some of the agricultural activity and the city grew. It is guessed that the city was continuously occupied right up until the Spaniards came in the mid-1500s. At the peak of their trading years, the Maya of Santa Rita included the Rio Hondo and the New River in their territory. They called their city **Chetremal**.

There were two significant **burial chambers** found at the site. One contained an elderly woman decorated with turquoise jewelry. In the other was a warrior from around AD 500. He had a flint bar and stingray spine in the tomb with him.

The main attraction, however, is a smaller pyramid that had a **ceremonial room** from the late classic period. In this room, offerings were made to the gods. This pyramid and ceremonial room are a good example of the architecture from that time and the offerings were an indication that the people were fairly prosperous.

But even more impressive (for me) is the **jade mosaic mask** that was found in one tomb. The mask, now in the National Museum, is 11 cm (four inches) by 16 cm (six inches) and has pieces of jade pasted onto a base. The eyes and mouth are made from shell and iron pyrites. A vase found in the same tomb dates from the early classic period (about AD 500-600) and has exquisite decorations painted in dark brown paint on a cream background. The painting is of glyphs inside rectangles. The vase can now be found in the National Museum.

It is believed that in the late classic period the Maya from this site traded with people as far away as the Aztec cities in Mexico and the Aymara cities in the Andes. Pottery found on-site supports this theory.

THE NORTH

Cerros Ruins

Cerros ruins are located across Chetumal Bay from Corozal. To reach them you need to hire a boat; approach anyone with a boat at the dock behind the museum in town. Exploring the ruins (unless you are a professional) will take about two or three hours. The boat will have to wait for you. Tour agencies from other cities offer trips to the ruins. You can also contact **Menzies Travel Agency**, ☎ 422-2725, in town near the south end of the village. Also, a boat can be rented from Harman Pillaro, who is docked behind Tony's Resort at the west end of town. He charges US $60 for three people. These ruins are one of the few places in Belize where there is no charge to stomp around with camera poised.

Cerros (which means hill in Spanish) sits on 53 acres by a cliff overlooking the Caribbean Ocean, a setting much like Tulum in Mexico. The community was at its height between 400 BC and AD 100. At that time the people there specialized first in fishing and then in the marine trade along the coast. Some archeologists believe that salt was an important trade item. As other cities became more prominent, Cerros lost power. Today, the ruins are showing serious erosion due to their proximity to the ocean.

The largest building at the site stands 69 feet (21 meters) above the plaza floor; it still has some walls intact. It's one of the best examples of pre-classic architecture, with **sculptures** on the walls beside the stairs. The four friezes are named Evening Star Setting, Morning Star Rising, Sun Setting, and Sun Rising.

Around its outer perimeter Cerros had a **canal** almost 20 feet wide (six meters). The main purpose of the canal was to drain the surrounding land so it could be used for agricultural purposes. Encompassed by the canal were two **ball courts**, three **pyramids** and over 100 public and private buildings. Today, maintained trails go from the center of the ancient city out to the canal.

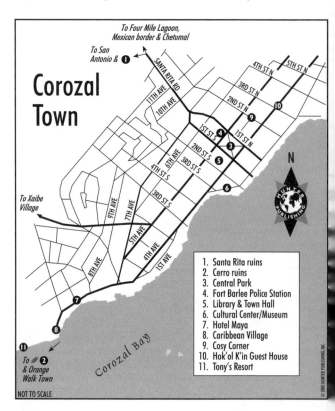

1. Santa Rita ruins
2. Cerro ruins
3. Central Park
4. Fort Barlee Police Station
5. Library & Town Hall
6. Cultural Center/Museum
7. Hotel Maya
8. Caribbean Village
9. Cosy Corner
10. Hok'ol K'in Guest House
11. Tony's Resort

NOT TO SCALE

© 2005 HUNTER PUBLISHING, INC.

Corozal Town

Across from the park on 5th Avenue is the Fort Barlee **police station** and the **post office** – once the hospital of Fort Barlee.

On 1st Street South is the **library** and **town hall**. Inside the hall is a mural painted by Manuel Villamor Reyes. He originally painted it in the 1950s, then decided to re-do a lot of the scenes within the mural when it was restored in 1986. Reminiscent of a Diego Rivera painting, the mural has a lot of historical detail, starting with the life of the Maya and covering major events up to the present sugar cane production.

The **Museum of Corozal**, also called the Cultural Center, is along the water between 4th Avenue and 1st Avenue. The museum is open from 9 to 12 and 1:30 to 4:30 pm, Tuesday to Saturday. The entry fee is US $5.

First built in 1886 as the Customs House, the building is the only colonial structure of this design in Belize. Everything in the building is made of iron that has been bolted and riveted together. When first built, it was the only legal entry place into Belize. The displays are well done. Many of the bottles on exhibit were found in the bay just offshore, left by the pirates of earlier days. There are ink, perfume, rum and medicine bottles of colored glass made in every shape. The most recent bottles date back to the mid-1800s.

Four Mile Lagoon

The lagoon is just four miles south of the Rio Hondo. Jump on your bike, take the Santa Rita road north and then branch off to the right onto a secondary road. There is a sign indicating the turn-off to the lagoon. Bike rentals are available from **Hok'ol K'in Guest House**, 89 4th Avenue/4th Street South, ☎ 422-3329, at US $5 per day. This is a deal. However, guests of the hotel get first dibs on the bikes.

People come to swim, windsurf and fish. Since the lagoon has fresh water, it is a treat to swim in after the ocean's salt water.

Bill Dixon owns the **Four Mile Lagoon RV** and **tenting** site that is fully serviced. To get there, follow the road going to Santa Rita and turn north (right) onto a gravel secondary road. The site is alongside the lagoon. Tenting is US $5 per person. On Sundays you can go to Riverol's Cool Spot along the beach for a beer, pop and/or snack.

◆ Places to Stay

Hotel Maya, between 9th and 10th Streets South on South Street, ☎ 422-2082, $$, is clean and friendly. The hotel first opened in 1980 with just two rooms. It did so well that there are now 20 rooms. There is air conditioning, cable TV and private bath with hot water in every room. The hotel is half a block from the beach. An on-site **restaurant** is open from 7 am to 9 pm daily.

❖   **HOTEL PRICING**

$	$10 to $20
$$	$21 to $50
$$$	$51 to $75
$$$$	$76 to $100
$$$$$	over $100

Caribbean Village, 7th Avenue, ☎ 422-2725, $, is two blocks southwest of Hotel Maya. Besides a hotel, there is an **RV park** and **tenting** places right on the water. There are also two thatched-roof cabins for rent; they are basic

THE NORTH

but have fans. An on-site eatery, **Haileys Restaurant**, ☎ 402-2045, $, makes staying here convenient. The food is good.

Corozal Bay Inn, ☎ 422-2691, www.corozalbayinn.com, $$, has four suites in a comfortable colonial-style home. They have a pool and a poolside lounge, a restaurant and safe parking. The suites have large bedrooms, living rooms, tiled kitchens and tiled bathrooms.

Cosy Corner Guest House, 2nd Street North, ☎ 422-0150, $$, has rooms with private baths and hot water, air conditioning and tiled floors. There is a swimming pool, garden in back, large common room, restaurant and bar. Operated by Darlene Bartlett, this well-run establishment has been recommended by many travelers.

Hok'ol K'in Guest House, 89 4th Avenue/4th Street South, ☎ 422-3329, maya@btl.net, $$, is near the water. It is clean, comfortable and highly recommended by those who like comfort without paying big bucks. The hotel has a nice porch where you can sit and watch the sunset (or sunrise) over the Caribbean while sipping on some rum punch. There is a **restaurant** on site, and they also have bikes for rent. Hok'ol K'in is wheelchair accessible.

Kich-Pam Ha Resort, 99 5th Avenue, ☎ 402-2625, $$, on the way to the border, has everything from hammocks on the porch to thatched-roof cabins. The name means "beautiful water" in the Maya language and the name refers to the view of the lagoon from the property. There are covered huts for picnicking, a games room and water wheelers (pedal boats) for rent.

Pirates Cave, ☎ 501-422-6679, dixiemoss@aol.com, $$$$$, is a 30-minute boat ride up the Rio Hondo, close to where pirates long ago went to hide. This tiny resort has two cabanas. Each cabana has two bedrooms so it can accommodate two couples in each. The cabanas are luxurious and tastefully decorated with Maya weavings. The price includes transportation to the lodge, meals, room service and tours on the Rio Hondo and along the Caribbean coast into Corozal.

Tony's Inn and Beach Resort, South End (on Corozal Bay Road) ☎ 422-2055, $$$, is the town's common landmark. It is about a half-mile down the bay from the center of town. The rooms are big, the service excellent, and the owners friendly. There is safe parking for your vehicle, as well as a bar and **restaurant** on the premises. Boats can be hired behind Tony's for a trip to Cerros.

Casa Blanca Hotel, PO Box 212, Consejo Village, Corozal, ☎ 423-1018, www.casablanca-bythesea.com, $$$. Chosen by Lan Sluder's *Belize Guide Book* as one of the 10 most romantic places to stay in Belize, Casa Blanca certainly deserves this status. The hotel is exceptionally comfortable and the rooms offer air conditioning, fans, private baths with hot water, satellite TV, queen-sized beds and exceptional views. There's a **restaurant**, postal service, e-mail facilities and tour office. The resort will also cater to weddings that can be held on its private beach. All-inclusive package deals offered.

Kayaking, waterskiing and windsurfing equipment is available for rent. The bay on which the resort sits is one of the best in the country for windsurfing but it hasn't yet been discovered by the crowds who seem to chase the wind around the Caribbean.

◆ Places to Eat

Al's Café, 5th Avenue between 2nd and 3rd Streets, $, is where the locals eat. The restaurant serves Belizean food: rice and beans with either pork, beef or chicken, but it is good rice and beans. However, the waitress can be a little impatient with tourists. Refrain from leaving a tip if she is this way when you are here.

❖ RESTAURANT PRICING	
$	under $5
$$	$5 to $10
$$$	$11 to $25
$$$$	$26 to $50
$$$$$	over $50

Hok'ol K'in Guest House, 89 4th Avenue/4th Street South, ☎ 422-3329. The restaurant is great if trying to escape the heat. It is clean to a sparkle and the salads are made with crisp fresh vegetables. One gentleman I spoke with enjoyed the rum punch far too much. He ended up staying in one of their rooms too. Hok'ol K'in offers bikes for rent at US $5 per day. Guests of the hotel get first dibs on the bikes.

Corozal to Santa Elena & the Mexican Border

THE NORTH

▶▶ *If leaving Corozal at Mile 79 on the New Northern Highway, go past the service station and bus terminal. Stay on the road, but do not go to the Santa Rita ruins (up the hill). Instead, veer to the right and continue to the junction five miles beyond Corozal. Turn right. It is four miles to Santa Elena and the Mexican border. From Corozal to the border takes about half an hour and the crossing is usually non-eventful. There is a fee of US $20 to leave Belize. There is no fee to enter Mexico.*

Belize **buses** cross the Mexican border and go as far as Chetumal. The money changers at the border are good. Get rid of your Belize dollars before crossing.

> **AUTHOR TIP:** *Do not take Belize dollars too far into Mexico unless you collect foreign currency.*

If coming into Belize from Mexico, there is no charge to enter. You will be given a tourist card that must not be lost. (Should you lose your card, you will need to go to the closest police station when you discover the loss and try to get another.) You will have an exit fee once you leave Belize.

 For information on **Chetumal** and the Yucatán Peninsula, see the award-winning book by Bruce and June Conord, ***Adventure Guide to the Yucatán, Cancun & Cozumel*** (2nd edition), by Hunter Publishing.

Directories

◆ General Directory

GENERAL DIRECTORY		
■ OUTFITTERS & TOUR OPERATORS		
Birding Pals		www.birdingpal.org
Fernando/Verde Tours	☎ 423-2085 or 423-2283	
Jungle River Tours	☎ 302-2293	
Paradise Inn (birding tours)	☎ 220-7044	www.adventurecamera.com
Rancho Luna	no phone	located in Corozal
■ ATTRACTIONS		
Belikin Brewery & Coca Cola	☎ 225-3195	
Belize Jungle Gardens/Aquarium	☎ 609-5523	
Burmudian Land. Baboon Sanct.	☎ 220-2181	www.howlermonkey.bz
Cuello Ruins	☎ 322-2141	
Crooked Tree Wildlife Sanct.	☎ 223-5004	www.belizeaudubon.org
Godoy's Orchid Garden	☎ 322-2969	
Travellers Liquors	☎ 223-2855	ww.travellersliquors.bz
■ TRANSPORTATION		
Novelo Bus	☎ 402-3034	
Venus Bus	☎ 402-2132	
■ GROUP RESOURCES		
Programme for Belize	☎ 227-5616	www.pfbelize.org
Tropical Rainforest Coalition		www.rainforest.org
Wildtrack	☎ 423-0232	www.raleightinernational.org
■ USEFUL WEBSITES		
Corozal District Information		www.corozal.com
Corozal Business & Tourist Information		www.corozal.bz
Belize Tourism		www.belizetourism.org

◆ Accommodations Directory

PLACES TO STAY		
Belize River Lodge ($$$$)	☎ 225-2002	bzelodge@btl.net
Bird's Eye View Lodge ($-$$$$)	☎ 225-7027	www.belizenet.com/birdseye
Caribbean Village ($)	☎ 422-2725	
Casa Blanca Hotel ($$$)	☎ 423-1018	www.casablanca-bythesea.com
Chan Chich Lodge ($$$$$)	☎ 800-328-8368	www.chanchich.com
Corozal Bay Inn ($$)	☎ 422-2691	www.corozalbayinn.com
Cosy Corner Guest House ($$)	☎ 422-0150	maya@btl.net
D' Victoria Hotel ($$)	☎ 322-2518	www.d-victoriahotel.com
Embassy Hotel ($$)	☎ 225-3333	www.embassyhotelbelize.com
El Chiclero ($$)	☎ 225-9005	soffit@io.com
Fernandos Rooms ($$)	☎ 423-0285	
Hill Bank Field Station ($$)	☎ 221-2060	
Hillside B & B ($$)	☎ 323-0155	
Hok'ol K'in Guest House ($$)	☎ 422-3329	
Home Stay Program ($)	☎ 220-2181	
Hotel Maya ($$)	☎ 422-2082	
Howler Monkey Lodge ($$)	☎ 220-2158	h_monkey@btl.net
Kich-Pam Ha Resort($$)	☎ 402-2625	
Krisami's Motel ($$)	☎ 423-2283	drisamis@msn.com
Lamanai Outpost Lodge ($$$)	☎ 223-3578	www.lamanai.com
La Milpa Research Station ($$$$)	☎ 323-0011	www.pfbelize.org
La Rosita Store/Rooms ($$)	☎ 323-0445	
Last Resort ($)	☎ 606-1585	see www.belizenorth.com
Maruba Jungle Resort ($$$$$)	☎ 322-2199	www.maruba-spa.com
Nature Resort ($$)	☎ 604-9286	naturer@btl.net
New River Park Hotel ($$$)	☎ 322-3987	
Paradise Inn ($$$$)	☎ 220-7044	www.adventurecamera.com /paradise
Pirates Cave ($$$$$)	☎ 501-422-6679	dixiemoss@aol.com
Pretty See Jungle Ranch ($$$$)	☎ 209-2005	
Pueblo Escondido	☎ 614-1458	www.pueblo-escondido.net
St. Christopher Hotel ($$$)	☎ 322-3987	
Sam Tillett's Hotel ($-$$$$)	☎ 220-7026	samhotel@btl.net
Shipstern Nature Reserve ($)	no phone	
Tony's Inn ($$$)	☎ 422-2055	

THE NORTH

◆ Restaurant Directory

THE NORTH – PLACES TO EAT	
Al's Café ($)	no phone
Baboon Sanctuary Restaurant ($$)	☎ 220-2181
Belize Road Chinese Restaurant ($)	☎ 322-3159
Bushey's Place Restaurant ($$$)	☎ 223-3578
Cornerstone Café ($)	☎ 323-0905
Diner, The ($$)	☎ 302-3753
El Chiclero restaurant ($$)	☎ 225-9005
El Pescador at Jungle Gardens ($$)	☎ 609-5523
Howler Monkey Lodge Rest. ($$)	☎ 220-2158
Juanita's Restaurant ($)	☎ 322-2677
Lily's Restaurant ($)	no phone
Maya Wells Restaurant ($$)	☎ 209-2039
Ms. Judith's ($)	no phone
Ms. Suzette's ($)	no phone
Tree & Vee's Restaurant ($)	no phone

The West

The Western Highway goes from Belize City to San Ignacio and on to Guatemala. The distance is 76 miles, with Mile Zero at the traffic circle on Cemetery Road and Central American Boulevard in the city.

Outdoor adventure is the most attractive feature of the Western Highway area. **Mountain Pine Ridge** is easily accessible and a real draw for the mountain bike enthusiast. Many of the **cave systems** are not far off the Western Highway and a run down the Macal River

will give every **whitewater** kayaker/canoer a thrill. Places like **Xunantunich and Caracol ruins** are must-sees, as is **Belize Zoo**. **Horseback riding** at the historical Banana Bank Lodge is the best in Belize, and photography around Roaring River provides unique opportunities for shutterbugs.

The landscape is diverse, ranging from swamp to savanna to mountains. And each landscape has different birds and animals.

The west is prepared for tourists and the area offers something for every budget. However, if you are going west during high season, Oct. to Feb., you may want to book ahead for places to stay.

Along the Highway

The road going west from Belize City is described below. When we come to secondary roads that lead to other places of interest, we will take a detour and explore them before returning to the highway.

Although there are few mileage signs on the Western Highway, people refer to locations by the number of miles along the road. To make things easy, I give all directions this way. If you lose track of where you are, just ask a local resident.

MILEAGE FROM BELIZE CITY TO TIKAL, GUATEMALA	
Mile Zero	Traffic circle at Cemetery Road & Central American Blvd.
Mile 5	**Beach** access
Mile 6	**Sir John Burdon Canal**
Mile 10	**Almond Hill Lagoon**
Mile 15.5	Turnoff to **Community Baboon Sanctuary** (see *The North*, page 77)
Mile 16	**Hattieville Village**
Mile 26	**Big Falls** turnoff
Mile 29	**Belize Zoo**
Mile 31.5	**La Democracia**
Mile 37	**Jungle Paw Resort** turnoff
Mile 47	**Banana Bank Lodge and Equestrian Center**
Mile 48	**Guanacaste Park** and **Belmopan**
Mile 50	**Carmelote Village**
Mile 52	**Teakettle Village**
Mile 52.5	**Roaring Creek** and **Xibalba**
Mile 54.5	**Warrie Head Resort**
Mile 57	**Spanish Lookout** turnoff
Mile 59	**Unitedville**
Mile 60	**Caesar's Palace**
Mile 66	**Georgeville**
Mile 69.6	Cristo Rey Road
Mile 70	**Santa Elena/San Ignacio/Bullet Tree** turnoff
Mile 71.2	**Clarissa Falls** turnoff
Mile 72	Hydro Dam Road
Mile 72.8	**Tropical Wings Nature Center**
Mile 73.1	**San Jose Succotz**
Mile 74.5	**Benque Viejo del Carmen**
Mile 76	**Guatemalan border**

Leaving Belize City

◆ How to Travel

To get anywhere along the highway by **bus**, take a taxi to the **Novelo bus** station at the main terminal in Belize City and buy a ticket for the town yo wish to visit. Buses stop anywhere along the road, except the express bus, which stops only in the major centers.

For those **driving, cycling or hitching**, I describe the simplest way to get out of Belize City, not the shortest. This is because of the many one-way streets requiring a lot of turns along the way.

From the swing bridge in Belize City, follow Albert Street to Eve Street. Turn north and continue along the road that skirts the water. Eve Street becomes Newtown Barracks Road. It curves and turns into Princess Margaret Drive. At the large traffic circle with many flags in its center, go straight ahead onto Central American Boulevard. Cross the Belcan Bridge (built by Canadians and Belizeans in the 1970s) and continue to the next traffic circle. Take the first exit off the circle. This is Cemetery Road and Mile Zero of the Western Highway.

◆ As You Leave Town

Following the **Western Highway** out of Belize City for five miles, there are two access roads leading south (left) to **Belizean Beach** and **Buffer Hole Beach**. At Belizean Beach is the **Florida Beach Resort** ($-$$) with a new hotel (almost finished when I was there), restaurant, RV park and tenting sites. There is a tiny, quiet beach for swimming or paddling a canoe. Along the same strip is **West Lake Beach Motel** ($$), a clean place with large rooms, a locked and secure gate, and hospitable owners. This motel is a 10-minute walk from the water. If you have a vehicle, it will be safe here.

These two little bays are a good place to cycle or take a bus to; if busing, you must walk the mile or so to the water.

Belize City to the Zoo

A Place to Stay

Another four miles along the Western Highway at Mile 9 is the **Almond Hill Motel**, ☎ 220-9018, $$, and the Almond Hill Lagoon. According to Emory King, this lagoon is believed to have been hand-dug by the Maya. Almond Hill has a population of 500, so few amenities are available. However, the motel has six clean rooms for rent.

▶▶ *The Western Highway continues to Hattieville at Mile 15.5. The Bermudian Landing Baboon Sanctuary turnoff is on the right (see* The North, *page 77).*

◆ Hattieville

Hattieville was originally a temporary settlement for the refugees left homeless after hurricane Hattie hit Belize. Some of the refugees stayed and made this their permanent home. Today the population is around 500 people.

> ### ❖   HOMES FOR THE HOMELESS
>
> Many of the houses between Belize City and Hattieville have been built by Habitat for Humanity, an organization that believes everyone should have an acceptable place to live. If a family has insufficient funds to live decently and they qualify under the organization's mandate, Habitat will build them a home. These homes are simple, with two or three bedrooms, and a small porch. They are constructed from cinder blocks. Should you wish to support this worthwhile cause, contact **Habitat for Humanity**, #146 E. Collet Canal, Belize City, ☎ 227-6818, habelize@btl. net, www.habitat.org. Habitat loves visitors.

The scenery continues to improve as the Western Highway rises into rolling, rocky, forested country. At Mile 26 there is a secondary road going north to the little village of **Big Falls**. If there is even a single cloud in the sky, I would suggest you not try this road as it can disintegrate quickly. Instead, take the road going through the Bermudian Landing Baboon Sanctuary.

▶▶ *At Mile 29 of the Western Highway you will reach the Belize Zoo and the Tropical Education Center. If you don't have your own transportation, **public buses** are the easiest way to reach the zoo and the Tropical Education Center. Take any bus going west from the main terminal and ask the driver to drop you off at the zoo. The walk from the road to the zoo is short, but the walk down to the Tropical Education Center is about 1.8 miles. Follow the signs on the opposite side of the road to the zoo.*

◆ Belize Zoo & Tropical Education Center

This zoo, built in 1983, is considered the best in Central America. It was originally built to accommodate 17 animals that were used in the making of a film called *Path of the Rain Gods*. Tamed and no longer able to fend for themselves in their natural environment, the animals were housed in a temporary zoo after the film was made. When the official zoo was built, these 17 animals were the first conscripts. Now there are over 150 different animals and birds.

Today, the zoo will accept only those animals whose life is in danger. They will not accept animals captured from their natural habitat to be sold.

What makes this zoo more attractive than most is that many of the animals are kept in jungle-like surroundings with only a wire-mesh fence to keep them enclosed. They are not in cages behind concrete ditches.

An outspoken environmentalist, Sharon Matola, is the founder and present director of the zoo. She also contributes articles to a popular newsletter sent to members (sign up at www.belizezoo.org). The zoo offers a program that gives you the opportunity to adopt an animal. For example, for US $60 foreigners can adopt a howler monkey. The money goes toward your adopted animal's food and medicine and the upkeep of his home. You don't get to take the monkey home.

Besides April, the famous resident tapir, there are jaguars (both the spotted and black variety), deer, macaws, pumas, ocelots and monkeys. The birds include a barn owl called Screech who, during the visitors' night walks, loves to fly over and land on the hand of a staff member.

The 29-acre facility takes less than two leisurely hours to visit, ☎ 820-2004, www.belizezoo.org. It's open daily from 8 am to 5 pm, except during major holidays. The entry fee is US $7.50 for foreigners. Your tour can be stretched out to a full day if you walk to the Tropical Education Center and spend time there also.

The Tropical Education Center is across the road from the zoo and covers 84 acres of savanna. It has observation decks that can be used for bird watching, a labeled self-guided trail, and an iguana breeding center. Here, you can sign up for a half-day guided canoe trip down the Sibun River or join the zookeepers for a night tour of the zoo.

The center is geared toward environmental education and scientific research. For an added US $50 you can join in on the natural history lectures.

◆ Places to Stay & Eat

The Tropical Education Center, PO Box 1787, Belize City, ☎ 220-8003, $, has dormitory accommodations that can hold 30 people. There are showers and kitchen facilities.

There is a small **restaurant** at the zoo that can supply refreshments and a basic meal.

Cheers Restaurant, Mile 31, Western Highway, ☎ 614-9311, $, west of the zoo by about three miles, is the closest place to eat west of the zoo. The restaurant is open-air and it has a small gift shop.

 Belizeous Cuisine is a book put out by the LABEN Scholarship Foundation. Profits from the book are used to help needy kids further their education. The book sells for US $17.95 and can be ordered from LABEN, PO Box 191701, Los Angeles, CA 90019, ☎ 323-732-0200.

just beyond the zoo the **Western Highway** is joined by a secondary road called the Coastal Road or the Manatee Road. This goes to Gales Point and Dangriga farther south. It is a dry-weather, gravel road.

La Democracia to Guanacaste National Park

◆ Places to Stay & Eat

B's Watering Hole, ☎ 820-2071, $, at Mile 32 along the Western Highway, has very good food and is just a 10-minute stroll from the field research station.

To reach the **Jaguar Paw Jungle Resort**, ☎ 820-3023, $$$$$, turn at the sign at Mile 37 on the Western Highway and follow the gravel road for about seven miles, veering to the right whenever there is a junction. This will be either a long dusty ride or a muddy one, depending on the season.

The lodge is run by Donna and Cy Young. The 16 air-conditioned cabanas sit on 215 acres of jungle at the edge of the Caves Branch River. The lodge has all the amenities you could wish for, from large bedrooms with private baths to a bar where you can enjoy a rum punch. However, it is the exquisite African décor of the hotel that is intriguing. The décor adds to the romance of the jungle. The resort is also a privately owned nature reserve that offers **river tubing, hiking, mountain biking, birding** with a guide and instruction in **rock climbing**. Equipment is available at the lodge.

The **caves** on the property are thought to be 150,000-200,000 years old and show signs of use by the Maya. Trips to the caves located on the property are possible, but you may enter the cave only with a guide, available at the resort. Some caves are reached by tubing down the river.

> ❖ **BATTY FACTS**
>
> Bats mate for life and become distraught when separated from their partners for long periods of time. Bats can hibernate at will, especially during times of food shortages. They can soar at elevations of up to 10,000 feet (3,000 meters).

Farther along the Western Highway over Beaver Dam Creek at Mile 39 and past the village of Cotton Tree at Mile 42 is a sign pointing to the right (north) for the road to the Banana Bank Lodge. **Banana Bank Lodge**, Mile 47 of the Western Highway, ☎ 820-2020, www.bananabank.com, $$$$, sits on the Belize River. In the 1800s, the outpost was a *barquadier*, a place where mahogany logs were sorted and marked. Logs that were of the same quality were then tied together and floated down the river to Belize City. The main house of the lodge is the original house.

The thatched-roof cabanas each have two rooms with fans and a private bath with hot water. They can sleep four people comfortably and are great for families. Additional rooms in the main lodge, which come with either shared or private bathrooms, have been artistically decorated with cultural themes. The cost of a room includes breakfast and there is a **restaurant** ($$$) for lunch and dinner. The **Green Dragon Internet Café**, ☎ 822-2124, from San Ignacio, is also on site. This is the best café in Belize in which to buy a cappuccino, an ice cream, a latte or a plain old coffee while doing your Internet.

Birdwatching and trekking along the trails are encouraged, as is star gazing. Near the river is an observation tower with a 12-inch, computer-controlled, Schmidt Cassegrain telescope available for guest use. Here you can watch the stars unbothered by light pollution.

> **AUTHOR NOTE:** *In Belize the non-poisonous **snakes** outnumber the poisonous by six to one. To avoid an unpleasant encounter, never reach inside a hole without looking first and always check the unseen side of a log or rock before stepping there.*

On the property there are 4,000 acres of land, half of which is still virgin forest where birds nest and orchids bloom. But it is mostly the **equestrian** who is drawn to Banana Bank. There are over 70 horses, many of them with long pedigrees. Warrior Chief, for example, has a line almost as long as the Banana Bank's guest list. The animals are gentle and well trained.

Horses with Western or English saddles can be rented by the day or by the hour. You can go on a guided trip through the jungle or take lessons to learn how to run an obstacle course. Trips can last two or three hours or all day and range in price from US $50-$90 per person. The jungle trails seem to be the most popular. You need not be a guest of the resort to rent a horse.

An added attraction to Banana Bank is the resident jaguar, Tika, who has been around for quite a while. She is friendly and beautiful to photograph.

Banana Bank will arrange stays that include caving, riding, ruins, jungle trails, accommodations, and meals. Go to their website, www.bananabank. com, for more information or contact them directly, ☎ 501-820-2020.

▶▶   *Return to the Western Highway. At Mile 48 is the junction of the Hummingbird Highway going south. Guanacaste National Park is at the junction and just two miles north of Belmopan.*

◆ Guanacaste National Park

Guanacaste National Park is a mere 50 acres of tropical forest bordered by the Belize River on the north, Roaring Creek on the west and the Western Highway to the east. The northern boundary features a walking trail called **Rustlers' Walk**.

> ❖   **TWISTED BEGINNINGS**
>
> The park derives its name from a giant guanacaste tree with a triple trunk. During its youth, the tree's trunk split and, as it grew, became twisted. Loggers decided that it wasn't worth cutting down. The famous tree is found growing at the western end of the park near the junction of three walking trails.

The guanacaste tree is fast-growing and will often reach a height of 130 feet (40 meters), with a 30-40-foot (10-12-meter) trunk. The seed pods are dark brown, about three inches across and coiled into a circle. Their shape may be one reason why the tree is sometimes called the "monkey's ear" tree. The tree is not susceptible to worm rot and is often used for making dories or dugout canoes.

Adventures

The maintained hiking trails in the park are short and interspersed with seating areas and wooden stairs that help prevent erosion from walking traffic. Many of the trees are identified with labels.

Near the parking lot a **visitor center** has a display of natural flora and fauna found in or near the park. There is also a picnic site, washrooms and a few birding deck.

THE WEST

The **Riverview Trail** takes you down to the Belize River where there is a large pool for swimming, a popular spot with Belizeans. The marked **Guanacaste Trail** will take you to the celebrity tree and beyond along the **Amate Trail** to the Roaring River. When you arrive at the Amate Trail you can go either right or left. The trail to the right will take you to the river much quicker than the one on the left. However, even if you decide to walk all the trails in the park, it should not take you more than an hour or two, depending on how long you spend watching the critters hidden in the foliage.

The **leaf cutter ants** in the park are phenomenal. If you are at all interested in these little creatures, be sure to study them here. There are also **giant iguana, bats, rodents** and **opossums** roaming in the vegetation that includes trees such as the mammee apple, bookut and quamwood.

> #### ❖ LIFE OF A LEAF CUTTER ANT
>
> Leaf cutter ants started their quest to denude the jungle somewhere around five to 15 million years ago. Although they haven't succeeded, one colony can eat the foliage of a giant guanacaste tree (actually, they will eat any tree) in a single day. They chew the leaves (like snuff) and then spit the chewed leaf onto a leaf fragment. A fungus grows and the ants eat the fungus. The excretion from the ants helps to fertilize the rainforest.

The park is host to many types of birds, including the rare **blue-crowned motmot** and **black-faced antthrush**. I heard **woodpeckers** and **cuckoos** too when I was there.

There is no place to stay in the park. You can either continue on the highway to Belmopan (see below), or head back to the places mentioned above.

Belmopan

The capital city of Belmopan, with a population of 7,000, is growing and Belmopanians are hoping that the outskirts will reach the Western Highway in the near future. With their encouragement, I have included Belmopan along the Western Highway.

After hurricane Hattie wrecked Belize City, the government of Belize decided to move the capital inland where future destruction would be far less likely. Belmopan comes from the conjunction of Belize and Mopan. Mopan is the name of the Maya group living in the Cayo district.

Although the main government offices and the university have been moved to Belmopan, the people of Belize City weren't interested in following along. The city is considered the smallest capital city in the world and Belizeans occasionally refer to it as the Garden City.

Belmopan is built around a central plaza, much like a Maya city. **Independence Plaza** is surrounded by the Governor General's House, the Foreign Ministry, the National Assembly and Government offices. Grouped around the government buildings are the police station, the fire hall, the telephone office, the banks, the Belize Government Immigration Office, the market and the bus terminal. The entire city feels spacious.

To get anywhere in Belmopan does not take a long time, maybe 15 minutes to walk from one side to the other.

◆ Things to Do

The only thing of interest to visitors is the **National Archives**, 26-28 Unity Boulevard, ☎ 802-2247, open from Monday to Friday, 8 am to 5 pm. The Archives welcome researchers interested in the history of Belize.

The **agricultural fair grounds** are at the junction of the Western and Hummingbird Highways. There is a national fair here every year toward the end of May. Call the tourist office in Belize City for exact dates, ☎ 223-1913.

> **AUTHOR NOTE:** In Belize, "patchwork children" are kids from blended families.

◆ Places to Stay

Bull Frog Inn, 23-25 Halfmoon Avenue, ☎ 822-2111, bullfrog@btl.net, $$$, is clean and comfortable. The rooms have private bath, air conditioning, and cable TV. They have sheltered prominent people like the President of the Dominican Republic and Belize's Prime Minister Musa. There is a

❖ HOTEL PRICING	
$	$10 to $20
$$	$21 to $50
$$$	$51 to $75
$$$$	$76 to $100
$$$$$	over $100

drug store, travel agent and gift shop in the strip mall next door.

Belmopan Hotel, Bliss Parade and Constitution Drive, ☎ 822-2130, $$$, has the only swimming pool in town. Each room has air conditioning and private bathroom. The staff seems a bit indifferent. The parking lot is fenced.

El Rey Inn, 23 Moho Street, ☎ 822-2841, $$, has budget rooms with private baths. The owners are pleasant and the place is clean. This is the place I would stay if I had to spend time in Belmopan. It has an easy way about it.

◆ Places to Eat

Caldium Restaurant on Market Square, ☎ 822-2754, $$, is open from Monday to Saturday, 7 am to 8 pm. This air-conditioned establishment is the best in town and offers things like fresh conch soup, sweet and sour chicken, or shrimp Creole with coconut rice. The del Valle family takes pride in serving guests and makes you feel welcome.

❖ RESTAURANT PRICING	
$	under $5
$$	$5 to $10
$$$	$11 to $25
$$$$	$26 to $50
$$$$$	over $50

Bull Frog Inn, 23-25 Halfmoon Avenue, ☎ 822-2111, $$, has a restaurant open daily from 7 am to 9:30 pm. It serves many dishes, including treats like

THE WEST

tandoori chicken and curried beef, at reasonable prices (US $7-8). The bar is the most popular in town and offers live entertainment on Friday nights.

International Café on Market Square, no phone, $, is where you can pick up the latest travel information and/or exchange a book. They are open daily from 7:30 am to 4:30 pm. Besides ordinary foods like soup and sandwiches, they also offer many vegetarian dishes.

◆ Other Services

Market Square is where all **buses** servicing the west or the south stop to pick up and drop off passengers while the drivers have a meal. If in transit, you will have at least half an hour to poke around. Be sure to shop in **Market Square**, which has small stalls offering local crafts and often something just a bit different than you find in many other places. The **Caldium Restaurant** also has a gift shop and boutique, just in case you need a new pair of shorts or a cooler skirt.

Techno Hub, ☎ 822-0061, on the square, has an Internet service. **BTL** across the street and up about half a block, offers the same service but their two machines are often occupied.

Belmopan to Georgeville

▶▶ *Back on the Western Highway heading west, you will cross Roaring Creek Bridge and then, three miles farther at Mile 50, the village of Camelote, where a secondary road goes left (south).*

The sign at the corner gives directions for the **Roaring River Lodge**, ☎ 820 2037, rorivlodge@btl.net, $$$. The map says Roaring Creek but I agree with the lodge owners that it's more like a river. Follow all the signs as you go farther and farther into the jungle, about four miles. It takes 20 minutes by car and 45 by bike. At the end of the road there is a lodge with three cabanas surrounded by manicured lawns and mounds believed to be old Maya sites that have not been excavated. The cabanas have private bath and the rooms in the lodge have shared bath. All have hot water. Breakfast is included with the price of the room and other meals can be arranged.

There is a **birdwatching** deck over the Roaring Creek and there is a quiet pool where guests can swim. **Tubing** down the creek for a few hours is possible. Longer cave exploration trips can also be arranged. There is now a nine hole **golf** course next to the lodge. Clubs, transportation to and from the lodge and a round of golf runs US $40.

Because the lodge is a fair distance from the big city lights, the hosts offer meals, as long as they are ordered ahead of time.

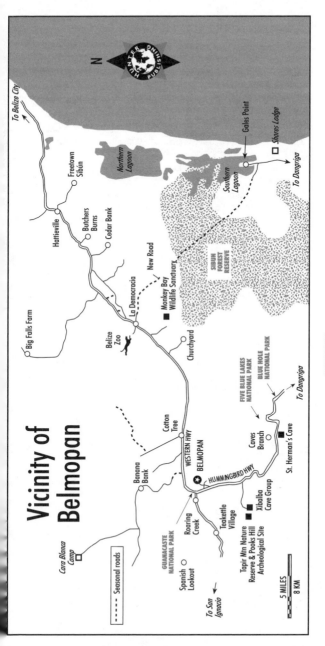

Vicinity of Belmopan

THE WEST

Seasonal roads

5 MILES
8 KM

◆ Caves at Roaring Creek, Xibalba

AUTHOR NOTE: *Even though you could reach these caves on your own, you are not permitted to enter without a guide. The reason for this is that Belize wants to preserve as much of this history as possible while allowing visitors to get a sense of Maya culture.*

My suggestion is to hire a tour company such as **Mayawalk**, ☎ 824-3070, www.mayawalk.com, from San Ignacio or come with a group such as **Slickrock**, ☎ 800-390-5715, www.slickrock.com, or **Island Expeditions**, ☎ 800-667-1630, www.islandexpeditions.com, from North America. They have climbing gear and strong lights so you can see. They also know their way around the caves so that you won't be wandering in the Maya underworld for eternity.

To get to base camp, commonly known as Xibalba (shee-BAL-ba) Hilton, walk 1.8 miles along Roaring Creek (there is no road). The alternative to walking is to take a canoe down river. Xibalba means Place of Fright.

This group of three caves splays out from Cahal Uitz Na ruins, a small site that was in use around AD 250-900. There is a plaza and a ball court at the ruins and six very weathered stelae. The name means Place of the Mountain House.

Before going into the caves be certain to have face masks (respirators) because of the bat guano (feces) that could contain spores that will cause serious illness.

Actun Tunichil Muknal

This is by far the most impressive of the three caves in this group. Some say it is the most impressive in all of Belize.

The entrance is often engulfed in mist and the Maya believed that the rain god, Choc, lived inside. The mist is suspected to be the reason the Maya called the cave the place of fright. This cave was especially popular during a period of drought that occurred just before the abandonment of many sites in Belize around AD 1000. Scientists believe that the Maya came to appease the rain god so he would end the dry spell. As the droughts got worse, the Maya went farther into the three-mile-long cave.

To enter the cave you must swim across a pool at the entrance. There are sharp edges and rocks in the water, so sandals must be worn. Although Water flowing through caves is usually cooler than surface water in creeks or the ocean. You may get cold. A second chamber is found about a third of the way in. This chamber has a stone altar and carved slate with many stingray spines.

All in all, there have been over 1,400 artifacts located in this cave, including about 200 ceremonial vessels. Some of the bones and artifacts have been cemented into the cave due to the calcification that occurred.

The final section of this cave is reached by climbing fixed ladders on a rock wall. You will then enter a huge chamber where the crystal sepulcher is located.

MYSTERIOUS MAYA: *Actun Tunichil Muknal means Cave of the Crystal Sepulcher. It was named after the calcified skull of a young woman that is in the chamber.*

A tour of this cave takes about three hours, longer for those who really want to poke around. Make certain your tour guide will stay as long as you do.

Actun Nak Beh

Acten Nak Beh is directly south of the Xibalba Hilton along Roaring Creek. It was found in 1997 by a worker who accidentally made a wrong turn and ended at a 25-meter (75-foot) wall that opens to passages leading to burial sites. Although much of this cave had been looted, the archeologists found one adult and two adults with a child in two separate graves. Because of the pottery found, the cave is believed to have been used by the upper classes who traded with others at Boiling Pot, Pook's Hill and Cahal Pech. There is also a causeway being uncovered and investigated.

Actun Uayazba Kab

Actun Uayazba Kab means "handprint" and the cave is named after the pictographs found inside. The entrance is .4 miles south of Xibalba Hilton along trails through the jungle. This cave opening is near the top of a cliff that rises about 200 feet (60 meters) above the jungle floor. It requires a steep uphill climb to the entrance. There is a large overhang at one of the two entrances and, from a distance, the two entrances make the wall look like a human skull. Inside, jugs were placed on ledges; you must use ropes to belay down in order to see them. Just inside the entrance is a carved turtle with its head missing.

THE WEST

 MYSTERIOUS MAYA: *It is believed that when boys were coming of age they climbed up one side of a turtle's back and once they got over to the other side they were transformed into men.*

Many of the passages along this cave system are so low you have to squirm through on your belly. Inside, some of the chambers have plaster floors. Petroglyphs depicting human faces and pictographs of handprints are etched into the walls of the cave. The remains of 11 people have been found in this cave system.

PLACE TO STAY

At Mile 54 of the Western Highway is **Warrie Head Lodge**, ☎ 227-7185, www.warriehead.com, $$$$. Located on the Belize River, this was once a logging camp. John and Elvira Searle purchased the property in 1988 and restored the old house. They cultivated the grounds and developed a botanical garden. The sugar mill's machinery was dug out of the ground and cleaned up and a Fowler engine, once used to move logs, was restored. Now visitors can **canoe** on the Belize River, **swim** in Warrie Creek or **hike** the mountain trail to a waterfall. Nothing offered here is strenuous and the artifacts scattered around give a real view of Belize history.

> **AUTHOR NOTE:** *During the 1700s Belize was called the Bay Settlement and people living here, mostly loggers, were called Baymen. The riverside logging camps were called "banks."*

▸▸ *Return the Western Highway. A short distance farther west is the village of* **Teakettle**, *Mile 52, where you have access to Pook's Hill Lodge and Pook's Hill archeological site.*

◆ Pook's Hill

Pook's Hill Lodge, ☎ 820-2017, $$$, www.pookshillbelize.com, is a 300-acre reserve that sits next to the Tapir Mountain Nature Reserve (not open to the public). To get here, follow the dirt road out of Teakettle for four miles. Turn right onto another road and follow it for .75 miles) to the border of the reserve. The lodge is another .7 miles along this road. There are signs.

The lodge is composed of a number of cabanas surrounding a small Maya residential plaza. The white plaster cabanas are screened and have fans and private baths with hot water. The cabins are decorated with traditional Maya weavings. There is a library available for guests. The bar and restaurant look like large cabanas and were designed in traditional Maya architecture. **Meals** ($$$) are European, with a splash of Caribbean influence.

The uniqueness of the lodge is its location, within walking distance (two hours) of the Actun Tunichil Muknal Caves and just steps from virgin forest.

For activities, there is **birding** and **swimming**. There are two **hiking** trails one that takes less than an hour and follows the river. The other takes about two hours and goes through the jungle with flagging tape for directional markers. It is advised to take either a compass or a guide on this trek. The lodge has **horses** for hire for US $40 per person, per day. They also offer an overnight jungle **tenting** excursion (US $150) that includes gourmet camp meals and a tour of the Actun Tunichil Muknal Cave.

❖ GREEN IGUANA PROJECT

This project started in 1996 and was designed to help increase the number of iguanas in the jungle. Members collect iguana eggs and hatch them under controlled conditions. Once the iguanas are big enough to fend for themselves, they are released into the wild. Pook's Hill has released about 100 green iguanas every year since the project was started.

◆ Pook's Hill Archeological Site

Besides the four main temples around a little plazuela at Pook's Hill archeologists found a **midden pile** tucked between temples 1 and 2A. A mid den pile is important because it gives us a view of what the ordinary person (as opposed to the kings and elite) was eating, using and throwing away.

Temple 2A was a banquet hall that was used for social gatherings. Here they found human teeth, grinding stones, ceramic figurines and musical instruments. On the opposite side of the plazuela, they found burial sites in front of the building. This type of mass grave was common after the main burial sites were full. So far, nine skeletons have been found in this grave.

Pook's Hill is believed to have been abandoned shortly after the caves at Roaring Creek. The pottery found in the caves is of similar design to that found at Pook's Hill.

 MYSTERIOUS MAYA: Popol na *means "Mat house" and the word seems to indicate a municipal building where public affairs were taken care of. Ah Hol Pop means "head of the mat."*

▶▶ *Back on the Western Highway near Mile 57, a road goes right (to the north), leading to Spanish Lookout.*

 MYSTERIOUS MAYA: *Scribes were from the elite of Maya society and served to record a king's spiritual and earthly superiority. This writing blatantly extolled the king's powers. Scribes captured by an enemy were bound, semi-nude and had the pads of their fingers clawed away before they were finally put to death.*

◆ Spanish Lookout Village

THE WEST

Spanish Lookout Village is six miles from the Western Highway. It's a fairly large Mennonite community that includes both traditional and modern believers. The community is bustling. The only health food store in the country is in Spanish Lookout and you can get anything there from vitamins to wholewheat flour. The biggest draw to the village is the **Western Farms ice cream parlor**. The home-made ice cream flavored with fresh fruits is the best in the country. They also make a delicious yogurt that will cure any stomach problems – even those contracted by traveling. The cheese should be purchased just so you have something really good to snack on.

If you would like to stay in the village for a few hours (there is no place to stay overnight in the village itself) there are two restaurants, **Golden Choice Buffet**, ☎ 823-0421, and **Braun's Family Restaurant**, ☎ 823-0196. There is also a grocery store and an old-fashioned hardware store that seems more like a museum than a store.

> **AUTHOR NOTE:** *Mennonite women wearing white caps on their heads are from the more progressive groups and those wearing black caps are from the more traditional groups.*

Anyone on a **bicycle** is likely to be hungry, so for cyclists especially I recommend the short cycle into Spanish Lookout for food.

▶▶ *Return to the Northern Highway. There is not much to see along this stretch. The next hamlet is Unitedville (Mile 59), then **Caesar's Palace** at Mile 60.*

Caesar's Palace, ☎ 824-2341, $$, has five rooms tucked well off the highway where it is quiet. The cabins are clean and spacious with fans and private bathrooms. There is a bar and **restaurant** on the property; these are so popular with both locals and visitors that if you come after seven you won't find a seat. Live jazz is featured on the first Saturday of every month. Internet service is also available. The hotel is set on five acres of groomed land with fruit trees throughout and a small creek in the back. If cabins are not what you want, you can also **tent** at the back of the property. There are four **RV sites** with full hook-up services available.

For carved wood products **Caesar's Palace Gift Shop**, ☎ 824-2341, www.belizegifts.com, is second-to-none in Belize. There is a woodworking shop on the property.

▶▶ *Return to the Western Highway at Mile 60 and continue west to Mile 66 in Georgeville. The **Chiquibul Road** (south/left) heads out to the Barton Caves and the Mountain Pine Ridge gate is 10 miles in. However, except as a way of seeing the Barton Caves I do not recommend this road as it is in deplorable condition. The Chiquibul Road and Mountain Pine Ridge area can be reached from San Ignacio. Although the road from San Ignacio is also rather rough, it is better.*

The Chiquibul Road

If you decide to take the Chiquibul Road, it will lead you through green, lush citrus farmland, acres and acres of it. The entire Mountain Pine Ridge is excellent **mountain bike** territory. Any enthusiast can spend an entire month exploring the many logging roads and interconnecting military roads throughout the area.

> **AUTHOR NOTE:** *Belize has 30,000 acres of good citrus farmland. This produces a total of 3,600,000 crates of fruit, 2,400,000 of them oranges and the rest grapefruit. Most of this is made into juice concentrate and exported.*

◆ Barton Creek Cave

You must have a canoe to go into the cave (available for rent at the entrance), and you should visit only with the services of a guide. To get here you must travel five miles along the Chiquibul Road. When you pass a large orange grove on your right, take the first left onto a one-track trail. You will have to drive through the creek and then past an Amish Mennonite community. Continue along to the end of the road and the opening to the cave. It is just beyond a pool of green water and is surrounded by jungle vegetation.

Inside the cave there are almost 1.2 miles of passages, partly inhabited by bats. Everything is eerily quiet, so you will find yourself whispering. The beauty of this cave is staggering. The river flows through a narrow canyon with walls about 150 feet high (45 meters) and in other places the river is 20 feet wide (six meters) wide.

There are many Maya artifacts and burial sites hidden inside the cave. Stalactites often come down so far from the ceiling that you will have to lie down in the canoe to pass by them. There is a natural bridge in the cave. Any touching of the cave walls is now discouraged.

The length of the trip depends on the time of year. Rainy season will result in more water in the cave, making the float through easier and also producing a waterfall. Visibility is possible if your guide brings a large light, powered by car batteries (a small head lamp is not sufficient). The trip inside should take about two hours. Doing this on your own would require access to a lot of gear, and tubing is no good because you would not be able to take enough light to see everything.

Green Hills Butterfly Ranch, Mile 8 on the Chiquibul Road, ☎ 820-4017, www.belizex.com/green_hills.htm, is getting a world reputation for its work with butterflies. It's open from 8 am to 5 pm and the entry fee is US $5 per person for a guided tour (min. of two people). A picnic spot is open to visitors.

◆ Mountain Equestrian Trails

MET is eight miles along the Chiquibul Road, ☎ 820-4041 or 800-838-3918, www.metbelize.com, $$$$$. This resort offers cabins decorated in Maya design. All cabins have private baths with hot water, mosquito nets over the beds, kerosene lights, and decks with tables and chairs. There is a bar and restaurant where meals can be purchased if they are not included in the price of the rooms. There is also a gift shop.

This is one of the few places in Belize where outdoor adventure in general and horseback riding in particular is part of the deal. The lodge has been rewarded for its efforts in these areas; last year, it received the Belize Eco Tour Award.

Marguerite Bevis, one of the owners, is a registered nurse (so less need to worry about snake bite) and an avid conservationist. Her husband Jim has lived in Belize since childhood and is at home in the jungle.

Horseback riding trips can be either full-day or half-day events. The full-day trips run to **Big Rock Falls** and back; along the way, you will be shown different plants used by the Maya for medicinal purposes. At the falls, you can jump from the surrounding cliffs into the pool below, just to cool off. The **River Cave Ride** will take you through Maya farms to a river where you can swim into the cave. Inside are shards of pottery from ancient times. The **Mountain Pine Ridge Cave** trip takes you through the karst region to a cave with Maya pottery. Along the way you'll see many interesting limestone formations as well as medicinal plants used by the Maya. **The Vega Trail** is a half-day trip through a lush valley to a small waterfall along the Macal River.

▶▶ *This is as far as we go on the Chiquibul Road. Return to the Western Highway at Mile 66 and continue west. It is another one mile to the turnoff for the privately owned Matthew Spain Airport. It is just another 3.6 miles along the Western Highway to the Cristo Rey Road from the airport turnoff.*

THE WEST

The Cristo Rey Road

The Cristo Rey Road forks at its beginning. The left fork goes to the Cahal Pech ruins, and ends there.

◆ Cahal Pech Ruins

Cahal Pech is open from 8 am to 5 pm,and costs US $5 to enter. Information pamphlets (US $2) are available. It takes no more than 10 or 15 minutes to walk to the ruins from San Igancio and touring should take no more than a couple of hours.

The site is believed to have been occupied by Maya from 1200 BC until the great collapse around AD 1000. Jade and obsidian from 100-600 BC have been found at the site. The acropolis on which the site stands is 900 feet (300 meters) above sea level.

If you walk from San Ignacio to the ruins, you will probably enter the site from the north onto Plaza B, where most of the **stelae** have been found. The earliest carved stele ever discovered in the Maya lowlands was found at this site. Besides the six stelae found here, 34 **ceremonial structures** have been uncovered, along with two **ball courts**. The old city is believed to have covered about 10 square miles during its peak. Structure A1, just to the west of Plaza B, stands at a height of 77 feet (23 meters).

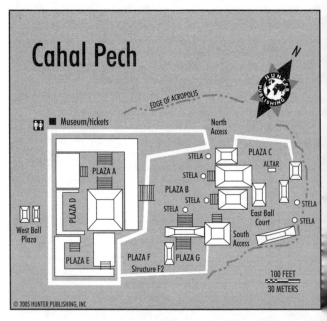

If you continue south from Plaza B you will see excavations taking place at structure F2. The diggers have unearthed some stairs facing Plaza F that lead to a platform with a door that opens to an interior room that measures three feet by nine feet (one meter by three meters). This room had traces of red paint on the walls. At first, the archeologists thought that the room would open onto Plaza G, but this has not happened.

A pre-Columbian plate with graffiti on it was found at Cahal Pech. Graffiti in Maya culture was very rare.

To the west of the main structures is a newly completed museum with some interesting diagrams. The grounds are kept in immaculate condition at this site and it is pleasant to walk around even if you are not an antiquities buff.

▶▶ *Return to the fork at the beginning of the Cristo Rey Road. The right fork goes to Christo Rey and San Antonio before it hooks into the Chibiquil Road at Mountain Pine Ridge reserve. From there, it passes through recreational country with caves, relaxing resorts, splendid waterfalls, the greatest mountain biking in the country, canoeing, white-water rafting and outdoor camping sites that can be reached only by horse.*

If you have a car or bike, the way is easy. If not, you could hitch all the way to the Caracol ruins, but do it only during daylight hours. You should have a plan as to where you will stay if you are unable to get a ride all the way in and/or out.

A bus goes to San Antonio from San Ignacio at 11 am, 1 and 6 pm daily. They leave San Antonio at 6 and 7 am and 4 pm daily. There are no buses going beyond San Antonio.

◆ Places to Stay

After half a mile along the Cristo Rey Road you will come to **Manfred's Farm Bed & Breakfast**, Box 141, San Ignacio, ☎ 824-2276, $$, on the east side of the road. There are two spacious cabins for rent. One is for a couple and the other is for a family. Each has a private bathroom with

❖ HOTEL PRICING	
$	$10 to $20
$$	$21 to $50
$$$	$51 to $75
$$$$	$76 to $100
$$$$$	over $100

hot water, a deck with hammock. This is a farm, so fresh milk and the best granola in Belize are available.

Another .3 miles past Manfred's Farm is **Maya Mountain Lodge**, Box 174, San Ignacio, ☎ 824-2164, www.mayamountain.com, $$$. It features white plaster and tiled cabanas that have fans and private baths with hot water. Tastefully decorated, these cabins offer privacy. There are less expensive rooms in the main lodge and there is a 40% discount for rooms during the off-season. Children are welcome and can stay for half-price up to age 12 and free up to age six. There is a pleasant **walking trail** behind the lodge where you can find over 100 edible plants. Being family oriented, the lodge has a pool and library, and offers special activities for kids, such as shows and story times.

There is a **restaurant** and bar on the premises. The food is high in quality and great in quantity. All tours for the Mountain Pine Ridge area can be arranged through Maya Mountain Lodge, who use some of the best guides available in the area.

Maya Mountain Lodge offers a combination of custom-designed, all-inclusive packages that can take in things like visiting caves, waterfalls, the cayes and the ruins at Caracol. Some include canoeing and horseback riding. Their packages run from US $150 to $200 per person per day, depending on what you do and how long you stay.

Crystal Paradise, Cristo Rey Village, Cayo, ☎ 824-2014 or 824-2772, www.crystalparadise.com, $$$, is just beyond Cristo Rey village, a Maya settlement at Mile 3. The family-run lodge has 20 units. There are thatched-roofed cabins, as well as traditional cabins and rooms in the main lodge. All have private baths, hot water, ceiling fans and verandahs. The décor of the cabins is in the Maya theme and the place is spotless. The Macal River flows behind the lodge.

Meals at Crystal Paradise are home-cooked and delicious. You can request traditional Maya dishes (in advance) and Mrs. Tut, the mother of the family, will try to accommodate you. Meals are served family-style in the central part of the lodge.

Several **birding** scopes are available to help you spot some of the 300 birds reported to live here. There are **horses** on the property, some of which can be ridden. To add to the beauty, the garden has over 150 plants, with about 50 species of orchids. If photographing flowers is your passion, this may be the best place around for you to do so.

◆ Shopping

Sac Tunich Gift Shop is another .3 miles down the road and is recognizable by the large carving of a Maya head on the upper stairs. The shop, located in a traditional Maya house, is run by local people and has many slate and wooden carvings that were made on the premises.

San Antonio

San Antonio, at Mile 10, ☎ 824-3266 (public phone that can be used for contact), has a population of about 1,500. This Maya hamlet is nestled in a farming community and is worth a poke around. Not only does the village house the world famous Garcia Sisters (see below), but until 1996 it also was the home of Dr. Panti, the medicine man who lived for 103 years acting as the spiritual leader of the community and healer to all in need. While in the village you can visit with a Maya chiropractor, a snake doctor, a massage therapist or a midwife to learn about these areas of Maya medicine. The **Pacbitun ruins** and **Noj Kaax Panti National Park** are within cycling/walking distance. San Antonio also offers a home stay program, allowing you to stay with a family and learn traditional skills like patting tortillas or grinding corn.

◆ History

The five **Garcia Sisters** are Maya ladies who, years ago (1983), were working in the field when they uncovered a piece of slate. At the same time as the
stone came to the surface, Pauahtun, the Maya God of art and writing, in-
spired them to carve on slate as their ancestors had done. Unable to control
their new passion, they took the stone home and started carving.

Today, there is an art gallery and shop at the Tanah Maya Art Museum in
the village where you can purchase some of these carvings (see below).

◆ Things to Do

Take lessons in the practice of **Zaxtuns,** a form of healing that includes medicinal plants, prayers and secret stones. Practiced and taught by the Garcia
Sisters' uncle Elejio Panti, this traditional way of healing is practiced not only
among the Maya but also by foreigners as an alternative medicine. You can
purchase herbs and tonics at the shop in the village.

Besides learning about the gathering and use of medicinal plants, you can
take a course in the art of slate carving using chisels, Exacto knives, hack-
saws and machetes to etch out your creation.

The small **Tanah Maya Art Museum** and Community Collection, www.
awrem.com/tanah/experience.html, is beside the Chichan Ka Lodge on the
way into the village. It has a collection of artifacts that have been donated by
local villagers for the preservation and promotion of their culture. A donation
of US $5 is requested to support the museum and to establish a botanical
garden in the village. Open 8 am to 4:30 pm daily.

The shop at the museum offers Garcia carvings that run anywhere from
US $50 to $1,000. There are also necklaces, rings, plates, bowls and
plaques, all with creative Maya designs.

Noj Kaax Panti National Park was inaugurated on Feb. 23, 2001. The
13,000-acre park was named after the famous Dr. Panti from San Antonio
who lived to 103 years of age and was the spiritual leader of the town until his
death in 1996. The boundaries of this park are along the Macal River to the
west, Barton Creek on the north, Mountain Pine Ridge on the east and Rio
Frio Caves on the south.

In the park are the **Kaamcatun Ceremonial Caves**, reported to have large
vessels inside. You will need a guide from the village to take you there. There
are also many old Maya and chicle trails that can be walked.

◆ Pacbitun Ruins

You can visit the Pacbitun ruins on your own, or with Mountain Rider tour operator (see below). If traveling independently, you will need to stop at Mountain Rider and pay the entrance fee of US $5.

Leave San Antonio and follow the Cristo Rey Road up the hill, veering to
the left at the fork near the top. Continue to Mile 10.5 and turn left onto a secondary road to reach **Mountain Rider**, ☎ 820-4036, where horses and a

guide can be rented. Jose Tzul, owner and licensed guide, can take you to the ruins, bathing pools and caves in the Mountain Pine Ridge area. Tzul's philosophy is that he uses horses to do interesting things, as opposed to riding for the sake of riding. His horses are as gentle as he is. You can arrange a half-day trip (US $35 per person) or full-day excursion (US $50 per person). Longer trips must be arranged in advance. Jose can accommodate children, but no younger than five years of age.

Pacbitun ruins are beyond the Mountain Rider property by half a mile. There is a sign indicating the road to the ruins. At the sign, turn right and follow the road for about three miles.

Pay your entrance fee at the home of the Tzul family, where Mountain Rider is located. You can wander by yourself, although the family would much rather take you in by horse.

The name Pacbitun means "stones set in earth." The city is believed to have been occupied about 1000 BC and to be one of the oldest cities in the country.

Found on 75 acres of land on a limestone outcrop in the foothills of the Maya Mountains, the ceremonial center has 25 pyramids, the tallest standing about 56 feet high (17 meters) high. This is a temple pyramid with a vaulted superstructure. There is also a ceremonial ball court, a causeway that is a half-mile long and an irrigation system. Because of the numerous musical instruments found here, it is believed that the city was occupied by an elite group of artists. The ocarinas, or wind instruments, made from pottery were the most common of the pieces, although drums were also found.

❖ MAYA GODS

- ❖ Itzamna – God of Creation
- ❖ Kinich Ahua – Sun God
- ❖ Akab – Moon Goddess
- ❖ Chac – Rain God
- ❖ Ix Chell – Goddess of Medicine
- ❖ Hacha – God of Fire
- ❖ Pauahtun – God of Writing & Art
- ❖ Ah Puch – God of Death
- ❖ Yumkaax – God of Corn
- ❖ Yum Kax-Ku – God of Mountains & Land
- ❖ Xaman Ek – God of the North Star

◆ Places to Stay

Chechan Kaa Resort, Box 75, San Ignacio, ☎ 820-4023, tanah-info@ awrem.com, $$, is located at the beginning of the village. These are decent accommodations in a traditional Maya house, where you can have a private room with or without private bathroom. Also meals are offered and include organically grown vegetables cooked in an open hearth. Most meals are traditional Maya foods that are often corn-based.

This resort is run by the Garcia sisters and a stay here is an unforgettable Maya experience.

Should you wish to stay in a **home** with a family, call the same number as the resort and ask about the home stay program. It is run by the Itzamna So-

ciety, first headed by Maria Garcia (one of the sisters). The society was originally set up to form the Noj Kaax Elejio Panti National Park.

◆ Places to Eat

Whether you eat at the **lodge** or at your **home stay** residence, search out a
glass of sugar-cane wine. This potent white wine is best sipped both slowly
and sparsely.

The Chiquibul/Cristo Rey Road

◆ Mountain Pine Ridge Reserve

▶▶ *Return to the Cristo Rey Road at Mile 10.5 and continue south for two miles.
You will see the gate to the Mountain Pine Ridge Reserve where the Cristo
Rey Road meets the Chiquibul Road that goes down to Georgeville on the
Western Highway; the Cristo Rey Road continues south to Caracol. I advise
you not to even consider trying the Chiquibul Road. It was not passable at
the end of the dry season when I was there. In rainy season you'd turn to
mould before getting out.*

NOTE: *The Cristo Rey Road and Chibiquil Road are the same route
and locals use both names. To save repeating both names in the
text, we use just Cristo Rey.*

The gate to the reserve is manually operated by a park warden who uses it to
keep track of those coming and going.

The reserve has 126,825 acres of controlled logging. However, in recent
years a highly aggressive species of pine beetle has infested and killed 90%
of the trees in the area and the hill tops in Mountain Pine Ridge look like they
have tooth picks sticking in them.

THE WEST

❖ UNDER ATTACK

The female pine beetle burrows into the bark of a tree so she
can lay her eggs. On her head, she carries spores that produce
a blue staining fungus. As she chews through the bark, she
drops the spores. The fungus grows and blocks the vessels of
the inner bark and the sapwood.

After the female successfully enters a tree and lays her 160
eggs, she spreads pheromones that attract males (for fertiliza-
tion of the eggs and other females so they too can drop their
eggs into a safe place. It takes two months for the life cycle of
the beetle to be completed and they can have three to four gen-
erations a year.

As the trees' sap stops flowing, the needles turn yellow and
then a straw color. Finally, they turn a reddish-brown and the
tree dies.

Woodpeckers like to eat developing larvae. Also, after a female sends off her pheromones, she attracts enemy beetles. But these enemies are not enough to save the trees.

The "toothpick tree" problem is being addressed by replanting. As of Aug., 2002 officials have planted seedlings that are a bit more resistant to the beetle than the present trees. The reforestation program will continue for four years. Pine trees grow fairly quickly. At the end of four years, some of the trees should be almost as tall as you.

▶▶ *Inside the gate, at Mountain Pine Ridge Reserve, the road splits. You are at Mile 14 of the Cristo Rey Road. Veer to the left and follow the road signs for Hidden Valley Falls and the lodges along that road.*

◆ Lodging, Waterfalls Included

Hidden Valley Inn, Box 170, Belmopan, ☎ 800-334-7942 or 822-3320, www.hidden valleyinn.com, $$$$$. This is an exclusive lodge that has 12 cabins semi-circled around the main building, where the **restaurant** is located. Each cabin has a zinc roof, screened windows, fan, private bath

❖ HOTEL PRICING	
$	$10 to $20
$$	$21 to $50
$$$	$51 to $75
$$$$	$76 to $100
$$$$$	over $100

with hot water, two twin-sized or one queen-sized bed, and tile floors. Rooms are tastefully decorated. The restaurant serves full-course meals at linen-covered tables decorated with fresh flowers, crystal glasses and candlelight. The price of the room includes meals.

The main draw, other than luxury, is access to the private waterfalls. Interspersed around 118,000 acres of private land are the **Tiger Creek** pools and falls, just a 30-minute walk from the resort, and the **King Vulture Falls**, a 45-minute walk away. The King Vulture Falls have a picturesque canyon on the opposite side of the river. **Bulls Point** allows a view all the way to Belmopan on a clear day. There is also a picnic shelter at Bulls Point. **Butterfly Falls** is a two- to three-hour round-trip hike. These falls drop 80 feet into a secluded swimming pool.

Lake Lolly Folly is a man-made lake 30 minutes from the lodge. If you catch fish here, the chef at the lodge will prepare it for your dinner.

Manakin Falls is 45 minutes along a two-mile trail. These falls were named after the bird frequently seen there. The luxury of these trips is that if you feel lazy, you can be driven close to each spot.

Hidden Valley Falls is just beyond the turnoff to Hidden Valley Inn, along the Cristo Rey Road and 4.5 miles from the gate. Follow the signs. The cost is US $2 per person. Tour buses frequent this site. The falls don't take long to photograph.

There is a washroom, a covered sitting gallery and a gift shop with local artwork at the site. The cabins belong to the Hidden Valley Institute for Environmental Studies. Four of the highest mounds that you see in the surrounding hills are unexcavated and unmapped Maya temples.

As you arrive at this government-controlled site you will see lush jungle, dying pine trees and the falls in the distance – .6 miles away. If it is raining or if there is a low mist, don't bother coming here as you will see nothing.

▶▶ *Return to the Cristo Rey Road at Mile 14 and go to the right.*

The first lodge along the way is **Pine Ridge Lodge**, ☎ 606-4557 or 800-316-0706, www.pineridgelodge.com, $$$$ (discounted in off-season). The lodge has seven fully screened cottages that have been refurbished to a sparkle and are decorated with Belizean pottery and Guatemalan textiles. The cabins have private baths with hot water. Some are made with materials gathered in the jungle, some overlook the river and some are just plain nice. The grounds are well kept and dotted with orchids. The open-air **restaurant** serves gourmet meals, specializing in Italian and vegetarian dishes. However, I have heard that their soups are the big draw. The meals are served in a jungle-type dining room lit with kerosene lamps.

To go to Vaqueros Creek waterfalls, you must stop in at the lodge and ask for directions. I suggest you also have "the last cold beer on the road to Caracol."

Just beyond the property is the **Little Vaqueros Creek** and its 85-foot waterfall. It takes about 15 minutes to reach by walking. The lodge is also just 2.5 miles from Big Rock Falls, an excellent day-hike or a cycling excursion.

Pine Ridge Lodge has numerous people working for it. Some are very familiar with the Chiquibul area, including its caves, logging roads and rivers. If you are looking for a guide to that area, this is the place to find one. Or, contact the lodge in advance. Their knowledge of the back country and their willingness to help you enjoy it is admirable.

Big Rock Falls on the Privassion River has a 150-foot drop into a swimming hole. To get there, go about one mile along the Cristo Rey Road, following signs toward the Five Sisters Lodge. Turn right onto a secondary road after one mile and go another two miles until you see a cleared parking spot on the right. From there, follow the trail downhill for 10 minutes. You will come to a clearing where horses have been kept. Cross the clearing and follow the second trail until you come to the river. The falls are on the left. All in all the Privassion River has about 10 falls, most of them on private property. This trail description was given to me by Gary Seewalk of Pine Ridge Lodge.

Blancaneaux Lodge, Box B Central Farm, Cayo, ☎ 820-3878, www.blancaneaux.com, $$$$$, is located .6 miles past Pine Ridge Lodge along the Cristo Rey Road (Mile 12.4 from San Ignacio) and is what film director and writer Francis Ford Coppola considers to be paradise. This is why he bought the place after he found it while hiking through the Mountain Pine Ridge area.

THE WEST

❖   **FRANCIS FORD COPPOLA**

Known for winning the Oscar at the age of 31 for the movie
Patton, Coppola also made such famous films as *The Godfather.*
He won first place at the prestigious Cannes Festival for *Conver-sation* and *Apocalypse Now*. It was the resemblance to the Phil-ippines, where he filmed *Apocalypse Now*, that attracted
Coppola to Belize.

The lodge is first class. Each thatched-roof cabin, set on a ridge above the
river, has antique colonial furniture, private Japanese bath, Maya weavings
and hardwood floors. The entire lodge is surrounded by rock, jungle and wa-ter. With advance reservations, you can be picked up at Belize City Interna-tional Airport in the lodge's private plane. Or, if you wish, you can drive.

The restaurant here will serve anything you want, but it specializes in the
Coppola family's Italian recipes, like Neapolitan pizza or mother-in-law
chicken. These are cooked on a wood fire in an oven imported from Italy.

There is also a Thai massage parlor and a grass thatched-roof building im-ported from Thailand, with authentic Thai therapists. Services include
aromatherapy, wraps and facials. But if these activities don't use up enough
energy, you can take a horse for a ride or hike along one of the jungle trails on
the property.

Next along the Cristo Rey Road is **Five Sisters Lodge**, ☎ 800-447-2931
or 820-4005, www.fivesisterslodge.com, $$$/$$$$. The lodge sits above the
Privassion River. The 14 screened cabanas have thatched roofs, hardwood
floors, mosquito nets over the beds and private baths with hot water gener-ated from a wood-burning boiler. There are also smaller rooms available in
the main lodge. A bar and **restaurant** serves excellent meals and a gift shop
sells souvenirs. The resort also offers tour options or all-inclusive packages.

The five acres of property has trails down to numerous waterfalls, some of
which drop more than 100 feet (30 meters). Bar service is available on the
Garden of Eden Island, where natural swimming pools are located.

A **nature trail** that leads around the lodge has labeled medicinal plants.
Bikes can be rented for a cycle to the Rio On and Rio Frio Cave. **Mountain
biking** in the Mountain Pine Ridge is excellent and Rio On is about four miles
past Blancaneaux Lodge along the Cristo Rey Road. The travel is slow but
worth the joggling and abuse you must take to get there. Rio On's parking lot
has a picnic shelter. You must go down about 100 cement stairs to the river
where it flows over granite rocks into a multi-faceted gorge. There are nu-merous swimming spots on the river although, during dry season, they have
far less water in them. There is no charge for entering this site.

◆ Rio Frio Cave

To reach **Rio Frio Cave**, turn right at the village of D'Silva, Mile 25 on the
Cristo Rey Road (going left will take you to the research station), and right
again at the first turnoff. Follow the signs and park at the end of the road.

The walk from the car park to the Rio Frio Cave is mystical (if by yourself) as jungle critters call like ghosts through the silence of the forest. There are numerous small caves at the side of the trail that you can explore. Take note of the scars on the sapodilla trees that were tapped for chicle many years before. It takes about 15 minutes to walk to the mouth of the cave, where you will find pools and sandy beaches along the river and the cave itself tucked into the side of a hill. The cave is huge and an easily followed path leads to the exit less than a quarter-mile in.

Continue along the river as it skirts the hill and you will find other caves. There is no charge to this site.

◆ Caracol

From D' Silva it is another 10 miles to the Caracol ruins. Travel along the poor road averages five-15 miles an hour and you should keep alert to logging trucks. During wet season, the travel is even slower and sometimes the road is impassible.

Close to Caracol is the Guacamallo Bridge over the Macal River. Guacamallo is the Spanish word for macaw parrot and Macal is the English Creole word for the same bird. The bridge marks the border for the Chiquibul Forest Reserve that houses the longest cave system in Central America. At the Chiquibul Reserve's border with the Bladen Forest Reserve stands **Doyle's Delight**, the highest peak in Belize. Until recently it was believed that Victoria Peak was the king (queen?) of the mountains in Belize, but that has since been disproved.

There are picnic tables and a toilet at the entrance to Caracol. The visitor center, built with the help of Raleigh International, holds maps and artifacts found at the site. This mini museum is worth visiting. If you are there while the scientists are working, you will be taken on an informative tour.

THE WEST

History

The information about Caracol has been brought to light mainly by two dedicated scientists, **Diane and Arlen Chase**, from the University of Central Florida. They started digging in Belize in 1979 (they were in Guatemala before that) concentrating on the Orange Walk district. It didn't take long for them to be drawn to the challenge of Caracol, the largest ancient Maya settlement in Belize. The site also contains the highest manmade structure in Belize.

HISTORICAL TIMELINE

1200-250 BC Caracol was a collection of small hamlets and farming sites.

900-600 BC The first signs of a city appeared.

AD 70 Temples and burial sites were being used. A ritual complex was also present.

AD 150 Elaborate burial sites were developed.

AD 250-900	The city was at its peak with a population of around 150,000 people. By 800 the decline had started.
AD 331	Evidence was found of a Royal dynasty existing.
AD 480	An unknown ruler was buried in the city.
AD 553	Lord Water becomes ruler. He is also mentioned at Tikal.
AD 562	Caracol's most prominent rival, Tikal, is defeated, either in a game or in battle.
AD 575-618	Smoke Ahau is born and comes to power.
AD 618	King Kan becomes the ruler.
AD 626-936	The Naranjo Wars (rival groups from Guatemala) start.
AD 658	Kan dies and Smoke Skull comes to power.
AD 680	The Naranjo's War of Independence.
AD 702	Ixkun is captured.
AD 859	The most recent date inscribed on a stele at Caracol.
AD 1050	Caracol is abandoned.

The city originally started as a small farming community. As it grew, there was a need for a central market place. The civilization became more sophisticated, temples were added near the market, burial sites were created and the need for a place of worship (rituals) was satisfied.

The city eventually became immense, covering over 88 square miles and holding over 30,000 structures. In the center plaza a pyramid was built that was higher than any other structure in the town. Its top still bursts out of the jungle canopy at a height of 128 feet (42 meters). From the top, you can see all the way to Guatemala. The city had no permanent water supply, so reservoirs were built and an observatory was erected. The ball courts took on a circular shape and stelae revealing the history of the city were inscribed.

As the wealth of the city grew, rival areas like Tikal fought with Caracol for power. At first, fights were common only among the elite classes. However, as the wars became more frequent and fierce, the lower classes were required to fight. The Naranjo wars continued for a long time until what is now Guatemala won its independence from Caracol.

In 895, for some reason, whether it was disease, famine or invasion, the city collapsed and the elite left. Some buildings were left unfinished and the body of a child was found in one room. The assumption is the parents didn't have the time to perform a burial ceremony. However, many of the peasants on the outskirts of the city remained.

Exploring the Ruins

As you enter the city from the visitor center, the imposing **Caana Temple** (meaning sky place) is on the far right, to the north. It stands at 128 feet (42 meters) and has 71 rooms, 45 of which had ceramic tile floors. It was in this

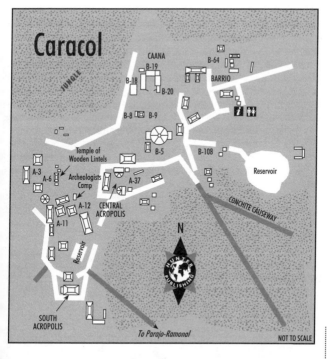

temple that the unburied body of the child was found. This building contained only storage vessels and no drinking, eating or working vessels.

There have been more than 200 burial sites found under Caana, some with family plots. One such plot contained two adults, a 15 year old, a six year old and a one year old. These ages are approximate. All of them had either filed teeth or inlays of jadite put into the teeth. In some of these tombs, fragments of the original paint can still be found.

Around Caana are structures **B18** and **B20**, palaces where the elite lived. **B25** dominates the eastern side of the plaza and it has a room inside that is 35 meters long and seven meters wide. The door to the room is three meters wide and has eight steps leading to it. Inside, benches are set around three sides of the room and numerous vessels are strewn about.

To the south of Caana is a **ball court**, where a marker was found that describes the battle with Tikal. **Altar 23**, the largest found at the site, is southeast of the ball court. The altar was inscribed in 810 and shows captured prisoners. The glyphs tell of the war with Tikal.

To the east or the back of Caana is the **Barrio complex**; B26 is the tallest building in this complex. A new building was being erected on top of an older one, but was never completed.

Continuing south of Caana, the main **acropolis** dominates the center of the city. It is surrounded by three plazas and two ball courts. **A39** had a bench inside similar to the one at Caana. This bench was painted red and inside the room were tripod plates, vases and a ceramic bird whistle.

Behind the central acropolis is the **temple of the wooden lintel**. The carved lintel was of sapodilla wood. Just to the west of this temple was the observatory where the elite studied the stars. To the north of this set of buildings is a **ceiba tree**, believed to be at least 600 years old. Its huge buttresses fan out far enough that they could be the walls of another temple. The Ceiba was sacred to the Maya, who believed it was the symbol of all creation.

Tombs and rooms throughout the city have been found with interesting treasures inside. One of the most interesting was a free-standing stucco statue of a person seated on a throne. Inside the statue's chest was a ceramic box. Both the box and the statue are rare objects for a Maya site.

One burial site found had a beehive chamber inside. The chamber at Saraguate, 1.2 miles from the center of Caracol, was looted, but the bones of a 25-year-old woman were not touched.

Of the interesting **stelae** found, one had a feathered serpent, and one describes a fire in 895. One of the altars suggests there was a female ruler for awhile. So far, 40 inscribed monuments covering 500 years of Caracol's history have been found. One held in the highest esteem is from 562, when people were rejoicing in the defeat of Tikal by Lord Water.

Hiking

Caracol is on the Vaca Plateau and stands at about 1,500 feet (450 meters) above sea level. The causeways around Caracol offer excellent walking and, if time permits, should not be overlooked. One of the causeways, an engineering masterpiece, still supplies water to the site.

Information

Caracol ruins, www.caracol.org, is open from 8 am to 4 pm and costs US $5 to enter (for foreigners). Belizeans do not pay on Sundays or any public holiday. The site was made into a national park in 1995 and shortly after it became a natural monument reserve.

There are **no facilities** or amenities at Caracol. Bring food and drink, plus enough gas to get home. If cycling (the best thing to do) you will need to camp between Caracol and town. You should have those arrangements made with one of the lodges (above) before you arrive.

◆ Chiquibul Caves

The Chiquibul (CHICK-ee-bull) Cave system starts eight miles past Caracol and weaves in and out of about 265,000 acres of jungle on the Vaca Plateau, across the Guatemalan border and back. So far, 40 miles of connected passages have been mapped and there's a suspected 20 miles still to be done.

Hardly accessible because of the lack of maintained roads, the caves can be reached on horseback (see below) following old logging tracks and stream beds. Water is often inaccessible along the route, so carry some with you until the Chiquibul River is reached. You must have a guide and a permit from the Department of Archeology in Belmopan, ☎ 822-2106 or 822-2227. Failing to obtain a permit is punishable by a jail term. The jails are crowded in Belize and there is no TV.

This is the longest connecting cave system in Central America and includes the largest cave chamber in the western world. The chambers, which can be as wide as 260 feet (78 meters), are connected by narrow passages. Some passages stretch for almost two miles. The Chiquibul River runs through these passages and, during rainy season, the water level can rise as much as 70 feet (20 meters), making passage quite dangerous.

By measuring a uranium isotope, scientists reckon that the caves were formed 800,000 years ago. The bones of a now extinct bear species, believed to have lived 10,000 years ago, were found in one of the caves. Bones from vampire bats dating to the same period were also found.

If you want a knowledgeable **guide**, inquire at the **Pine Mountain Lodge** (above), or contact **Peter Herrera**, a naturalist guide who has worked for Birds without Borders and assisted journalists on magazine assignments. His number in Belize City is ☎ 222-4802.

▶▶ *This is the end of the Cristo Rey Road. Return to the Western Highway at Mile 69.6.*

Santa Elena

The little village of Santa Elena, Mile 70, is on the east side of the Macal River. It is quiet and non-imposing as compared to San Ignacio on the other side of the Hawksworth Bridge, the only suspension bridge in Belize.

> **AUTHOR NOTE:** *From the Western Highway going west, turn right at the sign that says "Santa Elena," even if you are going directly to San Ignacio. If you go straight ahead, you will come to the Hawksworth Bridge and you will be going the wrong way. I did this and had to make an embarrassing U-turn in the middle of the road to the honking of numerous vehicles coming toward me.*

Once on the road to Santa Elena, go straight to the stop sign and turn left. Santa Elena is straight ahead. If going to San Ignacio, veer to the right after the stop sign and go down the hill to the wooden bridge.

Santa Elena has both hotels and restaurants.

◆ Places to Stay

The Aguada Hotel, ☎ 804-3609, www.aguadahotel.com, $$, is a first-class hotel in the center of town with very reasonable rates. Rooms are clean and have air conditioning, private baths and hot water. There is a swimming pool and a patio. The Aguada also offers Internet service and a good **restaurant**. The entire hotel is surrounded by jungle vegetation that also encompasses a nearby pond hosting birds, turtles and fish. For kids, there is a play house and small park.

The Touch of Class Comfort Inn, Perez Street, ☎ 824-4006, www. touchofclasscomfortinn.com, $$, is a two-storey motel-style building that has 10 rooms with air conditioning or fans, cable TV, and private baths with hot water. There is a bar and **restaurant** on the premises. The rooms are clean, the hotel quiet, the walk to town not far. To get there, turn left at the first street past the La Loma Luz Hospital. Follow the signs. The hotel is about four blocks down Perez Street. The Inn has mountain bikes and motorbikes for rent. They will also arrange tours for you.

The Log Cabins, on the Western Highway past the Cristo Rey Road turn-off, ☎ 824-3367, $$$, have rustic but clean cabins set in an orange grove. The nine cabins have private baths and hot water, fans and a deck. There is a swimming pool, bar, **restaurant** and gift shop on site. Internet service is also available. The owners offer packages that include meals.

San Ignacio

San Ignacio, often called Cayo, is on the western side of the Macal River. It has a population of about 15,000 people, making it the second-largest town in Belize.

The Western Highway goes through San Ignacio, but because the bridge is one way going east instead of west, you must turn right before the bridge and go toward Santa Elena. Instead of going into that village, take a left at the stop sign and then an immediate right onto the road going downhill. You will cross a wooden bridge and then come to the Savanna Sports Grounds in San Ignacio. Take any road to the left to get to the center of town. It becomes obvious once past the sports grounds.

◆ Introduction

[handwritten: resort has an AWESOME pool + view! $5 BZ to swim]

San Ignacio has a fair amount to offer. Nearby are the **Xunantunich ruins** with the towering palace of El Castillo. There are Maya medicine trails to walk and butterfly reserves to visit. **Cahal Pech**, an extensively excavated and well cared for ruin, is a short walk from the center of town. San Ignacio is also a place where guides can be hired to take you on specialty **adventures**, such as those to Barton Creek Cave or whitewater rafting down the Macal River.

Going to the different resorts and visiting their attractions like the medicine trail, the Belize Botanical Garden and the Museum at Chaa Creek, is easy to do. Taxis, buses or bikes are all possible means of transportation. Xunantunich and El Pilar ruins can be reached by bus or bike and caves can be visited by joining a tour. Canoeing down the Macal River is a great sport; canoes can be rented in town.

Nightlife is also exciting. There is a new **casino** and numerous hang-out bars where you can listen to local musicians. Coffee shops are located in garden settings and funky gift shops sell souvenirs. San Ignacio is also just nine miles from the Guatemalan border.

AVERAGE TEMPERATURES & RAINFALL		
	Daily temp.	**Monthly rainfall**
JAN	73.6°F/23.1°C	47.3 inches/120.2 cm
FEB	76.3°F/24.6°C	32.0 inches/81.3 cm
MAR	80.4°F/26.9°C	23.9 inches/60.7 cm
APR	81.3°F/27.4°C	16.9 inches/43.0 cm
MAY	84.2°F/29.0°C	27.9 inches/71.0 cm
JUN	83.7°F/28.7°C	84.8 inches/215.5 cm
JULY	82.2°F/27.9°C	88.6 inches/225.1 cm
AUG	82.6°F/28.1°C	62.9 inches/160.0 cm
SEPT	82.6°F/28.1°C	70.7 inches/179.8 cm
OCT	80.9°F/27.2°C	72.5 inches/184.6 cm
NOV	80.2°F/26.8°C	81.9 inches/208.2 cm
DEC	76.3°F/24.6°C	55.9 inches/141.9 cm

THE WEST

◆ History

Originally a **logging** community, San Ignacio during the mid-1800s became a sanctuary for the Maya fleeing from the Caste Wars in the Yucatán. They settled in the mountains and made money by selling their produce in San Ignacio.

After the logging market dropped off, **chicle** became the important commodity of the area. However, that too lost its attraction and now **citrus** or **cattle ranching** are the ways to earn a living.

◆ Getting Here & Getting Around

BY BUS: Novelo buses go to San Ignacio or Santa Elena from Belize City every day starting at 4 am. They run every half-hour until 9 pm and every 45 minutes during slack times. The cost is US $2.50. From San Ignacio, buses leave for BC every half-hour starting at 4 am. The last one leaves at 5 pm.

Buses to and from Benque Viejo go every half-hour starting at 3:30 am and run until 11:30 pm at a cost of US 25¢.

CAR RENTALS: Safe Tours Belize Ltd., 287 Western Highway, ☎ 824-3731 or 824-4262, cell 614-4476, dcpil@yahoo.com, has vans or Izuzu Troopers, most of which are four-wheel-drive and have air conditioning. The vans, some of which can hold up to 15 passengers, rent for US $100 per day or $87.50 per day if taken for more than four days. The Troopers go for US $75 a day or $62.50 per day if taken for more than four days. The vehicles are new and in good repair. These prices include insurance for driver and passengers (most companies do not include passenger insurance).

The company will pick up and deliver anywhere in the Cayo district free of charge. If delivering to the international airport near Belize City, there is an additional US $25 charge. You can save by taking the airport shuttle van (it meets all planes) from the airport to San Ignacio to pick up your vehicle.

You should book these vehicles about two weeks in advance, especially during peak season. Cancellation must be completed at least one week before pick up is due. Should you have problems with your vehicle, owner Emil Moreno will come out to where you are with a new one. This is a 24-hour service. The vehicles can take you almost anywhere you would want to go in Belize.

◆ Sights

Hawksworth Bridge, built in 1949, sits over the Macal River and joins San Ignacio with its sister city of Santa Elena. Often called the roller coaster because of the noise this metal one-way suspension bridge creates when vehicles cross, it is the only one of its kind in the country. Vehicles coming from San Ignacio and going east must use it. Historically, the bridge was used as a two-way bridge with only one lane of traffic. But when conflicts arose as to who had the right of way, the city decided to put in a traffic light. But the light was often out of commission so the conflicts continued. Finally, the city decided to detour drivers coming into San Ignacio over a smaller wooden bridge, while those leaving can have the Hawksworth at all times.

Foot and bicycle traffic can use the bridge both ways at any time. Sitting close to the bridge and watching the action is often better than watching television.

◆ Adventures

Birding

Birding Pals, www.birdingpal.org, is a networking group that tries to put birders from different countries in contact with each other. The purpose of the group is to have people share their special interest in birds and learn about one another's cultures. Since the list is growing daily, please check their website just before heading to Belize if you would like to develop such a friendship. There is a pal from San Ignacio who is registered.

The website also lists professional guides who can be hired for a fee. These listings give the qualifications of each guide so you can find one to meet your needs. This list is also growing rapidly.

Birding Pals was started in Apr., 2000 by Knud Rasmussen of Toronto, Canada. Since the group's inception, the list of members has become sub-

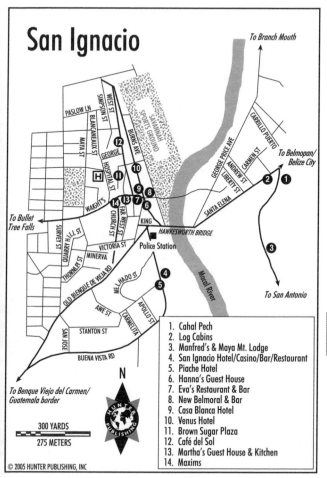

San Ignacio

1. Cahal Pech
2. Log Cabins
3. Manfred's & Maya Mt. Lodge
4. San Ignacio Hotel/Casino/Bar/Restaurant
5. Piache Hotel
6. Hanna's Guest House
7. Eva's Restaurant & Bar
8. New Belmoral & Bar
9. Casa Blanca Hotel
10. Venus Hotel
11. Brown Sugar Plaza
12. Café del Sol
13. Martha's Guest House & Kitchen
14. Maxims

300 YARDS
275 METERS

© 2005 HUNTER PUBLISHING, INC

stantial. There are over 1,500 pals in 166 countries. Mr. Rasmussen gets no funding for this nor does he charge for the immense amount of work he does. His motivation is due to his love of birds and he believes that birders are very special people.

Canoeing

The Belize Canoe Association was formed in Jan., 2001 with Elvin Penner, Julian Sherrard and Luis Garcia as the founding members. Membership has increased quickly and their mandate is to promote canoeing while preserving the environment. For more information, go to www.blackrocklodge.com/bcanoe.htm.

❖ CANOE RACE HISTORY

During the logging days and before locomotives, people moved around in Belize by river. In those days it took one week to go by boat from San Ignacio to Belize City, longer if paddling a dory.

For entertainment, the dory paddlers would race. Eventually, one-man dories were replaced with eight-man dories and, finally, 15-20 men paddled in a grueling race from San Ignacio to Gales Point, north of Dangriga.

There was often a serious competition with the winning cup sometimes going to Gales Point and other times going to San Ignacio. In 1975, the races came to an end and canoeing of any sort in Belize became unpopular.

In 1997 Luis Garcia wanted to revive the racing spirit so he started a small race called the Up and Down. The race went down the Mopan River to Branch Mouth and then up the Macal to San Ignacio, finishing at the Hawkesworth Bridge. It became so popular that it was eventually made into the now world famous Ruta Maya from San Ignacio down to Belize City.

CANOEING LOCALES

The Mopan and Macal rivers are interesting and both have a little white-water on them just to keep you on your toes. The Macal run starts at a gorge near Black Rock Resort and flows into San Ignacio down to the Branch Mouth, where it joins the Belize River for a run to the ocean.

The Mopan River run goes from the bridge at the Guatemalan border for 15 miles, through some bubbles but nothing too serious, until it joins the Macal near San Ignacio. This is a full day's run. If you wish to stop en route at El Pilar ruins near Bullet Tree, you must start very early.

Guacamallo Bridge to Negroman is a 21-mile run starting in the Vaca Plateau in the Mountain Pine Ridge. This rugged canyon run is for rafting or very skilled kayaking as there are numerous Class III and IV rapids, plus several Class V stretches. Portages take you around the two Class VI waterfalls. The run starts at the high end of the Hydro Dam Road and goes through the canyon, past Black Rock and on to Negroman, where the river flattens out.

Negroman to the Branch Mouth is an easy 11-mile float past white cliffs and good swimming holes. It ends at the car wash in San Ignacio.

You can rent equipment locally. See below.

Caving

This is the best caving area in the country and most caves are Maya ceremonial sites. The **Chiquibul Caves** (see page 146, the Cristo Rey Road beyond

Caracol) are the longest in Central America and they have rooms that are second to none for beauty. Some require that you rappel down on ropes or visit by boat. If a dry cave is your preference, head to nearby **Chechem Hah Cave** (see page 164), which can be visited independently. **Actun Chapat** and **Actun Halal** (see below) are also nearby. The architectural work inside Actun Chapat makes the exploration more interesting than at some other caves.

Actun Chapat, which translates as "Cave of the Centipede," is presently being researched by archeologists. It is about 20 miles south of San Ignacio, and you must have a guide to show you inside. The trip requires travel along old logging roads and a walk in the jungle.

First discovered in 1982, the cave has been mapped. There are two entrances with a chamber that is about a quarter-mile long in between. The most interesting objects are the terraced platforms, stairways and shelves. There is even a bench carved into the cave wall in one room. One tiny room has resident ghost-faced bats, an endangered species (so leave them alone).

Actun Halal, in the Macal River Valley, is a small cave with two entrances. It's more of a rock shelter than a cave. The entrances are connected by a passage that measures about 75 feet (26 meters) long. The petroglyphs inside are what make Actun Halal interesting. In one room is a wall that has a calcium carbonate waterfall flowing down it. Shine your light and you'll see it sparkle. There are five petroglyphs carved on this wall and more in the smaller room nearby.

At least one cave trip is a must when in Belize, and San Ignacio is the best place from which to do it. It matters not whether you hire a guide for a customized trip or join a tour and share the excitement with others. See below for recommended guides.

THE WEST

Swimming

Cool off in the pool and then relax on the deck and enjoy some home-cooked meals at **Crystal Paradise Lodge**, Cristo Rey Village, ☎ 824-2014 or 824-2772. The cost for swimming is US $2.50.

Tour Companies

Cave touring is the thing to do while in Cayo. There are dry and wet caves (with rivers), some with exceptional formations, others with Maya artifacts. The most appealing aspect of exploring in the Cayo region is that guides and tour operators will cater to what you want, rather than vice-versa. Regardless of what you choose, expect to pay US $50-$80 for the day.

Manfred Lohr, on the Cristo Rey Road, ☎ 824-2276, is, in my opinion, the best guide in the region. He knows his way around the caves and has a few exceptional hikes on which he can take visitors. You must be in good physical condition and want an adventure if you book with Manfred. He also speaks German. Because he is good, he is busy. Book ahead.

George Luzero, 66 George Price Avenue, ☎ 824-3627, is an excellent guide who has his own vehicle. Whether you want a trip to Caracol or a run down the Macal River, George can fix it up for you. If you are lucky, he will take you himself.

Easy Rider, 24 Burns Avenue, San Ignacio, ☎ 824-3734, www.belizex. com/easy_rider.htm, runs horse trips in the Mountain Pine Ridge area. The owner, Charlie Collins, offers half-day excursions for US $25 and full-day excursions for US $40. The horses are gentle, so children can be accommodated. He will also arrange visits to caves, ruins and waterfalls.

Belizean Sun Travel and Tours, Box 180, San Ignacio, ☎ 824-4853 or 603-3271, specialize in cave tubing and visiting dry caves. They also run jungle night walks with overnight camping, which allows you to see nocturnal animals and try to sleep as the howlers sing their lullaby. BST also likes to do bike tours, especially with small groups.

Mayawalk, 19 Burns Avenue, ☎ 824-3070, www.mayawalk.com, is a one-stop shop. Aaron Juan offers tours that are high adventure, involving activities like spelunking in a cave after rappelling down the canyon wall. Or mountain biking to a jungle river and camping overnight to the music of the howler monkey. The trips are not for the out-of-shape adventurer. If whitewater is your desire, this is also a good company to arrange kayaking/rafting trips on the Macal River. Mayawalk has an impeccable reputation. They also hire Manfred Lohr (above) as one of their guides.

Belize Close Encounters, Box 1320, Detroit Lakes, MN 56502, ☎ 888-875-1822 or 218-847-4441, www.belizecloseencounters.com, has been operating in Belize for over 13 years and knows the country well. They represent over 60 resorts and can combine a number of activities with suitable accommodations. Their best skill is creating custom trips, whether it be caving or diving, museums or horseback riding. The San Ignacio area is their specialty.

Equipment Rentals

Black Rock, ☎ 824-2341, rents canoes for US $30 a day. If staying at Black Rock Lodge, you get the advantage of a vehicle pickup after the run out from the resort to San Ignacio.

Belizean Sun, ☎ 824-4853, offers kayaks for US $30 a day, plus pickup and delivery. Tube rentals are US $5 for 2.5 hours on the river. Bike rentals are US $7.50 per day. Valid ID or credit card must be left as security. They also offer tours with guides (to Xunantunich and elsewhere) for US $50 per day.

◆ Nightlife

Brown Sugar Plaza has a **movie theater** so you can take in the local latest. The **Blue Angel Night Club**, ☎ 804-4309, next to the post office, starts to bop around 11 pm on weekends and the **World Culture Club** (no phone) upstairs at the bus station, is an open-air bar facing the Macal River. **Mi Amor** (no phone) is air conditioned and sits over Courts Store. They often have well-known DJ's and popular bands.

The **Stork Club**, 18 Buena Vista Drive, ☎ 822-2034, San Ignacio Hotel, is the place for a drink before you have your steak in the restaurant. The club has a happy hour every evening, but it is especially popular on Friday.

> **ODD FACT:** *In 1806 a law was passed that required all heads of families to have six fire buckets, one ladder and one hook with a rope attached in their homes. This law is still on the books.*

Cahal Pech Tavern, Cahal Pech, ☎ 824-3380, features a wide variety of local bands. The drinks are not costly and the place is popular with travelers.

The **Casino** is in the San Ignacio Hotel on Buena Vista Drive, although it's not part of the hotel (it rents space there). It's a good spot to lose a couple of dollars. If boredom is a problem, this can be a lively place.

◆ Shopping

Cocopete Bar - hot spot

This is your last chance to shop in Belize if you are headed to Guatemala and your first chance if you are coming from there.

The **Indita Maya Gift Shop**, West Street, ☎ 824-4346, is a small shop well stocked with local artwork.

The **Belize Gift Shop**, West Street, ☎ 824-4159, has a wide selection of gifts and souvenirs in all price brackets. The people are friendly – that's the biggest draw.

◆ Places to Stay

THE WEST

The San Ignacio Hotel, 18 Buena Vista Drive, ☎ 824-2034, www.sanignaciobelize. com, $$$$. The 25-room hotel sits on 14 acres of land that overlook the Macal River. Each room has private bath with hot water, fan or air conditioning, and cable TV. There is also a gift shop, a pool, a basketball court and a very good steak house.

❖ HOTEL PRICING	
$	$10 to $20
$$	$21 to $50
$$$	$51 to $75
$$$$	$76 to $100
$$$$$	over $100

The Casa Blanca Guest House, 10 Burns Avenue, ☎ 824-2080, $$, is new, clean and comfortable – the best bet in town. Each tastefully decorated room has private bath with hot water, tile floors and fans. The owners are friendly and helpful and guests can use a kitchenette to make a cup of tea or a sandwich. This hotel is probably the most secure in downtown San Ignacio.

The New Belmoral, 17 Burns Avenue, ☎ 824-2024, $$, has 11 clean, comfortable rooms, all on the second floor. Some have private baths. If you can, pick a room not overlooking the street, as those are a bit noisy. There is a common sitting area and a balcony that overlooks the action below. The operators of this hotel will do everything they can to make your stay pleasant.

The Hi-Et Hotel, West Street, ☎ 824-2828, $, is a family-run budget hotel. Rooms have a balcony and shared bath, but there is no hot water. Despite that, this quiet hotel is popular.

Irva's Place, West Street, just below Pacz Hotel, no phone, $, is exceptionally clean. Of the five rooms available, three have private baths. Although I have not been able to make a personal visit, those who have stayed here say it's a good deal.

The Pacz Hotel, 4 West Street, ☎ 824-4538, $$, is another bargain for those willing to share a bath. Clean and comfortable, this is a tiny place with only five rooms. One draw is that you can get complimentary coffee in the morning.

The Piache Hotel, 18 Buena Vista, ☎ 804-2032, $$, is not on the same property as the San Ignacio Hotel, even though they share an address. The Piache is on the opposite side of the street. It's a comfortable establishment, with a beautiful garden. Rooms are tiny but clean, and come with fans and private baths with hot water.

Tropicool Hotel and Bike Rentals, 30 Burns Street, ☎ 824-3052, $$, is clean and bright. There are shared bathrooms, ceiling fans in each room, a common room with TV, and a laundry facility.

◆ Places to Eat

Brown Sugar Plaza on West Avenue has a food court that serves excellent ice cream in every flavor you could want. The **Coffee Press** is the first restaurant open in the mornings, usually around 6 am. It serves coffee and muffins and has good Internet access.

❖ RESTAURANT PRICING	
$	under $5
$$	$5 to $10
$$$	$11 to $25
$$$$	$26 to $50
$$$$$	over $50

Café del Sol, ☎ 822-4899, $$, serves coffee in a garden. Their yogurt smoothies are a must and the French toast is served with lemon cream-cheese in the center. There is a **book exchange** and **gift shop** at the café. The gift shop here has some artistically designed crafts that are worth a look.

Erva's Restaurant, Far West Street below Pacz Hotel, ☎ 824-2821, $. The food is gourmet, and this place remains a favorite for its seafood and pizzas. The coffee is good and the hash browns are superb. The chicken Cordon Bleu, with mushrooms and a cream sauce, is highly recommended, as are the shrimp cooked in butter and tons of garlic. There are also many vegetarian dishes from which to choose.

Eva's Restaurant & Bar, 22 Burns Avenue, ☎ 804-2267, $, is the best place to make connections, collect information, find someone to share a trip or check your e-mail. However, it can be a bit noisy and some find it difficult to concentrate at the computer. It's often hot, too, so sitting outside at the tables on the street is a good option. Stewed chicken with rice is the most popular dish. There is a book exchange and a gift shop. They serve instant coffee and I think the place is slightly overrated. *awesome tajitas! pretty cheap*

Green Dragon Internet Coffee Shop, #8 Hudson Street, ☎ 824-4782, serves the best cappuccino in town. They also have ice cream that kids believe comes from the Magic Dragon. They sell health foods, books, gifts and arrange tours. It's open from 8 am to 8 pm every day except Sunday. This is a "must stop."

Hannah's, 5 Burns Street, ☎ 822-3647, $$, across from the Casa Blanca, has good Indian curry. It is all freshly made and served in the best of Indian style. Foods with sauces are the best, as you get far more spice for the price.

Pop's on West Street across from Martha's (which you should avoid), $, serves the best breakfast in town, especially when it comes to waffles. The restaurant is tiny and doesn't have fancy décor, but the breakfasts are exceptional. Pop's also has a good selection of ice cream.

The Running West Steak House, 18 Buena Vista (at the San Ignacio Hotel), ☎ 822-2034, $$$, sanighot@btl.net, is the place to go for steak. They have imported wines and serve some delightful dinner drinks. There is also one vegetarian meal on the menu. Have a drink at the Stork Club bar (downstairs), go to the restaurant for a steak and then sleep in one of their rooms.

The Serendip Restaurant, 27 Burns Street, ☎ 822-2302, $$, has south Indian foods. They specialize in seafood, Indian-style. Meals are reasonable and the portions acceptable.

The Aguada Hotel, ☎ 804-3609, www.aguadahotel.com, $$, in Santa Elena, offers the best meals available in the two towns. Everyone I spoke with constantly reminded me that this was the place to go. The food is good, the portions ample and the prices reasonable. _german bakery + house of pastries_

San Ignacio to Bullet Tree Falls

THE WEST

Bullet Tree Falls is northwest of San Ignacio. From the wooden bridge between Santa Elena and San Ignacio, follow the road and keep traveling west. Pass the sports grounds and, instead of turning to go into downtown San Ignacio, keep going straight.

If you do not have your own car, take a taxi (US $7.50) or a *collectivo* (50¢) from the bus station in San Ignacio.

> ❖ **SAFETY ALERT**
>
> The road to Bullet Tree Falls is not recommended for cycling or hiking. There have been some hostages taken and some tourists have been robbed by gun-wielding thugs. Women have also been raped. Although it seems that the crimes are targeted toward the higher-end traveler, I think everyone should take care. But things change and robbers get caught. Check in town for the latest information before heading this way by bicycle.

Bullet Tree is a tiny Spanish-speaking village of 2,000 people. It is five miles from San Ignacio. Just beyond the village is where you will find the Maya ruins of El Pilar.

◆ Things to Do

Be Pukte Cultural Center, in Bullet Tree on the San Ignacio side of the Mopan River Bridge, is open Friday to Monday, 9 am to 3 pm. The center's name, Be Pukte, means Bullet Tree. Inside, it has a model of El Pilar done to scale. The center also sells handicrafts made by locals. There are wood carvings and slate carvings, but my favorite are the corn-husk dolls. These make a great gift.

El Pilar ruins are seven miles north of the Mopan River Bridge. There are numerous signs indicating where to go along an all-weather road. The drive or cycle uphill is steep, a total of 900 feet (300 meters) elevation gain to the ruins. Once at the site you will see a building with a green roof, the caretaker's house. Stop here to pay the US $2.50 entry fee that includes a map of the trails. There is a picnic area and washroom facilities at the entrance.

El Pilar is on 100 acres of land and the ruins are divided into four sections, with the western section set within Guatemala and thus not accessible from Belize. A huge causeway links the eastern and western sections of the city. It measures 100 feet (30 meters) across in places and is walled on both sides. The purpose of the wall hasn't been established and the final destination of the causeway has not been found. Some suspect that it linked Tikal with El Pilar, since the two centers are only 28 miles apart.

The site, believed to have been occupied from 500 BC to AD 1000, has 25 plazas and numerous temples that stand 50 to 70 feet (15-20 meters) above the plaza floors. The **Wing Temple** in Plaza Copal had eight plaza floors beneath it, indicating about 3,000 years of occupation. Some plazas are up to 1.5 acres in size and the north plaza, called **Nohal Pilar**, has four pyramids and a ball court around it. There is a huge staircase on the north side leading to the plaza and a ramp on the south side.

North of Nohal is **Xaman Pilar**, with palaces that feature underground tunnels and stairways. There is only one door to Xaman Pilar. This, too, is unusual as numerous exits are always present in Maya buildings, especially in places where the elite resided.

El Pilar has several corbel vaults where each layer of stone juts out over the one below until the two sections of wall meet at the top. This creates a cramped space. Many of the stairways were made with quarried limestone.

Masewal Forest Garden, 1.5 miles down the Paslow Falls Road, belongs to Don Betto, a Maya. Don is knowledgeable in medicinal plants, a skill he learned from his father, who was a famous snake doctor in the area. Betto's 15-acre garden has more than 500 plants. You can go on a guided tour with him and ask all the questions you like, for US $5.

Midas in SI is a cool little place just outside the town. Has bungalows for pretty cheap ($60 $52) owner Roger is very helpful + nice. Can order breakfast!

◆ Places to Stay

Hummingbird Hills, Paslow Falls Road, ☎ 614-4699 or 413-527-4363, www.hummingbirdhills.com, $$, is located on 12 acres of replanted ranch land. They have three cabins, made of hardwood and thatch. Two cabins sleep four and have private baths and hot water, fans and mosquito netting. One cabin sleeps only two and has a shared bath. There is also a tenting site and restaurant on the property. The owners have a unique craft; they make jewelry out of recycled copper.

    Aguallos Place, ☎ 822-3945, $, is near the Mopan River. They have a safe camping site with **hammocks** or small **tents** for US $5 and large tents for $10. There are clean washrooms with hot showers, and kitchen facilities with fridge space for your food. There is also a TV for anyone missing that form of entertainment. Pets and kids are welcome. Aquallos, the owner, is well known in the village. Just ask for directions. Aquallos speaks English and Spanish.

        AUTHOR NOTE: *The Maya weave fibers from the agave plant to make hammocks.*

The Parrot Nest, ☎ 820-4058 or 614-6083, www.parrot-nest.com, $$, is on the way into Bullet Tree from San Ignacio. Take a *collectivo* to the village and walk 10 minutes to the lodge. This unique place has two treehouses built in the tips of guanacaste trees. There are also four other on-the-ground cabins and two bathhouses. Cabins have fans and all but one has shared bath facilities. Three sides of the property are bordered by the Mopan River and, since the water is calm, it is a good place for swimming. The on-site **restaurant** serves breakfast (US $4) and/or dinner (US $8) on the verandah, which overlooks the jungle. The owners will cater to dietary needs if you let them know ahead of time.

THE WEST

San Ignacio to San Jose Succootz

▶▶ *Return to the Western Highway and continue from Mile 70 at San Ignacio to the border. The road is good, the resorts first class and the rolling hills a pleasure to watch.*

◆ Places to Stay

The first place you will reach is **Mayaland Villas**, Box 137, Belize City, ☎ 223-1409 or 824-2035, www.mayalandbelize.com, $$$$$. The 10 white plaster units are clean and spacious, with private baths, fans and front porches. The setting is lovely and the people friendly. There is also a gift shop, **restaurant** and Internet service.

    As you continue along the Western Highway, the road on the right (north) at Mile 71.2 leads to a resort on the Mopan River. **Clarissa Falls Resort**, Box 44, San Ignacio, ☎ 824-3916, $$$, www.belizereport.com/lodging/clarissa.

The lodge has 11 thatched-roof cabanas, all tastefully decorated with Maya weavings. Each cabana has a fridge, stove, private bath, hot water, fan and electricity. There is also a bunkhouse that is less expensive, a campsite for tenting and an RV park for motor homes. Barbeque pits and picnic tables are interspersed throughout the property.

The resort is neat and tidy, the lawn well kept, and the animals that cross the lawn are fun to watch. Nearby, on the Mopan River, tubing is the sport of choice. The lodge has tubes for rent at US $5 per day and transportation to the ruins, where you can start your float trip, can be arranged.

There is a very small **golf course** on the property where you can rent a club and ball and play the "where it lands" style of golf. Although there are only five holes, it takes skill to get yourself a hole in one.

The food at Clarissa Falls comes recommended by Belizeans. The most popular dinner is a spaghetti dish cooked with a good dash of garlic, and the *relleno negro* soup is a meal in itself. Each bowl holds a huge piece of chicken, some vegetables and an egg. For dessert, try the rum-soaked fruit cake.

Returning to the Western Highway, take the next road on the right, just a few hundred meters past Clarissa Falls turnoff. It goes to **Nabitunich Lodge**, ☎ 824-2096, www.nabitunich.com, $$$. Nabitunich means "Little Stone Cottage" in Mayan. The lodge and its five stone cottages are located near the banks of the Mopan River. From the garden you can see La Castillo at the Xunantunich ruins; it's a mere 10-minute walk away. There is a **restaurant** on site.

▶▶ *Back on the Western Highway, just after Nabitunich Lodge turnoff, is a secondary road to the left (south) at Mile 72 called the Hydro Dam Road.*

The Hydro Dam Road

Green Haven Lodge, Box 155, San Ignacio, ☎ 800-889-1512 or 820-4034 www.ghlodgebelize.com, $$$. The owners of the lodge are French, and these well-kept cabins have a taste of France in their décor. The larger rooms have hardwood floors, tiled bathrooms and Belizean-made furniture. There is a swimming pool or you can play volleyball, badminton or petanque (a game from southern France). If you need to wind down, you can take advantage of the masseuse services.

The **restaurant** offers real French cooking – dishes such as *boeuf bourguignon* or filet mignon – and vegetarian dishes. The desserts are exceptional. The restaurant has the only wine cellar in Belize, as far as I know. The service matches the quality of the food and the setting is romantic. You can eat inside or on the spacious deck, where there is always a breeze.

▶▶ *There is a fork in the road, the right goes to Black Rock, the left to the rest of the resorts.*

Follow signs for the **Black Rock Lodge**, Box 48, San Ignacio, ☎ 824-2341 or 824-3296, www.blackrocklodge.com, $$$. The lodge, nestled into 250 acres of jungle, was previously inaccessible by road, but can now be reached at any time of year. Set on a hill above the Macal River, this first-class hideaway overlooks Black Rock canyon and cliffs. Each of the slate and thatch cabins has screened, louvered windows, double beds, fans and Belizean art. Some cabins have shared bath. This resort is remote.

Visitors often take a **canoe** from the resort and run a few of the smaller rapids on the way into San Ignacio for a beer. The staff at the lodge will pick you and the canoe up once you are done. Or you can go to Vaca Falls for a day of swimming and cave exploring.

One of the things you can see near Black Rock is an oropendola's nest hanging from the trees. Julian Sherrard, the lodge owner (along with his dad), identified this nest for me.

❖ GOLDEN PENDULUM

Oropendola means golden pendulum. The bird is so named because of its long, bright-yellow (*oro*) tail feathers and its hanging nest. These nests, ranging in size from three to six feet (.9-1.8 meters) long, take nine to 11 days to build and there are often up to 40 nests on one tree. The bird uses palm frond fibers and grass to make the nest. These essentially black birds are polygamous and often the males will fight while protecting their harem. The female lays one or two eggs, which are incubated for 15 days. It takes one month of care before the young ones leave home. They eat insects, grain and seeds and are very gregarious.

Chaa Creek Resort is along the left fork a short way, ☎ 824-2037 or 820-4010, www.chaacreek.com, $$$$$. It sits on 330 acres at the edge of the Macal River. The 19 thatched-roof, Hansel and Gretel-style cabins are exquisite in design and comfort. They are screened, and have porches with sun decks, private baths, mahogany beds, tile floors and original art pieces.

An international reputation speaks for Chaa Creek. In 2002 they won the Condé Nast Ecotourism Award. In 2001 they won the America Society of Travel Agents Environmental Award and the Caribbean Sustainable Tourism Award. In 1998, they won the Green Hotel of the Year Award from American Express and the Caribbean Hotel Association. This year the resort was chosen by the readers of *Travel + Leisure* magazine as one of the 25 best hotels in Mexico, Central and South America. They have also been praised by numerous prestigious magazines (all articles are available at the lodge) and there isn't a local in Belize who won't tell you how superb the resort is. They are often featured on TV travelogues.

Chaa Creek has miles of maintained trails for guests to walk, as well as a **Natural History Museum** (open daily, 8 am to 5 pm, US $6 entrance), ☎ 824-2037. The museum displays flora and fauna and has a model of the

Macal Valley. You can also peruse the museum's archives and topographic maps of the area.

❖   HOWLING SUCCESS

Chaa Creek's Natural History Center, Yerkes Regional Primate Research Center and the Belize Zoo have worked together to re-locate some howler monkeys along the lower Macal River. Yel-low fever killed most of the population in Cayo around 40 years ago. Loss of habitation and low diversity resulted in the animals disappearing totally. However, now they are back. The reloca-tion project started with 16 animals being placed in the area. They have flourished and have spread as far as the village of Cristo Rey.

The **Blue Morpho Butterfly Farm** is included in the museum's entry fee. The farm was built so that guests could learn about the four stages the but-terfly goes through during its lifecycle.

❖   THE LIFE OF A MORPHO BUTTERLY

The blue morpho, with its iridescent blue wings, is found in rain-forests in Central and South America. With a wing span of 13-17 cm (five-seven inches), this king of the butterfly world can fold his wings at night and hang onto the bottom of a leaf or branch so his enemies can't see him. Morphos eat flowers, leaves, rotting logs, sap and juices. They love the sun and live from a few days up to eight months.

When in the caterpillar stage the morpho is red-brown in color, with patches of lime green. It is cannibalistic. The hairs on the caterpillar are irritating to the skin of humans.

The morpho's enemies are birds, fish, larger insects and people. We use the wings to make clothing. The wings are also used to make jewelry.

The resort has Trek-950 **mountain bikes**, **horses** and **canoes** available to rent. There have been more than 250 different birds spotted on the property, making it a big draw for birders.

However, the resort is not for only the very wealthy. There is a campground where **tenting** is permitted.

Ix Chel Tropical Reserve, which houses a medicine trail (see below), came into being because of the dedicated work of Rosita Arvigo and her hus-band Greg Shropshire. After moving to Belize in 1981, Rosita worked with Dr. Elijio Panti, the Maya healer from San Antonio who lived to the age of 103. Rosita learned both healing practices and spiritual traditions from Panti.

Besides working with scientific organizations that are researching the uses of medicinal plants for diseases like cancer and AIDS, Rosita and Greg go into areas that are going to be developed or logged to salvage any plants that they don't already have at Ix Chel. The plants are taken to the Terra Nova

Medicinal Plant Reserve, located adjacent to Ix Chel. This is a government-sanctioned area, encompassing 6,000 acres. The transplants are done just in case there is danger of the plants going extinct. Rainforest remedies, herbs and tonics can be purchased at the reserve.

Panti Rainforest Medicinal Trail, ☎ 824-3870, www.rainforestremedies. com, is open daily from 8 am to 4 pm and costs US $5.75 per person. Located above the Macal River and next to the Chaa Creek Lodge, it can be accessed on foot or by canoe. To canoe is easier, although more complicated to orchestrate.

There is a shelter at the trailhead, where you register and listen to a talk before going on a self-guided tour. You can also hire a guide for an extra US $7.50 to tell you about the plants. However, all the plants are labeled with common and scientific names and their uses are explained.

du Plooy's Resort, Big Eddy, San Ignacio, ☎ 824-3101, www.duplooys. com, $$$$. This is a small place with cottages dotted along the Macal River. There are four room choices. The first is a luxury duplex that has a wrap-around porch, large rooms, whirlpool bathtub, coffee maker and fridge. Rooms on the lower level of the duplex have two beds and a couch. The second choice is one of the detached cottages that have private baths and spacious rooms. The third option is a room in the lodge. Finally, there's a seven-bedroom Pink House designed for large families or small groups. Most prices include meals.

This is an ecologically minded resort, so they have tiled roofs instead of cutting palm thatch (to preserve trees), they have no beef on the menu because they don't want more rainforest destroyed for cattle grazing, they use no throw-away containers, and all their vegetable garbage is composted.

The property features the **Belize Botanical Garden** that holds over 120 species of orchids. There is also a nursery and two ponds where fish, birds and plants live together. The gardens are often visited by foxes, armadillos, gibnuts and a very shy tapir.

Ek Tun, ☎ 303-442-6150 or 824-2002, www.ektunbelize.com, $$$$, is almost at the end of the Hydro Dam Road. This remote little spot has two thatched-roof, hardwood cabins tucked into the jungle. There are private bathrooms with hot water, fans, lots of windows and oil lamps. Each cabin will sleep up to five people. Chosen by *Belize First Magazine* as one of the top 10 most romantic places to stay, and number four in the top 10 jungle lodges, Ek Tun will certainly give you a restful vacation. Meals are included in the price of the rooms.

Martz Farms is 7.9 miles in on the Hydro Dam Road, ☎ 824-3742, $$. This is the most remote place to stay near San Ignacio and has been recommended by many travelers. Commonly called the Water Hole by ex *chiclero* farmers, the 200 acres are dotted with fish ponds, pasture land and jungle plants. There's also a spring-fed creek that has a 90-foot (27-meter) waterfall that drops into a natural bathing pool (see *Vaca Falls*, below). The two thatched-roof cabins overlook the Macal River. Both have porches, private bath and fans.

THE WEST

◆ Things to Do

The Trek Stop and Tropical Wings Nature Center is on your left, ☎ 823-2265, www.thetrekstop.com, $. This is a small place with comfortable cabins and tenting pads interspersed throughout a 40-year-old orchard that has mango, avocado and coconut trees. Trails run throughout the 22-acre property, and signs identify plants.

The cabins are small but clean, and each bed has a mosquito net. Those who are tenting can rent a luxury-sized tent and pad or, if you have a tent, you can rent a place to pitch it. The center is close to the border and Xunantunich ruins, so it is an excellent spot for budget travelers. Grocery stores are within walking distance, and you have access to kitchen facilities, laundry and the Internet. Water here is heated by solar panels and there is a composting toilet.

The Trek Stop has two-person inflatable **kayaks** for rent for US $17.50, **mountain bikes** for US $10 and **inner tubes** for US $6 per day. The interpretive center and butterfly house cost US $2.50 to enter and are worth every penny.

The **restaurant** is one of the most reasonably priced in the area and offers French toast and fry jacks, hamburgers or vegetarian spaghetti, stir-fried vegetables or club sandwiches. If you crave calories, the cheesecake is a must. You can also get a packed lunch to take with you on a day trip.

◆ Chechem Hah Cave

This cave is one of the few with inside architectural work done by the Maya. If you have a car or bike, you can go on your own. Otherwise, you may need to hire a guide in San Ignacio (see page 169 for a list of guides).

To get here, go eight miles on the Hydro Dam Road or the Arenal Road (they are the same) until you see a small sign to the right. The road should not be driven without four-wheel-drive, especially in rainy season. You can walk down to the farm of the Moraleses and they will take you into the cave. There is a US $10 charge for the tour. A steep, 20-minute climb will take you to the cave opening. You should carry water with you.

The entrance is small and has been secured by stones. There is a locked gate to prohibit looting. The cave is about a quarter-mile long, with ladders and ropes placed to help you climb around. Inside the rooms you will find storage vessels, plates and a stele. It is believed that the cave dates back to 600 BC and was used for storage and as a ceremonial center. Although some things have been removed to the Archeological Center in Belmopan (and the museum in BC) many objects have been left in the cave.

◆ Vaca Falls

Vaca Falls are spectacular. They drop about 200 feet (70 meters) from the tiny creek (the one you crossed to get to the Chechem Hah cave) down into the Mopan River. There is a swimming pool near the bottom. The walk down is about 25 minutes and the walk up is only twice as long. Remember to carry drinking water. Also, dampen a scarf to place over your head for your climb back up. It will help keep you cool.

▶▶ *Back on the Western Highway, go to Mile 72.8 and turn left (south) onto a secondary road.*

San Jose Succotz

San Jose Succotz is at Mile 73.1 on the Western Highway. This town of about 1,200 people (most of them Maya) lines the banks of the Mopan River and many of the residents work at the Xunantunich ruins as laborers, caretakers or guides. The town's liveliest times are during fiestas, when traditional Maya dances, food, music and games are enjoyed.

There is a small restaurant, the **Plaza Café**, where you can get refreshments. The **Va Yang Restaurant**, ☎ 823-2460, and the **Rong Feng Restaurant & Bar**, ☎ 823-2688, are other alternatives. A **gift shop**, up the street from the Plaza Café, sells slate and wood carvings in Maya designs.

◆ Xunantunich Ruins   ↗ *tours with cruise ships sucks! worth it? maybe.*

These are the most accessible ruins in all of Belize, reachable by bus, car, bike or on foot. Whichever mode of transportation you choose, you'll have to take the little hand-operated ferry across the Mopan River (it carries cars). There is no charge for the ferry, but your entry ticket to the ruins must be turned over to the ferry operators on your trip back.

The ruins are open daily from 8 am to 5 pm and the cost is US $5 per person. The ferry quits for an hour every day during lunchtime. If your bags are getting heavy to lug around, leave them with the ferry operators.

There are numerous licensed guides at the ferry dock. If you are even remotely interested in archeology, hire one. The charge is US $15 an hour for two people.

After driving or walking the .6 miles uphill, you will be greeted by the imposing tower of El Castillo. At the entrance to the site are toilets, a picnic spot and a museum. Inside the museum is a reproduction of the ruins. There are also some stelae that were found at the site and a replica of the frieze found on El Castillo. The replica makes it much easier to identify what archeologists tell us is on the frieze.

Xunantunich means "Maiden of the Rock" in Mayan, but in the early part of this century the ruin was often referred to as **Benque Viejo**. The name Xunantunich comes from one of the carved monuments showing a ruler with a headdress.

Exploring the Ruins

The largest pyramid and the main attraction is **El Castillo**. It stands at 130 feet (40 meters) above the plaza floor. You can climb to the top for a look at

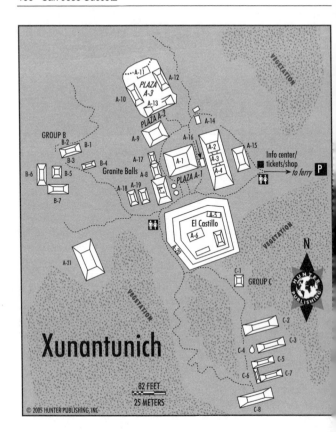

Xunantunich

82 FEET
25 METERS

© 2005 HUNTER PUBLISHING, INC

the surrounding countryside (well worth the climb). This is the second-highest structure in Belize; the highest is at Caracol.

It was on El Castillo that the famous **frieze** was found. Looking at the frieze, the man with the big ears and earrings is the Sun God, Kinich Ahua. Beside him is the moon and then the signs that stand for Venus. The frieze also incorporates signs for the different days in the Maya calendar. The carved stone, which went all the way round the pyramid, was covered in plaster and then painted.

There are six major **plazas** around Xunantunich and more than 25 **temples**. A **ball court** behind (south of) El Castillo is believed to have been abandoned early, maybe at the same time as Tikal fell. The ball court was about 30 by 60 feet (10 by 20 meters) – it was not an extremely big one.

Eight **stelae** and two **altars** have been found in the central group. Most are plain, probably because they were originally covered in plaster and painted with glyphs. Of the carved ones, two fell down. One landed face up and was weather-worn over the years, rendering the glyphs unreadable. Howeve carvings on the altar that landed face-down are still visible. They focus on fertility and warlords (apparently, warlords were a sign of fertility).

The group of buildings to the west of the main plaza is in disrepair. A small grave was found in one of the platforms. It was that of a female who had extensive dental work done, indicating that she may have been upper class. Her upper incisors were notched and her lowers were notched and then resurfaced. She had a ceramic whistle to accompany her to heaven.

> ❖ **MY MY MAYA TIME**
>
> According to the Maya calendar, each day of the 20-day month had a name and number and each month had a name and number. This resulted in each day having four titles; one for the number and one for the name of the day and then one for the number and one for the name of the month.

About 1.6 miles north of the main plaza is the city of **Actuncan**, which has a 27-meter (88.5-foot) pyramid. A stele found there indicates that the city was the predecessor of Xunantunich.

It was around AD 890-900 that Xunantunich was abandoned. Some believe this was due to an earthquake.

◆ Place to Stay

nice, secluded area
didn't stay - too pricey!

Across the highway from the ruins is the first-class **Royal Maya Resort and Spa**, ☎ 823-2497 or 888-271-3483, www.royal mayan.com, $$$$. Well-kept rooms come complete with TV, private bath, hot water and air conditioning. The spa offers a pool, gym, sauna, Jacuzzi (overlooking the ruins of Xunantunich) and a massage parlor. There is a **restaurant** and bar.

❖ HOTEL PRICING	
$	$10 to $20
$$	$21 to $50
$$$	$51 to $75
$$$$	$76 to $100
$$$$$	over $100

THE WEST

The resort will pick you up at the airport and arrange any type of tour you want, from horseback riding to caving to shopping. Special rates are offered for long stays and all-inclusive packages are possible.

Benque Viejo del Carmen

Benque Viejo del Carmen, Mile 74.5 of the Western Highway, is almost at the end of the road/country. The village of Benque has about 5,000 people and almost all are Spanish-speaking.

◆ History

The Maya living here are from the **Chan Maya**, the last to be subdued by the Spanish. This didn't happen until 1697. After the British came along, logging became the major industry of the area. The name remained Spanish and it means "Old Bank," with bank referring to a logging settlement.

Today, the town has a hospital, town hall, a number of government offices, a post office, church and cemetery. There are a few places to eat and stay, although most people go on to The Trek Stop (see page 164) in San Jose Succotz or into San Ignacio.

◆ Things to Do

The **El Ba'lum Art Gallery**, 43 Churchill Drive, is more of an art museum than gallery. It has many artifacts related to the art world that are of interest, from musical instruments to photographs.

The **Chechem Hah Cave** and **Vaca Falls** are also just south of Benque along the Hydro Dam Road (see page 164).

Poustinia Earth Art Park is three miles out of Benque. Contact David Ruiz, 43 Churchill St. ☎ 823-2084 or 822-3532, www.poustiniaonline.org, for more details. Located on 270 acres of land, this is where artists come to express themselves in the new medium called earth art. Earth art occurs when an artist creates a piece of work and lets the natural world, in this case the jungle, re-work the piece. This is when artist and nature unite in creation.

The two **Eldorado cabins** at Poustinia are fully equipped with stove, kitchen utensils, bed linen and towels. There is running water and generated electricity. A cabin will hold up to six people and the cost is US $30 for two and US $10 for each additional person. Transportation to Poustinia is available at a cost of US $2.50 per person each way. Call ahead.

◆ Shopping

Stonetree Records, 36 Elizabeth Street, ☎ 823-2241, www.stonetree-records.com, is a strong supporter of local music. They maintain a website that gives the history and a review of various Belizean musicians. The site also has a news page with the latest hot stuff on it. It's a good place to stop.

◆ Places to Stay

The Mopan River Resort, Riverside North, ☎ 823-2074, www.mopan riverresort.com, $$$$$, is an all-inclusive resort, meaning that the room, the food, the drinks and the tours are included in the price.

All 12 cabins are hardwood and thatch with large sitting areas, cable TV, fans, mini-bars, in-room safes and double sinks in the bathrooms. The main lodge has a huge open-air deck, where you can enjoy either Thai, Italian, Mediterranean or Mexican dinners. Hors d'oeuvres are served before every dinner, along with your evening cocktail. And homemade cinnamon buns are offered to help sweeten your coffee in the mornings.

There's a swimming pool, a 20-foot birding tower and live entertainment twice a week. You can canoe, kayak, raft or hike independently. One of the excursions included in the price is a day at Tikal, but it is offered only on Tuesdays and Fridays.

Woodland Resort, George Price Boulevard, ☎ 823-2553, $$, has nice rooms with fans. **Maxims Palace**, 41 Churchill Street, ☎ 823-2259, $$, has clean rooms with private baths and hot water. **Maya Hotel**, 11 George Street, ☎ 823-2116, $, has rooms with private bath and hot water.

◆ Places to Eat

Allan's Chinese Rest- aurant, George Price Street, ☎ 823-3275, serves Chinese and Western-style food. The same can be found at **Hai Yan Restaurant** on Kennedy Street, ☎ 823-3262, and the **Hong Mei**, 324 Church Street, ☎ 823-3098. The **Long Lucky Chinese Restaurant** (with grocery store next door) is on George Price Boulevard, ☎ 823-2546.

El Sitio Ice Cream Parlor, 37 Churchill Street, ☎ 823-2138. Stop for an ice cream. It is your first/last chance. The ice cream in Guatemala isn't recommended, but the ice cream in Belize is the best in Latin America.

Directories

◆ General Directory

GENERAL DIRECTORY		
■ **OUTFITTERS, GUIDES & TOUR OPERATORS**		
Belizean Sun Travel	☎ 824-4853 or 603-3271	
Easy Rider	☎ 824-3734 www.belizex.com/easy_rider.htm	
George Luzero	☎ 824-3627	
Manfred Lohr	☎ 824-2276	
Mayawalk	☎ 824-3070	www.mayawalk.com
Peter Herrera	☎ 222-4802	
■ **ATTRACTIONS**		
Belize Zoo	☎ 820-2004	www.belizezoo.org
Caracol Ruins		www.caracol.org
Green Hills Butterfly Ranch	☎ 820-4017	www.belizex.com/green_hills.htm
Monkey Bay Wildlife Sanctuary	☎ 820-3032	www.monkeybaybelize.org
Panti Rainforest Medicinal Trail	☎ 824-3870	www.rainforestremedies.com
Poustinia Earth Art	☎ 823-2084 www.angelfire.com/pe/poustinia	
Tanah Maya Art Museum		www.awrem.com/tanah/experience.html

THE WEST

GENERAL DIRECTORY		
■ TRANSPORTATION		
Safe Tours Car Rental	☎ 824-3731	dcpil@yahoo.com
■ GROUP RESOURCES		
Dept. of Archeology	☎ 822-2106 or 822-2227	
Habitat for Humanity	☎ 227-6818	habelize@btl.net
LABRN Scholarship Foundation	☎ 323-732-0200	
■ SERVICES		
Techno Hub (Internet service)	☎ 822-0061	
■ USEFUL WEBSITE		
Belize Tourism		www.belizetourism.org
■ SHOPPING		
Belize Gift Shop	☎ 824-4159	
Caesar's Palace	☎ 824-2341	www.belizegifts.com
Indita Maya Gift Shop	☎ 824-4346	

◆ Accommodations Directory

PLACES TO STAY		
Aguada Hotel ($$)	☎ 804-3609	www.aguadahotel.com
Aguallos Place ($)	☎ 822-3945	
Almond Hill Motel ($$)	☎ 220-9018	
Banana Bank Lodge ($$$$)	☎ 820-2020	www.bananabank.com
Belmopan Hotel ($$$)	☎ 822-2130	
Black Rock Lodge ($$$)	☎ 824-2341	www.blackrocklodge.com
Blancaneaux Lodge ($$$$$)	☎ 820-3878	www.blancaneaux.com
Bull Frog Inn ($$$)	☎ 822-2111	bullfrog@btl.net
Caesar's Palace $$)	☎ 824-2341	www.belizegifts.com
Casa Blanca Guest House ($$)	☎ 824-2080	
Chaa Creek Resort ($$$$$)	☎ 824-2037	www.chaacreek.com
Clarissa Falls Resort ($$$)	☎ 824-3916	www.belizereport.com/lodging/clarissa
Crystal Paradise ($$$)	☎ 824-2014	www.crystalparadise.com
DuPlooy's Resort ($$$$)	☎ 824-3101	www.duplooys.com
Ek Tun ($$$$)	☎ 824-2002 or 303-442-6150	www.ektunbelize.com
El Rey Inn ($$)	☎ 822-2841	
Five Sisters Lodge ($$$)	☎ 820-4005	www.fivesisterlodge.com
Green Haven Lodge ($$$)	☎ 820-4034	www.ghlodgebelize.com

PLACES TO STAY		
Hidden Valley Inn ($$$$$)	☎ 822-3320	www.hiddenvalleyinn.com
Hi-Et Hotel ($)	☎ 824-2828	
Hummingbird Hills ($$)	☎ 614-4699	www.hummingbirdhills.com
Jaguar Paw Jungle Resort ($$$$$)	☎ 820-3023	
Log Cabins ($$-$$$)	☎ 824-3367	www.logcabins-belize.com
Manfred's Farm B&B ($$)	☎ 824-2276	
Martz Farms ($$)	☎ 824-3742	
Maxims Palace ($$)	☎ 823-2259	
Mayaland Villas ($$$$$)	☎ 223-1409 or 824-2035	www.mayalandbelize.com
Maya Mountain Lodge ($$$)	☎ 824-2164	www.mayamountain.com
Maya Hotel ($)	☎ 823-2116	
Mopan River Resort ($$$$$)	☎ 823-2074	www.mopanriverresort.com
Mountain Equestrian Trails ($$$$$)	☎ 820-4041	www.metbelize.com
Nabitunich Lodge ($$$)	☎ 824-2096	www.nabitunich.com
New Belmoral ($$)	☎ 824-2024	
Pacz Hotel ($$)	☎ 824-4538	
Parrot Nest ($$)	☎ 820-4058	www.parrot-nest.com
Piache Hotel ($$)	☎ 804-2032	
Pine Ridge Lodge ($$$$)	☎ 606-4557	www.pineridgelodge.com
Pook's Hill Lodge ($$$)	☎ 820-2017	www.pookshillbelize.com
Roaring River Lodge ($$$)	☎ 820-2037	
Royal Maya Resort ($$$$)	☎ 823-2497	www.royalmayan.com
San Ignacio Hotel ($$$$)	☎ 822-2034	
Touch of Class Comfort Inn ($$)	☎ 824-4006	www.touchofclasscomfortinn.com
Trek Stop ($)	☎ 823-2265	www.thetrekstop.com
Tropicool Hotel ($$)	☎ 824-3062	
Tropical Education Center ($$)	☎ 220-8003	
Warrie Head Lodge ($$$$)	☎ 227-7185	www.warriehead.com
Woodland Resort ($$)	☎ 823-2553	

THE WEST

◆ Restaurant Directory

PLACES TO EAT	
Aguada Hotel Restaurant ($$)	☎ 806-3609
Allan's Chinese Restaurant (n/k)	☎ 823-3275
Braun's Family Restaurant (n/k)	☎ 823-0196
Bullforg Inn ($$)	☎ 822-2111
Café del Sol ($$)	☎ 822-4899
Caldium Restaurant ($$)	☎ 822-2754
Cheers Restaurant ($)	☎ 614-9311
El Sitio Ice Cream Parlor (n/a)	☎ 823-2138
Erva's Restaurant ($$)	☎ 824-2821
Eva's Restaurant ($)	☎ 804-2267
Fantasy Bar (n/a)	☎ 823-3201
Golden Choice Buffet (n/k)	☎ 823-0421
Green Dragon	☎ 822-2124
Hai Yan Restaurant (n/k)	☎ 823-3262
Hannah's Restaurant ($$)	☎ 822-3647
Hong Mei Restaurant (n/k)	☎ 823-3098
JB's Watering Hole(n/a)	☎ 820-2071
Long Lucky Chinese Restaurant (n/k)	☎ 823-2546
Rong Feng Restaurant (n/k)	☎ 823-2688
San Ignacio Hotel facilities ($$$)	☎ 822-2034
Serendip Restaurant ($$)	☎ 822-2302
Va Yang Restaurant (n/k)	☎ 823-2460

Guatemala

The Belize-Guatemala border is at Mile 76, 1.2 miles from Benque, and you can either take a taxi or walk. Go out St. Josephs Street one block past the cemetery, turn left (south) and follow the road. Most people who cross here make the side-trip to Tikal.

Getting Here

◆ By Air

If it is rainy season, flying is better than traveling overland. You can fly to Flores, Guatemala by **Maya Air** (☎ 800-225-6732, 226-2435, www.ambergrisecaye.com/islandair) or **Tropic Air** (☎ 800-422-3435, 226-2012 in Belize, www.tropicair.com). Both airlines have two flights daily leaving from Belize City for about US $250 return. From Flores, the airlines will arrange ground transportation to Tikal.

◆ Organized Tours

Many tour companies offer trips to Tikal. Most are by van and most go only for one day. This option allows you a fairly knowledgeable tour guide but cuts your time at the ruins to a minimum.

◆ By Car

Driving a rental vehicle requires special insurance. Be certain that you have this before leaving Belize. See page 46 for a full list of rental agencies.

If driving your own vehicle, you will be issued a permit to drive in Guatemala. You must have a valid International, Canadian or American drivers license and registration papers for your vehicle. The Guatemala driving permit is valid for 30 days and can be renewed in major centers (there are no places where you can renew between Tikal and Belize). You can purchase liability insurance in the major centers in Guatemala, but all other coverage must be bought in your home country.

GUATEMALA

◆ By Bicycle

Cycling should be done during daylight hours only. The roads can be rough, so your speed may be slower than the usual six mph. Plan the stages of your trip and pace yourself so that you are in a village before dark. It is 37 miles from Melchor on the border to Los Cruces junction (also called Ixlu Junction) and another 1.2 miles to El Remate. Tikal is an additional 20 miles past Remate. From the border, it is a long cycle in the heat on a gravel road.

Money

Once at the border you can obtain currency with **money changers** or you can go to an **ATM** in Flores. The exchange rate is eight quetzales for one US dollar. Dealing with money changers, you may get a bit less than the going rate at the bank, but the more you exchange, the better the rate. Using US cash for exchange will also result in a better rate than changing Belize dollars or trying to cash traveler's checks.

There is a **bank** on the Guatemala side of the border that is open from 8:30 am to 6 pm on weekdays, but it doesn't have an ATM. There is also a service charge for changing traveler's checks that, if they are American Express checks, will be refunded once you are home. Keep receipts (see page 37, *Banking/Exchange*).

If going to Tikal, you should have enough quetzales to last until you get to a bigger center, such as Flores, or you return to Belize. There are no money changers or banks at Tikal itself and, although the big hotels take charge cards, they will not give you a cash advance. If you plan to visit Flores, you will need money for transportation, food and a room.

Once across the border, you will find everything is cheaper than in Belize, sometimes 50% less. However, there is far more bartering for goods and services. Being a foreigner, you will be expected to pay more.

Customs & Visas

I have always found the border guards from both countries easy to deal with I have never argued with the Guatemalan guard over the service charge must pay for his overtime, but I have often thanked him for not charging me. depends on the guard as to whether you will have to grease his palm and don't know what they use as a determining factor.

Everyone needs a visa to enter Guatemala. Travelers from develope countries like America, Canada and Europe should have no problem gettin one at the border. You simply pay your shekels and away you go. Peopl from developing nations such as Botswana, Yeman, Moldova or Banglades must apply to the Guatemalan Immigration Department for a pre-approve visa. I've always got mine at the border with no problem, but I have heard c others who were turned away. Since this procedure changes periodically, check with the consulate on Church Street in Benque, ☎ 823-2531.

You will be charged an exit fee and a Conservation Fee when leaving Belize, a total of almost US $15. If you plan to return to Belize, keep the receipt for the conservation fee; it need not be paid again if you are leaving for a second time within 30 days.

In Guatemala

◆ Over the Border

Once over the border, **Spanish** is the language so you'd better pull out your dictionary. Buses will be waiting at the border or at the market in Melchor, a short walk away. They go when full or almost full. Also, minivans and taxis go to Tikal and Flores/Santa Elena on a regular basis. The cost is US $10 per person. This is the easiest way to go.

Food is always offered in or near markets. Women have plates of tortillas, sandwiches, fruits, eggs and empanadas. Soda is safe to drink, as is mineral water. The bus driver will stop for bathroom breaks anytime you wish.

◆ Destinations

Decide where you want to go. **Santa Elena** is on the shore of **Lake Petén Itza** and **Flores** is on an island connected to the mainland by a causeway. Flores is the more popular destination. There is every possible class of hotel in Flores and numerous cafés in which to eat and hang out. Tour agencies claim to provide any kind of trip you want, but many can't deliver what they promise.

If you're going directly to **Tikal**, then you have the option of staying in **El Remate**, just 1.2 miles north of El Cruces (if it is light enough you can walk to El Remate from El Cruces) and 20 miles farther to Tikal. Or you can go all the way into Tikal and stay there. There are no accommodations at El Cruces.

Tikal National Park

Tikal National Park occupies 226 square miles of ruins and jungle in the northern Petén region of Guatemala. For me, Tikal is the most mystical place on the planet. Although I haven't been to every interesting site on earth, I found Tikal more special than the Great Wall of China, the Pyramids of Egypt, the temples of Thailand, the monasteries of Tibet, or Machu Picchu in Peru. If you are able to visit early in the morning, just at sunset or during a full moon, you too will come away with a feeling of splendor. I am not the only one who believes that Tikal is splendid – about 25,000 tourists a year come to the park.

GUATEMALA

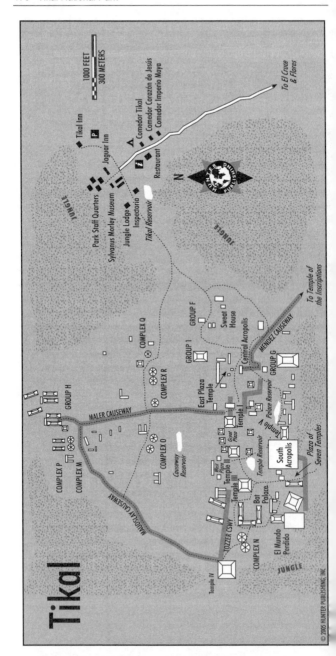

Tikal

Tikal not only has impressive restored pyramid temples in the main plaza, but also some wild jungle that clutches onto parts of the city. Birds and animals hide in these jungles, as do snakes. And the site is huge – it takes hours to walk around the main plazas. If you want to really explore, it takes days.

◆ Exploring the Park

The park covers 142,328 acres and the central city fills 10 square miles. There are 344 people employed in Tikal in positions of administration, resource management, education, research and research assistance. There are also grounds keepers and trail clearers, guards and caretakers. A daily entrance fee of US $10 is collected as you come into the area. If you arrive after 3 pm you will be given a ticket for the next day. Dogs and firearms are not allowed in the park. Parking of a vehicle is US $4 a day. Inside the park you will find three hotels, all of which have restaurants. Besides these eateries there are three *comedores* that offer basic meals at reasonable prices.

AUTHOR NOTE: *Carry water at all times. The atmosphere can be dehydrating.*

The **Sylvanus Morley Museum** is open Tuesday to Sunday, 9 am to 5 pm. Admission is US $2 per person. Morley was an archeologist who worked in the Petén between 1914 and 1928. He was interested in the inscriptions of the Maya and, under the Carnegie Institute of Washington, managed to record many of the works at Piedras Negras and Uaxactun. He wrote two books, *Ancient Maya* (1946) and *Inscriptions of Petén* (1938).

The museum displays artifacts from tombs, such as ceramics and jade, bone and stone carvings. It also has replicas of stelae and friezes from Tikal. But the best exhibit is a reproduction of Temple I, where King **Jasaw Chan K'awiil** was laid to rest upon jaguar and ocelot pelts. There were over 16 pounds (seven kg) of jade jewelry on his body and he wore a cape covered in pink and orange seashells. The original museum was built in 1965 and was called the Tikal Museum. It has since been restored and renamed.

The **visitor center** is at the entrance to the ruins. It has a coffee shop and a gift shop that sells high-end Guatemalan crafts as well as William R. Coe's book *Tikal*, published by the University Museum, University of Pennsylvania, first printed in 1967. I purchased my copy in its 12th printing and that was in 1985. It is still the best guide to the ruins and the one from which I learned the most.

Next to the visitor center is the scale model of Tikal. This is well done. There is also a center holding some of the stone works found at the site.

❖ MAYA TIME
600 BC – Pre-Classic Period starts
AD 250 – Early Classic Period starts
AD 550 – Late Classic Period starts
AD 900 – Post-Classic Period starts

◆ The Ancient City of Tikal

Tikal is the modern name for the city, but a glyph deciphered by Schele and Matthews gives the original Maya name as **Mutul**. They translated this from what they believed to be the city's emblem, the back of a head with hair hanging straight down. The hair is knotted in place with a band of hair that comes from the front and sides of the head.

Tikal was a ceremonial and bureaucratic center. It controlled trade between those living in the Yucatán peninsula and those in the Caribbean. To show their power, the kings of Tikal built monumental temples and great plazas. They had their priests and elite adorned in elaborately designed robes and rich jewelry.

Ball games and human sacrifice were common. Slaves taken in battle and utilized by the kings were considered signs of wealth. Scribes were honored members of the educated classes.

As you enter the ruins of Tikal, a path leads left to the central acropolis, the sweat house and the Mendez Causeway. Veer to the right and you'll pass complexes O, Q and R sitting on each side of the path. The two pyramids (Q & R) were built by Hasaw Chan K'awil to mark the passing of a katun (close to 20 years). Unlike Belize, Guatemala reconstructs its ruins so these two pyramids have, in front of them, reproductions of the stelae and altars that were there centuries ago.

At the end of the path, turn left and walk along the Mailer Causeway to the North Acropolis, where the Great Plaza and Temples I and II are located. Since this site is huge, I will cover only the main temples and a tiny bit of history. If you need more detailed information or want to explore farther, purchase William Coe's book, *Tikal*, sold at the visitor center.

There are over 3,000 buildings in Tikal, some dating to 600 BC and others as recent as AD 900. During its height of power, Tikal had over 100,000 citizens.

The **Great Plaza** has **Temple I** on the east side facing Temple II on the west side. Temple I towers majestically at 170 feet (52 meters) above the plaza floor. It was called the Temple of the Giant Jaguar, so named because of the jaguar carved on one of the lintels and because of the crouching jade jaguar ornament found much later inside the tomb. The temple was built around AD 700, during the late classic period, with nine terraces (nine was a sacred number for the Maya) supporting the building platform and a three-room temple on top. The stairway features high steps that must have been a horrid climb for the short Maya kings and priests, especially when they were dressed in heavy robes.

The temple chambers at the top are corbel-vaulted. Interior wooden beams and the lintels are made of zapote, a rot-resistant wood. Inside, there are handprints on the wall, probably made by a bunch of kids fooling around after the city was abandoned (this is my opinion, not that of archeologists). Below the temple was a grave, and above the grave a pit filled with broken pottery, incense burners and animal bones left by those living in the area after the collapse of Tikal.

In the temple's tomb was Jasaw Chan Kawiil, who was placed at ground level and had the temple built over him. Some of the human bones found here have dates carved on them, the last date being 731. This is close to when archeologists suspect he died.

The ceremonial rooms were also corbel-vaulted. At one time, Temple I had Jasaw Chan Kawiil's face inscribed on the surface.

The tomb was found by a Harvard student working on his thesis. His name was N.M. Hellmuth and, with the luck of a beginner, he found the richest tomb in Tikal. Inside was the jade jaguar, plus 180 other pieces, some jade, some bone. The bone fragments were carved with inscriptions and pictographs of gods in canoes paddling to Maya heaven. The lines of these carvings were filled with cinnabar, a mineral found with mercury.

Once you climb the stairs of the temple you will see Temple II across the plaza to the west with the Central Acropolis beside it. The North Acropolis, built about AD 200, is to the right and the Eastern Plaza is behind you.

Temple II is on the west side of the plaza and stands at only 125 feet (42 meters) above the plaza floor. It is believed that this temple was built before Temple I, because the base is lower than that of Temple I, and that it originally stood at 140 feet (42 meters) above the plaza floor. Temple II is commonly called the Temple of the Masks because of the two masks carved on each side of the third terrace. Of the three lintels on the top, only the center one is carved. Inside there is graffiti. One scene from the graffiti is of a bound victim being impaled by a spear. At the base of this pyramid was the largest stele ever found in Tikal, standing at nearly 12 feet (3.6 meters). Its accompanying altar was also found; both were smashed but have since been restored. To date, no tomb has been found under Temple II.

> **AUTHOR NOTE:** *Although graffiti is usually destructive, that found at the temple is considered historical data.*

The Great Plaza also had two rows of stelae and altars placed along the south boundary. Some of these stones were used to record historical information. Others were plain and were probably covered in plaster and paint. The second stele from the left (Stele P21) on the Great Plaza came from the West Plaza, 330 feet away (99 meters). It was transported without the use of wheels. All told, there were 70 stelae and accompanying altars in this plaza during the late classic period.

Carved stelae were always laid side-by-side with carved altars while plain stelae were always with plain altars. It is believed that when a line of priests and kings declined, the following rulers would destroy the stelae and altars, along with the stories inscribed upon them. Beneath all the stelae and altars were sacrificial items, such as nine pieces of chipped flint, nine pieces of obsidian or nine sea shells.

The North Acropolis is the biggest so far found in the Maya world, with a base covering about 2.5 acres. Started about AD 200, most of the acropolis was used as funeral structures for the elite. Some of these were Jaguar Paw, Curl Nose and Stormy Sky.

Temple IV stands alone beyond the west plaza and is being consumed by the jungle. It is the job of the grounds keepers to hack away at the foliage to allow visitors to see even part of this temple. It's the highest temple in the city, standing at 212 feet (65 meters) above the plaza floor. It is also the one least excavated. Archeologists have estimated that 250,000 cubic yards of material was used to build this temple and its platform. Some of the interior walls are 40 feet thick (12 meters). The hieroglyphs on the lintels say that the building was built around AD 741 and give a record of dynastic successions. There is also a portrait of Jasaw Chan Kawiil with his son Yik Chan Kawiil.

You must climb up jungle vines and rickety ladders to get to the top of Temple IV, but the view is like nothing else you have seen. If you are fortunate enough to be in the area when no one else is around, this is the place to sit and read a book while the monkeys come to entertain you.

Temple V is presently being excavated and restored at the cost of 7.2 million quetzales, a price shared between Guatemala and Spain. The temple stands at 190 feet (58 meters) and has a tiny room at the top measuring 2.5 feet wide (one meter). The rear wall of this room is 15 feet thick (five meters). Another interesting feature of this building is that it has rounded corners.

The Temple of Inscriptions requires a walk through the jungle along the Mendez Causeway. Built around AD 736, the temple is topped by a 40-foot (12-meter) comb covered in hieroglyphs. It is suspected that Yik Chan K'awiil is entombed here.

Lost World (Perdido Mundo) is south of Temple IV. This very high pyramid at one time had four staircases decorated with huge masks. It is worth the climb to look at the rest of the city rising above the green vegetation.

The Plazas were often market places. East plaza, flanking the back of Temple I, is one such place. The **Central Plaza** covers an area of four acres and was built over a 500-year period. The structures around this plaza were used for administrative purposes. To date, five reservoirs have been found. (Proximity to a water source was never an attraction for the Maya when they chose building sites; they probably collected rain water, much the same way people in the area do today.) The two main causeways connecting the plazas and temples of the city are now used as walkways.

A **Sweat House** (near complexes O, Q and R) was used by the Maya for rituals. Priests went there before performing special rites and ball players went there before a game. The **ball court** at Tikal is not very impressive (go to Copán in Honduras to see a really good one). Located between Temple I and the Central Acropolis, the court has been partly excavated and restored.

The Story

Everywhere you walk in Tikal you will find a stele or an altar, a carved lintel or a stone mask. All these items, along with the pottery and stone carvings found in the tombs, tell the story of the Maya in general and Tikal in particular.

We know that the ruler Yax Chaktel Xok, also known as the First Scaffold Shark, died about AD 200. Chak Toh Ichak, Jaguar Claw the 1st, was the ninth ruler of Tikal and he died in 378. He led the city to victory over Uaxactun and died on the day of victory.

We know that Lord First Crocodile, also known as Curl Nose, ruled until 420. He is buried in the North Acropolis. His son Siyal Cahn Kawiil became the 11th ruler.

Tikal suffered under 137 years of war with Calaknul. Of the city's 11 rulers, we know the names of eight. In 554, Lord Water from Caracol and Double Bird of Tikal had a battle and Caracol won. In 562, Tikal was ruled by Lord Lizard Head and he also lost a battle to Caracol.

Tikal went to war in 672 against Dos Pilos under the leadership of Shield Skull, the 25th ruler of the city. Finally, Jasaw Chan Kawiil came to power and won over Jaguar Paw 2nd, the leader of Calaknul. During Jasaw's rule, and his son's rule, Tikal saw the building surge that resulted in Temples I and IV being built. There is an inscription in Temple II that suggests Lady Twelve Macaw, wife of Jasaw, was the ruler.

But then Tikal declined. Wars between cities ended. It could have been due to drought, loss of men at war, pestilence or overpopulation. Whatever the reason, form your own stories as you walk through this mystical place gathering the snippets of information that most interest you.

◆ Places to Stay

Jungle Lodge, ☎ 502-926-1519, $$-$$$, is the most popular place to stay and eat. The bungalows are duplex style, with tile roofs and plaster walls. Outside are decks and a swimming pool. The grounds are well kept, with pathways that lead between the buildings. The restaurant serves the tastiest

❖ HOTEL PRICING	
$	$10 to $20
$$	$21 to $50
$$$	$51 to $75
$$$$	$76 to $100
$$$$$	over $100

meals and the largest portions in the area. It does this at the lowest price. Service is slow in the morning.

Hotel Tikal, ☎ 502-926-0065, $$-$$$, has both rooms in the hotel building and bungalows around the grounds. Hot water and electricity is available from 6 to 11 pm, but this isn't guaranteed as electricity throughout the Petén is sporadic. The restaurant is expensive and the portions are small.

Jaguar Inn, no phone, $-$$, www.lacasadedondavid.com, has cabins, dorms and tenting. If tenting or in dorms, you can rent lockers for your gear. Cabins have large windows, decks, fans, cable TV and hot water in private bathrooms. This hotel has been around for a long time. The **restaurant** here also sells snacks.

El Remate is a small village 20 miles south of Tikal on the east end of Lake Petén Itza. It is home to about 200 families and offers 14 places to stay. Prices range from US $10 to $70 for a double. Camping is anywhere from US $2 to $6. **Casa de Don David**, ☎ 502-306-2190, $, is the most popular choice. His hotel overlooks the lake and the rooms, complete with private baths and hot water, are clean and comfortable. There is a restaurant open daily from 6 am to 9 pm and the meals cost no more than US $5 per person.

◆ Places to Eat

You can eat in any of the three big hotels, or choose from three *comedores*, which have been around since the early 1980s when I first came to Tikal. In those days the first *comedore* served chicken, the second served eggs and the third served chicken or eggs. Now I understand that beans have been added to all three choices. The atmosphere of these little *comedores* is typically Guatemalan.

Also consider **Santa Elena/Flores**, which has a selection of places to stay and eat. The restaurants are great for those wanting to meet people, make connections, and spend a night drinking, exchanging stories and enjoying great food.

Directory

GUATEMALA DIRECTORY		
■ **PLACES TO STAY**		
Casa de Don David	☎ 502-306-2190	
Hotel Tikal	☎ 502-926-0065	
Jaguar Inn	no phone	www.lacasadedondavid.com
Jungle Lodge	☎ 502-926-1519	
■ **INFORMATION**		
Guatemalan Consulate	☎ 823-2531	

The South

You will be using three highways to go south.

The **Manatee Highway**, or **Coastal Highway**, starts at Mile 30 of the Western Highway just west of the Belize Zoo. It leads to Gales Point and then continues south to Dangriga. The road has a rough gravel surface, but I have heard that it may be paved in the near future.

The **Hummingbird Highway** starts at Mile 47.7 of the Western Highway. The route runs past the city of Belmopan and down to Dangriga (also known as Stann Creek) on the coast. The Hummingbird Highway is a paved route.

The **Southern Highway** starts at Mile 48.7 of the Hum-

mingbird Highway and goes south to Punta Gorda on the coast. At Mile 21.3 of the Southern Highway, a road goes off to Placencia, located at the end of a long peninsula. Placencia is approximately halfway along the coast between Dangriga and Punta Gorda. The Southern Highway is paved beyond the Placencia turnoff, but not all the way to Punta Gorda.

Each of the highways has its own set of attractions, from small coastal towns to large cities and nature preserves. Most destinations can be reached by bus, although many travelers enjoy the flexibility of hiring a car and heading out independently to explore.

Along the Highways

◆ Coastal (Manatee) Highway

MILEAGE ALONG THE COASTAL HIGHWAY	
Mile Zero	The turnoff at La Democracia on the Western Highway, where the Coastal (Manatee) Highway starts.
Mile 2.3	**Sibun River Bridge**
Mile 12.8	**Corn House Creek**
Mile 19.6	**Big Creek**
Mile 28.7	**Mullins River Bridge**
Mile 36.1	**Gales Point**

◆ Hummingbird Highway

The mileage is measured from the turnoff on the Western Highway where the Hummingbird Highway starts. Some road signs along the highway are confusing as they start from Belize City. I have started Mile Zero at the beginning of the highway.

MILEAGE ALONG THE HUMMINGBIRD HIGHWAY	
Mile Zero	The turnoff at Guanacaste National Park on the Western Highway, where the Hummingbird Highway starts.
Mile 5	**Roaring River Estate**
Mile 11.4	**Jungle Lodge Caves Branch & Jaguar Creek**
Mile 12.4	**St. Herman's Cave**
Mile 13.6	**Blue Hole National Park**
Mile 14	**Premitus B&B**
Mile 32	**St. Maragaret's Village & Five Blue Lakes National Park**
Mile 46.2	Gales Point turnoff
Mile 48.7	Southern Highway splits from the Hummingbird Highway
Mile 54.7	**Dangriga**

◆ Southern Highway

The mileage is measured from the turnoff on the Hummingbird Highway where the Southern Highway starts. I have started Mile Zero at the beginning of the highway.

MILEAGE ALONG THE SOUTHERN HIGHWAY	
Mile Zero	The turnoff on the Hummingbird Highway where the Southern Highway starts.
Mile 6	**Mayflower Ruins**
Mile 8	**Silk Grass**
Mile 10	**Hopkins Junction to Sittee River**
Mile 12.5	**Sittee River to Hopkins**
Mile 15	**Maya Center/Cockscomb Basin**
Mile 21.3	**Placencia Peninsula**
Mile 42	**Monkey River Town**
Mile 73	**Indian Creek & Nim Li Punit Ruins**
Mile 83.2	**Maya Villages, Lubaantum Ruins, Rio Blanco, Blue Creek**
Mile 100	**Punta Gorda**

The Coastal Highway

Follow the Western Highway from Belize City as far as La Democracia at Mile 29.9 just west of the Belize Zoo. The road crosses many creeks – Corn House Creek, Mahogany Creek, Soldier Creek, Big Creek – on its way to the Caribbean. Citrus fruit trees grow in the fields along the way and rocky limestone cliffs hide unexplored caves.

At Mile 36, you can make a right turn (north) or a sharp left turn (south). The road north goes for 2.5 miles to Gales Point.

◆ Gales Point

Gales Point is a tiny Creole village of about 500 people. It is located on a spit that flows into Southern Lagoon. Staying in Gales Point will give you a unique experience that mixes culture with wildlife. The area has the best turtle nesting grounds in the western world, the best large-bird breeding areas in Belize's south and the purest Garifuna culture in Central America. You have access to both freshwater lagoons and the Caribbean Sea. There are caves in the Peccary Hills and unexcavated Maya ruins close by.

THE SOUTH

History

In the mid-1700s Jamaican refugees, called **maroons**, settled at Gales Point and other isolated places in Belize. They lived quietly, fishing in the ocean and lagoons and gathering food from the nearby jungles. They wanted a peaceful life.

The **Baymen** came to cut the trees. They employed (virtually enslaved) the blacks living in the Belize River, Sibun River area and some of the Maroons of Gales Point. In 1820, a revolt was led by two slaves named Will and Sharper. They managed to stave off their oppressors for over a month. Eventually, the maroons negotiated peace for freedom. Those who came from Gales Point returned to their dwellings and lived quietly, integrating their African culture with that of the Baymen. Today, those people with maroon background are fiercely proud and practice their customs with confidence.

Getting Here

BY CAR: Driving to Gales Point from Belize City is no problem; you can get there in a few hours. However, the road is rough and there are not many services along the Coastal Highway until you reach its end, Gales Point.

BY BICYCLE: Cyclists will find it is a long way to go in one day, especially in the heat. If you decide to do it, be certain to have sustenance and lots of water.

BY BUS: Some Buses use the Coastal Highway to go directly from Belize City to Gales Point. **Richie Bus**, ☎ 522-2130, located at the main terminal in Belize City, runs two buses daily that stop in Gales Point. Other buses take the Coastal Highway to Dangriga without stopping at Gales Point. If you jump on one of these and get off at the turnoff, you must walk the last 2.5 miles to the village.

Still other buses take the Hummingbird Highway to Dangriga. From there, you can catch a second bus to Gales Point. Buses leave regularly from 6 am to 5 pm for Dangriga from Belize City. The cost is US $5. Three buses go from Dangriga to Gales Point each day.

BY BOAT: Boats can be hired in Belize City to take you to Gales Point. The spectacular three-hour trip travels up the Belize River to the Burdon Canal and through the Northern Lagoon. Finally, you down to Gales Point, or go halfway down the lagoon and out to the ocean at Manatee Bar River. You would then follow the coast to the village. Book with a tour operator in Belize City (see page 72).

Things to Do

Gales Point Manatee Community Sanctuary covers 170,000 acres around Gales Point that includes cayes, ocean, beaches, mangrove swamps, tropical and pine forests, lagoons and karst hills. The main purpose of this sanctuary is to protect the manatee. The Northern and Southern Lagoons provide a safe environment. There is freshwater coming in from the Manatee River, Soldiers Creek and Corn House Creek and salt water through the Bar River. The salt water carries fresh food for the manatee.

The Southern Lagoon has a depression, fed by an underground spring, that is believed to be the home of about 50 manatees. It is here that you have the best chance of seeing one, but patience is needed. A manatee can stay underwater for 25-30 minutes before coming up for a breath of air. Manatees exchange 98% of their lung capacity in one breath, which allows them long periods of time between breaths.

Manatees weigh around 1,000 pounds (450 kg) and can be as heavy as 3,000 pounds. They eat about 150 pounds (67 kg) of vegetation a day, most of it sea grass. They hear well. While watching for manatees, listen for the sound of a snorkeler – it could be a manatee breathing. They sound the same.

There are two cayes on Northern Lagoon that are prime nesting places for birds and crocodiles. **Bird Caye** consists mostly of red mangrove and is home to egrets, herons, cormorants and white ibis. The unnamed caye just south of Bird Caye is also a nesting place for these birds, plus the caye hosts the king vulture and the brown booby. Nesting takes place from Mar. to July.

Once nesting is over for the birds, the Morelet's crocodiles move in and nest from December to Feb. After the eggs hatch, young crocodiles can often be seen sunning themselves along the shores.

The hawksbill turtle has prime nesting grounds along the deserted shores of the Caribbean just north of Gales Point. There are about eight miles of un-inhabited sandy beach where 200 hawksbill nests have been found. This is very rare. The largest community found before this was 16 nests. The nesting period for the hawksbill is between June and Aug., but turtles have come ashore as early as Apr. and as late as Oct.

Richard Slusher of Gales Point worked as a researcher with American Biologist Greg Smith and together they established the **Turtle Protection Program**, ww.communityconservation.org/Belize/html, for this nesting area.

To view turtles nesting or hatching you must go to the **Gales Point Tour Guides Cooperative** (no telephone number, ask in town) and hire someone to show you where they are. It is against the law to harass these creatures in any way. If caught doing so, you will be jailed. Remember that Belize jails are very crowded and have no TV.

Ben Loman Cave is a multi-roomed limestone cave with an underground stream running through it. The trip up the lagoon and through the jungle takes three to four hours. The cave is found between the two lagoons and two hills, on the north arm of Jenkins Creek. Be sure to hire a guide for this trip.

Fishing in the Manatee Bar River is excellent (the maroons have been doing it for about 250 years). Tarpon is the best catch but, since you have access to both the freshwater lagoons and the ocean, you can pretty much choose your catch.

Places to Stay

Gales Point Cooperative, no phone; ask in town, $$, has five rooms in a large house on the lagoon. The rooms are all on the second floor so they catch the breeze, and each has two beds and a private bathroom. Food is made by the villagers and eaten in the communal dining room.

❖ HOTEL PRICING	
$	$10 to $20
$$	$21 to $50
$$$	$51 to $75
$$$$	$76 to $100
$$$$$	over $100

There are also rooms in private houses. Miss Alice has two rooms and a large backyard in which to sit. Miss Elain has four rooms and a meeting place for small groups. Miss Iona has four rooms upstairs and Miss Bridget has three rooms on the second floor. All Miss Bridget's rooms have a nice view. Miss Hortense has two rooms with fans. All ladies offer meals with the family.

Gentle's Cool Spot, no phone, on the main road in town where the buses turn around, has basic accommodations that cost less than the private houses. It also has a nice little bar where you can sit and drink while gathering information and making connections.

Manatee Lodge, Box 1242, Belize City, ☎ 877-462-6283 or 220-8040, www.manateelodge.com, $$$, has eight rooms in a large colonial building situated at the very tip of the peninsula. The spacious rooms have hardwood floors and private baths with hot water. The property is huge and encompasses mangrove swamp, savanna and jungle. Canoes are available for guests to use on the lagoons. The **restaurant**, $$$, serves American and Belizean foods and the bar serves great rum punch.

Place to Eat

Orchids Café, ☎ 220-5621, $$, the best place to eat in town, serves good international, Belizean and vegetarian meals. A comfortable deck overlooks the lagoon. Like Gentle's Cool Spot, Orchids is also an information center.

The Hummingbird Highway

To reach the Hummingbird Highway going to Dangriga (as well as the Southern Highway to Punta Gorda) follow the Western Highway from Belize City to Mile 47.7. Mile Zero is at the junction where Guanacaste Park is located.

> **AUTHOR NOTE:** *I have covered **Belmopan** in The West chapter (see page 124) because it is near the junction, at Mile 1.3 of the Hummingbird Highway.*

The Hummingbird Highway, in the heart of the limestone cave country, goes up and down and around curves, beyond which lie rich farmland and citrus groves. There are karst outcrops riddled with caves and numerous wildlife sanctuaries to visit along the way. The road is seal coated as far as Dangriga and is in excellent condition for driving. Travel is relatively fast and traffic is low. However, if cycling, your elbows (not to mention your bottom) would get a bit sore. Seal coating makes for good driving, but is very bumpy for cycling.

◆ Armenia & Vicinity

At Mile 8 is the village of Armenia, where **Garcia's Bunkrooms and Cabanas** will give you fairly basic accommodations. The cost is US $7.50 for a dormitory-style bed and US $25 for a cabana that will hold more than one person. No phone.

Things to Do

Jungle Lodge and Adventure Center, Box 356, ☎ 822-2800, www.cavesbranch.com, $$$$, is at Mile 11.4 of the Hummingbird Highway and .6 miles on a secondary road. On the secondary road, take the left fork part way in. Tucked into 58,000 acres of jungle setting, part of it on the Caves Branch River, this is an adventurer's destination. There are cabanas, dorms or tenting spaces (US $5) for rent. Tours offered at this rustic spot are spectacular. You can take just a place to stay or opt for an all-inclusive package. Buffet-style meals are available: breakfast is US $12 per person and dinner is US $17.

I found the guides working for owner, Ian Anderson, pleasant; I found Ian himself unapproachable. Ian has taken some Canadian mountaineering rescue techniques and adapted them for jungle rescue. He has started the Belize Search and Rescue Organization and trained his guides in both first aid and the skills of rescue.

Their most spectacular trip, called the **Black Hole Drop**, is just as it suggests – a rappel into a sinkhole that drops 300 feet (90 meters). You will spend the night in the sinkhole. First-rate equipment is included in the cost of the trip. Anderson offers easier cave trips, but he is interested mostly in hard-core adventurers.

▶▶ *Return to the Hummingbird Highway. At Mile 12.4 is St. Herman's Cave on the right (west). From the cave you can walk the 1.8-mile trail over to the Blue Hole National Park, where you can swim in a cenote. You can also drive the highway to the Blue Hole.*

 MYSTERIOUS MAYA: *The Maya believed that cenotes were openings to the underworld.*

◆ St. Herman's Cave

St. Herman's Cave is probably one of the easiest caves to visit in all of Belize. To get there (other than by driving or cycling), take any bus from Belize City or Belmopan heading south and ask the driver to let you off at the cave.

Stop at the **visitor center** and pay your US $4 entry fee – good for both the cave and Blue Hole National Park. Managed by the Belize Audubon Society, the area is open from 8 am to 4 pm. If you would like to go all the way through the cave and out a second opening, you will need to hire a guide, available at the visitor center. Near the center are picnic tables and washrooms.

> **AUTHOR NOTE:** *For exploration of this park you will need good walking shoes or boots and a flashlight. Bring a bathing suit too, if you would like to swim.*

First established in 1965 as a tourist attraction, the 575 acres of jungle has seen, at last count, over 7,500 visitors each year. The limestone karst topography features a number of caves joined by underground rivers that eventually flow into the Sibun River.

Hiking Trails

The visitor center, where the **self-guided tour** starts, has numerous displays describing the life cycle of bats found in the area. There are also descriptions of some birds and many of the animals that haunt the forests nearby. If you go only 1,000 feet (300 meters) into the cave, a guide is not required. The honor system is practiced here.

A 10-minute walk along a maintained trail brings you to the small entrance of the high-ceilinged cave. A stairway that was first carved by the Maya leads down into the cave. The entrance is about 60 feet wide (18 meters), but it gets bigger as you walk and the cave's center measures 120 feet across (36 meters). Inside, use a flashlight to follow the trail markers. The gigantic stalactites and stalagmites have taken eons to form; they grow about one inch in 800 years. Tiny cracks in the ceiling of the cave occasionally add an eerie light. With a guide, you can go into the cave and come out at a second opening, where a trail leads back to the start.

From the cave, follow the trail to the hilltop observation tower, where you can spot some of the 200 bird species found in the area. The tower gives you a great view of the surrounding landscape. This is a one-hour walk from the cave. If you want a longer jungle hike, follow the trail to the rear entrance of the cave and back to the visitor center. This will take about three hours, total.

The park has over five miles of trails. If you follow the **Nature Trail** beyond the park border, you will come to Mountain Cow Cave, which can be entered for a few feet (more with a guide). Two trails lead from the cave to the Blue Hole. The **Hummingbird Trail** goes up a steep hill, through lush jungle and over to the change room at the hole. The second trail follows the highway just inside the cover of the forest. On either trail, it is just under two miles from the visitor center to the Blue Hole.

The Blue Hole

The Blue Hole was actually green when I was there. This sinkhole (a cave with its roof caved in) measures 300 feet across and 100 feet down (90 x 30 meters) from the top of the rocks to the pool's bottom. The pool itself is only about 24 feet deep (seven meters).

The water in the sinkhole comes from an underground stream that flows into a cavern, the opening of which forms an odd echo chamber.

Places to Stay

A **campsite**, for those with their own tent, has picnic tables and an outhouse. It is a two-hour, 2.5-mile hike to the site from the visitor center.

Ringtale Village, just south of the Blue Hole, has the **Primitas Farm Bed and Breakfast**, Box 80, Belmopan, ☎ 220-8259, pascott@btl.net, $. It's on the opposite side of the highway. This is a working farm where agronomist Patrick Scott grows produce such as cashew, cocoa, bread fruit, guava, mango and avocado, as well as many different citrus fruits.

The farmhouse has four rooms, each with two twin beds. Two rooms have private baths with hot water. The morning breakfast holds the promise of fry jacks and/or Johnny cake, along with freshly squeezed fruit juice.

Staying at this B & B gives you easy access to the Blue Hole and St. Herman's Cave, as well as the **Sleeping Giant** and **Five Blue Lakes Park**. The Sleeping Giant is a couple of peaks rising above a small waterfall that, from a distance, look like a sleeping person. The hills are shown as part of the watermarks on Belize dollars. This area is 10 minutes from the farmhouse.

Follow the Hummingbird Highway to Mile 18 and turn onto the road for the **Sibun River Rainforest Station**, ☎ 800-548-5843, www.ize2belize.com. The lodge at the station is located on the Sibun River in front of a clear pool. The lodge is in a three-storey building with huge windows and natural woods. There is a dining room, lab, library and observation area. The bathhouse is in a separate building. The area is ideal for birders, cavers, hikers, and cyclists. The cost is US $85 per day, per person, including meals.

▶▶ *Following the Hummingbird Highway south, at Mile 29 you will cross the Hummingbird Gap, the pass leading from the mountains down to the ocean. Turn east at Mile 32 of the highway to St Margaret's Village and Five Blue Lakes National Park. If you are cycling or walking, this place is a must.*

◆ Five Blue Lakes National Park

St. Margaret's Village is the gateway to the national park. To get there by bus, take any southbound bus from Belmopan and ask them to let you off at St. Margaret's. The cost is US $1.50 per person. You can also catch a bus going north from Dangriga (US $2). Driving or cycling from Belmopan can easily be done in a day.

The **visitor center**, ☎ 822-5575, swa@btl.net, for the park is in the village. It's open from 8 am to 4 pm. Since the work in the park is mostly voluntary, the park fees (US $2.50 per day) go totally to maintenance.

Five Blue Lakes National Park was established on Earth Day in 1991. The 4,200 acres of broadleaf forest features a collapsed cave or cenote that covers an area of 7.4 acres and reaches a depth of about 200 feet (70 meters).

In ancient times, the Maya are believed to have used these waters as sacrificial wells (not for humans).

The lake gets its name from the different depths of water that cause the different colors, rather than the number of lakes there are. Surrounding three sides of the lake are hills and limestone rock faces riddled with caves. Maintained trails can be followed from near the visitor center in the village to and around the lake.

Things to Do

One favorite place to visit in the park is an **orchid-rich island**. To reach it, you must walk along a sunken limestone ridge. There is a lookout tower and a changing room near the lake should you wish to swim. The picnic area has a covered shelter and the tenting area has an outhouse.

The **River Trail** crosses and follows the river for a bit and then goes to the **Duende Caves**, where you will find the uncommon lesser dog-like bat hanging near the entrance. They always roost where there is light.

At the very back of the lake are numerous **sinkholes** with walls up to 100 feet (30 meters) high that are decorated in clinging plants. Many caves can be seen with connecting tunnels that run for miles. The possibility of getting lost is very real. Unless you have a guide, do not go far inside. But even a short walk into some of the rooms will be a feast for your eyes.

To date, 167 species of **birds** and over 20 species of **bats** have been spotted here. **Fishers** can try their luck for bay snook and tuba, which hang out near the drainage point of the lake at Indian Creek.

When I was here, the howlers made me nervous with their serenade.

GUIDES

Guides who are knowledgeable in cave exploration, herbal medicine healing methods and local folklore are available at the visitor center. The cost of hiring a guide and equipment runs anywhere from US $50 to $100 per day. If you want to do some very difficult climbing and cave exploration in this region, contact **Manfred Lohr**, ☎ 824-2276, in San Ignacio.

Where to Stay & Eat

At the park's visitor center in the village you can book a room, rent a tent space (US $2.50 per night) or **rent bicycles**, so you need not walk the six miles to the lake. There is also a **canoe** kept locked up at the lake that can be rented from the center; you'll get the key upon payment. You can also opt for a home stay, $$, at the village. The **Hummingbird Tourist Connection**, ☎ 822-2005, handles some of the bookings. The **Hummingbird Cabanas Women's B & B** has over 20 places for visitors to stay. The meals offered by these families are reasonably priced and are authentic dishes belonging to the culture of the host family. You can request a stay with a Maya, Creole, Hispanic or Garifuna family.

▶▶ *Back on the Hummingbird Highway, past St. Margaret's Village (Mile 46.2) and to the left/north, is the turnoff to Gales Point. Another 2.5 miles to the right (south) is the turnoff to Placencia and Punta Gorda. The road straight ahead goes for six miles to Dangriga. This section of the road is surrounded mostly by citrus fruit farms that were established by the end of World War II. They now account for almost 15% of the nation's total citrus production.*

AUTHOR NOTE: *The sacks you see covering bananas hanging on the trees are to prevent the fruit from insect damage.*

◆ Dangriga

Dangriga, with a population of about 10,000, is at the end of the Hummingbird Highway and on the ocean. It's bordered by Stann Creek to the north and Havanna Creek to the south. Populated mostly by Creole and Garifuna, Dangriga becomes nicer the farther into the town you go.

AVERAGE TEMPERATURES & RAINFALL		
	Daily temp.	**Monthly rainfall**
JAN	75.6°F/24.2°C	11 inches/27.9 cm
FEB	78.4°F/25.3°C	8 inches/20.3 cm
MAR	79.3°F/26.3°C	6 inches/15.2 cm
APR	81.5°F/27.5°C	4 inches/10.2 cm
MAY	83.5°F/28.6°C	7 inches/17.8 cm
JUN	83.8°F/28.8°C	14 inches/35.6 cm
JULY	83.3°F/28.5°C	16 inches/40.6 cm
AUG	83.5°F/28.6°C	16 inches/40.6 cm
SEPT	83.3°F/28.5°C	18 inches/45.7 cm
OCT	80.0°F/26.7°C	15 inches/38.1 cm
NOV	78.1°F/25.6°C	14 inches/35.6 cm
DEC	80.1°F/27.2°C	12 inches/30.5 cm

Source of above data: Historical and current records at the Melinda Forest Station situated nine miles from Dangriga Town in the Stann Creek District.

THE SOUTH

History

Alejo Benni was an escaped slave living in Cristales Village, Honduras in 1823 when he and others sided with the Spaniards during an uprising. Fearing for reprisals, he and 27 other adults and 12 kids hopped into a couple of dugout canoes and headed across the Bay of Honduras toward Belize. Two days later, while paddling along the shore, they saw some clear creek water flowing into the ocean. They stopped and drank.

Benni called the water **Dangreugeu Grigeu**, or "Standing Creek." The name was shortened to Stann Creek by the British and it wasn't until Independence that it was changed to Dangriga.

Prior to the arrival of the Benni clan, there were a few English settlers living in the area, trading with the native Indians and growing vegetable gardens. They neither resisted nor welcomed the arrival of the Garifuna.

Getting Here

BY CAR OR BICYCLE: Take the Hummingbird Highway. By bus, you can travel by the Hummingbird or the Coastal Highways. Southern Bus Company bus leaves from Belmopan at 8:30 am daily and costs US $3. From Belize City, a bus leaves every hour from 6 am until 5 pm from the main terminal and costs US $5. These buses stop at Belmopan to pick up passengers.

BY AIR: The two local airlines (**Tropic Air**, ☎ 800-422-3435, and **Maya Air**, ☎ 522-2659) offer five flights a day. Flights cost US $46.50 one way.

BY BOAT: If going to the cayes from Dangriga, go to the southern bank of Stann Creek across from Riverside Restaurant and talk to the men who have **boats** for hire. I did not negotiate my trip to the cayes from here so I have no recommendations.

> **AUTHOR NOTE:** *The grass seen along the road that looks like sugar cane is actually elephant grass.*

Things to Do

Garifuna Settlement Day is Nov. 19th, but is celebrated on the weekend closest to the 19th. It is the biggest party in all of Belize. If you are in the area on this date, book a hotel ahead of time and join the festivities. Starting the night before the celebration is the Garifuna drum and "jump up" (dance), which lasts until just before dawn. Every barbeque barrel in the district is hot and cooking something authentic. Everyone in town is "dragging the gut" (drinking beer), eating and dancing to the beat of the Punta drum.

It is said that the women, when dancing, can do up to 200 hip rolls a minute. Some call this provocative, some call it back-breaking. It is supposed to be a re-enactment of the cock-and-hen mating dance, where the one dancer tries to outdo the other. It should also be noted that there are about 20 women to each man doing this dance.

Traditionally, the music was composed by women who sang about cheating husbands, sick kids, oppressive landowners and any other social commentary that came to mind. The music has a repetitious double-metered beat and the singers do a call-and-answer type of song.

At dawn dugout canoes are loaded with food, drink, drums and masked people dressed in brightly colored traditional clothes. They paddle to the shores of Dangriga, climb out of the boat and ask officials if they can settle on the land. Permission is given and they go to the church where they celebrate their arrival in exuberant chants and music. After that, the real party begins, with more food and drink and a parade with bands and flower-decked floats.

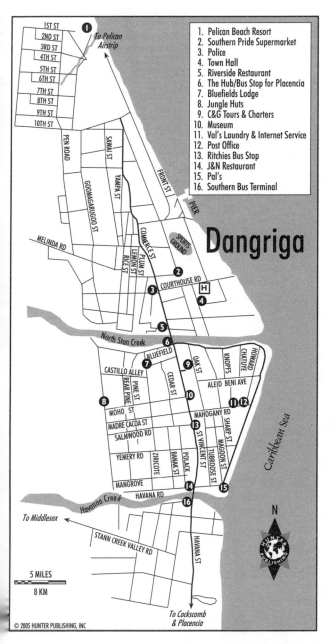

1. Pelican Beach Resort
2. Southern Pride Supermarket
3. Police
4. Town Hall
5. Riverside Restaurant
6. The Hub/Bus Stop for Placencia
7. Bluefields Lodge
8. Jungle Huts
9. C&G Tours & Charters
10. Museum
11. Val's Laundry & Internet Service
12. Post Office
13. Ritchies Bus Stop
14. J&N Restaurant
15. Pal's
16. Southern Bus Terminal

Dangriga

THE SOUTH

5 MILES

8 KM

© 2005 HUNTER PUBLISHING, INC

❖ PUNTA ROCK

Punta Rock was started in 1980 in Dangriga by Pen Cayetanno, a self-taught musician and painter born in 1954. He played music in Mexico and Guatemala before he realized the uniqueness of his own culture. He came home, and together with Mohobub Florez, Myme Martinez, Bernard Higinio, Peter Jeep Lewis, Faltas Nolberto and Calypso Lopez, put a band together. They quickened the sound of the traditional music they remembered from childhood, added an electric guitar and some turtle shells and three years later were recognized at the International Jazz Festival in New Orleans. Cayetano's studio is at 74 St. Vincent Street and he invites music and art lovers to visit.

RECORDED PUNTA MUSIC: The following are just a few artists whose CDs you may enjoy. The most famous for all Punta Music is **Andy Palacio's** *Til Da Mawnin*. Another is *Keimoun*. **Cayetano's** recordings are *In Mi Country, Sweet Africa, Punta Rock* and *The Beginning*. **Brad Pattico's** recordings are, *Ethnic Boon n Chime* and *Belizean Boom n Chime Band*. Another famous Punta Rock recording artist is **Nelson Gil**. His albums are *Baila Punta* and *Giving My Love*. Almost as famous as Palacio is **Mohobub**. Traditional women's songs are recorded in the CD called *Garifuna Women Voices*, which includes music from Belize, Guatemala and Honduras.

If you're interested in going birding in the area, contact **Birding Pals**, www.birdingpal.org, the birders' networking group. There is a Birding Pal in Dangriga. You can read more about the group and its history on page 87.

Gra Gra Lagoon is just two miles south of Dangriga and is good for birding. Go to the beach in town and head right (south) until you come to a fairly decent-sized creek flowing into the ocean. Yemeri Creek borders private property. Do not cross it, but head upstream to the lagoon. Gra Gra is a small lagoon and estuary that is the nesting site of numerous birds. The lagoon is under protection for both birds and crocodiles. The walk will take about an hour.

You can cycle to **Mayflower ruins**, a total of 15 miles each way. See *The South*, page 198, for a description of the ruins. The ruins themselves are not spectacular but the jungle is and bird sightings are good.

TOUR AGENCIES

C & G Tours and Charters, 29 Oak Street, ☎ 522-3641, cgtours@btl.net, $$, has tours to the reef and the ruins. A city tour that includes a visit to a drum crafting shop, a Garifuna Temple, a cassava farm, a hot sauce factory and the Green Bottle Winery is recommended. You may also get to meet a Bouyei (High Priest) at the temple. This is a full day's tour for US $50.

C & G also specializes in a **Mayflower Bocawina National Park** trip. Go with them if you don't want to do it yourself. They will point out birds and plants, animal prints and animals that may not be spotted by the untrained eye. They offer two hikes; one goes along Silk Grass Creek to a waterfall and takes only half an hour. The second, the **Antelope Falls Trail**, is a moderately strenuous climb with an elevation change of 300 feet (100 meters). Once at the falls, those with energy to spare can climb to the top of the mountain. The best feature of this tour company is their cultural knowledge.

Shopping

Garifuna culture is represented in the **Gallery of Benjamin Nicholas**. Nicholas is one of Belize's most famous artists.

Besides Nicholas's works, drums made by **Austin Rodriguez** are on display. The gallery is located at 32 Tubroose Street, ☎ 502-3752, and is open from 8:30 am to 4:30 pm every day, except Sunday. For authentic Garifuna foods, **Mrs. Felicia Nunez**, 5 Southern Foreshore, ☎ 522-2385, has been recommended. **Mrs. Williams**, another famous artist in Dangriga sells handmade baskets and hats. **Sabal's Farm** (just out of town) makes cassava bread for purchase. Eating cassava bread at least once is a must while in the south.

Places to Stay

Chaleanor Hotel, 35 Magoon Street, ☎ 522-2587, chaleanor@btl.net, $$, is one block west of the main post office. The hotel is clean and comfortable with friendly hosts. A new section has spacious rooms with private baths, hot water and tiled floors. The rooftop **restaurant** and bar serves good

❖ HOTEL PRICING	
$	$10 to $20
$$	$21 to $50
$$$	$51 to $75
$$$$	$76 to $100
$$$$$	over $100

food, both international and Belizean, at reasonable prices. During high season Garifuna drummers perform at the hotel.

Jungle Huts, 4 Ecumenical Drive, ☎ 522-3166, $$, has 10 rooms, all with private baths and hot water. Located some distance from the beach, this is a good place to stay if you need a touch of quiet, especially during the Settlement Day celebrations.

Bonefish Hotel, 15 Mahogany Street, ☎ 522-2243 or 800-798-1558, www.bluemarlinlodge.com, $$$, is just up from the waterfront. The rooms have fans and private baths with hot water.

Pelican Beach Resort at the north end of Dangriga, ☎ 522-2044, www.pelicanbeachbelize.com, $$$$. All rooms are on the second floor of the main building and have private baths with hot water, telephones, cable TV and air conditioning or fans. A second building, also of colonial design like the main one, has eight additional rooms.

There is a beachfront **restaurant** and bar, a gift shop and an interesting aquarium in the lobby. The restaurant offers numerous seafood and vegetarian dishes. In the morning, complimentary coffee is usually ready by 5:30 am. A sister hotel is located on South Water Caye, just 14 miles from Dangriga.

THE SOUTH

Bluefield Lodge, 6 Bluefield, ☎ 522-2742, $$, comes highly recommended by more than one traveler I met. The rooms are clean and most have private bathrooms with hot water. Some rooms have TVs.

Pal's Guest House, 868 A Magoon Street, ☎ 522-2095 or 522-2365, $$, palbze@btl.net, has rooms set right on the beach. All have private baths and hot water, as well as fans and TVs. There are also rooms in the older building suitable for budget travelers. Only some of these have private bathrooms.

Places to Eat

The Riverside Restaurant on Stann Creek near the bridge is open every day except Sunday. It offers a plate of Creole foods for less than US $5.

J & N Restaurant, 18 Havana Street, ☎ 522-2649, is a new place just opposite the bus station. It has great meals and, judging from what I heard, is the best eatery in Dangriga.

Other Services

Val's Laundry and Internet Café, 1 Sharp Street, ☎ 502-3324. This is a great concept – do your laundry while communicating with those at home (although Internet access is expensive). Val's is kitty-corner to the Bonefish Hotel.

The Southern Highway

To follow the Southern Highway that goes from the Hummingbird Highway to the southern tip of Belize, join the road that is six miles west of Dangriga. There is a service station on the corner. The junction will be considered Mile Zero. It's not paved all the way to Punta Gorda, but the unpaved part is only about nine miles. The road should be completed by the time this book is published.

This is the road that will take you to the Jaguar Preserve, Sittee River, Hopkins and numerous wildlife preserves. You can also catch a ferry to either Guatemala or Honduras from Punta Gorda.

Follow the Southern Highway for six miles and turn right (west) to the Mayflower ruins. After 4.5 miles on the secondary road you will come to the Mayflower. The ruins and surrounding 7,100 acres have recently been made into a national park called the **Mayflower Bocawina National Park**. Bocawina is the mountain seen beyond the ruins.

◆ Mayflower Ruins

Mayflower is a small site that has been partially excavated. It has two **pyramids**. One had a large amount of sand and boulders brought in to make the base for numerous platforms. This was topped with a thatched-roof ceremonial building. In front of this pyramid, known as Maintzunun (meaning small

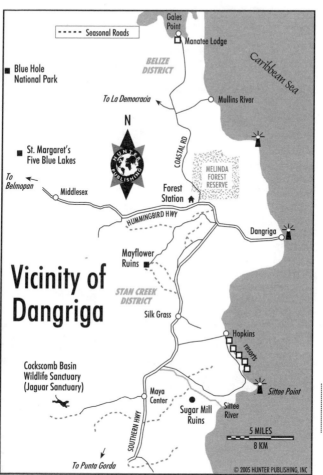

Vicinity of Dangriga

Legend and labels:
- - - - Seasonal Roads

Gales Point
Manatee Lodge
Blue Hole National Park
BELIZE DISTRICT
Caribbean Sea
To La Democracia
Mullins River
N
HUNTER PUBLISHING
St. Margaret's Five Blue Lakes
COASTAL RD
MELINDA FOREST RESERVE
To Belmopan
Middlesex
Forest Station
HUMMINGBIRD HWY
Dangriga
Mayflower Ruins
STAN CREEK DISTRICT
Silk Grass
Hopkins
resorts
Cockscomb Basin Wildlife Sanctuary (Jaguar Sanctuary)
Maya Center
Sugar Mill Ruins
Sittee River
Sittee Point
SOUTHERN HWY
To Punta Gorda

5 MILES
8 KM

© 2005 HUNTER PUBLISHING, INC

hummingbird), was a pit where offerings to the gods were burned. During one of the later phases of occupation, the buildings at this pyramid were destroyed by fire. The second pyramid is much smaller and has just one level. It is called T'au Witz, which means Place of the Local God of the Hill. A small stele and altar were found here, along with some pottery shards.

A Place to Stay

Next to the ruins is **Mama Noots Jungle Resort**, ☎ 422-3666, www.mamanoots.com, $$$, tucked into 50 acres under Bocawina Mountain. The cabanas all have screens on the windows, fans, private baths with hot water and, from each balcony, a view of Antelope Falls. One cabana has two rooms that sleep three people each. Meals can be included or separate.

The best thing about being here is that **jungle hiking** starts at your cabin. You can visit **Three Sisters Falls**, a natural waterslide that is good for tubing (tubes can be rented from Mama Noots). You can also take the rewarding hike along Silk Grass Creek to Antelope Waterfalls. If you want a long day hike, a trail goes from the lodge up Back Ridge Creek. All hikes in this area will result in numerous bird and animal sightings. The resort also runs horse and buggy rides around the area for those interested.

▶▶ *Return to the Southern Highway and drive/cycle to the village of Silk Grass. This is at Mile 8.* **Silk Grass** *is a small community of fewer than 500 people. It has a medical center, church, school and some houses. Silk grass is what people once used to make rope.*

Continue along the Southern Highway to Mile 10 and a secondary road called Hopkin's Junction. This is the turnoff to Hopkins. The secondary road heads east, makes a half circle through Hopkins four miles from the turnoff, and turns south past a strip of luxury hotels to Sittee River. It then goes west to join the Southern Highway, again just 2.5 miles south of Hopkin's Junction.

◆ Hopkins

Hopkins has a population of about 1,000 people. For a restful time, a good introduction to the Garifuna culture and finally the possibility of trying some Garifuna food, plan a stop at Hopkins. If your time there is during a festival or on a Saturday night, you will be especially lucky as the local people are receptive to strangers joining them while they drum and dance to Punta Rock.

Hopkins has one main street that goes north and south along the coast. The secondary road leading from the Southern Highway comes into the village at the center of this road. If you would like to learn more about the town, visit www.hopkinsbelize.com

History

Originally, a community called Newtown, settled in the 1800s, was located a few miles to the north of present-day Hopkins. But a hurricane hit in 1942 and demolished that town, so the residents moved a bit south and renamed the town after a bishop who had drowned in the area 20 years before. Since the town was built, little has changed; the people are still fishers and farmers who work all week, socialize on the weekends, and go to church on Sundays.

Getting Here

BY BUS: Three **Southern Bus Line** buses go into Hopkins from the junction on the Southern Highway. They pass through Hopkins and Sittee River each day at 12, 3 pm and 5 pm. You can also catch any bus going south and get off at Hopkin's Junction; anyone with a vehicle will give you a ride into town.

BY BICYCLE: Cycling is safe and easy.

> ❖ **GRACIOUS GREETINGS**
>
> When greeting anyone after 2 pm in Belize, you should say,
> "good evening." If greeting anyone after dark, you should say,
> "good night." North Americans find it hard to use "good night" as a
> greeting, and find 2 pm a bit early to be saying "good evening."

Things to Do

There is not much to do in Hopkins except hang out at the beach, eat, drink,
rest and enjoy the Garifuna culture. However, the **bamboo** stands around
the area are worth a look. Walk along any stretch of road and you will see
them. You can also rent a **kayak** and paddle up or down the coast and up
Boom Creek to spot some birds. The **jungle trips** are always spectacular.
You can also cycle to **Mayflower ruins** or take a taxi for US $12.50 to the
Jaguar Preserve and hike their trails (see page 207 for a full description of
this unique preserve).

Just across from Tipple Tree Beya at the south end of the village is
Hopkins Laundry, with a variety store next door.

Jungle Dunes Golf Course is located at the Jaguar Reef Lodge, just one
mile south of the village. It is a challenging par three course. The par three
holes average 150 to 200 yards, all built on natural sand dunes surrounded
by jungle. The new clubhouse has a bar and restaurant. Clubs are available
for rent and a practice green allows for warm-up. The greens fees are about
US $40 per person. Call the Jaguar Reef Reserve, ☎ 800-289-5756, to
make reservations.

You may see black and white t-shirts for sale in town. They cost US $10
and the profits go toward the **School Book Awards**. These awards are given
to students with the best essay. The title of the essay must start with "Why I
deserve." Besides winning the essay contest, a student must have a year of
high marks in all subjects to win the prize, which is US $100.

> **AUTHOR NOTE:** *The water supply in Hopkins can be disrupted at
> any time, so it is advisable to always keep a full bottle. The water,
> when running, is chlorinated and safe to drink from the tap.*

Equipment Rentals

Many places offer bikes and kayaks to their guests, but **Tipple Tree** (see below) actually rents bicycles to one and all for US $15 a day and kayaks for
US $20 a day. **Jungle Jeanies** (☎ 523-7047) also offers kayaks for US $20
a day.

Nightlife

It is best to be in Hopkins during the weekend, when you are more likely to
run across a fund-raising party that could feature a local band. If some sort of
sports game has ended, there's usually a party. All nightlife includes Punta
Rock.

THE SOUTH

The Watering Hole Bar and Tropical Inn, in the center of town (no phone), has pool tables to help wile away the hours. Although these are popular bars with the locals, they don't rock until all hours, except on Saturday night.

Places to Stay

IN HOPKINS

Tipple Tree Beya, ☎ 520-7006, www.tippletree.net, $$, is near the south end of the village on the beach. The comfortable cabins have private bathrooms with hot water, fans and hardwood floors. Each cabin has a coffee maker, a fridge to keep the beer cold and a verandah from which to watch the ocean. Owner Trish Sturman is a strong supporter of local culture.

❖ HOTEL PRICING	
$	$10 to $20
$$	$21 to $50
$$$	$51 to $75
$$$$	$76 to $100
$$$$$	over $100

> ### ❖ TIPPLE TREE WHAT?
>
> **Tipple Tree Warri** is an African/Caribbean pit and pebble game. Boards are available at Tipple Tree Beya and Trish will help you learn the game. The board has two rows of six warri (houses) that are actually indentations in a hardwood board. Each player has 24 pebbles or seeds; four are placed in each warri. The players take turns moving in a counterclockwise direction. No dice are used. Each player can move only the seeds on his side of the board. A player starts by moving four of his seeds. The idea is to keep the warris with more than two or three seeds. If the seeds are moved and there are one or two seeds in the warrie, then the seeds are captured. When all six warries are empty on a player's side, his opponent must move so as to give up seeds. If a player captures all his opponent's seeds, he wins the game.
>
> The game is so complicated that I don't quite understand my own and Trish Sturman's instructions. However, it is fun to play. Be sure to try it while in Hopkins.

The Hopkin's Inn, ☎ 523-7013, www.hopkinsinn.com, $$, sits on the beach. These two cabins can hold eight people and a new cabin (in process) will hold four more people. The white stucco cabins with red tile roofs are exceptionally clean and comfortable. They feature hardwood floors, fridges, coffee makers, private baths and fans, as well as screened windows. Breakfast of coffee, fruit and homemade bread is included in your room rate. German is also spoken.

Ransoms Cabanas, ☎ 523-2289 cabanabelize@hotmail.com, $$, has two cabins with two beds in each, kitchens, cable TV, radios, and seaside showers on their private beach. There is also a well-kept garden and a book exchange. Bicycles and kayaks are available for guests.

Jungle, ☎ 523-7047, $$, jungle@btl.net, has cabins on stilts with comfortable porches. The windows are screened, the beds are single and the private bathrooms have hot water. The cabins are close to the ocean. There is also **camping** space available for US $7.50 per person. The owners have windsurf boards and kayaks for rent.

Lauruni Cabins, $$, on the north side of the road, are also basic, but they are a good deal. The clean rooms come with a double and a three-quarter-sized bed, good for three people (four if two kids share the three-quarter-sized bed), private baths with hot water, fans and cable TV. If no one is there when you arrive, go to Innies Restaurant and ask for Marva.

Caribbean View, ☎ 523-7050 $/$$, just north of the police station, has eight rooms at different levels of comfort. There are basic rooms with shared bath, spacious rooms with private baths and hot water, and beachfront cabins. All have fans and sitting areas (some just a small table with chair). Rates can be negotiated for long-term stays.

Heartland Inn, ☎ 523-7153, $$, on the beach, has two cabins with private baths, hot water, fridges and screened windows.

La Furaru Weyu, ☎ 614-2069, $$, has rooms on the beach. Each has a private bath with tiled floors, twin beds and fans.

Wabien Guest House, ☎ 523-7010, $$, has singles or doubles with private bathrooms and fans. The owners are eager to make you feel welcome and will prepare authentic Garifuna food for you if you contact them ahead of time.

SOUTH OF HOPKINS

Hamanasi, Box 256, Dangriga, ☎ 520-7073 or 877-552-3483, www.hamanasi.com, $$$$, is set on 17 acres with 400 feet (125 meters) of groomed beachfront. There are eight beachfront rooms, four beachfront family suites and four tree house cabanas in the forest. The rooms are spacious. All have eight-foot porches, fans, screened windows, air conditioning, hardwood furnishings, local folk art and tiled bathrooms with hot water.

A 50-foot freshwater pool sits in front of the colonial-style restaurant and reception center. There is a wrap-around porch and a patio on the roof. Included in the price is a breakfast of fresh fruit, juice, tea/coffee and a basket of fresh bread. The bar serves everything, including imported wines. Dinners, $$$, are served on tables decked out with crisp linen and fresh flowers.

Two-tank daytime dives are available for US $70, and there's also a PADI certified instructor, diving courses and a dive shop. Dive trips usually head north of Tobacco Caye and include such sites as The Cathedral, South Cut, Carrie Bow Ridges, South Water Wall and The Abyss. Night dives are also offered and bikes and kayaks are available for guests.

Jaguar Reef Lodge, ☎ 800-289-5756, www.jaguarreef.com, $$$$$, has exquisite white stucco and thatched cabins (14 in all) tucked inside a garden. Each spacious room has tile floors, mahogany furniture, a mini-bar and fridge and hot water in the private bathroom. There's a private pool and bikes and kayaks are supplied. In the evenings you can watch the stars through their Ultima 2000 computer-driven telescope. The restaurant, $$$, serves both local and international dishes.

Pleasure Cove Lodge, ☎ 520-7089, www.pleasurecovelodge.com, $$$, is a tiny place with only five rooms placed around a pool. Each room has a TV and VCR, private bath, tiled showers, air conditioning and fans. The owners offer bikes, kayaks and golf carts for guest use. There's an on-site bar and restaurant, $$$, which features international or Belizean cuisine.

Pleasure Cove can arrange many types of tours, but they specialize in fishing – fly, spin or trolling. They know the location of the best permit flats in the world (not far from the lodge).

Beaches and Dreams, $$, ☎ 523-7078, www.beachesanddreams.com, $$$, is two miles south of Hopkins, right on the beach. It has four luxury rooms with hardwood floors and walls, 14-foot ceilings, rattan furniture, fans, verandahs and private bathrooms with hot water. Guests are offered complimentary use of kayaks and bicycles.

It is the Canadian hospitality and the food, $$$, that is the draw to this place. I heard about the meals long before I came here. Their menu includes waffles with Canadian maple syrup, shrimps on skewers and numerous kebabs. The seafood dinner is also popular. Dessert is a must – fried bananas. Even if you are not staying here, try to stop in for a meal.

Places to Eat

❖ RESTAURANT PRICING	
$	under $5
$$	$5 to $10
$$$	$11 to $25
$$$$	$26 to $50
$$$$$	over $50

You can eat in someone's home as long as you order ahead. Meals seldom cost more than US $10. **Wabien Guest House** will also take special requests. Hopkins is one of the best places to get typical Garifuna food, such as areba, bundiga, tapau or sere. What are they? You'll have to try them and let me know what you think.

Another option is to take a stroll or cycle down the beach to one of the bigger hotels, like **Beaches and Dreams**, where the food is legendary.

Sarita the Sweet Bun Lady supports herself and her children with her backyard baking. Be certain to buy one of her pastries. Ask in town which is her place.

Wine made by residents from local fruits and berries is worth seeking. A bottle from grape concentrate is about US $5 and one made from local fruits and berries is about US $9.

Iris' Place, north of town on the main drag, serves the best breakfast, lunch and supper, all of which can be enjoyed on a nice porch. The hamburgers are small and require two to satisfy some appetites. The fries are delicious.

Innies Place is farther north than Iris', but offers similar food and service. Getting special dishes is possible as long as you let them know ahead of time. It is best to go either the day before or in the morning of the day you would like a meal and let them know what you want and when you will want it. Ask a local to point out Innies' house.

Marva's, close to the center of town, is the other good place to eat. If you get tired of Iris' or Innies' then switch to Marva's. Innies', Iris' and Marva's are establishments owned and operated by local people. They are all good, and I recommend them.

◆ Sittee River

Continue past the resorts south of Hopkins for about four miles to Sittee River, a tiny Creole community located on the deepest river in Belize. The Sittee estuary heads inland for 10 miles from the Caribbean Sea. Here, you'll see freshwater fish and plants near the surface and manatees, stingrays and saltwater fish in the deeper water.

The Sittee, host to so many interesting birds and animals in its green waters, is my favorite river in Belize.

Getting Here

BY BUS: Three **buses** (Southern Bus Lines) go from Hopkins Junction through Hopkins and past Sittee River each day. They come by the junction at noon, 3 and 5 pm. The road is rough gravel dotted frequently with potholes.

Things to Do

Paddle up the Sittee River and look for manatees, toucans, crocodiles, stingrays and green or orange iguana. The river is wide and slow and should be paddled early in the mornings when there are more birds and animals around. There are also the **Betsy Snowdon** and **Sapodilla lagoons** to visit. Paddling downriver, past the gas station, you will see a small channel on the right (south). This leads to the Betsy Snowdon Lagoon, where numerous birds nest. Since this is not an often-visited lagoon, your chances of spotting wildlife are better than they are in many other places. You can continue through the lagoon to the mangrove swamps near the ocean and then up the ocean to Sapodilla Lagoon. As you paddle these lagoons, the highest mountain to the south is Victoria Peak, now recognized as the second-highest mountain in Belize (Doyle's Delight is the highest).

To return, paddle into the ocean and then back up the river to your starting point. Visiting both lagoons would be an all-day excursion. Be certain to take water and food.

Canoes can be rented from Glover's Guest House (☎ 520-7099, beside the dock) and at Toucan Sittee (☎ 523-7039, birdcity@btl.net).

Miss Minn (Minerva McKenzie), ☎ 523-7072, an herbal specialist and snake doctor, lives next door to Glover's Guest House. You can order meals from her if staying in Lamont's dorm. The food is Creole, spicy and good. You need to order a few hours ahead of time.

THE SOUTH

Possum Point Biological Station is on the opposite side of the river from Glover's Guest House, so you need a boat for access. The station is on 23 acres of land and is used mostly by scientists and educational groups. However, you are more than welcome to paddle across and walk along the one mile of **trails** they have going through the jungle.

Serpon Sugar Mill is now a park with a cut trail that leads to the mill. The path starts 1.8 miles east of the Southern Highway and .6 miles west of Sittee River. A strangler fig near the mill has a 100-foot circumference. The mill was functioning in the 1860s and the main piece of machinery to see from that era is a steam-powered cane crusher made in Richmond, Virginia. The mill, which was originally operated by an ancestor of Belikin Beer's Bowan family, is the oldest in the country.

You can **sail to Glover's Reef** on the Lamont family's sailboat, which was built in the 1850s by Jones Dock & Co. in Belize City. Constructed out of sapodilla and pine wood, the vessel was made to carry sand to construction sites along the coast. It is used during calm weather to sail to Glover's Reef. It carries up to 50 people and the trip can take anywhere from four to six hours one way, depending on the weather. The cost is US $50-75 per person.

Second Nature Divers, Box 91, Dangriga, ☎ 523-7038, www.belizenet. com/divers.html, is based on the Sittee River close to its mouth. The people here specialize in diving trips to South Water Caye Marine Reserve, but they also like the Grand Channel, Hole in the Wall, The Crack and Elkhorn Crossing. For more experienced divers, they offer a run to Sharks' Cave, where black tip and grey reef sharks can be found.

Second Nature has equipment for rent, offers lessons and can arrange for any land tours you may want. It will also make reservations for you at different cayes.

Places to Stay

Glover's Guest House, ☎ 520-7099, $, owned by the Lormont family, is beside the dock and next door to Miss Minn's. The house offers dormitory-style accommodations and can sleep 13 people. Each bed has a mosquito net. The property is hospital-clean and there is a shower house next to the dorm. You can also camp on the grounds if you have a tent. There are canoes for use. Again, in my opinion, exploration of the river is a must.

If a dorm is not what you want, stop at the **Toucan Sittee**, ☎ 523-7039, birdcity@btl.net, $, next door (walk along the roadway from Lomont's toward Hopkins). The hotel is clean, tidy, and friendly. It features five rooms, all different. The dorm has five single beds, each for US $9.50. One room has two double beds and two single beds; you share a bathroom with one other room. There is a minimum of two people to this room and the cost is US $16 per person. The apartment is good for two to four people. There are two double beds, a kitchen and private bathroom. The cost is US $64 for two people and $5 more for each additional person. A second apartment has one double bed, a kitchen and a private bath for US $48 and is good for one or two peo ple. Then there is a small room with one double bed and its own bathroom located outside the room. It goes for US $20 for one or two people. All rooms have a fridge. You can order meals from here; breakfast is US $4.75 and supper is US $9. They also rent canoes and bicycles.

Lillpat Sittee River Resort, ☎ 520-7019, www.lillpat.com, $$$$, is half a mile from the sugar mill on 50 acres of groomed yard surrounded by jungle. They have only four double rooms, all of which are luxurious. There is air conditioning, private bathrooms, wicker furniture, satellite TV and a swimming pool. The price of the room includes breakfast. The restaurant, $$$, offers European, Italian and American foods.

Places to Eat

A truck comes to Sittee River every Saturday evening or early Sunday morning to sell in-season **produce** that you can take out to the cayes or to eat while in town. The produce is fresh and reasonably priced.

Miss Minn's and Glover's Guest House, $, offer family-style meals – both places are recommended. If staying more than a day or so, be certain to have a meal at **Toucan Sittee** up the road (see above).

The **grocery store** up the road has some basic products and lots of cold soda.

▶▶ *Return to the Southern Highway at Mile 10 and continue south. The Sittee River turnoff is at Mile 12.5 of the highway. The next landmark is the Kendall Bridge that goes over the Sittee. At Mile 15 is the Maya Center and turnoff to the right (west) for the Cockscomb Basin Wildlife Sanctuary and Jaguar Reserve, Belize's showcase reserve.*

◆ Cockscomb Basin Wildlife Sanctuary & Jaguar Reserve

Maya Center Village will likely be your home base when you visit the reserve. It has a total of 138 residents.

You must stop at the village and purchase a ticket (US $5 for foreigners) before entering the park. The ticket booth is at the entrance to the village.

Cockscomb Basin Wildlife Sanctuary and Jaguar Reserve is six miles up the hill past the village. Since most of the way is steep, walking would take all day and cycling would take at least a couple of hours.

A **taxi** from the village to the sanctuary/reserve for one to five people will cost US $12.50 and $2.50 per person extra over five. To Dangria, the fare will be US $125, and to Hopkins, US $40.

Call **Hermalino Saqui**, ☎ 520-3034, or **Julio Saqui**, ☎ 520-2042, for taxi service. **Julio and Ernesto Saqui**, ☎ 520-2021, are also certified guides, who can take you to Victoria Peak, as can **William Sho**, ☎ 520-2042, another certified guide. These men are the best, but if you are not able to get hold of them, go to the grocery store/bar and talk to the proprietor. He will be able to rustle up a guide with whom you will be happy.

AUTHOR NOTE: *The word yaguar in Mayan means "he who kills in one leap." The Spanish pronounce a "y" like a "j" so it is easy to see from where the word came.*

History

Wildlife research scientist **Alan Rabinowitz** conducted a study in 1982 that two years later resulted in 3,000 acres being declared a "No Hunting" zone. It took another two years of hard work to have the area declared a reserve. This was the first land on the planet ever dedicated to the preservation of the jaguar and it got the attention of the world.

It is believed that the reserve is habitat for 30 jaguars and that there are as many as 200 in the adjacent reserves (Chiquibul National Park to the west and the Maya Mountain Forest Reserve to the south). To keep these animals company (and well fed), 15 howler monkeys were relocated from the baboon sanctuary up north (see page 77) in 1992 and another 23 added in 1993.

Terrain

This moist tropical forest contains the headwaters of three important water ways: the **Swasey River, South Stann Creek** and the **Sittee River**. The Swasey is a tributary of the Monkey River.

The jaguar, a nocturnal creature, is the third-largest member of the feline family. An adult male can grow to 6.5 feet (two meters) long and weigh up to 220 pounds (100 kg). Females are about two-thirds as large as males. Jaguars are territorial and each male keeps about 16 square miles of territory. When walking on the trails, you will see lots of jaguar tracks, even if you never see the animal. The park also has 55 mammals, including pumas, margays, ocelots, jaguarundi, peccaries, brocket deer and pacas. There are armadillos, the jaguar's favorite meal, and otters, coati, kinkajous, anteaters and tapirs. There have also been 300 birds recorded in the area and one small Maya ruin is hiding in the jungle.

The **visitor center** at the entrance to the park marks the site of a vanished logging village called Quam Bank. Outside the center is a mahogany tree planted by Prince Philip of England in 1988. Close to that is an "earth ant truck (now being taken over by the jungle) that once belonged to Alan Rabinowitz, the founder of the park. Inside the center are displays of the region's geology, flowers and animals.

Hiking

Just beyond the visitor center numerous trails lead into the jungle. The short **Plane Wreck Trail** leads to a wrecked plane that crashed during a wind storm because the pilot never saw one of the high trees. He lived.

To make the four-day hike up and down **Victoria Peak** you must have permit (US $5) from the Forestry office in Belmopan, ☎ 822-3412. You must also hire a guide. The cost of camping on the trail is US $5 per day and guide is US $12.50 a day. Pay your fee at the Department of Forestry. Firs

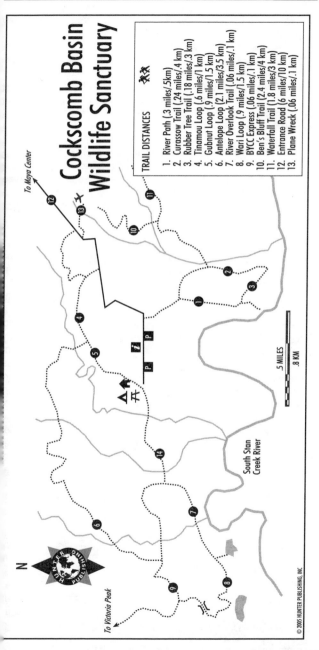

Cockscomb Basin Wildlife Sanctuary

To Moya Center

To Victoria Peak

N

South Stann Creek River

TRAIL DISTANCES

1. River Path (.3 miles/.5km)
2. Curassow Trail (.24 miles/.4 km)
3. Rubber Tree Trail (.18 miles/.3 km)
4. Tinamou Loop (.6 miles/1 km)
5. Gubnut Loop (.9 miles/1.5 km)
6. Antelope Loop (2.1 miles/3.5 km)
7. River Overlook Trail (.06 miles/.1 km)
8. Wari Loop (.9 miles/1.5 km)
9. BYCC Express (.06 miles/.1 km)
10. Ben's Bluff Trail (2.4 miles/4 km)
11. Waterfall Trail (1.8 miles/3 km)
12. Entrance Road (6 miles/10 km)
13. Plane Wreck (.06 miles/.1 km)

.5 MILES
.8 KM

THE SOUTH

© 2005 HUNTER PUBLISHING, INC.

climbed in 1888 by Goldsworthy, Victoria Peak was then considered the highest in Belize. Now that credit goes to Doyles Delight in Chiquibul Reserve. If you wish to hike this trail, do so during dry season. In wet season the climb up is slippery and dangerous, and there are also more mosquitoes.

It was recommended to me that the hike be done in rubber boots. I have never hiked in rubber boots, but it sounds as if blisters would develop before the end of day one. However, wearing wet leather boots for three days sounds almost as bad. Start hiking early, when it is cool, and be sure to carry lots of water. A tent will keep the bugs off while you sleep. You can rent a tent in Maya Center Village to take with you up the mountain. The cost is US $10 per tent. Bring water tablets to purify stream water for drinking.

The trail to the summit of Victoria was recently cleared. There isn't much change in elevation to the first camp at the Sittee River, eight miles in. Here you will find a kitchen shelter and outhouse. Day two will take you to base camp at Mile 12. Although much shorter in distance, day two is grueling as you go up and down hills. You must cross a rocky knoll prior to dropping down into campsite two. You will sleep here two nights. The ascent to the summit will be done with only enough food and equipment to sustain you for the day. Day three's ascent will take five hours, minimum. Part of the walk requires boulder-hopping up a creek bed. Near the end, you must crawl up through a gorge and then onto a ridge.

In these three days you will have climbed 3,543 feet (1,080 meters) in elevation. From the top, you can look over the jungle to a second peak, called Molar Peak. As all hikers know, the views will make the work worthwhile. The descent back to camp takes almost as long as the ascent because of the steepness of the climb. Day four could get you all the way out, but it would be a long day.

A shorter, one-day hike takes you to **Outlier Peak** only four miles one way, with an elevation change of 1,800 feet (600 meters). It will take you six hours to get to the top, which translates into an average of .6 miles an hour – that's pretty slow walking. The first part of the hike isn't too bad, but the last 45 minutes requires quite a bit of vine and root climbing. Near the top you will see both Victoria and Molar Peaks. It takes about three hours to return. Water must be carried and a guide is recommended, although not essential.

There are other trails available, named so you can guess what you will see – Tiger Fern Trail, Ben's Bluff Trail, Antelope Trail, Gibnut Trail and the War Loop. Some have waterfalls in which to cool off, while others seem only to have tons of leaf-cutter ants. Some trails take as little as 10 minutes to complete.

The park director is Ernesto Saqui, ☎ 520-3033. Call him for any detail you may need that the warden at the visitor center can't help you with.

Places to Stay

You can stay at the park if you wish. **Dorm-style beds** (US $20) sleep six to room and there are also private **cabins** (US $50 a night). All guests have use of a well-equipped kitchen. **Tenting** sites are also available for US $5 per person. Halfway up the road to the park is a white house that offers rooms for US $55 per person. This is luxury. Call Ernesto Saqui, ☎ 520-3033, to make arrangements for staying in the white house. If staying in the park, see the warden at the visitor center.

The village runs a **home stay program**, which is also organized by Ernesto Saqui, ☎ 520-2021, nuukcheil@btl.net. The cost is US $20 per person and it includes one dinner and one breakfast. Meals only are available for US $5 per person if you are not staying in a home but need to eat.

All of the places listed below are in the Maya Center Village.

Nu'uk Che'il Cottages, ☎ 520-2021, $$, features a group of cottages at the end of town closest to the reserve. Each cottage is a white plaster, thatched-roofed building with two rooms. They are basic, but clean, and the rooms have fans and electricity. There are separate bathroom facilities.

Mejen Tzil Lodge, ☎ 520-2020, isaqui@btl.net, $, has a row of rooms with a shared porch. The rooms are basic but, again, clean and comfortable. None offers a private bathroom; the toilet is an outhouse. You can get meals here even if you're not a paying guest. The **H'men Herbal Center and Medicine Trail** is on Nu'uk Che'l Cottages grounds and you can walk it for US $2. The lodge supplies a handout so you can guide yourself. Alternate attractions include Maya spiritual healing prayers, acupuncture, a snake doctor, chiropractor, midwife and herbal doctor. You can learn a lot by speaking with these people. There is also a gift shop at the center.

Nu'uk Che'il Restaurant, $, ☎ 520-2021, provides local dishes like corn tortillas, tamales, corn porridge and corn biscuits. Maya tea is also offered. They have a delivery service up to the sanctuary and reserve. You must order in town and they will deliver the meal when you want it.

▶▶ *Return to the Southern Highway at Mile 15. Continue south for 6.3 miles, over the South Stann Creek River Bridge, until you come to the road to Placencia at Mile 22.2.*

➔ Placencia Peninsula

Placencia Peninsula is a 16-mile strip of sandy beach that has resorts all the way to the tip. Seine Bight is the only village. Placencia has replaced Caye Caulker and Ambergris Caye as the most popular beach destination in Belize. For the most part, places along the coast here are less expensive and the services are better than they are at any other beach locale in Belize. Close proximity to the ocean gives you the opportunity to enjoy all water activities. Plus, you are closer to land destinations you may wish to visit, like caves and ruins.

Placencia itself went through hell on Oct. 8th, 2001, when Hurricane Iris hit and destroyed almost everything. But, like the phoenix, Placencia rose out of her ashes to reign again.

THE SOUTH

Most of the action is on the left (east) side of the road going to Placencia, because the ocean and beaches are the main attraction. The water to the right (west) is referred to as "the lagoon" and is popular with birders.

I have tried to list the hotels as they occur along the strip. Most places offer something unique and I am certain there is something for everyone. For information on Placencia, the absolute best website is www.placencia.com. It offers objective information about services on the peninsula and there is almost nothing that can't be answered on this site.

We'll follow the peninsula from Riversdale to Placencia town.

Getting Here & Getting Away

▶▶ *Turn left at Mile 22.2 off the Southern Highway. Drive/cycle for 1.5 miles and stay right at the curve. It is another 10 miles to Riversdale and the start of the strip. Turn right (south). The Placencia Lagoon will be on your right (west), visible for part of the drive down, and the Caribbean is on your left (east), visible for the other part.*

If you would like to get to the mainland and continue south, hop on the **ferry** that goes from Placencia over to Independence or Mango Creek (the same town split by a creek). From there, it is only five miles to the Southern Highway. The ferry goes twice a day; once mid-morning and once mid-afternoon and it meets the buses traveling north and south along the Southern Highway. If going south, it's a waste to travel all the way up the peninsula and then back down again. All buses along the Southern Highway stop at Mango Creek.

Gulf Cruise Boats leave from the dock in Placencia for La Ceibe, Honduras every Friday and return every Monday (US $25). There are also private boats that will take you. For further information, go to the dock and enquire.

Things to Do

Besides lying on the beach and tanning, **swimming**, drinking beer and eating, you can try **snorkeling**, **diving** or **fishing**. You can play coconut **bowling** or go for a **booze cruise**. You can write postcards or go sailing. For diving or snorkeling, explore the more than 20 miles of underwater canyon and mountains dotted with fish of every size and color imaginable. Twenty dive sites close by cater to all skill levels. You can also visit some of the cayes – Laughing Bird, Pumpkin, Ranguana and Silk cayes are all close to Placencia.

There is **windsurfing**, **sea kayaking** and **bird watching** on the lagoon along with grand slam **fishing** opportunities. Most hotels along the strip have tour offices and some have equipment rentals or dive shops.

See *Tour Operators*, below, for tours, equipment rentals and prices.

The **Lobster Fest** celebrates the opening of lobster season and is usually held on the weekend following June 15th. Check with the tourist office, located at the most southeast end of the town, or go to their website, www.placencia.com, for the latest information. The festival features a fishing tour nament, races, a parade, dancing, food and concerts. Proceeds from the festival are used for community improvements. I also recommend that you enter in the draw, which offers prizes such as airline tickets to the US and all-expenses-paid weekends at luxury resorts in Belize.

The **Booze Cruise** is for those who just want to lie back and spend a day on the deck of a boat sightseeing. On the way up the peninsula, you will stop for refreshments (cost extra) at some of the more famous lodges like Jay Birds, Rum Point Inn and Robert's Grove. The trip ends at Mango's in Maya Beach, at which time you return to Sugar Reef for a complimentary cocktail on their deck overlooking Placencia Lagoon. This tour is offered by Cayescape Tours, ☎ 523-3285 (see below).

Anyone with a boat will likely be willing to take you on a **river trip** – the Monkey River is a popular choice (see *Monkey River Town*, below).

Cool Running Bike Rentals, on Placencia Road beside the lagoon (no phone) offers rental bicycles at reasonable rates.

Laughing Bird Caye Marine Park Visitor Center is open from 9 am to 4:30 pm. In order to visit the caye you must get a permit from the center first. It's located at the harbor end of town east of the town dock. See *The Cayes* chapter for more details.

Seine Bight is a tiny Garifuna village of about 800 people four miles north of Placencia. It's nestled between the sandy beaches of the Caribbean on the east and the Placencia Lagoon on the west, with the highway running through the center. Seine Bight offers a unique cultural experience with the Garifuna people. A four-hour historical/cultural walking tour is recommended.

In the center of Seine Bight, **Veras** offers traditional Belizean dishes of chicken, rice and beans. There is also the **Kulcha Shack** and **Lola Delgado's** if you'd like to listen to music as you eat.

Seine Bight has a church, a police station and a community center, as well as two **Dugu temples** where the Garifuna worship. Priests from the temples can rid members of things like bad luck or illnesses by singing, dancing, drumming, eating and drinking. Visitors are welcome.

The Placencia Airstrip is the next landmark on your way south along the peninsula, en route to Placencia (town).

Placencia has a population of about 10,000. It's known for its famous sidewalk that runs for 4,071 feet (1,221 meters). Named in the Guiness Book, it was originally built so that fishers could haul their day's catch up in wheeled barrels. The sidewalk was almost totally destroyed by Hurricane Iris, but residents are finding creative ways of raising money to rebuild the walkway and the town.

The tourist office has been operating since 1998 and is not just an information center. It publishes a community newspaper that sells for BZ $1 (or you can read it on-line at www.placenciabreeze.com). The office is open Tuesday to Saturday, 9 am to 5 pm and is located at the most southeast end of the town. They can give you an indication of what a room or tour will cost.

Tour Guides/Companies

You can fish with world-famous angler Charles Leslie of **Kingfisher Adventures**, ☎ 523-3323 or 523-3322, www.belizekingfisher.com. His 30 years of experience allows him to take you to places where you have the chance to earn the Grand Slam prize for catching permits, bonefish and tarpon all in one day. He owns Tarpon Caye, complete with a fishing camp, cabanas for rent, plus a clubhouse and fly tying shop. Lessons are offered. The cost is US $275 a day for fly-fishing and troll lessons, $450 for blue water, and $275 a day for light tackle.

> **❖   RECOMMENDED FLIES**
>
> Charles Leslie suggests using the following flies:
>
> ❖   Tarpon – Clouser Minnow, Cockroach Deceivers
> ❖   Permit – MacCrab del Mecken, Moe Fly
> ❖   Bonefish – Crazy Charlie, Bemini Bone, Snook Fly
> ❖   Barracuda – Cudo Fly, Fish Hair and Nylon Middlefish Balad.

UnBelizeable Adventures Ltd., ☎ 523-3179, www.unbelizeable adventures.com, specializes in arranging weddings, honeymoons and educational tours. These can be all-inclusive.

Destinations Belize, ☎ 523-4018, www.destinationsbelize.com. Mary Toy offers the usual trips to anywhere in the southern part of Belize, whether it be a hike to a Maya cave or a canoe journey up a jungle river. However, her specialty is in customized tours of the more rugged type. If you have camping equipment and would like to camp on the cayes, Mary can get you there. You can camp only on Silk Caye, North East Caye on Glover's Reef and in the Punta Ycacos area near the Punta Ycacos Lagoon. Rates vary depending on the type and length of your trip, but all details are provided on the website.

Guides must be used for many of the trips you take in Belize. You can hire one through a company or, on some occasions, you can request a specific one. In Placencia, **Captain Bobo**, ☎ 603-0342, is a favorite. He does run up the Monkey River (see *Monkey River Town*, page 223). This tour ends with a search for the ever-elusive manatee. Because Captain Bobo is so experienced, he often has success in finding the animals. An all-day tour for four people is US $250, including a cooked lunch.

If you are looking for something just a bit different, **Cayescape Tour** ☎ 523-3285, offers a trip on the Sennis River. Lunch is included in the US $50-$75 fee.

The same company offers a Booze Cruise (US $50), which starts at 10 am and goes up the coast, stopping at Sugar Reef, Jay Birds, Rum Point Inn, Roberts Grove, Wamasa Bar and Mango's at Maya Beach. The tour ends the Sugar Reef Bar with a complimentary drink (if you can take any more) and a glimpse at the setting sun.

Ocean Motion Guide Service, ☎ 523-3363 or 523-3162, www.ocean-motion.com, has been offering tours from Placencia since 1995. Most of their tours revolve around the water, and cost between US $50 and $75. They also have snorkel equipment for rent at reasonable prices.

Toadal Adventure, ☎ 523-3207, www.toadaladventure.com, offers sea kayaking trips for small groups (no more than 10). They want an active crowd and have all equipment, including North Face tents, Wilderness Systems Sealution kayaks, Seatwo closed-cockpit kayaks and Wilderness System open-cockpit kayaks. Life jackets are included with the rental. A six-day, five-night island kayak trip costs US $965 per person, while a four-day, three-night jungle river journey costs US $538.

Nite Wind Guiding Service, ☎ 523-3176, is located along the sidewalk close to the town dock. Local Calbert Gardiner has been guiding for 15 years and knows every good fishing spot close to Placencia. You can also charter a boat for any trip of any duration. The cost for a guide and boat is US $275 a day. Boats for hire must be negotiated.

Saddle Caye South, ☎ 523-0251, www.kayakbelize.com, has tents, snorkeling gear, kayaks, and dry and wet bags for rent. Discounts are available to those renting for longer than a day. To get to the office, walk along the path behind the basketball court near Wallen's Market. Turn left (south) on Rocky Road and continue to a small channel. Turn right onto a lane south of the channel. The SCS lodge and office is just at the end of the lane at the lagoon pond. Overnight kayak trips run US $200 per person, and day kayak rentals are US $30.

Sea Horse Dive Shop, ☎ 523-3356 or 523-3166, www.belizescuba.com, has three boats to take out divers for day or night trips. PADI and NAUI qualified divers offer instruction. A night dive costs US $75 per person; wall dives are US $75 and shark dives are US $100.

Places to Stay

PLANTATION BEACH

The first beach at the north end of the peninsula is called the Plantation. **Calico Jacks**, ☎ 520-8103, www.calicojacksresort. com, $$$, is the only hotel along this beach. A pirate-themed resort named after the 18th-century pirate, it has a rustic elegance. The hotel has seven thatched-roof cabanas on

❖ HOTEL PRICING	
$	$10 to $20
$$	$21 to $50
$$$	$51 to $75
$$$$	$76 to $100
$$$$$	over $100

the beach with private baths and fans. There is a swimming pool, restaurant and gift shop; all facilities are wheelchair-accessible. **One-eyed Jack's beachfront bar** is a favorite hangout. If sailing is your thing, you can rent the resort's 52-foot ketch for a stay on the water or try a kayak. If land touring is your thing, bicycles and cars are also available for rent.

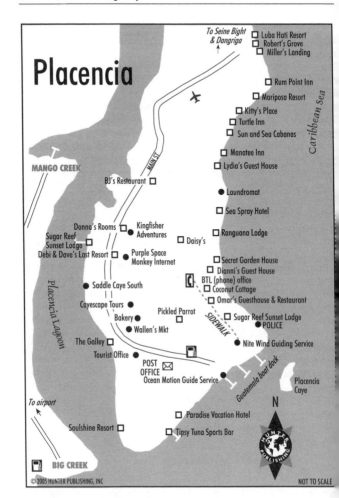

Placencia

To Seine Bight & Dangriga

Luba Hati Resort
Robert's Grove
Miller's Landing

Rum Point Inn

Mariposa Resort

Kitty's Place
Turtle Inn
Sun and Sea Cabanas

Caribbean Sea

Manatee Inn
Lydia's Guest House

MANGO CREEK

BJ's Restaurant

Laundromat

Sea Spray Hotel

Donna's Rooms   Kingfisher
Sugar Reef   Adventures
Sunset Lodge   Daisy's
Debi & Dave's Last Resort   Purple Space
                             Monkey Internet

Ranguana Lodge

Secret Garden House
Dianni's Guest House
BTL (phone) office
Coconut Cottage

Saddle Caye South

Cayescape Tours
Bakery   Pickled Parrot
Wallen's Mkt

Omar's Guesthouse & Restaurant
Sugar Reef Sunset Lodge
POLICE

Placencia Lagoon

SIDEWALK

The Galley
Tourist Office

Nite Wind Guiding Service

POST
OFFICE
Ocean Motion Guide Service

Guatemala boat dock

Placencia
Caye

N

To airport

Paradise Vacation Hotel

Soulshine Resort

Tipsy Tuna Sports Bar

HUNTER
PUBLISHING

BIG CREEK

© 2005 HUNTER PUBLISHING, INC

NOT TO SCALE

MAYA BEACH

Maya Beach is next along the peninsula. If staying along these beaches with
out transportation, local taxis cost $10 one way to Placencia. There are n
buses, but hitching is not a problem. **Mango's Bar** is the favorite waterin
hole in this area.

Maya Beach Hotel, ☎ 520-8040, www.mayabeach.com, $$, has fiv
rooms, each with paintings from local artists. They have ceiling fans, priva
baths and hot water. The **Calypso Café** offers tropical drinks to go with you
Belizean cuisine meal.

Joyce & Franks Bed and Breakfast, ☎ 561-683-3899, www.belizeb-andb.com/, $$$$, is a two-level house on the beach. Each air-conditioned room has a fridge, microwave, double bed and private bath with hot water. The dock has a thatch hut, a sun deck and a diving board. Inside, the dining room features a sitting area overlooking the Caribbean where you can break-fast, which is included in the cost. The owners are liberal-minded and love to sit and tell tales of the latest hot spot for birders or cyclists.

Maya Breeze, ☎ 523-8012, www.mayabreezeinn.com, $$$/$$$$, has cabins on the beach with nice-sized porches for lounging. There are four units in all, two with two bedrooms and the other two with one. All have air conditioning, and the kitchen has a fridge. Kayaks are available for rent and, on the side of the resort facing the lagoon, there is a café.

Barnacle Bill's Beach Bungalows, 23 Maya Beach Way, ☎ 523-8010, www.gotobelize.com/barnacle, $$$$, has two secluded bungalows with full kitchens. Actually, these are little houses, that can be rented for no fewer than three nights. They are good for honeymoon seclusion.

Singing Sands Resort, ☎ 523-2243 or 800-649-3007, www.singing-sands.com, $$$$, is nestled in a lush garden with a 40-foot pool in the center. Six thatched-roof cabins have fans and fridges inside. There's also a **restaurant** (dinner runs about $20), gift shop and equipment rentals on site. Birders staying at the resort can use canoes to go to the lagoon. There is a nice dock leading from the beach to a hut where you can get some shade.

Maya Playa, ☎ 523-8020, www.gotobelize.com/mayaplaya, $$/$$$, has three cabins that are available by the day, week or month. The thatched-roof cabins sleep four, with two in the loft. There are shared cooking facilities. The owners rent equipment and can also arrange for a trip to Laughing Bird Caye.

SEINE BIGHT

The only problem with staying at Seine Bight is that a taxi into Placencia costs $10 one way.

Blue Crab Resort, ☎ 520-4104, www.bluecrabbeach.com, $$$, has four air-conditioned rooms and two cabanas dispersed around five acres of land. The rooms feature hardwood floors, private baths, and each has a porch overlooking the water. The fan-cooled, thatched-roof cabins also have hard-wood floors. Children under 16, traveling with parents, stay free. The gardens house many birds, lizards, fox, possum, coati and raccoons. Bikes are available for rent and tours to other places can be arranged. The **restaurant**, $, right on the ocean, offers special Asian cuisine. Linn, the chef, was born in Taiwan and loves to prepare her specialties. She also cooks American dishes.

The attractive **Nautical Inn Adventure Resort** is owned by Americans-turned-Belizeans Ben and Janie Ruoti; ☎ 520-3595, www.nauticalinnbelize.com, $$$$. The hotel was one of the first on the peninsula and is still one of the biggest. There are 22 rooms, all with patio doors opening onto a pool. In addition to the nice rooms and pool, there is a gift shop, bar, and **restaurant**.

❖ IGUANA MAMAS

The Ruotis (of the Nautical Inn, ☎ 520-3595) are involved in the iguana-raising project. They collect eggs that are vulnerable to predators and place them in an incubator, where the eggs are kept under controlled temperatures until they hatch. The baby iguanas are fed twice a day for four months after birth, during which time they are never touched by humans. Once they reach maturity, the iguanas are sent to nature preserves around the country.

NORTH OF PLACENCIA AIRSTRIP

When receiving directions, you will be told that the following resorts are "north of Placencia Airstrip." After Seine Bight, the locals refer to the resorts along the road as either north or south of the airstrip.

Robert's Grove, ☎ 523-3565, in the US 800-565-9757, www.roberts-grove.com, $$$$$. Classified as a five-star resort, Robert's offers it all, from qualified diving experts to a luxurious swimming pool in the front yard. There are 32 rooms in all, 12 of them luxury suites. The resort has added a new 50-foot Newton dive boat to its fleet and expanded the marina on the lagoon. The fly-fishing center has also been enlarged to accommodate the growing number of fishers who are drawn to the area. Robert's Grove also has a massage parlor, steam room, whirlpool and a salon offering manicures, pedicures and facials. It has a fitness room, kayaks, canoes, windsurfing boards, sailboats and bicycles for guest use. In the restaurant, $$$, a professional chef offers a different type of pasta each night. Wednesdays are reserved for poolside barbecues that feature dishes like lobster kabobs and shrimp scampi. The meal is accompanied by Garifuna drummers and dancers or reggae bands.

Miller's Landing, ☎ 523-3010, www.millerslanding.net, $$$/$$$$, has three rooms in one building and another two buildings with upper and lower rooms. The upper rooms are the most luxurious and come complete with waterbeds. There is a pool, gift shop and **restaurant**, $$, which serves the best pizza on the entire peninsula. The bar often has live entertainment.

> **AUTHOR NOTE:** *Many kitchens advertised as "fully supplied," have microwaves but no stoves.*

Rum Point Inn, ☎ 523-3239 or 888-235-4031, www.rumpoint.com, $$$$$, is fairly large, with 12 rooms in the main lodge and 10 cabanas. Each room has air conditioning, fridge and a personal safe for valuables. A fish-shaped pool may tempt you. The beach has a private dock and thatched huts for guests. The use of bikes, kayaks and snorkeling gear is complimentary. After a day of touring, you can book a massage or visit the library. The owner is a librarian, so reading supplies are extensive and include magazines, newspapers, reference and history books and some good classics.

> **LOCAL LINGO:** *The Creole word "backra" means a white person and comes from "raw back" or sunburn.*

Luba Hati Resort, ☎ 523-3402, www.lubahati.com, $$$$$, is a beach-front resort with eight rooms in the main hotel and four units on the beach tucked into the surrounding vegetation. All rooms have private baths with hot water, air conditioning, fans and African art on the walls. Cabins feature fridges and stoves in the kitchens. Breakfast is included in the cost and is served in the rooms. Kayaks and bicycles are available without charge. There is a pool, a gift shop and **Franco's restaurant**, $$$, that specializes in Mediterranean cuisine.

SOUTH OF THE AIRSTRIP

Because jets don't land at the airstrip, the noise is of no consequence.

Mariposa Resort, ☎ 523-4069, www.mariposabelize.com, $$$$, has two cabins on the beach. The cabins are decorated with Maya glyphs and statues, Italian tiles, fans and queen-sized beds. There are private baths with hot water, and fully equipped kitchens with fridges, stoves (with four burners), microwaves, toasters and coffee makers. There are dishes and cookware so all you need is your food and drinks. Each cabin has its own thatched-roof hut on the beach and there is a beach shower. The cabins are within walking distance of the village.

Kitty's Place, ☎ 523-3227, www.kittysplace.com, $$$$$, has every combination you could wish for, from a cabin with kitchenette that sleeps four to six people, to regular rooms, Colonial suites, Colonial Rooms, Garden Rooms or Belize Studio Apartments with full kitchens. There are even two budget rooms that share a bath for US $30 (double). Most rooms have tile floors, fans, private baths with hot water, verandahs and kitchenettes. The luxury side of the hotel offers a spa, reflexology treatments, massage therapy and yoga lessons.

Turtle Inn, ☎ 523-3244 or 800-746-3743, www.blancaneaux.com, $$$$$, as 11 cabins with private baths, queen-sized beds, living rooms with pullout sofas, decks and outdoor beach showers. The beach runs along 650 feet (195 meters) of the coast. There is a pool, restaurant, dive shop and tour company. The **Gauguin Beach Grill**, $$$$, offers fresh seafood cooked over coconut husk coals.

Sun & Sea Cabanas, ☎ 523-3415, see the accommodations page at www.placencia.com, $$$, has three cabins on the beach. Each has private bathroom, a fan, a fridge and a kitchenette with cooking facilities. There is also a screened verandah.

PLACENCIA

Manatee Inn, ☎ 523-4083, www.manateeinn.com, $$, has six clean rooms off a common porch. Each has a private bath, fan and fridge. The building is made partly of local hardwoods and is situated right in town, close to everything.

Lydia's Guest House, ☎ 523-3117, see the accommodations page at www.placencia.com, $, has eight rooms in a nice house with a verandah. Each room has a fan and shared bath. There are limited kitchen facilities available, but breakfast can be ordered ahead of time.

Sea Spray Hotel, ☎ 523-3148, www.belizenet.com/seaspray, $$/$$$, has 19 rooms. There are a variety of accommodation choices, but every option has a private bathroom with hot water and fan. Some rooms accommodate two people only, with either a double bed or two singles. Some have fridges and open porches or beach decks. As you get more elaborate, the rooms have coffee makers and kitchenettes and are closer to the beach.

Ranguana Lodge, ☎ 523-3112, www.ranguanabelize.com, $$$, has five little cabins on the beach, right in town. They are clean and comfortable with porches. Each has a private bath with hot water, fans and a fridge.

Deb and Dave's Last Resort, ☎ 523-3207, see the accommodations page at www.placencia.com, $, has four basic rooms with fans and shared bathrooms. Although not on the beach, Deb & Dave's is very clean and the bus passes right by here.

Serenade Guest House, ☎ 523-3481, www.belizecayes.com, $$$, is a colonial-style house a block off the beach, behind Cosy's restaurant. The white plaster and bright tiles make it look clean at all times. All rooms have air conditioning and private baths. The owners of this guest house also own Frank's Island in the Sapodilla Cayes. Equipment rentals are available here.

Westwind Hotel, ☎ 523-3255, see the accommodations page at www. placencia.com, $$, has eight rooms with private baths, fans and fridges. On the beach there is a comfortable thatched-roof hut with hammocks. There are also two vehicles available for rent.

Secret Garden House, ☎ 523-3420, www.secretgardenplacencia. netfirms.com, $$, is a two-bedroom house on stilts. It's fully furnished and can sleep four comfortably.

Dianni's Guest House, ☎ 523-3159, $$, has six rooms with fans, fridges and private baths. A large balcony is adjacent to the rooms. Kayaks are offered for rent and Internet service is available. The staff will also do laundry for you.

Coconut Cottage, ☎ 523-3155, www.placencia.com/members/coconut. html, $$$$$, is on the beach toward the north end of town and near the air strip. These two spotlessly clean cabins have private bathrooms with hot water, fans and minimal kitchen facilities. **Harry's Cabanas** are also part of the operation. There are three cottages at Harry's for US $50 per night.

Omar's Guest House, ☎ 609-3135 or 609-2326, $, is along the sidewalk across from the school. The beach can be seen from the deck. Some rooms have private baths, and all rooms are clean and large with ceiling fans. There is a laundry service and a restaurant downstairs.

Paradise Vacation Hotel, ☎ 523-3179, paradiseplacencia@hotmail. com, $/$$, overlooks the town dock. It has 16 rooms with fans, some have private baths and hot water. Kitchen facilities are limited, but there is a lovely deck on the second floor.

Be Back Cabins, ☎ 523-3285, $$, are near the football field crossroad and are high in the air so they catch every little bit of breeze. If two are sharing a bed, these immaculate cabins are a good deal as the owners charge for the cabin, not per person. Cabins are totally equipped for comfortable living. Reasonable weekly and monthly rates offered.

Soulshine Resort and Spa, 1 Placencia Point, ☎ 877-700-7685, www.
soulshine.com, $$$$$. This is a spa in the old Roman style. There are the
usual amenities like a **restaurant**, bar, swimming pool and secluded beach.
Your package can be with or without meals. Sunshine offers reflexology,
aromatherapy, yoga or Japanese Reiki. You can have a Maya facial treatment that uses red clay and herb-scented towels or a scalp massage with
herb-drenched oils. Their best treatment is the ancient Maya bath. This takes
45-60 minutes and starts with a soak in herb-scented water, followed by a
shower and a warm pool soak. You then graduate to a hot pool soak, a cold
shower, a massage, another cold shower and a rest on the porch with a glass
of water. To reach Soulshine, go to the end of the peninsula and around the
point toward the lagoon. When you are across from the little island, you will
find a doorbell mounted on a pole. Ring the bell and the little ferry will come
across the 75 feet (22 meters) of water to get you.

Places to Eat

All of the bigger resorts offer dinner to non-guests. Most serve good food.
Check out the hotel listings above for additional places to eat.

Often-busy **Omar's Restaurant**, ☎ 609-3135 or 609-2326, $, on the side-
walk in Placencia, is well known and highly recommended for spicy Creole
food. The food is good and there is lots of it. Prices are reasonable.

Tutti Frutti Italian Ice Cream Shop, $, in Placencia, has 24 flavors of
homemade ice cream. Some of the more delectable flavors are vanilla chocolate chip, strawberry and mango delight. This is a must.

Purple Space Monkey Internet Café, $$, offers cappuccinos, lattés and
espressos as well as Internet access.

Nightlife

Placencia offers most of the nightlife on the peninsula. **Sugar Reef Sunset
Lounge**, 13 Sunset Drive, ☎ 523-3289, $$, has a 36-meter (120-foot) deck
overlooking the lagoon. This is one of the best places in Placencia. Besides
the daily happy hour there are other fun forms of entertainment, like a horse-
shoe competition (winner gets a bottle of rum).

Pickled Parrot, ☎ 523-3102, $$, is still serving their eminent tropical
blended drinks. Examples of this are the Blue Hole, the Yellow Bird, the
Belizean Hurricane or the always popular Parrot Piss. This place is famous.
After you've had enough Parrot Piss, try their pizza – it's a great combination.

Tipsy Tuna Sports Bar, ☎ 523-3179, is on the beach in Placencia. It has
ladies night and karaoke every Thursday. There's a big-screen TV and pool
tables.

> **LOCAL FLAVOR:** *A favorite drink is **rum bitters**, a concoction of
> special herbs and bark soaked in rum for days before you drink it.*

Seine Bight, **The Wamasa** is a nightclub and **Sam's Disco** is for the Reg-
gae crowd.

THE SOUTH

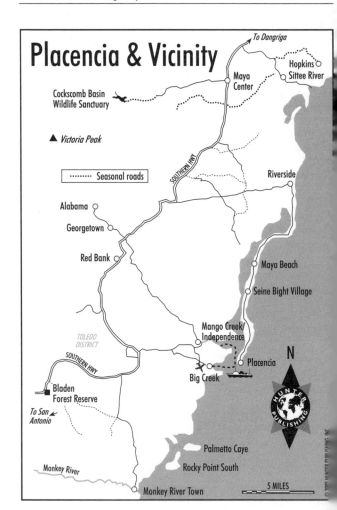

Leaving the Peninsula

To leave Placencia, you can cross over to Mango Creek/Independence by ferry, which runs twice a day; once mid-morning and once mid-afternoon. meets the buses traveling either north or south along the Southern Highwa If going south, it seems senseless to me to travel all the way up the peninsu and then back down again. All buses along the southern highway stop Mango Creek.

▶▶ *If you rejoin the Southern Highway at the turnoff to Placencia, continue
     south. The road to Red Bank is at Mile 32; turn right (west).*

Red Bank has a population of 700, most of them of Maya descent. The community is often referred to as the Holy Grail by birders because, from Jan. to
Mar., it is home to the scarlet macaw. Within 15 minutes walking time, you
are guaranteed to see at least two and as many as 92 of these endangered
birds. Villagers, trained as guides, admit that long ago they used to eat the
birds because they were so plentiful.

   If you wish to stay in the village you should phone in advance. There is a
village phone, ☎ 503-2233. Whoever hears the phone will answer, but it may
take a little while so give it a few minutes before you hang up. A four-room
guest cabin is available, $. It stands on stilts and is tucked into the jungle with
a freshwater creek running beside. Rooms all have double beds and window
screens. You must share a bathroom. There is no electricity; kerosene lamps
are used in the evenings. Meals can be ordered ahead and are minimal in
cost. However, if you want any extras, like a beer or snacks, bring them with
you. You can also book a room through the **Belize Audubon Society**,
☎ 223-4533, or the **Programme for Belize**, ☎ 227-5616, in Belize City.

▶▶ *Continue along the Southern Highway. If going into Mango Creek or Big
     Creek, take the turnoff at Mile 38.6. You'll be turning left (east).*

Mango Creek and **Independence** are the same town, divided by Mango
Creek. It has a shrimp processing plant and shrimp from here are sent all
over the world via Belize's deep-water port, Big Creek. The area also has a
lot of citrus farms that ship their produce from Big Creek. The road into Big
Creek is mostly for transport trucks.

   At one time there was a proposal to have a bridge built between Mango
Creek and Placencia but, to date, there is no funding. For the traveler, there
is little in Mango Creek or Big Creek.

▶▶ *Continue south along the Southern Highway to Mile 42 and turn left (east) to
     Monkey River Town. (The road signs may not correspond with this guide as
     they measure the distance from Belize City, while I measure the distance
     from Belmopan.)*

THE SOUTH

◆ Monkey River Town

Monkey River Town is an isolated Garifuna community with a population of
about 270 people. It offers just two places to stay, two bars to visit after the
sun goes down, two places to eat and two ways to get there. This really is a
"two-can" town.

   Monkey River Town is a wonderful little village that has simplicity as an asset. There is a large green sign near the harbor that says "Welcome to Monkey River," and somehow the greeting feels genuine. There is a police
station, a community center, a school and a church linked by sand streets.
Wood houses built on stilts dot the public places and there are no neon lights.
If you want something, you ask. To find anyone you must go to the dock,
where most people who aren't fishing or making meals are playing dominos.
This is a serious game; get involved in it while gathering information.

Getting Here

BY BUS: To reach Monkey River by bus is difficult. You could get off at the Southern Highway turnoff, but from there it is another 14 miles, too long for most to walk in a day. Avid walkers might manage it.

BY CAR OR BICYCLE: If you drive or cycle, continue straight along the Southern Highway to Mile 42 and turn left (east). Follow the secondary road for 14 miles to the Monkey River, where you will leave your car. At the river, holler for someone to bring you across in a boat. Just holler at the men playing dominos. You'll probably be the excitement of the day.

BY BOAT: The other option is to hire a boat and come down the coast or rent a kayak for a few days and paddle down from Placencia. It is about 20 miles, a long day's paddle even under good conditions.

Things to Do

A **Monkey River boat trip** can be done independently or with a tour from Placencia (see page 214 for list of operators). Dugout canoes are available for rent in Monkey River Town. Just ask. Prices will have to be negotiated, budget for US $7-10 an hour.

Paynes Creek National Park was established as a preserve in 1994 and a national park in 1999. It covers 11,600 square miles of wetland bordered by the Monkey River on the north, Ycacos Lagoon on the south, the Caribbean on the east and savanna on the west.

To get there you must paddle from Monkey River Town south along the coast to Punta Negra, a jut of land sticking out into the Caribbean with a tiny village on it. The distance from Monkey River is about 14 miles and then an additional hour from Punta Negra to Ycacos Lagoon. After going around Punta Negra, paddle down the coast to Punta Ycacos. It is less than six miles. **Punta Ycacos** is a distinct peninsula pointing south. Once there, look for a trail on the beach that leads to a boardwalk. Follow the walk that is lying over a marsh till you get to the lagoon. There is a ranger station beside the lagoon. It is about a one-hour walk on maintained trails from the station to the broad-leafed forests. Trail descriptions are posted at the ranger station.

Ycacos Lagoon is between four and nine feet deep (one and three meters), with mangroves surrounding most of it. Because this is such an isolated lagoon, the chance of spotting manatee or lagoon-nesting birds is good. About 300 birds have been sighted in the park. Hawksbill turtles also come here to nest. The lagoon also has some tarpon and permit. You can fish from the dock or from a canoe, but it's catch-and-release only.

The **Punta Honduras Marine Reserve** borders Paynes Creek National Park on the ocean side. This 327-square-mile reserve became a protected area in 2000. An estuary within the reserve was created by the outflow of seven rivers. On the water, there are about 135 mangrove islands and only 10% of them have dry land. One of them, Abalone Caye, is closest to the most sensitive area and will have a ranger's station built on it in the near future to help protect the mangrove and fish populations.

Underground Maya storage sites have been found on Wild Cane Caye, within the reserve. It is unknown if the water has risen since the early days of the Maya or if the land has sunk. Archeologists have also found some animal bones here. The bones are from fish, turtles and manatees, suggesting that the Maya ate these creatures.

❖   **MAYA MEMENTOS**

The Maya knew that if people didn't have salt in their diets they would become tired, feel aches in their joints and dehydrate. At Ycacos Lagoon, archeologists have found signs of Maya salt plants, where they would boil the brine from the lagoon to form salt cakes. These they traded for mountain products at Lubaantun, Nim Li Punit and Uxbenka.

Tour Guides

Clive (of Clive's Place, ☎ 709-2028, see below) has brothers and cousins who have lived in the area all their lives and can take you almost anywhere you wish to go. They will probably be successful in showing you what you want to see.

Elroy's Tour Guide Service, ☎ 523-2014, is a good place to start looking if you don't want to see all the tourist money going to Clive.

Percivil Gordon, ☎ 520-3033, is another long-time outdoorsman who knows the Monkey River area well. Both Elroy and Percivil are quiet, non-assuming people who know their stuff.

Places to Stay

Clive's Place, ☎ 709-2028 or 720-2025, www.monkeyriverbelize.com, $$, is officially called the Sunset Inn, but everyone calls it Clive's Place. It has eight rooms situated off a porch on the second floor of a wooden building. Each has a fan and private bathroom with hot water. You can take all your meals at Clive's for another US $15 a day. The downstairs bar and restaurant often feature drummers and dancers.

Bob's Paradise Hotel, ☎ 429-8763, $$$$/$$$$$, is a three-star hotel asking a five-star price. Bob's is also a mile out of town. It has six thatched-roof huts with private baths, hot water and fans. There's also a bar and **restaurant** attached.

Places to Eat

Alice's Restaurant, ☎ 520-3033, $, offers food for all the travelers who arrive on boat tours coming up the river. Ask for directions to Alice's. She will invite you in, offer you a seat and go off to prepare and, shortly after, serve your meal. You will be offered the same as she gives her family.

Of course, you can go around back of the village and eat at Clive's Place too. He will make you welcome.

▶▶ *Return to the Southern Highway at Mile 42 and drive or cycle south. The road meanders through milpa farms and citrus groves with the Maya Mountains to the west. There are numerous rivers to cross – the Swasey, the Bladen, Deep River and Golden Stream – before you reach Indian Creek Village at Mile 73.*

TERMITE TERRAIN: *The big gobs of amorphous dirt you see on the sides of trees, fenceposts and elsewhere are termite nests.*

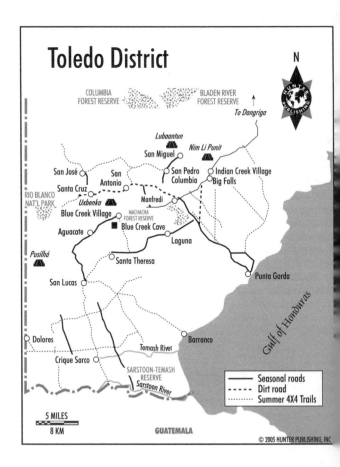

◆ Nim Li Punit Ruins

Indian Creek is a tiny Maya village with only one guest house (beyond the village), a gas station and a small grocery store. It serves as the gateway to Nim Li Punit ruins. The ruins and guest house are 1.25 miles west of the village along a hilly road. If coming by bus, ask the driver to let you off at the road to the village and walk the rest of the way (about an hour).

Exploring the Ruins

Nim Li Punit ruins is a small site known mainly for its **stelae**. Named after the longest stele found at the site, Nim Li Punit means Big Hat. That stele, which measures over 31 feet high (nine meters), had a carving on the front of a figure with a huge headdress. This stele is the tallest ever found in Belize and the second-tallest found at any Maya ruin.

There is a small **visitor center** at the ruins with some artifacts and a map of the site.

This ruin has three divisions, the west, east and south. The west has two **temples** with plazas at each. The eastern area has an **observatory**. Between the southern and eastern sections is a small but well-defined **ball court**. It is the southern section that is the most impressive. Here, archeologists found most of the stelae and three **royal tombs**. Inside the tombs were 36 pottery vessels, some of which are in the visitor center. Twenty-six **stelae** have been found, eight of them carved. One carving is of a ruler with some copal incense being thrown into a flame. Resin from the Copal tree, found in abundance throughout southern Belize, was burned as incense by the Maya. There are two other human figures on this stele, plus a mythical creature holding the pot with the flame.

 MYSTERIOUS MAYA: *The Maya carved on the front of stelae. Although glyphs appeared around the pictures, it is on the sides and backs that the text, the dates and stories were usually inscribed.*

THE SOUTH

Place to Stay

Indian Creek Guest House, ☎ 709-6324, info@belizelodge.com, $$, is situated across from the ruins (1.25 miles from the highway). It has eight rooms that can accommodate three or four people each. Two rooms share a bath. For a bit more privacy, consider renting one of 12 cabins located behind the guest house, on a hill. They have air conditioning, tiled bathrooms with hot water, fans and hardwood floors.

▶▶ *Continue along the Southern Highway from Mile 73 to Mile 83.2. At the gas station, turn right (west) for the Maya villages of San Miguel, San Pedro Columbia, San Antonio, Santa Cruz, Santa Elena and Blue Creek Village. There are also the ruins of Lubaantun, Uxbenka, and the Rio Blanco Forest Reserve and Blue Creek Cave, the Bladen Nature Reserve and the Columbia Forest Reserve.*

AUTHOR NOTE: *The road (I will refer to it as the San Antonio Road) that goes to the above places is rough. Most people go to Punta Gorda and then take a bus, which runs four times a week – on Tuesday, Thursday, Saturday and Sunday – to the village they wish to visit. Others take a bicycle, a taxi or a private vehicle.*

◆ San Pedro Columbia, Lubaantum & San Miguel

There are home stay programs in some of the villages, and San Antonio even has a guest house. But, generally, there are few amenities. If you want to have your meals with the Maya, you must order ahead. They will go out of their way to accommodate you.

▶▶ *For San Pedro Columbia, Lubantun and San Miguel, turn off at Mile 83.2 of the Southern Highway. Go west for two miles along the San Antonio Road until you come to the sign that indicates San Pedro Columbia and Lubantun ruins. Turn right (north) and follow the road.*

San Pedro Columbia is a Maya community with about 700 residents. The community has seven churches, a police station, a school and a small shop in town. The village is known for its hand embroidery.

People came to San Pedro from the Petén area of Guatemala, escaping from the oppression. They carried with them the statues of Santo Domingo, San Pedro and Santa Concepcion and settled in two locations before finding the clear waters of the Columbia River.

Things to Do

Mar. 19th is the **Feast of St. Peter**. The festival includes harp music, eating and dancing. To attend this celebration is a unique experience as the village is isolated and the festival is traditional. Mar. is also a good time of year to visit the Columbia River Forest Reserve.

The **Lubaantun ruins** are located at the top of a hill on manicured lawns. The parking lot is at the bottom of the hill and it doesn't take more than three minutes to reach the entrance. Stop at the new visitor center and pay the US $5 entrance fee (the caretaker is not always there so you may get lucky and not have to pay). There is also a bathroom and picnic table at the site.

"Lubaantun" means Place of the Fallen Stones. When looking at the construction – cut stones held together without mortar – it is simple to see why the stones have fallen. The roots of trees and the growth of plants have pushed and toppled the walls.

Lubaantun was built in three sections. The central core is the religious area where 11 **temples** have been found around five **plazas**. The middle ceremonial section consists of three **ball courts**. Three ball court markers and numerous pieces of pottery were also found. This has led archeologists to believe that Lubaantun was a popular sports center. Around the outer rim of the city were the residential homes.

The site ruled an area of 327 square miles that covered diverse landscapes, including mountains, ocean and farmland. The Maya from this city could get stones from the mountains for building and they could hunt and grow agricultural products in the foothills. The ocean offered them seafoods and medicinal plants. The availability of these products made Lubaantun fairly self sufficient.

❖ THE CRYSTAL SKULL

The most interesting story attached to Lubaantun is the tale of the Crystal Skull. Dr. Mitchell-Hedges and his daughter Anna were supposed to have been at Lubaantun in 1926 doing some research. On her 17th birthday, Anna spotted a glitter in the ruins that had not been excavated. It took six weeks to uncover the glitter, which turned out to be a crystal skull.

The skull was carved from one piece of clear quartz crystal and stood 5 3/16 inches wide by 4 7/8 inches deep and 7 7/8 inches high. It weighed 11 pounds, 13 ounces. When found, there was not a scratch on it. After another three months, they uncovered a jaw, which fit perfectly into the skull.

Supposedly, Anna was permitted by the native people living near Lubaantun to take the skull in trade for food and medicines. Around that time, a similar skull was obtained by the British Museum and put on display in England. The Mitchell-Hedges team claimed that their skull took 150 years to carve and that it was 3,600 years old. They also claimed that it was used by high priests in ceremonies that caused death to certain people.

Nick Nacerino, a researcher, became interested in the skull and its story in the 1980s. It didn't take him long to find inconsistencies in the tale. Crystal scratches easily, so it was highly unlikely that the skull had been lying in the ruins for centuries. He also found that the Maya people would never trade one of their icons for a few pieces of food or medicine. No elders remembered an American (Canadian actually) girl at Lubaantun during that period. Nacerino found that there was no record of the skull before 1943, an oddity for an archeologist to keep such a significant find a secret for that many years. Nacerino also found that in 1943 there was a bill of sale for the skull from Sotheby's to Dr. Mitchell-Hedges in the amount of £400. The skull was sold to Sotheby's by Eugene Babon, a known antiquities dealer and producer of fake items.

Finally, in 1996 a firm in Germany proved that the skull had been made within the last hundred years. Since this revelation, Anna Mitchell-Hedges has been unavailable for comment and the British Museum has removed their skull from exhibition.

an Miguel, a village of 380 people, is just beyond Lubaantun along the ame road. It has a library, a school, a church and a small store. Visitors are elcome.

Tiger Cave is about a half-hour walk from San Miguel. The story goes that a dog chased a jaguar cub into the cave and so it got its name. If you have a local guide, he will be able to show you the Blue Hole hot spring en route to the cave.

Tiger Cave requires a creek crossing; a canoe is left at the spot. The interior of the cave has ceiling holes so light seeps down to allow visibility inside. There is pottery on some of the ledges and a stream farther inside.

Place to Stay

San Pedro has a **home stay program**. Check with the village alcade in San Pedro or call ☎ 722-2470 to make advance arrangements.

▶▶ *Return to the San Antonio Road and continue west for another 1.5 miles just past Manfredi, an odd little community that has a sampling of just about every culture in Belize. Turn left (south) and go along the road for nine miles until you arrive at Blue Creek. You will pass a Mennonite farm that has tons of machinery. Obviously, they are not the fundamentalist Mennonites. Pass through the village of San Pedro and on to Blue Creek.*

◆ Blue Creek Village & Blue Creek Cave

Blue Creek Village is a Maya community of about 40 families situated on 500 acres of land. It has one hotel.

Getting Here

BY BUS: Buses arrive from Punta Gorda three times a week, on Monday, Wednesday and Friday. There are also **taxis** available in Punta Gorda that cost anywhere from US $50 to US $100 a day for four people.

Things to Do

Blue Creek Cave, called "Hokeb Ha" in Mayan, is a short walk from the lodge (see below), up slippery rocks along the creek. A walking stick should be used and good shoes are essential. If coming from the village, walk along the creek but do not cross the bridge. Instead, stay on the trail going up the creek. You will pass the lodge on the way.

The cave is big and the creek actually flows from it, causing water to run over the rocks at the entrance. In rainy season, there is a waterfall that washes some of the stalagmites and stalactites near the mouth. You will need lights to go into the cave any distance, but you can easily get to the pool, just a few feet inside. It's a great place for swimming. A ceremonial altar and some ceramics were found inside the cave.

A local resident, **Pablo Bochub** of Roots & Herbs in Blue Creek, ☎ 722-2834 or 608-2879, herbs@btl.net, can be hired to drive you to the caves.

Place to Stay

Blue Creek Rainforest Lodge, ☎ 722-0013, ize2belize@aol.com, has four wood cabins sleep two people each and have screened windows and fans; bathrooms and showers are in the main lodge. Tucked into the jungle and beside the creek, the cabins are within five minutes of the cave entrance. A **restaurant** at the site serves mostly typical Maya food. The cost is US $85 per person, including meals, jungle hikes, caving and river walks in the area.

▶▶ *To reach San Antonio, Santa Cruz Waterfall, Uxbenka ruins, Santa Cruz, Santa Elena and Rio Blanco National Park, you'll need to return to the San Antonio Road. Continue for about three miles west of Manfredi to San Antonio.*

◆ San Antonio

San Antonio is the largest Maya village in Toledo District with a population of about 1,000. It has a grocery store, two churches, a community center, a mission house, a health center and a hotel.

Getting Here

BY BICYCLE: Cycling to San Antonio is difficult as the road is rough, the way is long, and the hills become steep once past Manfredi. Also, there are few amenities.

BY BUS: A bus arrives from Punta Gorda on Tuesday, Thursday, Saturday and Sunday.

Things to Do

The **Uxbenka ruins** are also called the Santa Rita ruins. They are situated across from the water tower just outside San Antonio. It is a short climb up the hill to the unexcavated ruins.

First located in 1984, the site had 20 stelae, seven of which were carved. Today, there are 13 still at the site, lying in the ground eroded by weather and covered by moss and jungle. A tomb lies partially open – it looks like a hole in the ground with stones supporting the sides. There are plazas and temple walls at this tiny site, but not much excavation has been done. In the late 1980s a team of archeologists salvaged some artifacts and opened the tomb. There is no charge to visit this site and it takes less than 15 minutes to poke around.

Places to Stay

Bol's Hilltop Hotel, ☎ 702-2124, $$, is across from the stone church. It offers seven basic rooms with shared bathrooms. Meals can be arranged at the hotel or through the locals.

The TEA Guest House, ☎ 722-2096, $$, allows you to stay in a cabin shared with five other people. During the day, Maya guides lead excursions and teach you about the jungle. Your stay includes three traditional meals with a Maya family and, in the evenings, you can listen to their stories and music and watch some dancing. The TEA Guest House is similar to a home stay, only you – and the Maya family – have more privacy.

Home stay allows you to stay in a Maya home. You will work during the day with the family, whether it be chopping wood, harvesting coffee or making tortillas. For this program you can either check with the village alcade or call in Punta Gorda, ☎ 722-2470, for arrangements. The cost of this program is about US $5 per day, plus $2 per meal. This is a true immersion program.

◆ Santa Cruz

Santa Cruz village has a population of about 400 people and is just 1.25 miles past San Antonio along the same road. There are two **home stay** houses in Santa Cruz. One is with Marcus Sho and the other is with Santiago Ash. If you would like to stay with them, ask in the village or go to Rio Blanco National Park Visitor Center and inquire there.

Everisto Shoe and Venancio Canti have **horses** for rent. They are sanctioned by the Rio Blanco National Park to take visitors through on horseback. They need only one day's notice to prepare for a trip and can accommodate quite a few riders.

Santa Cruz Waterfall is about .3 miles out of Santa Cruz going west. This pretty waterfall is 30 feet wide (10 meters) and just as deep. There is a picnic area and a place to swim, making it a popular destination for the locals.

▶▶ *Santa Elena is at the end of the San Antonio Road about another1.8 miles beyond Santa Cruz.*

◆ Santa Elena & Rio Blanco National Park

Rio Blanco National Park is five miles past San Antonio. The cost to enter the park is US $2.50 for foreigners or 50¢ for locals. If hitching here, plan to return to town between 4 and 5:30 pm, when most traffic is on the road.

First established in 1994, the 105 acres of park are maintained by the people living in the area. This is a fairly new concept in Belize and it is called an Indigenous Peoples Park. With the help of the Peace Corps in general and Steve Roberts in particular, a park plan has been established and the group is working to fix a boundary and develop some walking trails.

The **visitor center** has some charts on display. There is also an arts and crafts room and two dorms that can accommodate six people in all Outhouses and a picnic table are nearby. There's also a tenting place.

The **trail** down to the river is well maintained and does not take long to walk. The river, even at the end of dry season, has plenty of water – enough in fact, to allow one to dive from an outcrop of rock 20 feet (six meters) above a deep pool.

Jaguar prints have been seen in the park and there are toucans peccaries, gibnuts, iguanas and other such animals.

Hiking trails are located on the far side of the river. A guide (you can rent a horse too) will be able to show you different medicinal plants that are used by the Maya.

 MYSTERIOUS MAYA: *The Maya believe that parrot bones carry rabies and if a dog eats the bones, he will die.*

▶▶ *Return to the Southern Highway at Mile 83.2 and continue south for another three miles. Turn west (right). In another three miles you'll reach the village of Laguna.*

◆ Laguna Village

Laguna Village has about 300 people, almost all Maya. There are two schools, two churches and one health post. The village has a home stay program in place, as well as a TEA Guest House. Nearby attractions include a cave and a lagoon. Staying in this village will give you a good Maya-life experience.

If you want to learn to **weave**, enquire at Miss Rosa's house in the village or at the office of the organizers of the home stay program in Punta Gorda, ☎ 722-2470. This is the only place in the entire country where I found someone willing to teach this skill.

Things to Do

Guides are available in the village. If staying at the TEA Guest House, guides for these hikes can be included in the cost of your stay.

Agua Caliente Lagoon, set on 6,000 acres of reserved land, is a two-hour walk from the village. Your walk there leads through pasture and milpas, across creeks and then enters a marshland. There's a ranger station at the marsh, but no services, only an outhouse.

This is known as a dirty hike – you will quite often be in mud up to your knees after you enter the marsh. Near the lagoon, the wildlife increases and the landscape has a backdrop of limestone hills. Wood storks, herons, egrets, ducks, cormorants and kingfishers are often seen here. The trip should be done with a guide because the trail disappears quite often and you could get lost.

Laguna Cave is a 1.5-hour hike from the village. You must cross a stream and go to the limestone mountain looming over the village. Once there, you will be faced with a 12-foot climb up a rustic ladder to the cave's entrance. This is a dry cave and cracks in the ceiling allow some light inside. As you enter, the cave slopes downward and you may notice some bats hanging around. At one time, the Maya used the cave, but artifacts have been taken out to the archeological holding pen in Belmopan. This cave was used to make offerings before planting started. It is a 20-minute walk through the cave to a second opening. This trip should be done with a guide.

THE SOUTH

Places to Stay

TEA Guest House, ☎ 722-2096, sleeps about eight people on bunks in two rooms. It is basic. It runs on the same basis as the one in San Antonio (see above).

There's also a home stay program. Check with the village alcade or call ☎ 722-2470 for arrangements. The cost of this program is about US $5 per day plus $2 per meal.

▶▶ *Return to the Southern Highway at Mile 86 and continue south to Mile 100 and the entrance to Punta Gorda.*

◆ Punta Gorda

Punta Gorda has a multicultural population of about 4,000 people. It has three streets that parallel the bay and it takes very little time to walk from one end of town to the other. This is the outback of Belize. If you want to hike or bike in the backcountry, then make Punta Gorda your base. You can immerse yourself totally in a culture by living a few days with the Maya or the Garifuna. Punta Gorda is also close to the sea, so snorkeling, diving and fishing are all possible.

AVERAGE TEMPERATURES & RAINFALL			
	Daily temp.	Monthly rainfall	Rain Days
JAN	75.0°F/23.9°C	.5 inches/1.27 cm	13
FEB	77.4°F/25.2°C	.2 inches/.65 cm	9
MAR	79.2°F/26.2°C	.2 inches/.65 cm	6
APR	82.6°F/28.1°C	.3 inches/ cm	6
MAY	83.7°F/28.7°C	.5 inches/.84 cm	9
JUN	83.7°F/28.8°C	1.9 inches/4.8 cm	20
JULY	82.4°F/28.0°C	2.3 inches/6.0 cm	25
AUG	82.6°F/28.1°C	1.9 inches/4.8 cm	23
SEPT	83.1°F/28.4°C	1.4 inches/3.7 cm	23
OCT	81.5°F/27.5°C	1.1 inches/2.7 cm	16
NOV	79.5°F/26.4°C	.8 inches/2.2 cm	16
DEC	77.2°F/25.1°C	.6 inches/1.6 cm	13

Source of above data: Historical and current records at the Belize College of Agriculture (Central Farm) situated five miles from San Ignacio Town in the Toledo District.

History

After the Maya civilization declined, the Toledo District was sparsely populated by the **Manche Chol Maya**. They remained unconquered by the Spanish until the end of the 1600s. Then disease hit and their numbers decreased. Those who survived were soon subdued by the British and sent to live in the highlands of Guatemala.

The next wave of people who came to the area were the **Garifuna**. They settled in Punta Gorda, Punta Negra and Barranco and their descendents are still there today, living mostly by fishing.

Finally, in 1868 some **Confederate soldiers**, looking for a safe place to live after the Civil War in the States, settled in Cattle Landing, just north of Punta Gorda. Within two years 12 sugar mills were erected to process the hundreds of acres of sugar that were planted. The area flourished. But when sugar prices dropped, the mills closed and those who remained were forced to live subsistence lives.

In the late 1800s and all through the 1900s the Maya living in Guatemala often escaped to Belize from the oppression and demand for more taxes. Today, the Maya make up 64% of the entire population of Toledo District.

Getting Here

The Southern Highway has only nine miles of paved way. The rest of the highway was ready for pavement, so I assume the completion date will be soon. Otherwise, the road is horrid for driving or riding a bus.

BY BUS: Two bus lines, **Southern** and **James**, have service from the main bus terminal in Belize City to Punta Gorda. Between them, they run buses every two hours from 6 am to 2 pm. There is one additional bus at 3 pm. The ride is scheduled to be six to eight hours, but it could take up to 12 hours, depending on the road and weather conditions.

Buses leaving Punta Gorda for Belize City start at 3 am and continue every hour until 6 am, then one leaves every two hours until noon. The cost is US $11 to Belize City and less for every destination before that.

> **AUTHOR NOTE:** *Belizean bus passengers love the excitement when buses stop for road construction. They become consultants and comment on what the contractors should or should not be doing.*

BY BOAT: Boats arrive in Punta Gorda from Puerto Barrios, Guatemala, every day and smaller motor boats often arrive from Livingston in Guatemala. Boats leave the harbor at Punta Gorda for Guatemala at least once a day for the one-hour run to Puerto Barrios. Motorboats also go to Livingston periodically. Check at the bulletin board on the dock to see if there is one scheduled when you want to make the trip. The cost depends on who you travel with and how full the boat is. Bartering is the name of the game.

> **AUTHOR NOTE:** *Be aware that many people climb into small dories and cross the Caribbean to Guatemala, but this is unsafe. If a sudden squall or storm breaks out, you could end up in the water.*

BY AIR: At least five **flights** a day to and from Belize City and Punta Gorda are offered by **Tropic Air** (☎ 800-422-3435, 226-2012 in Belize, www.tropicair.com) and **Maya Air** (☎ 422-2333). The price is less than US $100.

THE SOUTH

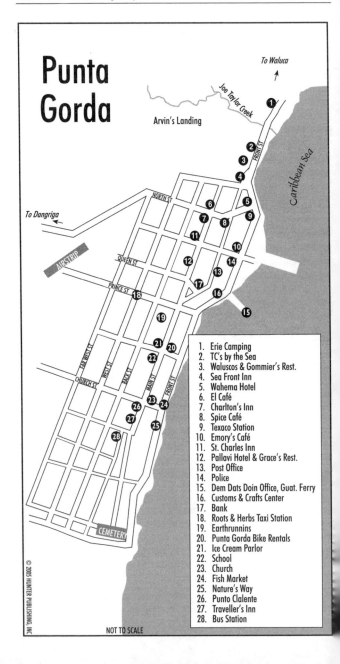

Punta Gorda

To Waluca

Joe Taylor Creek

Arvin's Landing

Caribbean Sea

To Dangriga

NORTH ST

QUEEN ST

PRINCE ST

AIRSTRIP

2ND WEST ST

WEST ST

BACK ST

MAIN ST

FRONT ST

CHURCH ST

CEMETERY

NOT TO SCALE

© 2005 HUNTER PUBLISHING, INC

1. Erie Camping
2. TC's by the Sea
3. Waluscos & Gommier's Rest.
4. Sea Front Inn
5. Wahema Hotel
6. El Café
7. Charlton's Inn
8. Spice Café
9. Texaco Station
10. Emory's Café
11. St. Charles Inn
12. Pallavi Hotel & Grace's Rest.
13. Post Office
14. Police
15. Dem Dats Doin Office, Guat. Ferry
16. Customs & Crafts Center
17. Bank
18. Roots & Herbs Taxi Station
19. Earthrunnins
20. Punta Gorda Bike Rentals
21. Ice Cream Parlor
22. School
23. Church
24. Fish Market
25. Nature's Way
26. Punto Clalente
27. Traveller's Inn
28. Bus Station

Things to Do

Fajina Craft Center, ☎ 722-2167. Market days are Monday, Wednesday, Friday and Saturday. Although not as colorful as the markets in Guatemala, Fajina has some interesting crafts.

   Internet service is available at the **Cyber Café** on Front Street. Alternately, go to **Dennis Bruce's** place (also on Front Street, close to the entrance of town). He has an eclectic business that includes renting one computer.

Tours/Equipment Rentals

Bike rentals are available at the Wahema Hotel, ☎ 702-2542, on Front Street near the entrance to town. The owner has numerous single-gear bikes for US $15 a day. He expects to have multi-geared bikes in the near future. You can usually negotiate a better price for longer usage.

   Punta Gorda Bike Rentals is on Main Street across from the ice cream parlor and just up from the school. They have one-gear bikes, too. If Wahema is rented out, try here.

   There are no car rentals in town, but you can hire a **taxi** to get you around, or ask anyone with a vehicle. The cost, including gas, is between US $50 and $100 a day. A taxi can hold four people, plus driver. The owner of the Charlton can and often will find you a vehicle with driver.

   Roots and Herbs on Back Street, ☎ 722-2834, will take you to caves, villages and ruins for US $75 for the day. Their vehicles are good for the backroads.

   Tide Tours, ☎ 722-2129, specializes in tours of southern Belize. They are happy to run custom excursions too; for example, you can ask for a guide, a cook, etc.

Places to Stay

Toledo Eco Tourism Association, 65 Front Street, ☎ 702-2096 (Nature's Way Guest House) is involved in promoting an elaborate home stay program for tourists. You can stay in a dorm that is shared with other visitors interested in a new cultural experience. The theory behind the separate

❖ HOTEL PRICING	
$	$10 to $20
$$	$21 to $50
$$$	$51 to $75
$$$$	$76 to $100
$$$$$	over $100

cabin (as opposed to the home stay where you live with a family) is that the dorm gives privacy to both you and the family.

   Your TEA cabin will have a private outhouse and some cabins have a shower house next door. In the day, you can go on a hike, a canoe trip, or a guided visit to a ruin or waterfall or cave. Your guide knows the plants and animals, the trails and the extra things that make a visit to a ruin special.

THE SOUTH

The final advantage to this program is that the participating villagers have been trained in story telling, dance demonstrations and music so when they perform for you, it is interesting and professional.

Other **home stay programs** can be arranged at the tourist office in Punta Gorda, ☎ 702-2029. The cost is US $5 per night and $2 for each meal. You can also arrange this stay with the local alcade (leader) of the village. Those programs are much less expensive than the TEA, but the focus is also different. With them, you get to sleep in the house with a Maya family. You help make meals, wash clothes or pick coffee beans. Whatever is in progress for that day becomes part of your day.

Nature's Way Guest House, 67 Front Street, ☎ 702-2119, $, is at the end of the road, almost on the water. This large wooden structure offers rooms with bunk beds, tables, chairs and fans. The bathrooms are shared. There's also a common room and a dining room, where you can order meals.

St Charles Inn, King Street, ☎ 702-2149, $$, has 13 rooms with private bathrooms. It's a funky little place, clean and comfortable. The grocery store downstairs is open until 9 pm. Go there to enquire about your room.

Charlton's Inn, 9 Main Street, ☎ 722-2197 or 702-2440, dwagner@btl. net, $/$$, is across from El Café. The rooms are clean and spacious, with private baths, cable TVs, air conditioning or fans and hot water.

Wahema Hotel, ☎ 702-2542, $, is on the water near the entrance to town. The rooms are basic, but clean, and have private bathrooms and fans. The owner is reasonable and will negotiate better prices for longer stays.

Pallavi Hotel, 19 Main Street, ☎ 702-2414, $$, has rooms with fans and private bathrooms. This is a newly renovated place and everything is hospital-clean.

Sea Front Inn, Front Street, ☎ 702-2300, seafront@btl.net, $$$, is at the north end of town. It is a large three-storey building with a blue tin roof and some stone siding. The quiet hotel has 10 spacious rooms with private baths, air conditioning and cable TVs. The restaurant serves breakfast only.

T.C's by the Sea, ☎ 702-2963, tcbythesea@btl.net, $$/$$$, is .6 miles north of town overlooking the ocean, in an area called Cattle Landing. It has six rooms, all with baths, and one unit with two rooms. Prices vary. The rooms are spacious and clean with cable TVs. There is a restaurant and bar on premises, at the back in a garden. The owner serves a killer steak for anyone needing some beef.

> **AUTHOR NOTE:** *In Belize electricity is called current and many houses are without it.*

Punto Caliente, Back Street, ☎ 702-2561, $$, puntacal@btl.net, has eight rooms with cable TVs, hot water and ceiling fans. Two rooms have air conditioning, and all have private bathrooms. A roof-top cabana overlooks the countryside. The hotel is 100 feet (30 meters) from the bus station. The owner is a non-assuming man who makes you feel comfortable right away.

Traveller's Inn, Back Street, ☎ 702-2568, $$$, is next door to the Punto Caliente. It is a clean, pleasant hotel, with a restaurant on site that serves breakfast only. The entire hotel is decorated with ceramic tile, which makes sounds echo.

IRIE Camping, $, at Cattle Landing, offers outside toilets and a shower house. The owners serve some vegetarian snacks and locally picked herb teas.

Places to Eat

Walucos Restaurant and **Gomiers** are both along the stretch between the north end of town and T.C.'s. Gomiers is highly recommended by people living and working in Punta Gorda as volunteers. He offers exotic vegetarian foods and specializes in organic and soy meals. A daily special is always available.

❖ RESTAURANT PRICING	
$.	under $5
$$	$5 to $10
$$$	$11 to $25
$$$$	$26 to $50
$$$$$.	over $50

El Café, on North Street, $, is a no-nonsense place that is almost too clean. The owner offers great breakfasts. I had a banana shake that was so thick I had to spoon it up. The specialty is Creole food. If spice is what you want, this is the place. Prices are reasonable. If you need a quiet place to read or think, you won't be bothered here.

Grace's Restaurant, 19 Main Street, $$, has the best Belizean dinners in the center of town. It's popular with local businessmen, so arrive before or after "rush hour" if you don't want to wait for a seat.

Earthrunnins, 11 Main street, ☎ 722-2007, $$, is popular with foreigners. The owner offers a variety of tasty American and seafood dishes.

Ice Cream Parlor, Main Street by the school, $, has the best (and only) ice cream in town and their hamburgers are good too. It's closer to the south end of town.

Spice Café, 6 Front Street, $$, has burritos and tacos that are reported to be tasty and the coffee is always good.

Emery's Café, North Street, $$, at the north end of town, is run by Carl Barona, a fly-fisher who has many fisher friends, so his dishes always feature fresh fish.

Nightlife

Nightlife in Punta Gorda is almost an oxymoron. You can go to the Spice Café and see if they have live entertainment. The huge deck at the **Cabin Creek Bar and Restaurant**, just north of the bridge, is the hangout spot in town, but even it was pretty quiet when I was there.

◆ Barranco

Barranco is a Garifuna village with about 150 citizens. It has electricity, plus one community phone, a store, a bar, a police office, a school and two churches. Barranco is part of the TEA and home stay programs. Besides en-

THE SOUTH

joying the lifestyle of the residents, you can participate in their evening drumming sessions or visit the Temash Sarstoon National Park with a guide. You can hire a guide in Punta Gorda or in Barranco. If taking a boat down to Barranco, hire the same boatman to take you to the park, rather than negotiate a second trip.

The place becomes almost eerie when you listen to the locals drumming in the evenings while sitting on the beach by a fire.

Getting Here

There is a rough, dry-season road for **4x4 vehicles**. Cycling is not advised. The distance is too long and there are no amenities along the way, not even a little village. The best way to get there is by **boat** – these can be hired at the dock in Punta Gorda.

Things to Do

Temash Sarstoon National Park, established in 1992, is 41,000 acres of remote land between the two rivers. The Sarstoon River borders Guatemala and the Temash borders the northern boundary of the park. In-between is a sandy marsh with white and red mangroves growing up to 100 feet high (30 meters). Orchids and bromeliads grow abundantly in this moist climate and the white-faced capuchin monkey has also been spotted, making this seldom-disturbed area its home. You must have a boat to visit the park. The easiest way to get there would be to hire a boat at the dock in Punta Gorda. Prices are negotiable, but US $75-$100 a day is reasonable.

Directories

◆ General Directory

GENERAL DIRECTORY		
■ OUTFITTERS, GUIDES & TOUR OPERATORS		
C & G Tours	☎ 522-3641	cgtours@btl.net
Captain Bobo	☎ 603-0342	
Cayescape Tours	☎ 523-3285	
Destinations Belize	☎ 523-4018	www.destinationsbelize.com
Elroy's Tour Guide Service	☎ 523-2014	
Jungle Jeanies	☎ 523-7047	jungle@btl.net
Kingfisher Adventure	☎ 523-3323	www.belizekingfisher.com
Manfred Lohr	☎ 824-2276	
Nite Wind Guiding	☎ 523-3176	
Ocean Motion Guide Service	☎ 523-3363	www.oceanmotion.com
Percivil Gordon	☎ 520-3033	
Roots & Herbs Taxi	☎ 722-2834	
Saddle Caye South	☎ 523-0251	www.kayakbelize.com
Sea Horse Dive Shop	☎ 523-3356	www.belizescuba.com
Second Nature Divers	☎ 523-7038	www.belizenet.com/divers/html
Tide Tours	☎ 722-2129	
Toadal Adventure	☎ 523-3207	www.toadaladventure.com
UnBelizeable Adventures	☎ 523-3179	www.unbelizeableAdventures.com
■ SHOPPING		
Fajina Craft Center	☎ 722-2167	
Gallery of Benjamin Nicholas	☎ 502-3752	
■ ATTRACTIONS		
Five Blue Lakes Visitor Center	☎ 822-5575	swa@btl.net
Jaguar Creek Ecological Site	☎ 820-2034	jagcreek@btl.net
■ GROUPS/ORGANIZATIONS		
Belize Audubon Society	☎ 223-4533	
Programme for Belize	☎ 227-5616	

THE SOUTH

◆ Accommodations Directory

PLACES TO STAY		
Barnacle Bill's Beach Bungalows ($$$$) ☎ 523-8010		gotobelize.com/barnacle
Beaches and Dreams ($$)	☎ 523-7078	www.beachesanddreams.com
Be Back Cabins ($$)	☎ 523-3285	
Black Point Retreat ($$$$$)	☎ 722-0166	www.blackpointretreat.com
Blue Crab Resort ($$$)	☎ 520-4104	www.bluecrabbeach.com
Blue Creek Rainforest Lodge ($$$$$)	☎ 722-0013	ize2belize@aol.com
Bluefield Lodge ($$)	☎ 522-2742	
Bob's Paradise Hotel ($$$$-$$$$$)	☎ 429-8763	
Bol's Hilltop Hotel ($$)	☎ 702-2124	
Bonefish Hotel ($$$)	☎ 522-2243	www.bluemarlinlodge.com
Calico Jacks ($$$$)	☎ 520-8103	www.calicojacksresort.com
Caribbean View ($-$$)	☎ 523-7050	
Chaleanor Hotel ($$)	☎ 522-2587	chaleanor@btl.net
Charlton's Inn ($-$$)	☎ 722-2197	dwagner@btl.net
Clive's Place ($$)	☎ 709-2028	
Coconut Cottage ($$$$$)	☎ 523-3155	
Deb & Dave's Last Resort ($)	☎ 523-3207	www.placencia.com
Dianni's Guest House ($$)	☎ 523-3159	
Glover's Guest House ($)	☎ 520-7099	
Hamanasi ($$$$)	☎ 520-7073	www.hamanasi.com
Heartland Inn ($$)	☎ 523-7153	
Hopkin's Inn ($$)	☎ 523-7013	www.hopkinsinn.com
Indian Creek Guest House ($$)	☎ 709-6324	info@belizelodge.com
Jaguar Reef Lodge ($$$$$)	☎ 800-289-5756	www.jaguarreef.com
Joyce & Frank's B & B ($$$$)	☎ 561-683-3899	www.belizebandb.com
Jungle Huts ($$)	☎ 522-3166	
Jungle ($$)	☎ 523-7047	jungle@btl.net
Jungle Lodge & Adventure Ctr ($$$$)	☎ 822-2800	www.cavesbranch.com
Kitty's Place ($$$$$)	☎ 523-3227	www.kittysplace.com
La Furaru Weyu ($$)	☎ 614-2069	
Lillpat Sittee River Resort ($$$$)	☎ 520-7019	www.lillpat.com
Luba Hati Resort ($$$$$)	☎ 523-3402	www.lubahati.com
Lydia's Guest House ($)	☎ 523-3117	www.placencia.com
Mama Noots Jungle Resort ($$$)	☎ 422-3666	www.mamanoots.com
Manatee Inn ($$)	☎ 523-4083	www.manateeinn.com

PLACES TO STAY		
Manatee Lodge ($$)	☎ 877-462-6283	www.manateelodge.com
Mariposa Resort ($$$$)	☎ 523-4069	www.mariposabelize.com
Maya Beach Hotel ($$)	☎ 520-8040	www.mayabeach.com
Maya Breeze ($$$-$$$$)	☎ 523-8012	www.mayabreeze.com
Maya Playa ($$-$$$)	☎ 523-8020	www.gotobelize.com/mayaplaya
Maya Village Home Stay ($)	☎ 520-2021	nuukcheil@btl.net
Mejen Tzil Lodge ($)	☎ 520-2020	isaquire@btl.net
Miller's Landing ($$$-$$$$)	☎ 523-3010	www.millerslanding.net
Nature's Way Guest House ($)	☎ 702-2119	
Nautical Inn Adventure Resort ($$$$)	☎ 520-3595	www.nauticalinnbelize.com
Nu'uk Che'il Cottages ($$)	☎ 520-2021	
Omar's Guest House ($)	☎ 609-3135	
Pallavi Hotel ($$)	☎ 702-2414	
Pal's Guest House ($$)	☎ 522-2095	palbze@btl.net
Paradise Vacation Hotel ($-$$)	☎ 523-3179	paradiseplacencia@hotmail.com
Pelican Beach Resort ($$$$)	☎ 522-2044	www.pelicanbeachbelize.com
Pleasure Cove Lodge ($$$)	☎ 520-7089	www.pleasurecovelodge.com
Primitas Farm B & B ($)	☎ 220-8259	pascott@btl.net
Punto Caliente ($$)	☎ 702-2561	puntacal@btl.net
Red Bank Guest Cabin ($)	☎ 503-2233	
Ranguana Lodge ($$$)	☎ 523-3112	www.ranguanabelize.com
Ransom's Cabanas ($$)	☎ 523-2289	cabanabelize@hotmail.com
Robert's Grove ($$$$)	☎ 523-3565	www.robertsgrove.com
Rum Point Inn ($$$$$)	☎ 523-3239	www.rumpoint.com
St. Charles Inn ($$)	☎ 702-2149	
Sea Front Inn ($$$)	☎ 702-2300	seafront@btl.net
Sea Spray Hotel ($$-$$$)	☎ 523-3148	www.belizenet.com/seaspray
Secret Garden House ($$)	☎ 523-3420	www.secretgardnplacencia.netfirms.com
Serenade Guest House ($$$)	☎ 523-3481	www.belizecayes.com
Singing Sands Resort ($$$$)	☎ 523-2243	www.singingsands.com
Soulshine Resort ($$$$$)	☎ 877-700-7685	www.soulshine.com
Sun & Sea Cabanas ($$$)	☎ 523-3415	www.placencia.com
T.C's by the Sea ($$-$$$)	☎ 702-2963	tcbythesea@btl.net
TEA Guest Houses/Home Stay ($$)	☎ 702-2096	
Tipple Tree Beya ($$)	☎ 520-7006	www.tippletree.net
Toucan Sittee ($)	☎ 523-7039	birdcity@btl.net
Traveller's Inn ($$$)	☎ 702-2568	

THE SOUTH

PLACES TO STAY		
Turtle Inn ($$$$$)	☎ 523-3244	www.blancaneaux.com
Wabien Guest House ($$)	☎ 523-7010	
Wahema Hotel ($)	☎ 702-2542	www.placencia.com
Westwind Hotel ($$)	☎ 523-3255	

◆ Restaurant Directory

PLACES TO EAT	
Alice's Restaurant ($)	☎ 520-3033
Earthrunnins ($$)	☎ 722-2007
J & N Restaurant (n/k)	☎ 522-2649
Nu-uk Che'il Restaurant ($)	☎ 520-2021
Omar's Restaurant ($)	☎ 609-3135
Orchids Café ($$)	☎ 220-5621
Pickled Parrot ($$)	☎ 523-3102
Sugar Reef Sunset Lounge ($$)	☎ 523-3289
Tipsy Tuna Sports Bar (n/k)	☎ 523-3179

The Cayes

Turquoise water under clear skies, white sand dotted with green palms, colorful fish of every size and coral swaying in the waves. These are common images of Belize. Diving, snorkeling, sailing, fishing, windsurfing and sea kayaking are what most people do in Belize. Other travelers read, tan, drink and eat seafood. For all this, we head for the cayes.

The cayes of Belize have the second-largest **coral reef** on the planet and their two atolls include some of the most challenging dive sites in the world. The area is huge, with only three cayes being densely populated. Many are uninhabited and others are uninhabitable.

Because of their fragility and unique natural contribution to the planet, parts of the region were set aside as preserves and parks. Then, in 1996, the seven sites were made into a UNESCO World Heritage Site. They are **Bacalar Chico National Park, Blue Hole Natural Monument, Half Moon Caye Natural Monument, South Water Caye Marine Reserve, Glover's Reef Marine Reserve, Laughing Bird Caye National Park** and **Sapodilla Cayes Marine Reserve**.

Fishing is always good here, whether you are a sports fisher, an underwater photographer, or a diver/snorkeler trying to spot a rare ocean inhabitant. The cayes of Belize are for the active and the sedate, the old and the young, the dreamer and the realist, the rich and the middle class.

If you want a **party scene** after a day playing on or in the water, then Ambergris Caye, Caye Caulker or Tobacco Caye are the places to go. If **seclusion** and quiet is what you seek, head to Glover's Reef or a resort on one of the privately-owned cayes. If you need **adventure** in the sun, go kayaking in the south.

The Cayes in a Nutshell

About 450 islands are bordered by 150 miles of reef that runs between 10 and 40 miles from the shoreline. The islands are of four types. There are the **wet cayes** that are mainly mangrove and are often partially under water. There are **coral islands** that are solid clumps of dead coral. The **sand cayes** are the most habitable. They are a combination of sand, coral and mangrove. Finally, there are three **atolls** – Glover's Reef, Lighthouse Reef and the Turneffe islands.

The corals that eventually form the reefs and, in turn, the coral and sand islands, are constantly producing more mass through a process that also helps clear the water. Except when a hurricane has just gone through, you can always see 50 feet or more (15 meters) down in the water and between Mar. and May you can often see up to 200 feet (60 meters).

Because of this natural beauty some of the areas have become preserves. On Glover's Reef, for example, there is an experiment in progress that has part of the atoll as preserve, while the other part is used for commercial and sport fishing. The success of this project is shown in the increased number of fish that are spilling over into the fishing area from the protected section.

◆ Natural History

It doesn't matter whether you are diving, snorkeling or walking along the beach, you will come in contact with coral and water creatures while on the cayes. **Corals** are alive. They are without backbones or vertebrae and are made up of moving polyps. These polyps have tentacles that reach out and trap small creatures floating by; they do this only at night. As a byproduct, they generate calcium carbonate that, after the coral dies, forms the reef structure.

In the waters of Belize there are 36 species of soft coral and 74 species of hard coral. Only hard corals make up coral reefs. Living with the coral is algae, which grows in the tissue of the polyps. The algae is what gives coral its different shades of green, brown and pink. Algae produces oxygen and other byproducts of photosynthesis that the coral consumes. Algae also rids the coral of its waste materials.

There is coral everywhere in the ocean, but the hard corals you are likely to see in Belize include the brain, short and long star, finger, elkhorn, staghorn and plate corals.

Corals

HARD CORALS

❖ **Pillar corals** form cylinders or spirals up to 10 feet long (three meters).

❖ **Boulder**, knob or mound corals are the bases for the reef structures in Belize. While growing, they resemble mountains, domes or knobs.

❖ **Brain corals** look like huge brains, usually cylindrical in shape with fissures like a brain. They are abundant in the waters of Belize.

❖ **Staghorn and elkhorn corals** look like their namesakes. They can be seen on the reef crests, the parts of the reef that are occasionally exposed. The back of the reef is the landward side and the fore reef is the side facing the ocean. Staghorn coral in Belize usually grows behind the reef, while the elkhorn, which grows on the other side, takes some of the wave action from the ocean.

❖ **Leaf and plate corals** look likes leaves or trees. Some are quite fleshy and the polyps become hidden in the flesh.

❖ BLACK CORAL ALERT

Black Coral is not one you will see in the waters of Belize. It takes about 100 years for a piece of black coral to grow one inch. The **Sustainable Sea Project**, partially funded by National Geographic, found that deep in the waters of the Caribbean, the black coral was "sparsely distributed, small and in marginal health." It is better not to purchase black coral jewelry and create a market for this rare coral.

SOFT CORALS

Soft corals include the hydro and octo-corals.

❖ One species of **hydro** coral is **fire coral**, which has a poison in its cells that causes burning on your skin when touched. These corals are tree-shaped.

❖ **Octo-corals** are soft corals that look like plants and are hard to tell from seaweed. Octo-corals include the **feather plume**, which can grow up to six feet long (1.8 meters); **sea fans**, delicate lace-like formations; and **sea whips**, which look like whips.

◆ Diving & Snorkeling

Because Belize is not overly crowded by locals or tourists, you may find yourself the only diver in the water at one of the walls or caves. The coral gardens and turtle grass beds often lie inside the reef and are seen just before the walls, caves and tunnels. Because of the complex cave systems throughout Belize, some of these caves extend under the ocean while others, like the Blue Hole, have actually caved in.

The coral is host for the rest of the marine life that can be seen around the cayes. Spotting a hawksbill turtle or a queen angelfish, a pork fish or a fairy basslet is as much a thrill as seeing the whale shark or barracuda. Jellyfish and sea urchins can often be seen from the shore. The fish trapped in tide pools formed by solid chunks of coral are numerous along the shores of some islands.

❖ CAVE ETIQUETTE

If going anywhere around the cayes and atolls, be certain to follow some basic rules.

- ❖ **Anchor** in the sand only.
- ❖ Don't collect **coral** or purchase products made from coral.
- ❖ **Don't move** or touch any of the corals or plants, as this can damage the coral and disturb the living creatures hidden within.
- ❖ Leave underwater caves and ledges within a short period of time as the **air bubbles** can become abrasive to delicate organisms. Have only one person enter the cave at a time to avoid crowding and coming in contact with some of the plants or corals.
- ❖ Be **conscious** of what you are doing. If you feel something touch you, don't panic and kick as this could possibly cause more damage. Move away carefully.
- ❖ **Do not feed** or "ride" with marine animals like rays or dolphins.
- ❖ Observe **fishing laws** and respect closed seasons. This includes avoiding lobster or conch during the closed season.
- ❖ **Do not disturb** in any way the nesting and hatching grounds of the sea turtles.

AUTHOR NOTE: *Diving after flying is quite safe. However, you should stop diving at least 24 hours before flying to prevent decompression problems.*

Dive Boats

Check the boats before hiring one. If the price sounds too good, it probably is. The cost of a dive is around US $50 and may decrease if you do more than one dive in a day. A higher number of participants may also decrease the costs.

A good boat should have radio communication in the event of an accident or problem. Legally, boats must have life jackets, compass, fire extinguisher and a spare motor. The boat should carry oxygen, a recall device and a first-aid kit. For strong-current dives, the crew should have a special descent line and for deep dives an extra tank should be hung at 15 feet (five meters).

> **AUTHOR NOTE:** *If going in a large group, make certain everyone's name is on the captain's list and that everyone is back on board before leaving the dive location.*

A **recompression chamber** is available only on Ambergris Caye. If diving at the more remote sites, be extremely cautious as it could take far too long to reach the chamber should you be in need. To help pay for the chamber and its support staff, dive operators donate US $1 from the cost of every tank that is filled.

Certification

Bring your **certification card** with you. No captain can give you a tank unless you have a card. If you are not certified, you can take lessons in Belize. There are as many qualified instructors as there are course options.

Divers are classified as **novice** if they have fewer than 25 dives under their belt (tank) and don't dive deeper than 60 feet (20 meters). **Intermediate** divers have anywhere from 25 to 100 dives under their tanks and dive up to 120 feet (40 meters). **Advanced** divers have logged over 100 dives. Your skill level will determine where you can dive while in Belize. A good dive master will not let a diver go down alone on her/his first dive, during which he will be assessing your skill.

If **snorkeling**, you will probably not go out beyond the reef, as the clearest and calmest water is within the reef or the lagoons of the atolls. The one danger for snorkelers is that the sun's rays may not be felt until it is far too late to prevent second-degree burns. Wear a t-shirt and put on waterproof sunblock.

Getting Here

There are only two ways to reach any of the cayes: by plane or boat. At each main city (or in the vicinity) along the coast, boats leave regularly for the cayes. You can also book special charters and live-aboard boats can be hired.

THE CAVES

Both **TropicAir** (☎ 800-422-3435, 226-2012 in Belize, www.tropicair.com) and **Maya Air** (☎ 422-2333) offer numerous flights every day to Caye Caulker, Amergris Caye and Chapel Caye, and the prices are less than US $50 each way.

The cost of a **boat trip** to any of the cayes depends on how many share the expense and how far you need to travel. Regular **water taxis** go to the most popular islands near Belize City. Some resorts include the cost of getting to their island in the total cost of staying there. Other resort operators or private boat owners offer trips on scheduled days to reach an island. For example, Glover's Reef can be reached by taking their boat from Sittee River and the cost is US $40 each way, but the service is available only on certain days. If you want to go out on a non-scheduled day, the cost is about US $250 for the boat. Reaching some of the islands can be quite costly – a boat to Blackbird Caye is US $400 each way.

Once on the islands you can usually walk or rent bikes and golf carts to get around. Electrically-powered carts are popular on Ambergris Caye.

Northern Cayes

◆ Ambergris Caye

Ambergris Caye is the largest and most densely populated island in Belize. It has hotels, restaurants, bars, discos, tour agencies, gift shops and tourists. The snorkeling and diving sites are numerous and spectacular, with most sites situated just half an hour's boat ride from San Pedro. The reef is only half a mile off the sandy beaches of the island. Although not widely done, windsurfing is excellent around Ambergris. The song *La Isla Bonita* by Madonna is about this island.

> **AUTHOR NOTE:** *The motto of Ambergris Caye is "No shoes, no shirt, no problem."*

It is believed that the island was named by British whalers, after the sperm whale's waxy gray secretions (called ambergris) found floating on the water. The secretions come from the sperm whale's intestine, and are used in making perfume. Read *Moby Dick* for an elaborate description.

The two main ocean sites to see on Ambergris are **Bacalar Chico** and the **Hol Chan Marine Reserve**. The most popular dive and snorkeling sites include the famous **Mexican Tunnel, Mexican Rocks and Mexican Cuts, Hol Chan Cut, Shark-Ray Alley** and **Bacalar Chico**.

Non-water people should visit the lagoons on Ambergris, where the wildlife hangs out. Because the island was once an extension of the mainland, many animals not normally seen on islands are found on Ambergris.

[handwritten note: ↓ take a tour to these 2 places. So WORTH IT! Jeffrey the tour guide is awes]

History

Pre-1500	Maya lived on Ambergris Caye, fishing and trading with mainland Maya.
1500	Spanish attempt to infiltrate the island, but are not successful.
1600	Pirates use secluded bays for a refuge.
1828	First record of British settlers on the island. The island is purchased by two Belize City business men by the names of Welsh and Gough.
1848	Maya fleeing from Caste War in Mexico arrive on the island.
1850	San Pedro village is named.
1873	James Hume Blake bought Ambergris Caye for BZ $625.
1880	Coconut business becomes important.
1893	Treaty signed giving Britain authority over Ambergris Caye.
1934	First freezer boat takes lobster to Florida.
1942 & 1953	Hurricanes destroy coconut trees.
1960s	Blake is expropriated off the island.
1965	Holiday Hotel opens and tourists arrive.

Getting Here & Getting Around

BY WATER TAXI: The most convenient way to reach Ambergris Caye is to catch the water taxi from Belize City. They leave from the Marine Building and from the Tourist Village. Just show up. Two companies run a total of 10 boats a day. Another company runs water taxis from Corozal. Their boats leave from the town dock in Corozal. In San Pedro, some boats arrive at the pier by Shark's Bar in the center of town, while others arrive at the back of the island just north of the airport. *$20 BZ one way*

BY AIR: There are 22 **flights** a day offered by Maya Air and Tropic Air. Planes depart from both the international and the municipal airports. Returning to Belize City from San Pedro, you have the same options.

GETTING AROUND: The caye is not so big that you need a car. However, there is no public transportation either. You can rent a **golf cart** or a **bicycle** (see *Equipment Rentals & Tour Agencies*, below). **Water taxis**, available at the town docks, will also take you up or down the island. San Pedro is the only village on the island.

THE CAVES

> **AUTHOR NOTE:** *If you take a taxi from the airport or the dock, and you ask the driver to take you to a hotel, he will take you to one where he gets 10% commission. That money will be hidden in the price of your room. If you went to the same hotel on your own, the cost would be 10% less.*

Sightseeing

Hol Chan Marine Reserve Office, Caribena Street, San Pedro, ☎ 226-2247, hcmr@btl.net, has numerous maps and charts to read. One that is really good is a side view of the cut at Hol Chan. The same chart shows how the water levels have changed in the past 7,000 years, which explains why some of the Maya ruins in the area are underwater today. Open daily from 9 am to 5 pm.

Ambergris Library, at the south end of Front Street in San Pedro, is open daily from 8 am to 4 pm. The library is small and could use additional books for both children and adults. It has some local poetry books and a limited selection of history books.

Rosie's Massage, ☎ 226-3879, is across from Ramon's and south of Steve and Becky's. Rosie will give you a combination massage and aromatherapy or deep-tissue massage, Swedish therapy, reflexology, shiatsu or a facial for US $25 an hour. She will come to your room to do these services. Rosie speaks little English; Spanish is her first language.

The Football Stadium, in the center of San Pedro, is used as an outdoor theater when entertainment comes to town. Otherwise, it is pleasant to sit at the stadium and watch the locals play their much-loved football (soccer). Near the stadium is the church with San Pedro standing watch over the fishers.

Go to see the **carving** at the San Pedro Holiday Hotel. The head was carved by the famous Belizean carver **George Gabb**, and depicts the ethnic groups in Belize – Maya, Creole and Mestizo. It is carved from zericote wood, the hardest wood known, and is so dense that it sinks in water. Gabb also has carvings at the Radisson Fort George in Belize City.

Tropica International Invertebrates Museum, ☎ 226-2701, www.tropicabelize.com/restaurant/crabs.htm, is part of the restaurant at the Tropica Beach Resort. The collection of crabs and lobsters was started in 1977 and includes invertebrates from around the world. The museum also displays fans and whips found on the coral reefs. The cost of the museum is a meal at the restaurant – both are a good deal.

Things to Do

Costa Maya Festival, www.ambergriscaye.com/festival, is the biggest celebration in San Pedro. It's held in Aug., but check the website for exact dates. If you plan on attending you will need to have a room booked well in advance. Literally thousands of people from every corner of the country arrive on Ambergris for the celebrations.

Each year the festival gets bigger. If you would like to taste Belize at its party best, this is a must.

The San Pedro Carnival is held the Friday to Tuesday before Ash Wednesday at the beginning of lent. It's the last binge before the 40-day fast that Catholics perform before Easter.

The carnival is fun and is the last true Mardi Gras-style festival in Belize. People dress in outrageous costumes, men often dress as women and fun is the requisite. What San Pedro-ans enjoy the most is the painting and splashing of each other in the streets. The party-goers use water colors and eggs to shmuck anyone going past.

St. Peter, the patron saint of fishers, has his own festival on June 27th (St. Peter's day) in San Pedro. It starts with a blessing at the church for all the fishers, followed by concerts, work shops, parades, lectures and dances.

Township Day is Nov. 27th. In 1984 San Pedro was raised in status from village to town. They celebrate with boat races, fishing derbies and parades.

NATURAL ATTRACTIONS

Bacalar Chico Marine Preserve can be visited only by boat. The most interesting way to do this trip is to include a circumnavigation of the island and stop at Hol Chan and Shark Ray Alley near the southern end of the caye. You can also have the pleasure of doing a bit of bird watching as you pass between the island's western side and Little Guana Caye Bird Sanctuary, a prime location for the blue heron and roseate spoonbills.

Boats can be hired from Belize City, San Pedro or Sarteneja in Orange Walk District (see *Equipment Rentals & Tour Agencies*, below).

Bacalar Chico is classified as a Zone A area, which means there is no fishing or collecting permitted at any time. Flora are not to be picked or removed and buoy moorings should be used whenever possible. All these restrictions mean that snorkeling is excellent.

The preserve encompasses 15,000 acres of marine land and 12,000 acres of coastal land at the north end of Ambrigris Caye. It became a preserve in 1996. Included in this area are Maya ruins, turtle nesting sites, a historical channel and walking trails.

Bacalar Chico is a channel cut through the mangroves that reminds me of the Everglades in Florida. This narrow channel was dug by the Maya 1,500 years ago so that they could take their canoes up to Chetumal Bay to trade without going all the way around the island. At Rocky Point, on the east side of the island, they would have had to enter the open sea and possibly dangerous or rough water.

The visitor center is open daily from 8 am to 5 pm (closed from noon to pm). The charge to enter the park is US $5 per person. There is a 12-foot (seven-meter) observation tower above the visitor center. From its top, you can see almost all the way to Tulum.

Hol Chan Marine Reserve is four miles south of San Pedro and hosts 0,000 visitors a year. It is one of the most popular marine sites in Belize. Hol han means "little channel" in Maya. The channel is about 10 meters wide 0 feet) and just about as deep. It is known for the moray eels that live in mall caves along the walls, but it is also rich in other wildlife.

Hol Chan became the first marine reserve ever recognized in Central merica. Established in 1987, it covers about five square miles and encompasses three different marine zones – reef, mangrove and sea grass beds. nce its inception the number of fish in and around the reserve has in-

THE CAVES

creased noticeably. Touching or disturbing any of the fish or plants is strictly forbidden. There is a park warden at Hol Chan watching what you do and collecting the US $3 fee required to visit.

MAYA RUINS

I describe these sites going down the island from the north. You will probably visit these sites in a boat and the cost usually includes a stop at the ruins. Check with your tour operator before you pay.

Near the visitor center of **Bacalar Chico Preserve** you will see a few mounds where the **San Juan** trading site was originally located. Parts of it jut into the water. There are pottery shards, tools, spearheads, obsidian, bones and bottles lying on the ground. It is illegal to collect or remove any of these pieces, but you may look. Some of the items found here (and taken to the museum) came from as far away as the Pacific coast of Guatemala and central Mexico.

Just through the mangroves is a trail that will take you up a hill to the **Santa Cruz** trading site. It has some wells that are secured around the rim by stones. There is also a plaza and some burial mounds.

After you leave Santa Cruz the Bacalar Chico Cut through the mangroves leads you to another site.

The **Chac Balam ruin** is not far from the cut. Originally, the Maya had to dig this harbor by hand. Today the harbor has again been cleared, although the trail to the ruin can be difficult and wet. There are deep holes just under the surface, so take a pole to check the ground before stepping. Once at the entrance to the ruin, you will see signs posted by the park officials indicating the names of trees.

Although Chac Balam is believed to have been a trading center, there are many shallow graves in the area, including burial mounds at the entrance. Some archeologists believe that this was a place where the Maya came to bury their dead.

The area of **Rocky Point** and **Robles Point**, just south of the Bacalar Chico Cut on the east side, are nesting grounds for the green and loggerhead turtles. Rocky Point is the only spot in Belize where the mainland touches the coral reef; you can see parts of the reef sticking up out of the water as you approach.

The **Marco Gonzalez ruins** are probably the largest of the sites on Ambergris. They are just 1.8 miles south of San Pedro. The city had a central plaza with several small courtyards. It is believed that the people from here traded with those at Lamanai. The most interesting thing about this site is that it i believed to have been occupied well into the 1200s, long after many of the other cities were abandoned.

Adventures on Water

DIVE & SNORKELING SITES

It is impossible in the scope of this book to describe the 50 or so different sites that I know of along the reef near Ambergris. The most popular snorke

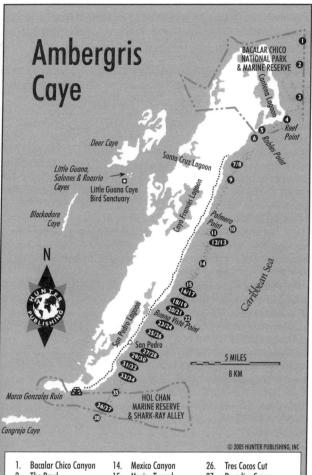

Ambergris Caye

BACALAR CHICO
NATIONAL PARK
& MARINE RESERVE

Bacalar Chico
National Park
& Marine Reserve

Cantena Lagoon

Reef
Point

Robles Point

Deer Caye

Santa Cruz Lagoon

Little Guana,
Salones & Roasrio
Cayes

Little Guana Caye
Bird Sanctuary

Blackadore
Caye

Cayo Frances Lagoon

Palmero
Point

N

HUNTER
PUBLISHING

Caribbean Sea

San Pedro Lagoon

Buena Vista Point

San Pedro

Marco Gonzales Ruin

5 MILES

8 KM

HOL CHAN
MARINE RESERVE
& SHARK-RAY ALLEY

Cangrejo Caye

© 2005 HUNTER PUBLISHING, INC

1. Bacalar Chico Canyon	14. Mexico Canyon	26. Tres Cocos Cut
2. The Bowl	15. Mexico Tunnel	27. Paradise Canyon
3. Franco Canyon	16. Mexico Rock	28. Tackle Box Canyon
4. Rocky Point Canyon	17. Mexico Cut	29. Toffee Canyon
5. Robles Canyon	18. Calalan Rock	30. Entrada San Pedro Cut
6. Tortuga Canyon	19. Mata Canyon	31. Dardanellos Cut
7. Bazil Jones Canyon	20. Punta Arena Canyon	32. Victoria Canyon
8. Bazil Jones Cut	21. Pescador Canyon	33. Cypress Canyon
9. Punta Azul Canyon	22. Pescador Tunnel	34. Cypress Tunnels
10. Palmero Canyon #2	23. Buena Vista Canyon	35. Boca Chica Canyon
11. Palmero Canyon #1	24. Cocao Canyon	36. Hol Chan Canyon
12. Palmero Cut	25. Tres Cocos Canyon	37. Hol Chan Cut
13. Santa Rita Canyon		38. Shark Ray Alley

ng/dive sites are Boca Ciega (for very advanced divers) and Bacalar Chico, Corral Gardens and Mexico Rocks, Mexico Tunnel and Mexico Cut for intermediate divers. But there are places like Buena Vista Canyon, Victoria Canyons, Palmero Canyon, Tres Cocos, Cypress Tunnels and more that are attractive and suitable for all skill levels.

The cost of a single dive is US $25-$40; if you book two or three dives for the same day, the cost decreases. Night dives are popular; snorkelers enjoy this sport also. The cost is US $10-$20 more per person for night dives.

In the sea grass beds at Hol Chan is the **Boca Ciega sinkhole**, or cave without a roof. The blue sponge fans and sea fans are abundant here. You must have permission from the warden to enter this area. Those diving along the cut should be aware that outgoing tides can create a strong current. All care should be taken not to drift with the tide into open water. This area should not be confused with Boca Ciega, just offshore from San Pedro, where you go about 100 feet deep (30 meters). The sinkhole dive is for intermediate levels.

Shark Ray Alley is a snorkeling site in shallow water just north of Hol Chan Cut. Fishers long ago used to clean their catch along this strip, thus attracting nurse sharks and stingrays, who came for the easy feed. Today, tour operators feed the fish so tourists can watch Caribbean sharks and stingrays.

> **AUTHOR NOTE:** *It will be your decision whether you approve of feeding animals. Ask the tour operators about their habits before paying to go. Personally, I believe that feeding any wild creature takes it away from its natural way of life and creates problems the animals can't cope with once the human has disappeared.* true

Mexico Rocks, with its shallow waters, was named after the coconut plantation that sat on shore above the site. Brain coral and sea fans are numerous as are small caves. The sea grass area is a good hiding spot for stingrays and batfish. Since the water is protected by the reef and the depth is only about 25 feet (eight meters), visibility (usually to the bottom) is almost always good. Close by is the spectacular pinnacle (near a canyon exit) called the **Mexico Rocks Pinnacle**. There is also a wall drop-off with tube sponges near the pinnacle and nearby are the **Mexico Tunnels**, suitable only for experienced divers. A light is needed and you must go with a dive master.

❖   **ECOLOGY**

Scientists have found, in the waters of Belize, that warning signs of ecological problems include the lack of plankton and plankton-eating fish. They also found that living conch are scarce, although there are a lot of empty conch shells in the waters. This would indicate that the waters were rich in marine life in the past.

The Pescador Cavern and Tunnels are only for the advanced diver. The dive is about 100 feet (30 meters) through a long tunnel, at the end of which is a 200-foot (60-meter) drop. This is a popular site. If there are too man people when you arrive, go over to **Punta Arena** just north of Pescador and you will find similar formations.

Palmeros is known for its huge limestone arches that house many of the larger fish. There is often a strong current here, so take care.

Buena Vista is an 80-foot (24-meter) dive that is good for the photographer. Many finger canyons here hide big groupers.

Tres Cocos and Cut is a 50-100-foot dive that has a healthy display of corals. The narrow gorges should be explored with caution. This is an intermediate dive.

The **Tackle Box** has typical spur and groove structures and huge canyons with parrotfish. Some walls are almost vertical. Look closely for the tube worms.

Don't let **Amigo's Wreck** lure you into believing you will see some great pirate's boat. This boat was sunk deliberately in 1996 (albeit by pirates) for the purpose of attracting divers. Stingrays, sharks and groupers are common.

M & M Caverns have coral mountains and tunnels that go 60 to 90 feet down (20-30 meters). It is the vibrant colors that attract people to this site.

Rocky Point is where the reef meets the land and the shallow canyons house tarpon and groupers.

PARASAILING

Parasailing is offered by **Fido's Fun Sports** in the center of San Pedro. The cost is US $50 if you go alone, $90 if you go tandem.

FISHING

SEASONAL FISHING CHART	
The following information was provided by Journey's End Hotel.	
BONEFISH	A year-round catch. Peak months are Mar.-Aug., but other months offer good opportunity too.
PERMIT	Mar. through to the end of Nov. offers excellent catches.
TARPON	The possibility of catching tarpon is fair for Dec., Jan. and Feb., good for Mar. and Apr. and excellent for the rest of the year.
BARRACUDA	Prime months for barracuda are Dec. through Mar. , although catches are taken all year.
SNAPPER	Snapper catches are good in Dec., Jan. and May to Sept., excellent from Feb. to the end of Apr., and then fair for Oct. and Nov.

Journey's End Hotel also provided the following equipment information. Bonefish rods should be between 5.5 and 6.5 feet long (1.6 and 1.9 meters) with reels holding 200 yards of six- to eight-pound test mono lines. The best lure is a 1/8 ounce jig with the hook pointing up in pink or brown/white.

THE CAVES

For fly gear, fishers should use #6 on a calm day and #8 or #10 in stronger winds. Reels should have 200 yards of 20-pound test Dacron backing plus floating fly line, neutral in color with a nine-foot leader. Tippets should be eight- to 10-pound test and clear. Flies should not be weighted and should be on a #6 hook. They should be orange or patterns of white, brown and pink.

Tarpon and permit like spinning or plug casting outfits that have lures from 1/2 ounce to one ounce. Line should be 12- to 14-pound mono or Dacron. For smaller tarpon, use two feet (60 cm) of 40-pound mono shock leaders. Fly rods for #8 or #9 lines are perfect. Tippets plus shock leaders of 50- to 100-pound mono are best. Flies should be Stu Apte in black/red/grizzly, black/red, white/red or yellow/red or Lefty's Deceivers in white or white topped with green. 1/0's are best.

Reef fishing is best done with stiff casting or spinning rods and reels with 17- to 20-pound test. White jigs are winners, tipped with plastic worms. Size should be 3/4 to 2 ounces for all depths.

WINDSURFING

For some reason, this sport has not really caught on in Belize, though the conditions are excellent. From Jan. to Mar. the winds are constantly 15 mph and the water is never below 80°F. Wetsuits are not needed, but sunscreen is. From Apr. until June the waters are calmer so the conditions are better for beginners. From Sept. to Dec. (hurricane season) the weather can be a bit touchy.

Lessons for windsurfing run about US $225 for eight hours. This includes equipment. The eight hours of lessons are spread out for two or three days. Day one for beginners starts with 15 minutes of dry-land practice and then 45 minutes of water practice with the instructor in a boat beside you. Straight board rentals cost about US $20 an hour for the long boards or $80 for five hours and US $25 an hour for short boards or $100 for five hours. See *Equipment Rentals & Tour Agencies*, below.

SAILING

Sailing, unlike surfing, is popular in Belize. For those learning, the conditions are optimum. Easy-to-operate sailboats like the Laser Pico, with or without jib, cost about US $20 an hour. Catamarans, which require a bit more skill cost about US $75 for half a day. See *Equipment Rentals & Tour Agencies* below.

Adventures on Land

CYCLING

A trip up to either end of the island is highly recommended. The sand is soft in places, so peddling can be difficult. If you cross the **San Pedro River** to the north of town, the cost is US 50¢ for a ride on the reaction ferry. The *reaction* is actually the action of three young men hauling on a rope that pulls a huge metal box across the water.

Cycling south will take you to the **Marco Gonzalez ruins**.

BIRDING

Just west of Ambergris Caye is the **Little Guana Caye Bird Sanctuary**, which includes Little Guana Caye and Los Salones Caye. These cayes were turned over to the management of the Green Reef Society (see below) in 1998. A non-profit, non-governmental organization formed in San Pedro in 1996 by concerned citizens, the organization has been working to preserve the nesting grounds inside the cayes of Belize.

On Little Guana you'll see blue herons, white ibis, tri-colored herons and reddish egrets, of which it has the largest colony in the Caribbean. Roseate spoonbills are no longer found here. An unnamed caye that sits between Sand Point and Mosquito Caye is a nesting site for many wading birds.

The entire western side of Ambergris Caye between **Laguna de Cayo Frances** and **San Pedro Lagoon** harbors a large population of birds that come to feed, nest and roost. It's a diverse group that includes the huge wood stork, the tiny hummingbird, reddish egret, brown booby and the tri-colored heron. Because the area between the two lagoons is not under protection, it is under threat and poaching of the juvenile wood stork has drastically decreased this bird's numbers. Fishing and unregulated tourism are other threats to these birds.

The **Green Reef Society**, 100 Coconut Drive, San Pedro, ☎ 226-2833, www.greenreefbelize.com, welcomes visitors interested in the conservation of the birds. Please stop in to give support and maybe learn the latest news about nesting birds in the area.

BUTTERFLY MIGRATIONS

The **sulfur butterfly** usually migrates at the end of June or early July from central Mexico over the Yucatán and down to Central America. As the food becomes scarce in Mexico, the numbers migrating south increase. One year at Caribbean Villas (see *Places to Stay*), Wil and Susan Lala estimated that there were 1,600 butterflies per hour passing their place.

The sulfur butterfly is a daytime flying species that is black with metallic green bands and long tails on its hind wings. Because the larvae feed on food not presently available in Belize it is believed that they migrate rather than make the area their home. Although it is common to see them in July, there have been sightings as late as Aug. in other parts of Belize like Cayo District and Monkey River Town.

According to lepidopterist Matthew Barnes, www.tropicalmoths.org, a specialist on the topic of moths and butterflies, there are many migrations through the country and much-needed studies are just beginning. It is believed by some scientists that the numbers of insects in tropical forests indicate the health of that forest. A study to prove this was conducted in the Rio Bravo area in the 1990s.

Jan Meerman did a study in Belize during that same period (along with numerous other people) and he concluded that some migrations have had up to one or two million butterflies/moths passing through Belize in a day. It is estimated that up to 1,500 species of moths and butterflies pass through or live

THE CAYES

in Belize at any one time. As conditions change and studies increase, so do the numbers sighted.

  The *Atlas of Neotropical Lepidoptera*, Volume 3, edited by J.B. Heppner, costs £49.

  If you can find it in a used bookstore, Bernard d'Abrera's *Introduction to the Butterflies of the Neotropics*, Hill House, UK, 1984, is about the best source of information.

Equipment Rentals & Tour Agencies

Joe's Bikes, ☎ 226-4371, and **Little Pete's** are across from each other on Middle Street. Both have bicycles for rent at a rate of US $10 a day. These are all one-gear bikes with wide tires, so traveling in the sand is okay but difficult, especially in the heat. Be certain to carry lots of water. You should also be aware that one-gear bikes do not have handlebar brake controls. To stop you must peddle backwards.

The Sail Sports, in front of the Holiday Hotel, ☎ 226-4488, www sailsports.net, offers boards and small sailboats. The cost of a windsur board is US $20 an hour; longer rentals receive a discount. They have a variety of boards to accommodate different ability levels. Sailboats rent for US $20-$45 an hour; lessons are US $60 per person. Sail Sports offers lessons (both windsurfing and sailing) that teach safety first and technique second.

> **AUTHOR TIP:** *Everyone carrying this book who deals with Sail Sports gets a **10% discount**. If you do enough with Sail Sports, you'll get back the cost of this book!*

Fido's Fun Sports, ☎ 226-3513, is on the beach just north of the football field and below Fido's Sports Bar. It rents kayaks for US $10 an hour or $50 a day. Sailboats cost US $20 an hour or $100 a day. Windsurfing boards cost US $70 a day.

Monchos Golf Cart Rentals, Middle Street, ☎ 226-3262, www monchosrentals.com, charge about US $12.50 an hour. These battery-powered vehicles are the way to go when on Ambergris, and you can rent either six- or four-seat carts. A full day's rental is eight hours and costs $60 for the bigger one and $45 for the smaller. For 24 hours, a large cart is $91 and the smaller one $61 (including a $1 overnight parking fee). An additional US $6 $4 per day provides a damage waiver for the cart.

Polo's on Front Street, ☎ 226-3542, is another rental company. The carts were in good condition.

All in all, eight companies rent carts on Ambergris. Shop around for the best deal. A ferry at the river can take you and the golf cart across so you can travel up-island. You must have a valid driver's license to rent and no children are permitted to drive.

> **AUTHOR NOTE:** *No vehicles are to be parked on Front Street on Friday, Saturday or Sundays, 6 pm to 6 am.*

Jungle Tours, ☎ 226-4555, www.jungletourbelize.com, is on the beach side of the Spindrift Hotel in the center of town. They offer tours using Seadoo

Each tour leaves the shop at 9 am, noon and 3 pm daily and they take you through the mangroves and allow time for snorkeling (they supply the equipment).

Amigos del Mar, ☎ 226-2706, is a dive shop along the beach that follows the "safety first" rules. This dive shop group has also been instrumental in putting buoys on the reefs to guide boats and divers.

Blue Hole Dive Center, ☎ 226-2982, www.bluedive.com, is on Front Street in the center of town. They offer numerous dive and snorkel trips, but they specialize in an overnight trip to the Turneffe Islands, Lighthouse Reef and the Blue Hole. All camping and sleeping gear is provided. You have a choice of sleeping on the boat, on the sun deck or in a tent. Park entry fees are not included in the price of this trip. Blue Hole Dive Center also has underwater camera gear for rent.

Tanisha Tours, on Pescador Drive and Middle Street, ☎ 226-2314, www.tanishatours.com, specialize in mainland tours. I recommend the boat ride up the Belize River to Altun Ha, a well-excavated site. For US $115, everything is included – breakfast, lunch, beer, rum punch, soda, water and park entrance fees.

Island Excursions Dive and Tours, at the north end of town, ☎ 226-4075, islandexcursions@btl.net, specializes in night dives, which allow you to see the phosphorescent effect that appears like sparks. The lights cost extra. This night dive runs about 2.5 hours.

Seaduced by Belize, ☎ 226-2254 or 226-3221, www.ambergriscaye.com/seaduced, is on Middle Street. Look for the purple picket fence. Seaduced offers cave tubing on the mainland. The trip starts by going up the Belize River, where there are crocs and iguanas. At the cave entrance you will be given lights and then you will start to float through the caves. The cost for this trip is US $140 for the entire day, which includes all park fees, breakfast, lunch, some rum punch or beer, and transportation.

Larry Parker's Reef Divers, on Front Street across from the Spindrift, ☎ 226-3134, offers a glass-bottom boat trip that includes a stop to snorkel at Hol Chan Marine Reserve and Shark Ray Alley. The cost of the trip is US $25 or half a day, plus US $5 park entrance fee. Your gear is included in the price. The boat leaves at 9 am and 2 pm daily.

Services

The Internet Place, ☎ 226-3434, next door to El Patio, has eight computer stations that run off satellite. The system is fast. The charge is US $7.50 an hour and it includes a cup of coffee. There is also an Internet service at **Bana Beach Hotel**, but the cost is US $1 for five minutes. This makes it US $12 an hour, the steepest I've come across in Belize.

THE CAVES

Downtown San Pedro

1. Sun Breeze Motel
2. Café Olé
3. Ruby's Hotel/Library
4. Mickey's Restaurant
5. Moncho's Golf Cart Rentals
6. Sail Sports
7. Holiday Hotel, Celi's
8. Cannibal Café
9. Coral Beach Hotel
10. Joe's Bike & Little Pete's Bike Rental
11. Belize Bank
12. Spindrift Hotel/Western Union
13. Police Station
14. Toucan Too
15. Post Office
16. Ambergria Art Gallery
17. Elvi's Restaurant
18. La Popular Bakery
19. Barrier Reef Hotel
20. Lion's Club
21. Jambel Jerk Pit
22. Fido's Courtyard & Funsports
23. Artesano
24. Reef Restaurant
25. Mario's Fruit & Veggies
26. Cyber Café (Internet)
27. Mayan Princess
28. Lilly's Caribbean Lodge
29. San Pedrano, Tomas Hotel/Marta's
30. Blue Tang Inn
31. Paradise Villas/Tradewinds Paradise

NOT TO SCALE

Shopping

There are many, many souvenir shops and kiosks on Ambergris Caye. Famous ones, like Toucan Too, will automatically attract you. Stores are usually open by 9 am and close at night by 9 pm.

Island Super Market, Coconut Drive at the south end of the village, ☎ 226-2972, sells vanilla for US $1.50 a liter, a great price. The store also sells alcohol and non-expired Kodak film.

Mario's Fruit and Veggies, on Middle Street, has the motto, "bueno, bonito y barrato" (good, beautiful and cheap). This is where you will find the highest quality produce at the lowest prices. Mario's also has seasonal fruit juices for US $2.50 a half-gallon.

La Popular Bakery, Back Street, ☎ 226-3242, is the place to stock up for a picnic lunch and snacks for your room.

Beauty of Nature Gift Shop is in the same shop as Tanisha Tours on Middle Street near Pescador Drive, ☎ 226-3310. Their brightly colored furniture, handmade by Rene Gerreo, breaks down for easy shipping. Rene also does custom orders.

Ambergris Art Gallery, ☎ 226-2695, ambergrisart@btl.net, at the Sun Breeze Hotel, carries works from the best painters in Belize. Large paintings sell for US $2,500 or more. If you are an art connoisseur, this is a good place to visit.

Artesano, ☎ 226-2370, opposite Fido's Courtyard on Front Street, has some exquisite ceramics painted by local artists. Artesano allows you to have your own art embedded into another medium so that you can keep it as a permanent image. They can take your photo, painting or computer-generated graphic and transfer it onto a ceramic tile.

Artesanos can also put images onto mugs, polyester fabric (like mouse pads), shirts, key chains, clocks and trinket boxes with inlaid ceramic tiles. Some of their t-shirts, calendars and mugs are sold in support of the local animal humane society. Tiles made here can be shipped to Canada and the US for no extra cost and to other places for a minimal charge.

Toucan Too, Front Street, ☎ 226-2445, sells Belize hot sauces, coffee and calabash art. Calabash is a gourd that is cleaned, dried and then painted. Coconut utensils and wine glasses are also unique at Toucan Too.

Nightlife

All of the nightlife takes place in San Pedro.

Crazy Canuck's Bar, ☎ 226-2870, is on the beach at Exotic Caye Beach Resort. The bar is popular, especially on Friday nights.

Bare Foot Iguanas, ☎ 226-4220, is a hopping bar that features exotic and erotic dancing girls with names like the "Energizer." There is a US $5 cover charge. Gentlemen's hours are from 5 to 9 pm on Friday nights and, since I'm not a gentleman, I don't know what that includes. This bar caters to a younger crowd.

Jaguar's Temple (no phone number available), a disco across from the football stadium, is moderate for noise. It attracts a young crowd who like to party longer and louder. The owners of discos like Jag's have had special sound-proofing put into their premises.

Fido's Sport's Bar and Courtyard, ☎ 226-3176, is undoubtedly the place to hang out from mid-afternoon to late evening. Live music – often local

eh, older crowd. lame music.

bands – is offered every night, starting at 8:30 pm. The bar overlooks the ocean and, with traditional art displayed, is inviting. I loved Fido's.

Wet Willy's, on the waterfront, ☎ 226-4054, has a beer-chugging contest every Friday night. It requires a team of five persons to enter the contest. Wednesday night is ladies' night, when each lady gets a complimentary shot of booze. You can also have breakfast from 7 am until 2 pm.

Pier Lounge, on the beach at the Spindrift Hotel, ☎ 226-2002, has the famous chicken drop every Wednesday night. At the event, up to 100 bets can be laid on the number that you think the chicken will drop his doodoo upon. Winner takes all. They have a happy hour from 4 to 6 pm daily and Friday night is ladies' night – that means a free kamakazee shot for us girls.

Palace Casino, ☎ 226-3570, is at the north end of town between Front and Middle Streets. It is a small casino with a few slots, a couple of tables for black jack and a wheel.

Shark's Bar, ☎ 226-4313, $$, is on the water where taxis dock. It's open from 7 am until 11 pm for meals and the bar stays open until 2 am. Bar stools sit around a fish tank that is in the ocean. This spot has live music and reasonable prices.

Places to Stay

IN TOWN

beautiful view! nice deck + clean rooms. Such a steal.

Ruby's, ☎ 226-2063, $$, at the south end of Front Street close to the library, is a popular place with the backpackers. The cost is US $25 for a basic single room without bath.

❖ HOTEL PRICING	
$	$10 to $20
$$	$21 to $50
$$$	$51 to $75
$$$$	$76 to $100
$$$$$	over $100

The other inexpensive places in town are **San Pedranos**, ☎ 226-2054, $$, **Marta's**, ☎ 226-2053, $$, and **Tomas's**, ☎ 226-2061, $$. These three are north from the wharf along Front Street. All have private baths and fans and cost around US $25 per person. During low season, you may be able to barter for a better rate. Of them all, Tomas's and San Pedranos' are the best.

Lily's Caribbean Lodge, ☎ 226-2059, $$$, is on the beach just north of Tomas's. There are 10 rooms, all withe private bathrooms and air conditioning. The porch is a popular place to sit and watch the ocean.

San Pedro Holiday Hotel, ☎ 226-2014, www.sanpedroholiday.com $$$$, is an historical icon as well as a hotel. It opened on June 15, 1965 and was the first hotel to be built in San Pedro. The present building has 14 rooms and two apartments. There is also a restaurant, a lounge, a deli, a dive shop and an air station. The hotel is the three-storey, pink and white building you see when you first come onto the island.

Spindrift Resort, ☎ 226-2174 or 800-688-0161, $$$, is in the center of town, on the beach. The 30 rooms are clean and simple with private baths and fans.

JAGUAR is the place to be! doesn't start getting busy til 11-1

Mayan Princess Resort, ☎ 226-2778, www.mayanprincesshotel.com, $$$, is a large hotel on the beach and in the center of town. All rooms have cable TV, phones, air conditioning and kitchenettes. There is a dive shop and gift shop on the premises, and bicycles and golf carts are available for rent.

Paradise Resort Hotel, ☎ 226-2083, $$$$, is in a quiet location at the north end of town just before the residential area. This white stucco resort is well maintained. There's a bar and a dive shop on the premises. You can choose a fan or air conditioning, and all rooms have private bathrooms with hot water. The deluxe rooms have king-sized beds, cable TVs and kitchenettes.

Blue Tang Inn, ☎ 226-2326, www.bluetanginn.com, $$$, has 14 newly renovated units, all with tiled floors, hardwood finishing and fully supplied kitchens. Fruit and coffee is served to guests every morning. There is no bar or restaurant on the premises, which makes it pleasantly quiet.

SOUTH OF THE AIRPORT

Sun Breeze Beach Hotel, ☎ 226-2191 or 800-688-0191, www.sunbreeze. net, $$$$/$$$$$, is across from the airport. It has 38 standard rooms in a two-storey structure built around the pool. There is a patio, bar and restaurant. Lush vegetation keeps the grounds quite cool. Each room has air conditioning, private baths with hot water, tile floors and television. The five deluxe rooms also have Jacuzzis. There is a gift shop, dive shop and dock at the hotel. **Caruso's Restaurant**, on site, serves the best Italian cuisine on the island.

> **AUTHOR NOTE:** *Places located near the airport do not have a noise problem because planes stop flying by dark and there are no jets, only prop planes.*

Ramon's Village, ☎ 226-2071 or 800-magic-15, www.ramons.com, $$$$/$$$$, is just beyond the airport on the water side of the road. The village has an immaculate garden setting with rustic thatched-hut cabins whose outside appearance hides the luxury. Ramon's dive shop is well equipped and the dive masters offer triple-tank and night dives at locations as far away as the Turneffe Islands.

Steve & Becky's Cute Little Hotel, ☎ 800-magic-15, $$$$, is across from Ramon's and is run by the same crew. All the services available at Ramon's are also available to those staying in the cabins. Each cabin has private bath and air conditioning. There is a tiny garden on the property.

Mata Rocks Resort, ☎ 226-2336 or 888-628-2757, www.matarocks.com, $$$, is a clean, comfortable place a mile south of town. The 11 rooms (two suites) are on the beach and have hardwood and tile finishings inside and stucco on the outside. There is a beachfront bar, complimentary use of bicycles and a pool. Breakfast is included. The owners are liberal-minded.

Changes in Latitudes B & B, ☎ 226-2986, www.ambergriscaye.com/latitudes, $$$, is a neat little house surrounded by a picket fence. It has six rooms with private entrances, private baths with hot water, air conditioning

THE CAVES

and fans, and tasteful décor. A full breakfast is included in the price. You can also use the kitchen facilities to make snacks or small meals.

Belize Yacht Club, ☎ 226-2777 or 800-688-0402, www.belizeyachtclub. com, $$$$$, is elegant and expensive. The suites have one to three bedrooms and come with air conditioning, telephone, cable TV, kitchenette and private, furnished balcony. Most have an ocean view. Within walking distance of the village center, the club has 40 suites, two **restaurants**, a full marina, a tour desk, a dive shop and a gift shop. There is also a fresh water pool. The tour desk can arrange for almost any trip you could want. There is a little patio restaurant with a few tables.

Hideaway Sports Lodge, south of the Yacht Club on Coconut Drive, ☎ 226-2141, www.hideawaysportslodge.com, $$$, is one of the older places off the beach. It has 20 clean rooms with private bathrooms. Some rooms have little kitchens.

Exotic Caye Beach Resort, ☎ 226-2870 or 800-201-9389, www. belizeisfun.com, $$$$$, is truly exotic. These rustic thatched-roof cabins are professionally decorated and interspersed around a large pool. Each bright cabin has a fully supplied kitchen, air conditioning and a living room couch that opens up to accommodate any extra member of your party. This beachside resort has a pool, dive shop, massage parlor, boat dock and volleyball court. They offer several packages.

Corona del Mar, Woody's Wharf, ☎ 226-2055, www.belizeone.com/ coronadelmar, $$$/$$$$, is a quiet place with no public bar or restaurant. The rooms have high ceilings, carved wooden doors, cable TV, telephones, living rooms, dining nooks, kitchens, combination bathtubs and showers, air conditioning, fans and balconies. The resort faces the ocean. Breakfast (included) consists of eggs with potatoes and toast, juice and coffee.

Tropica Beach Resort, ☎ 226-2701 or 888-778-9776, $$$/$$$$, has rooms with private baths, open porches, ceiling fans, air conditioning and louvered windows. On the premises is the famous International Invertebrates Museum (see page 252), a restaurant, bar, dive shop, 200-foot pier and freshwater pool.

Coconuts Caribbean Hotel, ☎ 226-3500 or 226-3677, www.coconuts hotel.com, $$$/$$$$, is set on the beach. All cabins can sleep four and come with private baths and air conditioning. A breakfast of fresh muffins, juice and coffee is included in the price.

Caribbean Villas, ☎ 226-2715, www.caribbeanvillashotel.com, is set on 4.5 acres on the beach surrounded by jungle vegetation that makes this a private bird sanctuary. The rooms were designed by the owner, so they have some efficient features like a spot to hide your suitcase under the counter. All rooms have air conditioning, mahogany wood trim and slatted windows, non-intrusive security systems, hideaway beds, fully furnished kitchens and ocean views.

Xanadu Island Resort, ☎ 226-2814, www.xanaduresort-belize.com, $$$$/$$$$$, features a variety of accommodations, from an attractive loft suite to a three-bedroom apartment. The kitchens are completely furnished and there is central air conditioning, cable TV, telephones, tiled bathroom and hardwood finishings. There is a freshwater pool, a dock, as well as complimentary use of bicycles and kayaks. There is no bar or restaurant.

Banyan Bay Resort, ☎ 226-3739, $$$$$, www.banyanbay.com, has 36 units with two bedrooms (one with Jacuzzi), two bathrooms, full kitchens, cable TV and air conditioning. The hotel has a pool, restaurant, dive shop, gift shop and 24-hour security.

Victoria House, ☎ 226-2067 or 800-247-5159, $$$$/$$$$$, is at the southernmost end of Coconut Drive and is the exquisite mansion seen from the water when approaching Ambergris Caye. The plantation-style rooms have mosquito nets, air conditioning, floor-to-ceiling windows, private baths, hardwood floors and mini-bars. Rooms open onto a wrap-around balcony. There is a freshwater pool, bar and restaurant on site.

Banana Beach Resort, ☎ 226-3890, www.bananabeach.com, $$$$, has 35 units, each capable of sleeping four. All have furnished kitchenettes with stove, fridge and microwaves, as well as cable TV, air conditioning, in-room safes and telephones. There is a garden pool, beach bar, dive shop and rental unit for kayaks and windsurf boards.

NORTH OF THE RIVER

Captain Morgan's, ☎ 226-2567 or 888-653-9090, www.belizevacation. com, $$$$$, is located 3.5 miles from town, with a private beach, no telephones, no TV, but lots of activities to keep you busy. The 35 palmetto and thatched huts have air conditioning, private baths, mahogany finishings, window seats and balconies. The on-site restaurant is expensive but high in quality.

> **AUTHOR NOTE:** *To follow true **Belizean marriage custom**, you must walk up and down the beach after the ceremony. Whenever you meet or see someone you must stop and kiss your new spouse while the onlookers clap and cheer.*

❖   MARRIAGE IN BELIZE

Marriage in Belize requires a license costing US $100 for foreigners. You must be in the country for three days before applying for the license and those under 18 years of age need parental consent. Anyone previously married must have documents proving divorce or widowhood. For more detailed information and valuable cautions, go to www.travelbelize.org/honeym.html.

THE CAYES

Journey's End Hotel, ☎ 226-2173 or 800-460-5665, www.journeysend-resort.com, $$$$$, is another luxury resort. Guests have complimentary use of tennis courts, kayaks, sailboats, windsurf boards and canoes. All units have air conditioning, mini-refrigerators, hair dryers and coffee makers. The 90-acre site also has a fully equipped dive shop and a tour office that can arrange a trip to any of the caves or ruins in Belize.

Capricorn Resort, ☎ 226-2809, www.ambergriscaye.com/capricorn, $$$, is three miles north of San Pedro. It has three air-conditioned beach cabins with hardwood ceilings, two double beds, balconies and private bathrooms with hot water. You also get the luxury of having priority for reservations at their world-class restaurant. Breakfasts are complimentary, as is use of kayaks and bicycles.

Places to Eat

IN TOWN

Celi's in the Holiday Inn Hotel, ☎ 226-2014, $$$, is reported to have good grouper cooked with three cheeses and covered in a white sauce. However, when I ate there, I found the prices far too high and the portions far too small. There were only a few items available on the menu and a large (but weak) rum drink cost US $5.

❖ RESTAURANT PRICING	
$.	under $5
$$	$5 to $10
$$$	$11 to $25
$$$$	$26 to $50
$$$$$	over $50

Lilly's Restaurant, ☎ 206-2059, $$$, is on the beach at the north end of town. The meals are good, but scanty, unless you order one of the specials of the day.

Elvi's Kitchen, ☎ 226-2176, $$$, is on Middle Street and has been over rated for a long time. The prices are high and the portions are small.

BC's Bar, ☎ 226-3289, $$$, on the south end of the island, has gring time on Sunday afternoons between noon and 4 pm when they barbequ things like chicken, sausage and ribs. The portions are large enough to shar between two.

Café Ole, ☎ 226-2907, is across from the airport. It's open for breakfas and serves strong coffee (not instant Nescafé) and fairly decent French toas with cream cheese and bananas for US $7.50. Café Ole seats about 25 pec ple and, because it is not air-conditioned, can be hot.

Early-risers will like the **Dockside Bar & Grill**, $$, at the Hustler Pie which opens at 6 am. It closes at 2 pm. Their morning fresh fruit platters ar recommended.

Jambel Jerk Pit, ☎ 206-2594, $$$, has jerk chicken that has the spice of true Jamaican cooking. Once you start eating, it is hard to stop, as evidence by the restaurant's popularity. It also makes vegetarian dishes.

Cannibal Café, $$$, is between the Holiday Inn and the Coral Beach H tel. Meat and seafood are the specialties. The atmosphere is pleasant ar prices aren't high.

Reef Restaurant, $$, at the north end of Middle Street, is a Belizean ea ery that serves large portions for reasonable prices. The average cost is u der US $4 for a meal, very low for Ambergris.

Caliente, ☎ 226-2170, $$, at the Spindrift Hotel in the center of town, h good ceviche, a wide variety of seafood and the best coconut chicken town. You'll find Maya, Mexican and Jamaican foods on the menu. This popular place.

Mickey's, ☎ 226-2223, $$, is on the backside of the island, just north of the airport. Its burritos are so big they overflow the plate. The cost is US $3.50. Go for lunch, but get there early as Mickey's is very popular.

> **AUTHOR NOTE:** *Lobster cannot be caught from Valentine's Day until mid-June.*

Lion's Club, on Front Street near the church and statue of San Pedro, has a chicken barbeque every Friday night. The proceeds go toward development of social amenities like the new clinic. The cost is US $2 for a plate of chicken and some salad.

Manelly's Ice Cream Shop, on Front Street, ☎ 226-2285, is open from 10 am to 8 pm. Manelly's has homemade ice cream and frozen yogurt. Especially good is the rum and raisin ice cream.

Blue Water Grill, ☎ 226-3347, $$, in front of the Sun Breeze Hotel, offers sushi on Tuesdays and has happy hour every day from 4 pm to 6 pm. *← not impressive*

Ruby's Café, ☎ 226-2063, $, beside the library on Front Street, has homemade pastries. *↳ awesome johnnycakes!*

SOUTH OF THE AIRPORT

Hideaway Sports Lodge is south of the Yacht Club on Coconut Drive, ☎ 226-2269, www.hideawaysportslodge.com, $$$. The steaks are famous on the island and he promises that each steak will be done to the exact request of the customer. The lounge often has live entertainment on Saturday night and there's a daily happy hour rum-drink special from 5 to 7 pm.

Purple Parrot, ☎ 226-2071, $$$, at Ramon's, has poolside dining with live music from 6 to 10 pm on Tuesday and Friday nights.

Victoria House Restaurant, ☎ 226-2067, $$$$, is at the south end of the island and overlooks the water. It has plantation-style décor and elegance. Reservations are a must. The menu is fairly extensive and the service refined to an art. You can order things like pork tenderloin served over vegetable stir fry with shrimp and peanut saté for US $16.50.

Jade Garden, ☎ 226-2506, $$$, at the south end of town, has a huge menu and serves the cheapest lobster in town. The Chinese food has been consistently good for years.

Blue Grill, $$, on the beach next to the Sun Breeze, has excellent breakfasts, good service and strong coffee. The portions and prices are decent.

> **AUTHOR TIP:** *Rick* is a blind man who walks around the streets of Ambergris pushing a cart and selling hot tamales. It is amazing how well he can manage on his own. Be certain to try at least a few of his homemade goodies.

Sheik's Restaurant (no telephone), $$, at the south end of town, serves Lebanese foods that include stewed lamb, hummus, falafels and couscous salad. Prices are reasonable; you can purchase a whole chicken for US $6.

Toucan's Pool-side BBQ is in front of the Coconut Beach Hotel, ☎ 226-2648, $$. The barbeque is offered from 6 to 10 pm every Tuesday evening and is popular. It features such dishes as Caribbean fish, pork ribs and

THE CAVES

shrimp kebobs, all for around US $10. Reservations are necessary in peak season. Open every day.

El Patio Restaurant, Coconut Drive, ☎ 226-3063, $$, has tables both inside and out. A roving musician plays a romantic tune while you eat. The most notable dish is a tropical chicken cooked in pineapple.

George's Country Kitchen, Coconut Drive, ☎ 226-4252, $$, is open from 6:30 am to 3 pm and again from 6 to 9 pm. This is a sparkling clean eatery that concentrates on quality of food rather than atmosphere.

Tropica Beach Restaurant, ☎ 226-2701, $$, located in the Tropica Beach Hotel, specializes in seafood. It offers vegetarian dishes and five types of salads. However, it is the International Invertebrates Museum inside the building that makes the trip to the restaurant a must (see page 252).

NORTH OF THE RIVER

Capricorn Restaurant, ☎ 226-2809, $$$$, is by far the most romantic place to eat on the island, and the quality of food cannot be met by any other restaurant on Ambergris. The only drawback is that they can take only 50 guests per night for dinner. This means that, during high season, you should book up to three days in advance. *Condé Naste's* Dine Out Section voted Capricorn one of three "must" places to visit in Belize.

Eating at the Capricorn is not simply appreciating a meal, it is an experience. While sipping wine, you can enjoy sun-dried tomato pesto drizzled over cream cheese and scooped up with spiced baguettes, or stone crab claws and roasted garlic. Take your time with a filet mignon marinated in red wine and portabello mushroom sauce with seafood served on the side. Finish it all with some boozy cake (rum chocolate) and a liqueur. The bill, excluding alcohol, will run about US $35-$40 per person.

Capricorn is three miles north of San Pedro so you'll need to arrive by water taxi or via the Capricorn's boat service. The restaurant is closed on Wednesdays.

Sweet Basil Restaurant, ☎ 226-3870, $$$, is on the north end of the island about a half-mile past the ferry. Although expensive, this restaurant, like Capricorn, is worth a visit. The owner imports a lot of her cheeses and is reported to have the best selection in Belize. She carries imported wines and offers a good medley of seafood. A large salad costs about US $12.50.

◆ Caye Caulker

Once a quiet backpackers' haven, Caye Caulker has changed a lot since I first saw it in the early 1980s. A few places (like Tom's and Edith's or Emma's have survived unchanged through the transformation, while other businesses (like Chocolate's boat service) have grown into large enterprises.

Caye Caulker is five miles long and only 1.2 miles at its widest point. The tiny island has 800 permanent citizens and 33 hotels that can sleep around 210 people, which means at any one time there can be no more than 1,200 people on the island. That translates into a fairly peaceful environment even when it's busy.

There are two drawbacks to Caulker. The first is the sand fleas and mosquitoes. If there is no breeze, you need tons of repellent. It seems that the south end of the island is worse than the north. The second drawback is that there are almost no places offering rooms to singles unless they pay the price of a double. This was a problem 20 years ago and it hasn't been rectified.

History

It has been only since the Caste Wars in Mexico that there have been permanent residents on Caye Caulker. In the late 1800s a man by the name of Luciano Reyes purchased the island for US $300 and soon started selling parcels of land to his relatives. One of his descendants is the owner of the Paradise Hotel.

Most people, since the first families arrived, earned their living by fishing. In 1961, Hurricane Hattie hit and caused the famous "split" at the north end of the residential area. During that storm, Hattie destroyed 82 of the 90 homes on the island. She also picked up and threw the schoolhouse that had 13 students inside hiding from the storm. All were killed.

Getting Here

BY BOAT: Seven boats run each day from the Marine Building and six arrive each day from the Tourist Village in Belize City. **Caye Caulker Water Taxi**, ☎ 203-1969 or 209-4992, www.gocayecaulker.com, offers the following:

- ❖ Belize City to Caye Caulker – 9 am, 10:30 am, 12, 1:30 pm, 3 pm, 5 pm
- ❖ Caye Caulker to San Pedro – 7 am, 8:30 am, 10 am, 1 pm, 4 pm
- ❖ San Pedro to Caye Caulker – 8 am, 9:30 am, 11:30 am, 2:30 am, 4:30 am
- ❖ Caye Caulker to Belize City – all taxis leave Caye Caulker half an hour after they leave San Pedro. It takes 45 minutes to reach Caye Caulker from BC and an additional 30 minutes to go from Caulker to San Pedro. The cost is $7.50 one way.

coming by boat, you may be met at the dock by a "helper" who will offer to nd you a hotel room. Be aware that this person will be paid a commission for king you to the hotel and you will be paying that commission in the cost of e room, making it more pricey than if you came to the hotel on your own. otel owners know who their touts are, but you won't.

When leaving Caye Caulker, boats go from both the front dock and back ocks. The last water taxi to Belize City leaves around 3 pm from the back ock and around 5 pm from the front. They will stop at Caye Chapel and St. eorges Caye on request.

BY AIR: There are also a dozen flights a day available from the two local airlines – **TropicAir** (☎ 800-422-3435, 226-2012 in Belize, www.tropicair.com) and **Maya Air** (☎ 422-2333).

Ragamuffin Tours-
Jimmy Jones

Adventures on Water

WINDSURFING

There are usually 20 days a month where the wind conditions are at level 6 on the Beauford Scale. Most days average between 4.5 and 6.8, which means conditions are great for bumping and jumping (windsurfing terms).

On Caye Caulker, an area known as the **Swash** offers runs of about a mile. It sits outside the reef, so big swells and waves are common. To the north of this area is the **Washing Machine**, where tidal currents, waves and rocks can present even the experienced with a challenge. Those with less experience can go inside the reef where there are runs of up to two miles on flat water.

You can even surf out to some nearby **islands**. This should only be done with a guide (the rule is never sail in unknown waters without a guide).

See *Equipment Rental & Tour Guides*, below.

SAFETY FOR WINDSURFERS

❖ If you fall off your board, stay with it. Your board floats.
❖ Never sail alone.
❖ Know the national distress call.
❖ Know your wind directions. Only very skilled surfers can go against the wind to get back to shore. The idea is to travel sideways against the wind.
❖ Watch for boat traffic and avoid heavily used areas.

DIVING & SNORKELING

When you look for a dive operator, be certain that they are licensed by the Belize Tourist Association. Non-licensed guides will give you a deal, but often they do not have safety training or equipment like jackets or radios.

Ask to see guides' official government identification cards, which guides should carry at all times. If they have the necessary documentation and the boats have all the safety equipment, they are probably okay. Often, guides will approach you privately rather than through a tour company. This is free enterprise. If you feel okay about dealing directly with a guide, then do so.

DIVE SITES: Stingray Village is similar to Stingray Alley off Ambergris Caye. It became popular with the rays when fishers cleaned their daily catch and threw the unwanted parts into the water. The rays soon learned to stick around. The site is not visited by as many tourists as the one on Ambergris Caye. Snorkelers get a chance to see big fish at Stingray Village.

The Split on the north end of the island before the mangrove swamps begin is a great place to take your own snorkeling gear and just poke around. Swimming is okay also. The split was caused by a hurricane and it separated the sandy beach area from the mangrove swamps. On the mangrove side the island is seething with bird life. To visit, you should rent a **kayak or canoe** and paddle around. See *Equipment Rental & Tour Guides*, below.

The mangled cement sidewalk just before the split is an example of the powerful force a hurricane can produce.

The **North Cut** and **Wreck** are at the same place. Because of the fast currents, these coral canyons are popular with drift divers. The dive goes down to 130 feet (40 meters) and people often see groupers, yellowtail snappers, moray eels and nurse sharks. The Wreck is a 50-foot (15-meter) boat that sits at 70 feet (20 meters).

Sponge Avenue slopes down 40 feet (12 meters) and has deep cracks and crevices to the edge of the wall along the reef across from Caye Caulker.

The Pyramid Flats and **The Tunnel**, east of the caye, often have stingrays, eaglerays and loggerhead turtles tucked between the star and brain corals. There are a fair number of spur and groove formations close by. The tunnel offers divers the possibility of seeing copper sweepers and horse-eyed jacks. Visibility is good, going down to 200 feet (60 meters) on clear days.

Many dive shops will take you to **Sergeants Caye** and **Goff's Caye**, about 35 miles south of Caye Caulker. See *Cayes near Belize City*, page 280.

CANOEING

Allie Ifield of **Toucan Canoe**, ☎ 226-0022, toucancanoe@yahoo.com, has canoes for rent at US $25 a day. Allie advises serious paddlers to bring their own paddles, which are easy to store while traveling.

An avid canoeist from northern Canada, Allie is working in Belize to promote women canoers. For more about canoeing in Belize, see page 151, or go to www.blackrocklodge.com.

Adventures on Foot

HIKING

Hike the 1.5-acre **SIWA-BAN Forest Preserve**, at the south end of the island (no phone). The preserve is named after the black catbird that actually meows rather than trills. There have been 150 species of birds spotted in this littoral forest.

On an island in the preserve you'll see plenty of salt-tolerant plants. Along the maintained trails, many of the trees are labeled. The visitor center is manned by volunteers and hours are a bit erratic.

Just beyond the preserve is a graveyard with Spanish-style graves that sit above ground. Past the graveyard is the airport.

Equipment Rental & Tour Guides

Toucan Canoe, ☎ 226-0022, toucancanoe@yahoo.com, has canoes/kayaks for US $25 a day or $10 an hour. This is a great deal – either paddle up to and around the mangrove area of the island to bird watch, or paddle around the island as fast as you can to prepare for the local canoe race in June.

Paradise Down, ☎ 226-0437, at the north end of the island on Front Street, was recommended in *Sports Diver Magazine* in May, 2002 as a PADI approved company. They offer an overnight trip to the Blue Hole for US $145 per person. It was the enthusiasm of the dive master that drew me to this place.

> **AUTHOR NOTE:** *Although it is not recommended, the thrill of diving under water and having a shark come close enough for you to grab his fin, let him pull you along and feel his muscles wiggle is a sensation never to be forgotten. Many companies offer this trip.*

Anwar Snorkel Tours, ☎ 226-0327, at the north end of the village, offers many tours, almost all of them involving snorkeling. Their most successful tour is to a manatee-protected area on Swallow Caye, where they can find these elusive animals in their natural environment. From there, they go to Goff's Caye, where you can snorkel as a prelude to a Shark Ray Alley visit. The tour goes from 9:30 am to around 5 pm and costs less than US $100 per person.

E-A Boy Tours, ☎ 226-0349, offers safe snorkeling tours for beginners.

Star Tours, ☎ 226-0374, www.startours.bz, is a snorkel and dive shop located at the Tropics Hotel. Star specializes in mainland tours to places like the Belize Zoo and on jungle river trips. The cost is about US $10 per person per full day.

Frenchie's Diving Services, ☎ 226-0234, www.belizenet.com/frenchies html. They have a lot of equipment for rent. Depending on the dive you choose, prices run between US $100 and $ 150 per person, per day.

Tsunami, ☎ 226-0462, www.tsunamiadventures.com, has a good boat that can take you out fishing or island hopping. Their snorkeling trips go to popular sites. Tsunami is open to charters should you want to customize a trip. This is a good outfit. Costs vary according to the type of trip, but prices are competitive.

Paradise Down Scuba Diving, ☎ 226-0437, www.paradisedown.com offers good prices and knows of some unique spots. The cost is about US $50 for half a day.

Winnie Estelle Charter Cruises, ☎ 226-0394, are great for those who can get a group together and hire the boat for longer periods of time. For an example, an eight-hour trip to Hol Chan Marine Reserve, the Coral Gardens, Shark Ray Alley and the Manatee Reef costs about $660 for 12 people. That is cheaper than individual bookings and, during low season, these prices can be haggled over.

Services

Caye Caulker Internet Service, on Middle Street south of Vespucci's, charges US $2.25 for half an hour and $4.25 for an hour – a lot cheaper than many I found in Belize. The **Caye Board** on Middle Street offers Internet service for US $2 for 20 minutes, $6 for an hour and $10 for two hours.

The **laundry** place is behind Habaneros, going toward the back dock. It offers coin-operated machines for US $2 a load, which includes wash and dry. The second laundromat, behind Wish Willies, is cleaner.

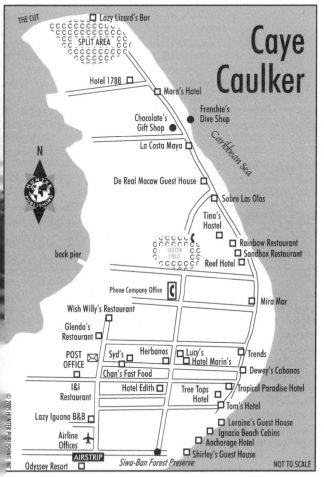

Shopping

Shopping is not the big thing at Caye Caulker but there are craft and art shops along the main streets. During high tourist season the shops are open from around 9 am and close around 9 pm every day.

Herbal Tribe offers natural solutions (other than a breeze) for those sand fleas and mosquitoes. This shop is located at the north end of the village.

Chocolate's, near the north end of town, has more imported goods than local art. There are batik sarongs and silver jewelry imported from Bali and woven bags and place mats from Guatemala.

Galeria Hicaco, at the south end of town, has more Belizean products. The bigger hotels often carry a few choice items.

Nightlife

Caye Caulker has good nightlife, but there's no special gathering spot. Many establishments offer live music. Since the noise bylaws have been introduced, loud entertainment must be confined behind specially sealed doors and windows so the neighbors are not disturbed.

Lazy Lizard, located on the south side of the split, is a great place to have a drink and howl at the birds across the way. It is the last wooden building in the village. The bar is open from midday to 11 pm.

I and I Bar is just off the south end of Middle Street. This neat three-storey thatched-roof building bounces at night.

Places to Stay

Tom's Place, ☎ 226-0102, $$, is along the beach, south of the water taxi dock. The rooms, which you must pay for before you move in, are clean and spacious, but they are hotter than Hades. My fan barely turned. Every time someone along the hall opened or closed a door, the echo was nerve shattering. The shared bath had only cold water, which was appropriated.

❖ HOTEL PRICING	
$	$10 to $20
$$	$21 to $50
$$$	$51 to $75
$$$$	$76 to $100
$$$$$	over $100

Sea View Guest House, ☎ 226-0205, www.belizenet.com/seaview/, $$ has four rooms facing onto a verandah. Each has a double bed, ceiling fan, table and chairs, dresser and private bath with hot water. The hotel is very clean. English, German and Spanish is spoken. They also offer windsurfing lessons and equipment rentals.

Loraine's Guest House, ☎ 614-9012, $, has seven tiny yellow cabins on stilts. The cabins are available for doubles only. Each cabin has a private bath, a double bed and a chair. It is certainly clean enough, but the cabins are very hot. The owner is friendly.

Ignacio's Beach Cabins (no phone or website), $$, has 21 private cabins. They are close to the airstrip, there is no hot water and the grey water drains into the sand below. Towels and toilet paper are not included. However, the screens on the louvered windows are good and the fans work.

Shirley's Cabins, ☎ 226-0145, www.shirleysguesthouse.com, $$/$$$ has nine cabins in a fenced yard on the beach beside the new forest pre serve. Each cabin has a fan, fridge, stove, coffee pot and private bath with hot water. This place is clean and comfortable.

Lazy Iguana, ☎ 226-0350, www.lazyiguana.net, $$$, has four tastefully decorated rooms that splay off a common sitting room. The two-storey building, near the back of the island close to the airport, is immaculate. If you want fine décor, a quiet room and isolation from the action, this is a good place. However, if there is no breeze (rare in the dry season) the mosquitoes and sand fleas are horrific. Breakfast is included in the price.

Anchorage Resort, ☎ 226-0391, anchorage@btl.net, $$$, has 12 double rooms with private baths and hot water, fans, two double beds, fridges, cable TVs and private balconies. I'm not sure what to say about this place except that it was alright.

Tropics Hotel, ☎ 226-0374, www.startoursbelize.com, $$, is across from the beach. It has clean rooms with air conditioning, private baths and hot water. Overall, it is neat and tidy.

Rainbow Hotel, ☎ 226-0123, $$, has slightly overpriced rooms. They face the ocean and have air conditioning, cable TV and private bathrooms with hot water. There is a small **restaurant** and bar on site.

De Real Macaw Guest House, ☎ 226-0459, www.derealmacaw.com, $$, has four clean and tastefully decorated rooms with private bathrooms and hot water. This new facility is on the beach at the north end of town. The rooms have tiled floors, fridges, and air conditioning or fans. There is a wrap-around porch with hammocks for guest use. The owners go out of their way to make you comfortable and, for the price, you won't get better in Caulker.

Sobre Las Olas ("On the Wave" in English), ☎ 226-0243, $, has four basic units with private bathrooms and fans. The rooms are spacious and very clean. Located on the north end of the village.

Hotel 1788, ☎ 226-0388, www.cybercayecaulker.com/motel1788.htm, $/$$. Toward the backside of the island on the last street before the split is this motel-style place with rooms around a pleasant courtyard. Each room has either a fan or air conditioning, private bath with hot water and cable TV. The hotel is clean, well maintained and even has a new dock out back for your use. A clean beach house comes with basic rooms and shared bath.

La Costa Maya, ☎ 226-0432, $$, is a fairly new building of blinding-white stucco (good for keeping things cool) just off the street near the split. It's clean and each room has a fridge, stove and private bathroom with hot water. There is tile on the floor and and a balcony accessible from each room.

Tina's Backpacker's Hostel, ☎ 226-0351, www.staycayecaulker.com/hostel.html, $, is near the split. There are four dorm-style rooms that sleep six each, plus kitchen facilities, lockers and a pleasant sitting room.

Diane's Beach House, ☎ 226-0083, www.staycayecaulker.com/beach-house.html, has two condo-type houses that have two bedrooms each and easily sleep five. There are fully supplied kitchens and all are newly painted with bold colors. The décor uses soft colors.

Mara's ☎, ☎ 226-0056, $, just before the split, has six individual cabins that are tiny, but clean. Each has cable TV, double beds and private bathrooms with hot water. The front porch of each cabin also has a hammock.

THE CAYES

Dewey's Seaside Cabanas, ☎ 226-0498, www.seasidecabanas.com, $$, are on the beach close to where the water taxi docks. The central bar, with rooms built around it, closes at 10 pm, making it quiet so people can sleep. Each wooden cabin has a thatched roof, private bath with hot water, good lighting (essential with wood walls), writing table and coffee maker. Some cabins can hold up to four people. Prices depend on the number sharing a cabin; price range here is for each person.

Trends, ☎ 226-0094 or 226-0306, www.gocayecaulker.com/members/trends.html, $, across from Dewey's, is a wooden two-storey structure that is clean and neat. There is a good book trade library and the hotel can accommodate wheelchairs. Rooms are for two, but even for a single person this is a good deal. Each room has private bath and some have air conditioning.

Lucy's, ☎ 226-0110, $, on Middle Street, hasn't changed in 20 years – it's still clean and inexpensive. The wooden building has been kept up and you have a choice of either private or shared bathrooms.

Island Hotel, $, (no phone number available), is at the south end of Middle Street. It's new, and the rooms are built on stilts. All have fans and private baths with hot water.

Tree Tops, ☎ 226-0008, www.treetopsbelize.com/misc.html, $$, is a cosy place, only 50 yards from the water, with clean and tastefully decorated rooms. This wooden building is bright. Two rooms have a shared bath and two have private baths. There are fans, cable TV, fridge and tiled floors.

Odyssey Resort, ☎ 226-0309, www.belizeodyssey.com, $$$, is beyond the airport on a large piece of land. Each room has a private balcony, air conditioning, cable TV and private bath with hot water. They have 12 rooms presently available and are working on 10 more. Plans are to have the dock dive-shop, gift shop and entertainment center ready soon.

Iguana Reef Hotel, ☎ 226-0213, $$$, has 18 rooms with fans, fridges, private baths, hot water and air conditioning. There is a bar and good restaurant on the premises. Long-stay rates are especially good. The price for a double (singles are the same price) is US $100 per night, but the discounted rate for a week is just over US $70 for a double.

Chocolate's Guest House, ☎ 226-2151, $$$, at the north end of the island, has one room with private bathroom and hot water, tile floors, fan and a coffee maker. The property features a porch with a hammock.

Places to Eat

There is a lot to choose from on this island, but be careful. Often, a popular restaurant goes on reputation rather than being consistent in quality. I found many places that were charging far too much for what they offered. Although I've tried to be brutally honest with my recommendations, things do change. Ask other travelers for their opinions.

❖ RESTAURANT PRICING	
$	under $5
$$	$5 to $10
$$$	$11 to $25
$$$$	$26 to $50
$$$$$	over $50

The kids selling coconut breads, Creole bread, Johnny cakes and brownies are safe and highly recommended. **Snake** (real name is Erral) drives around on his golf cart every day selling meat pies, empanadas, tamales and key lime pie. **Bones** comes to town every afternoon and sells brownies with a coconut topping. Both sell food that is tasty and safe to eat.

Habañeros Herbs and Spice, on Middle Street up from the front dock, is popular. The cost for a large dinner is US $12.50 and you won't get better on the island. They specialize in hot peppers and also serve homemade pastas and island-famous fajitas with tortillas. Habañeros opens at 2 pm, happy hour goes from 4 pm to 5:30 pm.

Glenda's Bakery, $, located in the blue house on Middle Street just before the airport, is the best place to get fresh baked goods. Think cinnamon buns, but think early as they are usually gone by 9 am. The little area where Glenda serves her meals is spotless. The bakery opens at 7 am during the week and is closed on Sunday.

Rasta Pasta, ☎ 206-0356, $$, relocated from Placencia, serves vegetarian foods, chicken fish, seafood, turkey bacon, ham and sausage. Breakfast is served till noon. Maralyn Gill is known throughout Belize for her homemade granola, breads, cheesecakes, coconut chocolate chip macaroons, and brownies. For main courses she serves things like conch fritters, huge burritos and Thai curries. Rasta Pasta is next door to the police station (this keeps you in line). It opens at 7 am and serves food until 9:30 pm. However, the bar serves things like homemade ginger beer and piña coladas until midnight. Happy hour, from 4 to 7 pm, includes free appetizers.

Chan's Fast Food is between Front and Middle Streets up from the dock. The meals are reasonably priced (chow mein for US $3) served in Styrofoam and eaten on the go.

Dave's Bar & Grill, on Middle Street across from Lucy's, has excellent food at reasonable prices. The owner is a fisher and he catches what he serves. If you are hungry, come here and get filled up.

Chinese Restaurant, no phone, $$, at the north end of town just before the Municipal Park, is very popular, with good food and large portions.

Syd's, ☎ 226-0994, is the supper version of Glenda's. It's located on Middle Street and offers burgers (spiced with his own sauces) and fries for US $3 and huge burritos for US $1. The lobster here is the best-tasting and least expensive on the entire island.

Tropical Paradise Restaurant, ☎ 226-0124, is one of the oldest restaurants on the island and one of the better places to go for breakfast. They open at 7 am. The French toast or pancakes are good and the cost is about US $3 a meal. This is a good deal.

Wish Willey's serves spicy hot Thai/Cajun shrimp or chicken shish kebob or about US $7. Going for dinner is like going to a friend's place. The owner will ask how hot you like your meal. Be very careful with your answer.

Sand Box, ☎ 226-0200, $$, located in the center of town, is open from 7 am until 10 pm and is one of the more popular places on the island for meals and drinks. They offer dishes like curried fish and conch ceviche or seafood salad for reasonable prices. Vegetarians can munch on things like stuffed eggplant with mushrooms. Happy hour is from 3 pm to 6 pm daily.

Cayes near Belize City

Almost all tours, dive trips and boat excursions are offered by the resorts themselves. Most of these are quite expensive, but travelers with just two weeks for vacation seem to like this option. There are also some all-inclusive operators (see *Outfitters Who Do All the Work*, page 43).

◆ Chapel Caye

This caye is privately owned by businessman Larry Addington from Kentucky. He developed the island to accommodate corporate meetings. If you are curious about this very high-end spot (US $1,000 per person, per night, without food or drinks), put on your best running shoes or hiking boots and go have a look. The island is open to the public when the resort is not booked by large corporations.

Besides poking around the resort or playing a game of golf (see below), look for old **graves** of some of the Spanish who were killed at St. George's Caye during the famous battle of 1798.

Golf

An 18-hole golf course undulates for 7,000 yards across Caye Chapel. The front nine holes are tight and there is a water trap on every one. The back nine holes have more variety and one is a 600-yard par 5. Sand is a hazard on all holes. Greens fees are US $75 for 18 holes and $50 for nine and that includes your clubs and cart, lunch, drinks and a visit to the pool. However the price is soon expected to go as high as US $200 a day. You'd better check first.

> **ENVIRONMENTAL NOTE:** *There was some controversy about the pollution damage a resort like this creates, but apparently the grass is a variety called paspalum, which uses 50% less fertilizer and pesticides than does ordinary grass.*

The clubhouse, when finished, will cover 23,000 square feet, with tiled floors and high ceilings. An Olympic-sized pool, tennis court, basketball court and workout gym are all in the plans. For US $1,000 per person, per night, you can stay in one of the 12 villas that offers two master suites with baths and private hydro spas. There are even separate dressing areas, and a sun terrace leads out from each bedroom. If this is a bit pricey for you, rent a cheap place for a mere US $379 per person, per night. I have heard that each suite has its own private butler. At time of writing the restaurant wasn't open. Contact them for an update, ☎ 226-8250, golf@btl.net.

◆ Sergeant's Caye & Goff's Caye

Sergeant's Caye and Goff's Caye are just south of St. George's Caye, near Belize City. These two islands sit on top of the reef. There are three others that are similar in the Turneffe Island area.

Sergeant's Caye covers about 1,000 square yards and has exactly three coconut trees on it. The water around this island is shallow, with 20-35-foot drop-offs. This is a good place for beginning snorkelers to see big vase sponges. The royal gramma (fairy basslet), a rarely seen fish, has been spotted in these waters. You may also spot an old bathtub that was left by previous inhabitants after a hurricane went through.

Goff's Caye is close to Sergeant's. In contrast, it receives over 500 tourists a week that arrive in about 40 boats. On the island, barely 200 feet across (60 meters), is an open-sided, thatched-roof hut that can be used for shade. There is also a bit of vegetation above the water line.

When the manatees are caring for their young, they often come to this island to feed on sea grasses. Most of the water around Goff's Caye is shallow and a good place for snorkelers to see fans and coral. Inexperienced snorkelers should not head to the outer side of the reef, which offers deep water and good visibility. There are both spur and grooves and solid drops near this island.

◆ Rendezvous & Paunch Cayes

Rendezvous and Paunch Cayes are tiny islands barely 1,100 feet across (330 meters), but the snorkeling available here makes these little islands a popular destination. If things are too busy at Goff's or Sergeant's Caye, then these are a good second choice.

◆ St. George's Caye

St. George's Caye is nine miles from Belize City, 20 minutes by boat. The U-shaped island has only 20 permanent residents, so a wild time is not what you will find here.

Originally the capital of Belize from 1650 until 1784, this tiny island still exudes an ambiance of colonial life. There are old houses with manicured lawns, some dotted with cannons and many enclosed in picket fences. The island is only 1.5 miles long and less than a mile wide. It has a **historical cemetery** at the south end and **Fishermen's Town**, to the north, where the fishers live.

History

Many times during the 1700s, the Spanish invaded St. George's Caye and took residents as prisoners. Some were sent to a prison in Havana and kept here for over 40 years, while others were taken to Honduras. Then after some saber rattling, on Sept. 10th, 1798, the Spanish decided to invade St.

George's Caye once and for all. They had 32 ships loaded with cannons, ammunition and 2,000 men. The British had 117 sailors on HMS *Merlin*, 50 men on two sloops and 112 men on seven gun flats. The residents lay in wait to defend their little island. The Spanish fired their cannons, inspiring 200 Baymen on the mainland to jump into anything that floated and join those defending the island. The battle was successful for the British; they didn't lose one man and the Spanish fled, never to return to the island again. Some of the Spanish who died in the battle are buried on Caye Chapel.

Things to Do

You can **sail**, **windsurf**, **snorkel** or **dive**. If you're here on Sept. 10th, you'll be able to enjoy the fun of **St. George's Day**, when people dress in red, white and blue to show their patriotism.

For divers, the caye offers a coral wall decorated with sea fans and whips. The depth is anywhere from 45 to 130 feet (13 to 39 meters). Groupers, moray eels, blue tangs, horse-eyed jacks and sergeant majors frequently hang around the coral. This is considered a good/intermediate diving spot.

Places to Stay

The **Cottage Colony**, ☎ 220-2020, $$$, cabins are wooden colonial-style buildings that circle around a central courtyard. The suites have kitchens, sitting rooms and air conditioning, while the smaller rooms have fans, private baths and hot water. Each cabin has a nice porch. There's a **restaurant** on the second floor of the main building.

    St. George's Lodge, ☎ 220-4444, www.gooddiving.com, $$$$, had the first dive shop in Belize. One of the draws for divers is the practice of using Nitrox (a mixture of oxygen and nitrogen) for diving. This is believed by some to be less dangerous than the traditional method. The lodge has 10 rooms and six cottages with thatched roofs, hardwood floors, private baths and an endless amount of quiet.

◆ Swallow Caye

This mangrove caye is close to Belize City, and increased boat traffic from there in recent years has left places like Swallow Caye or the **Northern Drowned Cayes** inundated with traffic. Their manatee populations were being reduced as many animals were being cut and sometimes killed by the passing boats.

    The 9,000 acres of water that include Swallow Caye and some areas of the Northern Drowned Cayes now have signs around them to warn the boaters that animals may be around. There is a resting hole where the manatees can often be found and a narrow creek in the mangrove where they swim.

    Many bottlenose dolphins, American crocodiles, upside-down jellyfish and other marine life live in or near the sanctuary.

One of the things you can do as a visitor to the area is make certain your boat operator does not race near the islands or harass or grab one of the animals. Anchors should be carefully placed. Even swimming in the area is prohibited. Make a deal with your boat driver. If he breaks the rules (make them clear before leaving port) that protect the marine life, you don't pay.

◆ Spanish Lookout

Ten miles east of Belize City, this is 186 acres of mangrove and buttonwood forest, sea grass bed and coral sand. Other than watching birds fly and manatees swim, there isn't much to do except dive, fish, eat and drink.

Spanish Bay Resort, ☎ 220-4024, www.spanishbaybelize.com, $$, has housed many divers, fishers, shellers and marine scientists. Its 10 cabins have fans, hardwood paneling and private bathrooms. You can also rent an apartment with a kitchen for US $40 per day. You can cook for yourself or arrange to have food included in the price.

The dining room, decorated with charts and maps on the walls, has a wrap-around deck but no electricity. If you dine here, the vegetables that are served are mostly grown on the island. The resort uses solar panels for some power and generators for compressing the tanks.

Diving and **fishing** trips can be included in the price of your accommodation or paid for separately. Transportation from Belize City is US $25 per person, with a minimum of two people in the boat. Visiting Spanish Lookout is a good deal, especially if you want to be able to return to Belize City quickly and inexpensively, yet avoid the crowds of the bigger islands that are closer to the city.

◆ Turneffe Islands Atoll

The Turneffe Islands is an atoll 25 miles east of Belize City. The central lagoon, dotted with about 200 mangrove cayes, is eight miles wide and 30 miles long. The mangroves have created a rich environment for marine life and this is where every level of diver can find rare species of fish and corals. The visibility level is always between 100 and 150 feet (30-45 meters).

The lagoon is inundated with flats and the mangrove nutrients attract so many fish that anglers are almost guaranteed a grand slam if they come at the right time of year. The winds and tide currents move the nutrients from the islands around the central lagoon area and to the flats.

There are four cuts for boats to enter into the lagoon. The first is the eight-foot-deep North Cut located about 400 yards from Coco Tree Cayes. The South Cut is about 150 yards from Big Caye Bokel and is also about eight feet deep (2.4 meters). The southwest entrance is at Pirates Creek, just above Caye Bokel and the last one is at Blue Creek, two miles north of Big Caye Bokel. The last two cuts are about five feet wide and eight to 13 feet deep.

THE CAYES

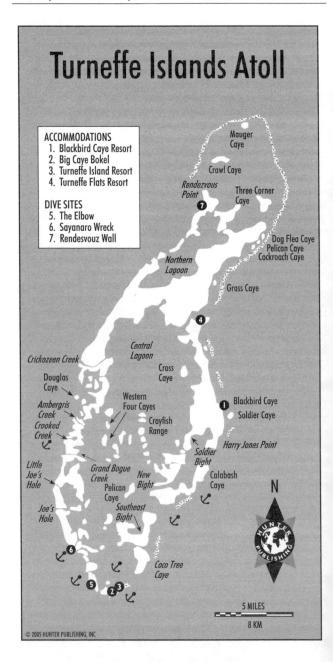

Turneffe Islands Atoll

ACCOMMODATIONS
1. Blackbird Caye Resort
2. Big Caye Bokel
3. Turneffe Island Resort
4. Turneffe Flats Resort

DIVE SITES
5. The Elbow
6. Sayanaro Wreck
7. Rendesvouz Wall

Mauger Caye

Crawl Caye

Rendezvous Point ❼

Three Corner Caye

Dog Flea Caye
Pelican Caye
Cockroach Caye

Northern Lagoon

Grass Caye

❹

Central Lagoon

Cross Caye

Crickozeen Creek

Douglas Caye

Ambergris Creek
Crooked Creek

Western Four Cayes

Blackbird Caye
Soldier Caye

Crayfish Range

Harry Jones Point

Little Joe's Hole

Grand Bogue Creek

New Bight

Soldier Bight

Calabash Caye

Pelican Caye

Joe's Hole

Southeast Bight

N

❻

❺   ❷❸

Coco Tree Caye

5 MILES
8 KM

© 2005 HUNTER PUBLISHING, INC

Diving

Because of this healthy environment, the schools of fish are huge. It is normal for a diver to brag about seeing over 30 rays swimming together. Turtles and dolphins are also common. White-spotted toad fish, eagle rays, jewfish, morays, groupers and horse-eye jacks are often seen here.

Although the north is not very good for diving and the west side of the atoll has too many wide grooves and very few coral spurs, there are other sites that do offer interesting challenges. The eastern reefs are a varied terrain with abundant sea life; the south is for the experienced, offering walls and currents that challenge even the best divers.

The most famous site is **The Elbow** at the southern tip. Here, dog and cubera snappers, Bermuda chup and horse-eye jacks are common. The reef reverses direction here, creating spurs that average 60 feet (18 meters) and groove formations 100 feet deep (30 meters). Seas at this spot can be rough and the current often sweeps divers toward open water. Control of buoyancy and air consumption is essential for this dive, which is best done as a drift. As this area is home to the predators, on a good day you will see up to 50 eagle rays swimming together. Yikes!

The **eastern reef** is a continuous vertical reef that measures 35 miles long. Parts of this wall slopes out about 100 yards and then, at about 50 feet down (15 meters), it drops. There is also a ridge at about 250 feet (75 meters) that shows the wave patterns causing the reef's erosion. At about 80 feet (24 meters) you will likely see some huge tuna and king mackerel, and occasionally an Atlantic blue marlin or a sailfish will whiz by.

> **AUTHOR NOTE:** *Many sites at the Turneffe atoll are good for intermediate divers. Some are really good for snorkelers too. The best website I found describing the various sites was www.ambergriscaye.com/pages/town/diveturneffe.html.*

The **Sayanaro** Wreck is a passenger/cargo ship that was sunk in 1985 by a local. The wood frame is rapidly deteriorating, but it is a good place to practice wreck dives. Other places, like the **Rendezvous Wall,** have overhangs with holes. The hole at Rendezvous was caused by rain dripping on the limestone when the oceans were lower and the rock was exposed. It connects to the lagoon in the center of the atoll, allowing freshwater to flow out into the salt water. Unfortunately, this causes death to the surrounding coral, which turns white. Divers, being creative creatures, refer to this white coral as icebergs.

This atoll is also covered in little patch reefs that are often like tiny tide pools just under the water.

THE CAYES

Places to Stay

The **Turneffe Island Resort**, ☎ 800-628-1447, http://angleradventures.com/TurneffeIsland/Turnefls.htm, is on Big Caye Bok at the southern tip of the atoll. This is a diver's/fisher's resort at which, for US $300 per person per day, you can have three dives plus all your meals included. Fishers can be out on the water for about six hours a day, but their package costs more than the diving package. Anyone wanting single occupancy in a cottage must pay almost the same as for a double. If you don't want to dive or fish, other less-expensive packages are available. The dive shop offers Nitrox

❖ HOTEL PRICING	
$	$10 to $20
$$	$21 to $50
$$$	$51 to $75
$$$$	$76 to $100
$$$$$	over $100

(mix of oxygen and nitrogen) tanks for US $7 each. The week-long package also includes a day at the Blue Hole and one night dive.

The resort has cabins that were built in the 1960s and have since been remodeled. Each cottage has a private bathroom, screened porch, fan and air conditioning. The food includes things like fresh-baked bread and freshly caught fish. The resort also has a library, kayaks and windsurfers.

Blackbird Caye Resort on the east side of the atoll, ☎ 888-271-3483, www.worlddive.com/destin/land/belize/blackbird.htm, $$$$$, is an hour and a half from Belize City. The resort offers a choice of 10 cabins on 166 acres of island. Each cabin has a sitting area, two beds and private baths with showers. The cabins are made of coco palm and thatch and all have porches. There is a choice of dive/fish packages. Fishers are asked to bring their own equipment as there is none for rent. Dive packages include three dives a day and fish packages include two trips a day with a guide. There are also sailboats, windsurfers, kayaks and canoes for the guests to use at no extra cost.

The island also has cabins that belong to the Oceanic Society. In conjunction with Texas A & M University, National Geographic Society and the Fort Motor Foundation, the society has been studying the behavior patterns of the bottlenose dolphin. You can join the researchers at the field station for around US $200 a day.

Turneffe Flats, ☎ 800-815-1304, www.tflats.com, on a secluded island on the northeast side of the atoll, also caters to fishers, divers and snorkelers. Their packages include pick-up and delivery to and from Belize City, one week on the island, and three dives every day or, if fishing, a 16-foot fishing boat with a guide (there must be at least two anglers in the boat to avoid an additional charge). All meals are included in the packages. For one week fishing, the cost can be up to US $3,700; one week's diving costs about $1,550; and a non-activity package with nothing scheduled costs $1,425 per person.

The remodeled cottages all have air conditioning, private baths and showers. The food is either Belizean or American. There is a gift shop that sells flies and tackle, among other things.

◆ Lighthouse Reef Atoll

Lighthouse Reef atoll lies 40 miles southeast of Belize City. The lagoon inside this reef is probably the most famous of the three atolls in Belize. It is home to the famous **Blue Hole**. The southern end hosts the **Half Moon Cay Natural Monument**. Lighthouse Reef is also famous for its fishing opportunities, both on the flats and in the deeper waters outside the reef.

Of the five islands in the lagoon, **Hat Caye** and **Long Caye** have no permanent residents, but the diving close to the cayes is popular among those who have intermediate skills. **Sandbore Caye** is an easy paddle by kayak from Lighthouse Reef Resort on Northern Caye. Just a few fishers and a lighthouse keeper live on the island. The lighthouse is an 80-foot structure that can be climbed to get an overview of the atoll.

Long Caye is a mature mangrove swamp with three internal lagoons that house saltwater crocodiles and a huge population of nesting egrets. However, Long Caye is mostly a diver's spot.

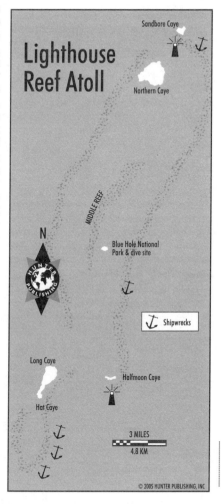

Places to Stay

Lighthouse Reef Resort, ☎ 800-423-3114, www.scubabelize.com, has 11 units on the water – five cabins with fans and private baths plus six luxury villas that rent for a little more than the cabins) with two double beds, tiled floors, fans, fridges, air conditioning, mini-bars, porches and private baths. The price for accommodations includes transportation from Belize City to and from the island, all meals and up to 17 dives (the goal) for the week. The cost for this is around US $300 a day.

The dining room is in a central building with a wrap-around porch. Occasionally, the resort puts on barbeques, to which guests are invited. Although the meals are not gourmet, they are well prepared and substantial in size. The central building has a TV, stereo, VCR and library.

Diving

Lighthouse is not just a diver's paradise; fishers too love it here. The flats are great for bonefish and the unofficial record for a catch is held by an American woman; the fish was 12 pounds (5.4 kg). If you just want to rest, the resort has 500 feet (150 meters) of beach and 15 acres in which to wander.

In addition to the Blue Hole and Half Moon Caye dive sites (profiled below), over a dozen well-known sites run along the eastern wall of the atoll. Some popular ones are **Captains Choice, Black Coral Forest, The Abyss** (that has a two-lipped wall), **Quebrada, Pete's Palace, Tres Cocos** and **The Aquarium**. They are all intermediate dives that go to 130 feet (39 meters).

Half Moon Caye

This natural monument is a 45-acre island that stands a maximum of eight feet (2.4 meters) above sea level. It's made from crushed coral, some of which has cemented together to form tide pools around the shore. The island's east end has coconut palms and the west end is thickly vegetated, mostly with the orange-blossomed ziricote tree, the gumbo limbo with its peeling skin, and the spider lily. The island is host to many birds whose droppings enhance the growth of these plants.

As your tour operator pulls up to the dock, you will see a welcome sign and the visitor center. There is no water on the island so you should have some with you. Pets are not allowed and fishing and hunting is strictly forbidden. Register at the center and pay your US $5 to enter the preserve. The center is open from 8 am to 4:30 pm.

Half Moon Caye, established in 1982, was the first marine preserve in the country. At one time, it had a **lighthouse** station, built in 1820, but it collapsed and a second was built in 1848 using the foundation stones from the first. This one didn't collapse, but it was eventually de-activated until, in 1931, the station was again put to use and a steel tower added. Today, the lighthouse is solar powered. It is not climbable because it is falling to pieces. The lighthouse is located at the southeast corner of the island.

The island was first made a reserve in 1928 and then a national monument in 1982. The reserve status was necessary to protect the **red-footed booby**. This is one of only two places in the world (Tobago is the other) where boobies have white plumage, rather than the common dull brown. The birds nest in the ziricote thickets at the west end of the island. To view the boobies, take the **walking trail** that leads from the visitor center to a viewing platform. The island gets an average of 120 visitors a week so staying on the trails is essential.

Boobies nest in mid-Dec., the eggs hatch in Mar. and the chicks are grown within two months. The birds leave the island by mid-Aug. The boobie population has fluctuated since the late 1950s. In 1958 there were 1,389 boobies; by 1988/89 that figure had dropped to 889. The last count I could find was done in 1991/2 when the population was again up to 1,325 birds. However some reports say there are up to 4,000 that frequent the island now. Boobies are constantly harassed by the ubiquitous **frigate bird**.

According to one source, another 98 species of birds have been seen on the island and 77 of those are migrants. Seventeen of those migratory species are seen often enough to indicate that they are spending the winter on nearby islands.

Half Moon Caye is also host to **iguanas**. One species is known as the "bamboo chicken" because of its good meat. It is red, with black bars on its back. Wish Willy, another common species, grows to three or four feet long (1-1.2 meters) and is yellow with black bars. The green iguana has been spotted here too. It is only the male who is green; females are orange.

The **giant anole**, a lizard, is found on all the cayes around Lighthouse Reef. The male is colorful, with a white throat, blue forehead, pink dewlaps and green body. Anoles are real chameleons who can change to a gray/black within minutes.

But the big draw is the **Belizean atoll gecko**, found nowhere else on the planet. Like many geckos, this one is nocturnal. **Loggerhead** and **hawksbill turtles** also nest on this island.

Diving near this caye offers a coral ridge at about 25 feet (7.5 meters), after which the wall drops for thousands of feet and is dotted with caves, bridges, canyons and tunnels.

Blue Hole

The Blue Hole, another national monument, is about a quarter-mile across and 480 feet deep (144 meters). Two narrow channels in the walls allow boats to reach the hole's center.

The Blue Hole is an eroded sinkhole that was a land-cave around 10,000 years ago. As the sea levels rose and covered the cave, the roof crashed in and the corals grew around the rim. It is believed that an earthquake caused the reef to tilt about 12 degrees, causing overhangs with stalactites and stalagmites to sit at precarious angles. Snorkeling at the rim is spectacular, but it is divers who really enjoy this site.

Divers will see the first stalactites and stalagmites at about 25-50 feet (7.5-15 meters). The water at this level is a bit murky and a light is needed. However, once you hit lower depths, visibility improves. The water temperature stays around 76°F (24°C). The first ledge is at about 150-165 feet (45-49 meters) and some of the cuts go back about 15 to 20 feet (4.5 to 6 meters). Some ledges form V-shaped tunnels that narrow toward the back. The farther down one goes, the better the formations.

This is for the skilled diver only. Your dive master should be with you at all times. Because decompression time is around 10 to 15 minutes, the operator should leave a spare tank at the 20-foot depth. Buoyancy control is essential.

On the west side of the hole at 150-200 feet (45-60-meters), a tunnel leads to a cave that goes on to a second tunnel and cave. This, in turn, leads to a third cave. Some believe that this cave system works its way back to the mainland. However, no one has gone through. Exploration of these caves is dangerous as the silt on the bottom is easily disturbed which causes visibility to drop.

There are no whirlpools in the Blue Hole. In fact, because water movement is almost non-existent, there is little marine life – one must stay near the rim to see anything alive. There you will see anemones, shrimp, angel and butterfly fish, elkhorn coral and purple sea fans. One diver reported lobsters up to four feet long (1.2 meters).

> ❖ **THICK LIPS, HARD-MINDED**
>
> During one study in 1970 a strange phenomenon was observed. A huge number of conch migrated in a southwest direction. They were all adults with thick shell lips. If one was taken out of the water and sent in a different direction, it soon turned itself and continued in the southwest direction. The studies could give no reason for this.

Cayes near Dangriga

◆ Tobacco Caye

Tobacco Caye is 9.7 miles east of Dangriga and it takes about 45 minutes by boat to get there. This five-acre island is similar to what Caye Caulker was in the early 80s, a laid-back tourist party spot. If you want good diving or fishing, plus a bit of nightlife, this is the place.

Tobacco Caye can be reached from Riverside in Dangriga. Two boats go to the caye on a regular basis. Captain Buck (pronounced "book") leaves from the dock in front of the Riverside Café every day at noon and leaves Tobacco Caye every day at 9 am. He is also available for fishing trips or touring of the cayes. Elwood Fairweather is the other person who comes to Tobacco Caye on a regular basis. He leaves Riverside Tuesday and Friday and charges US $15 each way. Mr. Fairweather also rents rooms on Tobacco Caye for US $25. This price includes meals.

> **AUTHOR WARNING:** *There have been unscrupulous "helpers" who offer boat rides. After they have your money, the boat never appears. Be certain to book your boat at the Riverside Café with a recommended guide.*

Snorkeling is good right from shore on Tobacco Caye. However, stay out of the channel where boats pass. One woman was killed in early 2002 when a motor boat passed over her. Locals have now put up buoys, but you must also be careful. The dive site closest to the caye is **Shark's Cave** and is for advanced divers only (a cave full of sharks sounds like suicide to me). There's a shore dive at **Tarpon Channel**, at the south end of the island where the reef curls around the island. Between Mar. and Nov., this cut is full of tarpon that can weigh up to 300 pounds (135 kg) and measure up to eight feet (2.5 meters) in length.

Tobacco Channel is just a mile or so off the east side of the caye. If you stay close to the reef, you may see large nurse sharks hovering in a few sand gullies. Stingrays and eagle rays are common.

Two popular **birdwatching** spots are **Bird Caye** and **Manawa Caye**.

Places to Stay

Tobacco Caye Lodge, ☎ 520-5033 or 227-6247, www.tclodgebelize.com, was originally called Island Camps. It features six single-, double- or triple-occupancy cabins on the beach along the west side of the island. Each has a fan, private bath, electricity from solar panels and a rain-water shower.

❖ HOTEL PRICING	
$	$10 to $20
$$	$21 to $50
$$$	$51 to $75
$$$$	$76 to $100
$$$$$	over $100

During high season, the cost is US $80 for a single, US $120 for doubles and US $180 for triples. This includes all your meals and transportation from and to Dangriga. During low season the prices are about 75% lower.

Reef's End Lodge, ☎ 522-2419 or 520-2037, www.reefsendlodge.com, is run by Saint Malo (the bad Saint). The rooms are large, with three beds in each, two doubles and a single. The cost is US $60 a day, which includes all meals and use of canoes. There is also a catering service should you wish to eat in your room.

Ocean's Edge, ☎ 522-9633, oceansedge@btl.net, has seven cabins with private baths and hot water for US $45 per person, including meals.

Gaviota Coral Reef Resort, ☎ 520-5032, has rooms for US $50 a day, including all meals. It sits in the middle of the island and looks well run. There are shared baths only, and a bar.

Tobacco Caye Diving, ☎ 509-9904, info@tobaccocayediving.com, has rooms with fans, private baths and electricity. It offers packages for US $1,000 per week that include two dives each day, two night dives, all meals and transportation from Dangriga.

◆ Cockney Island

There is a tiny lagoon at one end of the island. If seclusion is what you are looking for, this is definitely a quiet place. **Cockney Island**, ☎ 522-0334, www.belizeseaclub.com, is a new resort on a freshly cleared mangrove island. The owners were still bringing in and rearranging the sand when I was there. The round thatched-roof huts are spacious and well decorated. Each has a private bathroom and electricity generated from solar panels. The price is US $50 a day ($85 for double occupancy), including three meals. Although Cockney Island has a bar and restaurant, there is no dive shop. Additionally, arrangements for transportation must be made independently.

THE CAYES

◆ South Water Caye

South Water Caye is a 15-acre island 14 miles east of Dangriga that is a part of the South Water Caye Marine Reserve (see below). There are three main hotels on South Water and the reef is close enough that you can easily swim to its edge.

A beautiful caye, South Water is inundated with pelicans who perch on almost every post or pole on the island. I spoke with some people staying at Pelican Beach Resort and they couldn't say enough about how good it was – the food, the sea, the snorkeling, everything.

South Water Caye Marine Reserve

This 62-square-mile reserve includes numerous islands, 10 mangrove cayes, two mangrove ranges and a twin caye. A ridge of reef runs the length of the park and is the longest reef ridge in Belize.

The eastern border of the reserve is just east of the drop-off along the reef. The northern border includes the **Man-O-War Caye**, a red mangrove island that houses over 350 nesting frigate birds every year, one of the largest colonies in the Caribbean. Other residents include brown boobies, yellow-crowned night herons and tons of pelicans.

Just south of the Man-O-War is the **Carrie Bow Caye** where, since 1972, the Smithsonian Research Station has been located. The Smithsonian has conducted huge studies on sponges and medicines derived from the ocean. Between Carrie Bow and **Wee Wee Caye** is a sand bore rise, where areas of exposed rock are occupied by nesting sooty terns. Beneath these exposed rocks are huge barracudas and rays.

Twin Cayes has a seaweed farm, the first in Belize and the second in the Caribbean. Run by the Dangriga Development Initiative, the farm was established to replace the fishing business lost when the area was made into a reserve.

Wippari and **Rendezvous Cayes** form the southern boundary of the marine reserve.

Places to Stay

Blue Marlin Lodge, ☎ 520-2243 or 800-798-1558, www.bluemarlinlodge.com, offers all-inclusive packages for either eight days or five days. They have three unique dome-shaped igloos for rent, painted a cool ice blue. There are also nine standard rooms and three upscale cottages. But it

❖ HOTEL PRICING	
$	$10 to $20
$$	$21 to $50
$$$	$51 to $75
$$$$	$76 to $100
$$$$$	over $100

was the dining room that impressed me the most about this place. Everything was spotless and the food was tempting. The drink list included some very nice wines. The cost, US $225 per person, per day, includes two or three dives a day and meals.

Pelican Beach Resort, ☎ 520-3044, www.pelicanbeachbelize.com, is at the southern end of the island. The grounds are spacious and well kept in traditional colonial style. The dining room is in a wooden building. Five rooms are on the second floor, above the dining room. All rooms have fans and partial bathrooms; the showers are in a separate building. The price, including all meals and transportation to and from Dangriga, is US $100 a day based on double occupancy. If staying in a cottage, it's another $27 per person. Any activities like diving or snorkeling are extra.

International Zoological Expeditions, Leslie Cottages, ☎ 520-5030 or 523-7076, www.ize2belize.com, was one of the first ecological/educational destinations in Belize. Five cabins are available at a cost of US $135 per person, per day, meals included. Each has a fan, a private bath and hot water. Two of the wooden cabins sit over the mangroves. Satellite **Internet** service is available to anyone at IZE for US $5 for 30 minutes.

At the southern end of the South Water Caye Marine Reserve is **Wippari Caye**, ☎ 522-3130, which has four basic cabins available for US $20 each, $50 with meals included.

> **AUTHOR NOTE:** *All the tiny skiffs you see floating in calm waters belong to conch divers. Wait a moment and you will see a diver surface, usually with a conch in hand.*

◆ Glover's Reef Atoll

This remote atoll is protected as a UNESCO World Heritage Site. The atoll sits about 30 miles east of Dangriga and can be reached from Dangriga, Hopkins, Sittee River or Placencia.

Glover's is the smallest of the atolls in Belize. It is about 20 miles long and seven miles wide. In addition to remoteness, it offers some of the best walls in the world for divers and over 700 patch reefs for snorkelers. Because it is a marine reserve, fishing is restricted. The deepest point of the lagoon is about 50 feet (15 meters) and the clarity of the water is exceptional.

Underwater, the reef has more than 60 species of stony coral, over 200 species of fish and uncountable numbers of invertebrates. The 50 miles of walls start at around 25 feet (7.5 meters) and drop to 2,600 feet (780 meters).

The eastern side of the atoll is a wall with a sheer drop of 2,600 feet (780 meters). The western side has a sloping reef. The entire area is on the Bartlett Trough, a fault line.

The biological diversity of Glover's is another draw for wildlife enthusiasts. The reef has nesting sites for turtles and rare birds, such as the white-capped noddy, white ibis or boat-billed heron. From Mar. to May, whale sharks are frequently seen and, due to the marine reserve status, the numbers of fish and crustaceans have drastically increased.

There are four islands on this atoll. One has a marine biological station and the others have resorts that offer accommodations ranging from a Robinson Crusoe experience to a lush hotel.

THE CAYES

Glover's Marine Reserve includes the entire atoll, as well as all the surrounding waters to a depth of 600 feet (180 meters). There is a no-fishing zone over the southern 20% of the atoll. The rest of the reserve is closely monitored by rangers to ensure that restrictions are adhered to.

Northeast Caye is one of my favorite places in Belize. This is where I can play at being Robinson Crusoe, where children are welcome and safe, where remoteness and isolation are a fact, where hospitality is at the exact level that I need and where the marine life is exceptional.

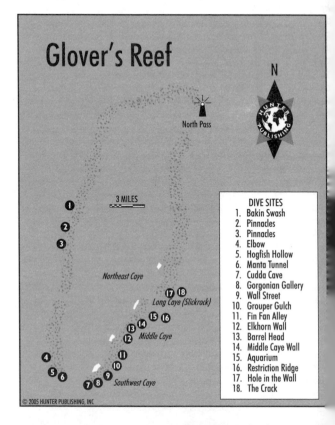

Glover's Reef

North Pass

N

3 MILES

Northeast Caye

Long Caye (Slickrock)

Middle Caye

Southwest Caye

DIVE SITES
1. Bakin Swash
2. Pinnacles
3. Pinnacles
4. Elbow
5. Hogfish Hollow
6. Manta Tunnel
7. Cudda Cave
8. Gorgonian Gallery
9. Wall Street
10. Grouper Gulch
11. Fin Fan Alley
12. Elkhorn Wall
13. Barrel Head
14. Middle Caye Wall
15. Aquarium
16. Restriction Ridge
17. Hole in the Wall
18. The Crack

© 2005 HUNTER PUBLISHING, INC

The nine-acre island is owned by the Lomont family, who came to Belize in the 1960s and made it their home. The family purchased the caye in 1978 from Nel Morgan, a descendent of the famous Captain Morgan. Nel's grandfather (not Captain Morgan) is buried on the island beside the big gumbo limbo tree.

From Sittee River or Dangriga, boats to Northeast Caye cost US $250 for up to six people or US $40 per person if taking the scheduled run. If coming from Placencia, the cost is US $300 and from Belize City the cost is US $500 for up to six people. Contact Glover's Atoll Resort, ☎ 520-5016 or 614-8351, www.belizemall.com/gloversatoll.

Accommodations offered at **Glover's Atoll Resort** on Northeast Caye, ☎ 520-5016 or 614-8351, are varied. The palmetto huts on the beach have thatched roofs and kitchen facilities. On the porch are hammocks and inside are two beds, a table and mosquito nets. The cost is US $199 per week, per person. The kitchen is below the sleeping area and is basic. There are kerosene stoves and tarps around the upper half that can be lowered if it gets windy. All kitchen utensils are supplied. Becky Lomont bakes bread on Tuesdays and Thursdays and offers it for sale. Drinking water can also be purchased from the resort, although the first five-gallon jug is included in the price. Night lighting is from kerosene lamps and toilets are the composting kind. Showers use well water, which can be a bit murky, as it is salt water that has filtered through sand. On its journey from the ocean to the well, the water loses its salt but it gains some of the alkaline products from the roots of the palm trees. The Lomonts come in on Saturday and return to the mainland on the following Sunday. It is possible to make an international flight on the same day as leaving the island.

Dorm beds are also available. They come with a fully equipped kitchen and cost US $149 a week, including transportation to and from Sittee River. Finally, the Lomonts also have camp sites for a mere US $99 a week, including the boat trip. Even if everything is full, the Lomonts will always find you a place to sleep.

Another advantage of staying on this island is that you can make your own meals or enjoy a meal with the family (you must give advance notice). Dinners of fresh fish (I had many) cost US $12 per person and are always cooked to perfection. You must bring your own alcohol as there is no bar on the island. There are **kayaks** and **canoes** for rent.

The dive master will take divers to some of the best wall sites in the world and will show them where the rare marine life hangs out.

Snorkeling is good right from shore and can especially be enjoyed by children. The Lomonts will give you a map of the island showing the best snorkeling spots. While I was there, we went to the wall and in a very short time I saw wahoo, king makerel, dolphin, barracuda, grouper, Spanish makerel and tuna. We also saw spotted and southern stingrays, parrotfish, gray angelfish, sergeant majors, banded butterfly and barrel sponge.

Divers can go out twice a day and take one night dive.

The Lomonts have a well-supplied dive shop with a compressor that is run by a generator. Some snorkeling sites are so close that you can wade to the

THE CAYES

drop-off from your cabin. A two-tank dive will cost US $36 and a one-week package including accommodations, meals, transportation from Sittee River and 14 dives cost US $850.

Long Caye Wall dive site was once rated by Jacques Cousteau as one of the three best dives in the world. It has giant elephant ear sponges, Atlantic spadefish, tons of rays, spiny lobster and much more. Other famous sites around Glover's Reef are **The Abyss, Middle Caye Wall, The Crack** and **The Pinnacle**s. The water is so clear that you may be tempted to go deeper than you should. Be aware that the nearest decompression chamber is at Ambergris Caye, a few hours away by fast boat.

Fishers love the flats here, which are seething with permit and bonefish just waiting to give you the fight of your fishing life. Tarpon have been recorded to grow up to eight feet long (2.4 meters) at Glover's Reef. Note that marlin are fished on a catch-and-release basis only.

> ❖ **FISHY FACTS**
>
> Parrotfish swim as a harem with only one male. When he dies, the strongest female changes color and her sexual orientation. She becomes the ruler of the harem.

Long Caye is close to Northeast Caye and can be reached by kayak or canoe for a day's activity. This is the island where Slickrock Adventures takes their kayaking groups for a few days' camping. Long Caye and Northeast Caye are the types of islands you see on postcards. Long Caye has the **Off the Wall Dive and Gift Shop**, ☎ 614-6348, offthewall@btl.net, where you can purchase some unique tie-died garments. The shop also offers diving courses for all levels. Although I didn't dive with them, I understood that safety was a major concern. Dive prices are reasonable. One dive costs US $40, six dives cost $195 and 12 dives cost $385. Their courses run from US $210 for the "adventure diver" (it takes 1½ days) to $385 for full open water (four days). Rental gear is also inexpensive.

The rustic accommodations at the other end of the island belong to Slickrock.

Middle Caye is owned by the Wildlife Conservation Society that is dedicated to research and conservation and has actively been researching marine life in Belize for more than 20 years. They purchased this 15-acre island in 1994 to establish the Marine Research Station and to provide a Para Headquarters base for the Belize Fisheries Dept.

The station's fish preservation program, under the leadership of Belizean scientist Dr. Charles Acosta, has been (in my opinion) hugely successful. The theory to begin with was that if an area was left to its own devices with no fishing/harvesting permitted, fish numbers would increase. Within a short period of time, the no-touch area's conch and lobster increased in number. So did the fish. When the area started getting crowded, some fish moved over to the unprotected area. This in turn resulted in increased catches for fishers and made tourists happy because they started seeing more marine life.

During daylight hours you are welcome to visit Middle Caye and learn about their latest studies and conservation beliefs. You will be made more than welcome. If you feel that you would like to support this organization and their work, buy one of their fund-raising items (a t-shirt or a hat).

Southwest Caye has two resorts. **Isla Marisol Resort**, ☎ 520-2056 or 520-0319, www.islamarisol.com, is owned by the Usher family who have owned the island since the 1940s. This small, intimate resort has five cabins, all wood, all new and designed for couples. Each has fans, louvered windows and private bathrooms with hot water. The restaurant serves excellent foods, often featuring conch, lobster or spicy chicken. The vegetables are brought in fresh from the family's farms on the mainland. A bar sits over the water, away from the cabins.

Manta Resort, ☎ 888-271-3483, www.mantaresort.com, $$$$, has rooms with air conditioning, fans and private bathrooms with hot water. This is a diving/fishing resort where package deals are the best option. The cost is US $240 per person for a room, three dives a day, all food and locally produced alcohol, as well as transportation from Belize City to the caye and back. Manta also has sailboats, kayaks, canoes and sailboards for guests. There is a gift shop, volleyball court, horseshoe pit and a restaurant.

Close to Southwest Caye are numerous dive sites, including **Hole in the Wall, the Barrel Head, Fin Fan Alley** and **Wall Street**. If those names aren't creative enough, how about **Hogfish Hollow**? You can also take diving lessons from dive masters here.

Cayes near Placencia

◆ Laughing Bird Caye

This national park is the southernmost island of the Central Lagoon in Belize's barrier reef. It sits 11 miles east of Placencia on a coral shelf called a faro or shelf atoll. It is made up of 1.8 acres of palm, littoral thicket and mangrove swamp measuring only 1,400 feet long and 120 feet wide (420 x 36 meters). It drops steeply on the side walls like an atoll. There are only a few like it in the world.

The island once was home to laughing gulls. However, with increased human traffic, the gulls have moved to another island. Laughing Bird Caye was designated a protected area in 1981 and a national park in 1991 in the hope that the birds would return. Since the park has been established, camping has been abolished and mooring buoys have been secured to avoid boat damage to coral. There is a charge of $4 to enter the park.

THE CAYES

> ### ❖ LAUGH A LOT BIRD
>
> The laughing gull is white with gray wings and a black head. The bird is about 15 inches long (42 cm) and has a distinct hahaha call. A beggar, the laughing gull will crash a picnic party or scoop up garbage that is thrown off fishing boats. It also eats shellfish, crabs and shrimp. Female gulls nest in colonies in tall grasses or on open ground. Every year they lay one to three green/brown eggs that take about 20 days to hatch. The young leave the nest by the time they are five or six weeks old.

Although the laughing birds aren't plentiful at present, there are still tons of frigates and boobies here, and the area around the island offers excellent snorkeling for beginners. Close to the island the reef has been damaged by El Niño, hurricanes and humans, so visibility drops to 100 feet (30 meters). However, farther out the staghorn and elkhorn corals are good. There are also patch reefs and coral ridges close to the island.

◆ Lime Caye

Lime Caye often has many tourists from Livingston, Guatemala visiting. As many as 9,000 come to these islands each year. It's only a few minutes from Hunting Caye, where there is a military base and a customs station. This is where people traveling by boat enter and leave the country. Lime Caye is part of the Sapodilla Cayes Marine Reserve. If you wish to stay on the island bring your own food and camping equipment as there are no amenities.

◆ Hunting Caye

Hunting Caye has a wonderful beach shaped in a half moon on its eastern shore. This is a favorite nesting place for the hawksbill turtle. Offshore, manta rays and dolphins are often seen and whale sharks are reported to congregate near here during the full moons in Mar., Apr. and May. There is also lighthouse, an immigration post and a BDF station.

> ### ❖ TURTLE TRIVIA
>
> Hawksbill turtles nest for six months, from July to Oct. Each female will nest about four or five times during the season and each nesting will be about 14 days apart. She lays around 140 eggs each time, each one measuring about 1.5 inches (4 cm) in diameter. They hatch within 60 days. This means that you could either see a turtle lay her eggs or see the little ones hatch for eight months of the year.

Serenade Island Resort, ☎ 523-3481, www.belizecayes.com/island.html has three cabins dotted over four acres of privately owned island, secluded from civilization yet with amenities like electricity, running water, a restaurant and a bar. Although they are not the most luxurious cabins, they are comfortable and clean. Different packages are available. A four-night stay with meals and a complimentary one-hour massage is US $800. Camping is also available. You can eat in the restaurant or bring your own food and cooking utensils. The resort runs **fishing** trips for US $250 a day, $125 for half a day or $35 an hour. There are jackfish and spadefish, and the great fighting bonefish on the flats near the cayes.

The restaurant sits over the water so you can watch sea life while eating dinner.

The resort has a well-supplied **dive shop** that carries fishing gear. There must be at least two persons per diving trip and the cost is US $65 per person. Snorkeling costs $25 per trip; gear is included. You can also rent a canoe to get close to other islands and snorkel from there. Canoeing to the other islands, some that are less than 1.2 miles away, is good for birdwatchers, especially around the mangrove islands. Canoes cost $10 per day.

Hunting Caye's dive spots offer the chance to see Atlantic mantas and spotted eagle rays. The predominant corals are staghorn, elkhorn, finger and brain coral.

> **AUTHOR NOTE:** *A fishing license is required for non-nationals and costs US $25. It can be purchased at most tackle shops.*

Directories

◆ General Directory

GENERAL DIRECTORY		
■ **OUTFITTERS, GUIDES & TOUR OPERATORS**		
Amigos del Mar	☎ 226-2706	
Anwar Snorkel Tours	☎ 226-0327	
Blue Hole Dive Center	☎ 226-2982	www.bluedive.com
E-A Boy Tours	☎ 226-0349	
Fido's Fun Sports	☎ 226-3513	
Frenchie's Diving Services	☎ 226-0234	www.belizenet.com /frenchies.html
Island Excursions Dive & Tours	☎ 226-4075	islandexcursions@btl.net
Joe's Bikes	☎ 226-4371	
Jungle Tours	☎ 226-4555	www.jungletourbelize.com
Larry Parker's Reef Divers	☎ 226-3134	
Off the Wall Dive Shop	☎ 614-6348	offthewall@btl.net
Paradise Down Scuba Diving	☎ 226-0437	www.paradisedown.com
Sail Sports	☎ 226-4488	www.sailsports.net
Seaduced by Belize	☎ 226-2254	www.ambergriscaye.com /seaduced

THE CAYES

GENERAL DIRECTORY

■ OUTFITTERS, GUIDES & TOUR OPERATORS, CONT.

Star Tours	☎ 226-0374	www.startours.bz
Tanisha Tours	☎ 226-2314	www.tanishatours.com
Toucan Canoe	☎ 226-0022	toucancanoe@yahoo.com
Tsunami	☎ 226-0462	www.tsunamiadventures.com
Winnie Estelle Charter	☎ 226-0394	

■ SHOPPING

Ambergris Art Gallery	☎ 226-2695
Artesano	☎ 226-2370
Beauty of Nature Gift Shop	☎ 226-3310
Island Super Market	☎ 226-2972
Toucan Too	☎ 226-2445

■ SIGHTS/ATTRACTIONS

Hol Chan Marine Reserve	☎ 226-2247
Tropica Invertebrates Museum	☎ 226-2701

■ GROUPS/ORGANIZATIONS

Green Reef Society	☎ 226-2833

■ GOLF

Chapel Caye Golf	☎ 226-8250

■ TRANSPORT

Caye Caulker Water Taxi	☎ 203-1969

■ SERVICES

Internet Place	☎ 226-3434
Monchos Golf Cart Rentals	☎ 226-3262
Polo's Golf Cart Rentals	☎ 226-3542
Rosie's Massage	☎ 226-3879

■ USEFUL WEBSITES

www.ambergriscaye.com
www.placenciabreeze.com

◆ Accommodations Directory

PLACES TO STAY		
Anchorage Resort ($$$)	☎ 226-0391	anchorage@btl.net
Banana Beach Resort ($$$$)	☎ 226-3890	www.bananabeach.com
Banyan Bay Resort ($$$$$)	☎ 226-3739	www.banyanbay.com
Belize Island Lodge (n/k)	☎ 223-6324	www.belizelodge.com/island.html
Belize Yacht Club ($$$$$)	☎ 226-2777	www.belizeyachtclub.com
Blackbird Caye Resort ($$$$$)	☎ 888-271-3483	www.worlddive.com/destin/land/belize/blackbird.htm
Blue Marlin Lodge ($$$-$$$$)	☎ 520-2243	www.bluemarlinlodge.com
Blue Tang Inn ($$$)	☎ 226-2326	www.bluetanginn.com
Capricorn Resort ($$$$)	☎ 226-2151	www.ambergriscaye.com/capricorn
Captain Morgan's ($$$$$)	☎ 226-2567	www.belizevacation.com
Caribbean Villas (n/k)	☎ 226-2715	www.caribbeanvillashotel.com
Corona del Mar ($$$-$$$$)	☎ 226-2055	www.belizeone.com/coronadelmar
Changes in Latitudes B & B ($$$)	☎ 226-2986	www.ambergriscaye.com/latitudes
Chocolate's Guest House ($$$)	☎ 226-2151	
Cockney Island ($$)	☎ 522-0334	www.belizeseaclub.com
Coconuts Caribbean Hotel ($$$-$$$$)	☎ 226-3500	www.coconutshotel.com
Cottage Colony ($$$)	☎ 220-2020	
De Real Macaw Guest House ($$)	☎ 226-0459	www.derealmacaw.com
Dewey's Seaside Cabanas ($$)	☎ 226-0498	www.seasidecabanas.com
Diane's Beach House (n/k)	☎ 226-0083	www.staycayecaulker.com/beachhouse.html
Exotic Caye Beach Resort ($$$$$)	☎ 226-2870	www.belizeisfun.com
Gaviota Coral Reef Resort ($$$)	☎ 520-5032	
Glover's Atoll Resort ($$-$$$$)	☎ 520-5016	
Hideaway Sports Lodge ($$$)	☎ 226-2141	www.hideawaysportslodge.com
Motel 1788 ($-$$)	☎ 226-0388	www.cybercayecaulker.com/motel1788.htm
Iguana Reef Hotel ($$$)	☎ 226-0213	
International Zoological Expeditions	☎ 520-5030	www.ize2belize.com
Isla Marisol Resort (n/k)	☎ 520-2056	www.islamarisol.com
Journey's End Hotel ($$$$$)	☎ 226-2173	www.journeysendresort.com
La Costa Maya ($$)	☎ 226-0432	

PLACES TO STAY		
Lazy Iguana ($$$)	☎ 226-0350	www.lazyiguana.net
Lighthouse Reef Resort ($$$)	☎ 800-423-3114	www.scubabelize.com
Lily's Caribbean Lodge ($$$)	☎ 226-2059	
Loraine's Guest House ($)	☎ 614-9012	
Lucy's ($)	☎ 226-0110	
Manta Resort ($$$$)	☎ 888-271-3483	www.mantaresort.com
Mara's Place ($)	☎ 226-0056	
Marta's Place ($$)	☎ 226-2053	
Mata Rocks Resort ($$$$)	☎ 226-2336	www.matarocks.com
Mayan Princess Resort ($$$)	☎ 226-2778	www.mayanprincesshotel.com
Ocean's Edge ($$)	☎ 522-9633	oceansedge@btl.net
Odyssey Resort ($$$)	☎ 226-0309	www.belizeodyssey.com
Paradise Resort Hotel ($$$$)	☎ 226-2083	
Pelican Beach Resort ($$-$$$$)	☎ 520-3044	www.pelicanbeachbelize.com
Rainbow Hotel ($$)	☎ 226-0123	
Ramon's Village ($$$$-$$$$$)	☎ 226-2071	www.ramons.com
Reef's End Lodge	☎ 522-2419	www.reefsendlodge.com
Ruby's ($$)	☎ 226-2063	
St. George's Lodge ($$$$)	☎ 220-4444	www.gooddiving.com
San Pedranos ($$)	☎ 226-2054	
San Pedro Holiday Hotel ($$$$)	☎ 226-2014	www.sanpedroholiday.com
Sea View Guest House ($$)	☎ 226-0205	www.belizenet.com/seaview
Serenade Island Resort	☎ 523-3481	www.belizecayes.com/island.htm
Shirley's Cabins ($$-$$$)	☎ 226-0145	www.shirleysguesthouse.com
Sobre Las Olas ($)	☎ 226-0243	
Spanish Bay Resort ($$)	☎ 220-4024	www.spanishbaybelize.com
Spindrift Resort ($$$)	☎ 226-2174	
Steve & Becky's Little ($$$$)	☎ 800-magic-15	
Sun Breeze Beach Hotel ($$$$-$$$$$)	☎ 226-2191	www.sunbreeze.net
Tina's Backpacker's Hostel ($)	☎ 226-0351	www.staycayecaulker.com /hostel.html
Tobacco Caye Diving ($$$)	☎ 509-9904	info@tobaccocayediving.com
Tobacco Caye Lodge ($$$$)	☎ 520-5033	www.tclodgebelize.com
Tomas ($$)	☎ 226-2061	
Tom's Place ($$)	☎ 226-0102	
Tree Tops ($$)	☎ 226-0008	www.treetopsbelize.com/misc. html

PLACES TO STAY		
Trends ($$)	☎ 226-0094	www.gocayecaulker.com/members/trends.html
Tropica Beach Resort ($$$-$$$$)	☎ 226-2701	
Tropics Hotel ($$)	☎ 226-0374	www.startoursbelize.com
Turneffe Flats ($$$$$)	☎ 800-815-1304	www.tflats.com
Turneffe Island Resort ($$$$$)	☎ 800-628-1447	http://angleradventures.com/TurneffeIsland/Turnefls.htm
Victoria House ($$$$)	☎ 226-2067	
Xanadu Island Resort ($$$$-$$$$$)	☎ 226-2814	www.xanaduresort-belize.com

◆ Restaurant Directory

PLACES TO EAT		
Bare Foot Iguanas	☎ 226-4220	
BC's Bar	☎ 226-3289	
Blue Water Grill ($$)	☎ 226-3347	
Café Ole ($)	☎ 226-2907	
Caliente ($$)	☎ 226-2170	
Capricorn Restaurant ($$$$)	☎ 226-2809	www.ambergriscaye.com/capricorn
Celi's ($$$)	☎ 226-2014	
Crazy Canucks Bar	☎ 226-2870	
El Patio Restaurant ($$)	☎ 226-3063	
Elvi's Kitchen ($$$)	☎ 226-2176	
Fido's Sport's Bar	☎ 226-3176	
George's Country Kitchen ($$)	☎ 226-4252	
Hideaway Sports Lodge ($$$)	☎ 226-2269	www.hideawaysportslodge.com
Jade Garden ($$$)	☎ 226-2506	
Jambel Jerk Pit ($$$)	☎ 206-2594	
Lilly's Restaurant ($$$)	☎ 206-2059	
Manelly's Ice Cream Shop	☎ 226-2285	
Mickey's ($$)	☎ 226-2223	
Moho Caye Restaurant (n/k)	☎ 223-5350	
Palace Casino	☎ 226-3570	
Pier Lounge	☎ 226-2002	
Purple Parrot ($$$)	☎ 226-2071	
Rasta Pasta ($$)	☎ 206-0356	
Ruby's Café ($)	☎ 226-2063	

THE CAYES

PLACES TO EAT	
Sand Box ($$)	☎ 226-0200
Shark's Bar ($$)	☎ 226-4313
Sweet Basil Restaurant ($$$)	☎ 226-3870
Syd's ($)	☎ 226-0994
Toucan's Pool-side BBQ ($$)	☎ 226-2148
Tropica Beach Restaurant ($$)	☎ 226-2701
Tropical Paradise Restaurant ($)	☎ 226-0124
Victoria House Restaurant ($$$$)	☎ 226-2067
Wet Willy's bar	☎ 226-4054

Appendix

Emergency Contacts

◆ Embassies

EMBASSIES
Republic of China, 20 North Park Street, Belize City, ☎ 223-1862 or 227-8744
Columbia, 12 St. Matthew Street, Belize City, ☎ 223-5623 or 223-3025
Costa Rica, 11A Handyside Street, Belize City, ☎ 223-6525
Cuba, Urban Ave./Manatee Drive, Belize City, ☎ 223-5345
El Salvador, 49 Nanche Street, Belmopan, ☎ 822-3404
Guatemala, 8A Street, Belize City, ☎ 223-3150 or 223-3314
Honduras, 22 Gabourel Lane, Belize City, ☎ 224-5889
Mexico, 18 North Park Street, Belize City, ☎ 223-0194 or 223-0193 and Embassy Square, Belmopan, ☎ 822-0497 or 822-3837
United Kingdom , Belmopan, ☎ 822-2146 or 822-2717
United States, 29 Gabourel Lane, Belize City, ☎ 227-7161
Venezuela, 19 Orchid Garden, Belmopan, ☎ 822-2384 or 822-2789
European Commission, Eyre and Hutson Streets, Belize City, ☎ 223-2070

◆ Consulates

CONSULATES
Austria, 16 Regent Street, Belize City, ☎ 227-7070
Belgium, 126 Freetown Road, Belize City, ☎ 223-0748
Brazil, 8 Miles Northern Hwy, Ladyville, ☎ 225-2178
Canada, 80 Princess Margaret Street, Belize City, ☎ 223-1060
Cezch Republic, 6 Westby Alley, Orange Walk, ☎ 322-3373 or 322-2225
Chile, 109 Hummingbird Hwy, Belmopan, ☎ 822-2134
Costa Rica, 7 Shopping Center, Belmopan, ☎ 822-3801
Denmark, 13 Southern Foreshore, Belize City, ☎ 227-2172
Dominican Republic, 10 Roseapple Street, Belmopan, ☎ 822-3781
Ecuador, Mile 1.5, Arenal Road, Benque Viejo, ☎ 823-2295

CONSULATES

France, 109 New Road, Belize City, ☎ 223-2708

Germany, Mile 3.5, Western Hwy, Belize City, ☎ 222-4371 or 222-4369

Guatemala, Church Street, Benque Viejo, ☎ 823-2531

Guyana, 7 Barrack Road, Belize City, ☎ 223-2469

India, 5789 Goldson Avenue, Belize City, ☎ 227-3991

Israel, 4 Albert/Bishop Streets, Belize City, ☎ 227-3991 or 223-1432

Italy, 18 Albert Street, Belize City, ☎ 227-8449

Jamaica, 4 Eve Street, Belize City, ☎ 223-5672 or 19/21 Ambergris Avenue, Belmopan, ☎ 822-2183

Korea, 120 A New Road, Belize City, ☎ 223-5924

Lebanon, Mile 2, Western Hwy, Belize City, ☎ 224-4146

Morocco, Mile 2, Western Hwy, Belize City, ☎ 224-4154

Netherlands, 14 CA Blvd/Banak Street, Belize City, ☎ 227-3612

Nicaragua, 49 North Front Street, Belize City, ☎ 224-4488

Norway, 1 King Street, Belize City, ☎ 227-7031

Panama, CA Blvd./Mahogany Street, Belize City, ☎ 222-4551

Peru, 33 Freetown Road, Belize City, ☎ 223-2098

Russia, 18 A Street/Princess Margaret Drive, Belize City, ☎ 223-1151

Suriname, 5789 Goldson Avenue, Belize City, ☎ 223-4487

Sweden, 2 Daly Street, Belize City, ☎ 224-5176

Switzerland, 41 Albert Street, Belize City, ☎ 227-7363 or 227-7185

Trinidad & Tobago, 56 Regent Street, Belize City, ☎ 227-1697

Turkey, 42 Cleghorn Street, Belize City, ☎ 224-4158

Index